BIG CITY GOVERNMENT IN INDIA

MONOGRAPHS OF THE ASSOCIATION FOR ASIAN STUDIES

Published by and available from: The University of Arizona Press
Box 3398, Tucson, Arizona 85722

XXXI. *Big City Government in India: Councilor, Administrator, and Citizen in Delhi,* by Philip Oldenburg. 1976. $9.50 cloth; $4.95 paper.

XXX. *The New Jerusalem: Aspects of Utopianism in the Thought of Kagawa Toyohiko,* by George B. Bikle, Jr. 1976. $8.95 cloth; $4.95 paper.

XXIX. *Dōgen Kigen—Mystical Realist,* by Hee-Jin Kim. 1975. $8.95 cloth; $4.95 paper.

XXVIII. *Masks of Fiction in DREAM OF THE RED CHAMBER: Myth, Mimesis, and Persona,* by Lucien Miller. 1975. $7.95 cloth; $3.95 paper.

XXVII. *Politics and Nationalist Awakening in South India, 1852–1891,* by R. Suntharalingam. 1974. $7.95 cloth; $3.95 paper.

XXVI. *The Peasant Rebellions of the Late Ming Dynasty,* by James Bunyan Parsons. 1970. $7.50.

XXV. *Political Centers and Cultural Regions in Early Bengal,* by Barrie M. Morrison. 1970. $7.50.

XXIV. *The Restoration of Thailand Under Rama I: 1782–1809,* by Klaus Wenk. 1968. $7.50.

XXIII. *K'ang Yu-wei: A Biography and a Symposium,* translated and edited by Jung-pang Lo. 1967. 541 pp. $14.50.

XXII. *A Documentary Chronicle of Sino-Western Relations (1644–1820),* by Lo-shu Fu. 1966. xviii + 792 pp. $14.50.

XXI. *Before Aggression: Europeans Prepare the Japanese Army,* by Ernst L. Presseisen. 1965. O. P.

XX. *Shinran's Gospel of Pure Grace,* by Alfred Bloom. 1965. $2.50 paper.

XIX. *Chiaraijima Village: Land Tenure, Taxation, and Local Trade, 1818–1884,* by William Chambliss. 1965. $5.00.

XVIII. *The British in Malaya: The First Forty Years,* by K. G. Tregonning. 1965. O. P.

XVII. *Ch'oe Pu's Diary: A Record of Drifting Across the Sea,* by John Meskill. 1965. $4.50.

XVI. *Korean Literature: Topics and Themes,* by Peter H. Lee. 1965. O. P.

XV. *Reform, Rebellion, and the Heavenly Way,* by Benjamin B. Weems. 1964. $3.75.

XIV. *The Malayan Tin Industry to 1914,* by Wong Lin Ken. 1965. $6.50.

Earlier-published AAS Monographs

XIII. *Conciliation and Japanese Law: Tokugawa and Modern,* D. F. Henderson. Univ. Washington Press, 1965.

XII. *Maharashta Purana,* E. C. Dimock, Jr., and P. C. Gupta. East-West Center Press, 1964. O. P.

XI. *Agricultural Involution: The Process of Ecological Change in Indonesia,* C. Geertz. Univ. California Press, 1963.

X. *Bangkhuad: A Community Study in Thailand,* H. K. Kaufman. J. J. Augustin, 1959. O. P.

IX. *Colonial Labor Policy and Administration, 1910–1941,* J. N. Parmer. Augustin, 1959.

VIII. *A Comparative Analysis of the Jajmani System,* T. O. Beidelman. Augustin, 1959.

VII. *The Traditional Chinese Clan Rules,* Hui-chen Wang Liu. Augustin, 1959.

VI. *Chinese Secret Societies in Malaya,* L. F. Comber. Augustin, 1959.

V. *The Rise of the Merchant Class in Tokugawa Japan: 1600–1868,* C. D. Sheldon. Augustin, 1958. O. P.

IV. *Siam Under Rama III, 1824–1851,* W. F. Vella. Augustin, 1957. O. P.

III. *Leadership and Power in the Chinese Community of Thailand,* G. W. Skinner. Cornell Univ. Press, 1958. O. P.

II. *China's Management of the American Barbarians,* E. Swisher. Far Eastern Pubs., Yale, 1951. O. P.

I. *Money Economy in Medieval Japan,* D. M. Brown. Far Eastern Pubs., Yale, 1951. O. P.

The Association for Asian Studies: Monograph No. XXXI
Paul Wheatley, *Editor*

BIG CITY GOVERNMENT IN INDIA
Councilor, Administrator, and Citizen in Delhi

Philip Oldenburg

 Published for the Association for Asian Studies by
THE UNIVERSITY OF ARIZONA PRESS
Tucson, Arizona

095487

About the Author . . .

PHILIP OLDENBURG received his Ph.D. from the University of
Chicago in 1974. In addition to his work on municipal government
in India, he has written on United States policy toward India and
Pakistan during the 1974 crisis and joined other scholars in preparing introductory materials on Bangladesh. He has taught in the
Department of Political Science and the Center for Asian Studies
of the University of Illinois at Urbana-Champaign.

The publication of this volume has been financed from a revolving
fund that initially was established by a generous grant from the
Ford Foundation to the Association for Asian Studies.

THE UNIVERSITY OF ARIZONA PRESS

I.S.B.N.-0-8165-0553-5 paper
I.S.B.N.-0-8165-0554-3 cloth
L. C. No. 76-4426

Contents

Maps and Diagrams

Tables

Preface

This study is a revised version of my Ph.D. dissertation, completed in August 1974 for the Department of Political Science of the University of Chicago. The revisions have been confined mainly to the substitution of data from the 1971 Census of India for the 1961 census data used in the dissertation. I have retained the title of the original work for this study. In the revision I have added some references to works published after the dissertation was written, and taken note of some of the more important events in the recent history of the Delhi Municipal Corporation. I have attempted to eliminate the many errors of the original study; I fear, however, that many persist, and these are, of course, my responsibility alone.

While this revision was in preparation, the Delhi Municipal Corporation was superseded, for the period of a year, in March 1975. Moreover, the effects of the proclamation of a state of emergency in June 1975 are bound to penetrate into the entire political system of India. The use of the present tense in much of the study does not imply a description of the current system of government of Delhi, but rather the descriptive analysis of an observer in 1969-70, the year of my research there.

There are no English equivalents for many of the Hindi and Urdu terms (for things such as house types) found in this study, and such terms are best defined in context. A page reference for

where the term is first used and defined is given
in the index. The translations from Hindi and Urdu
are my own.

The listing of my debts to others for the
formation of the ideas which went into this study,
the support given during the research, and the help
rendered during the writing, must begin with that
due to Lloyd Rudolph, the chairman of my dissertation committee. He has helped shape my work from
before its inception through its completion with
unfailing attention and skill. I am grateful also
to David Greenstone and McKim Marriott, the other
members of my committee, for the time they took to
read and comment on my work.

The members--faculty, students, and staff;
far, far too numerous to mention--of that marvelous
scholarly community which is the group of South
Asianists at the University of Chicago, contributed
immeasurably to my understanding of India. The
staff of the library and those who struggled to
teach me Hindi and Urdu deserve special thanks. A
similar group of scholars and staff at the Center
for Asian Studies of the University of Illinois at
Urbana-Champaign helped me through the tasks of
completing the dissertation and the revised study.

The year and a half of field research in
India was financed by a grant from the Foreign Area
Fellowship Program (which also provided for six
months of study before I left and six months of
writing time after I returned) for which I am very
grateful. The Program is not, of course, responsible in any way for the views expressed in the
study. This final version owes much to those who
read and criticized the dissertation; to the editor
of the Monograph Series, Paul Wheatley; and to the
staff of the University of Arizona Press. Even
more is owed to Dorothy Osborne, who prepared the
final transcript, and to Christopher Müller-Wille,
who prepared the charts and maps.

In Delhi, with almost no exceptions, I was
given cooperation cheerfully and with open hands.
I owe most to the councilor of "Kucha Khirkiwala"

(the pseudonym of the municipal ward I studied in detail) for permitting an outsider to peer in on him and his work, and to the councilors and officers of the City Zone who consented to interviews. Mr. H. B. Dass, the O & M officer of the Delhi Municipal Corporation in 1969-70, steered me clear of many incorrect judgments, with good humor and keen insight; my debt to him is particularly great. My stay in Delhi was enriched by my affiliation with the Indian Institute of Public Administration, and by the help given by its faculty and staff, particularly the members of the Center for Municipal Training and Research -- G. Mukharji, A. Datta, and M. Bhattacharya, among others.

This set of acknowledgments is hardly complete. I have mentioned few names here, not because others were not important in shaping my thought and helping me complete this work, but because most of my Delhi informants and friends must remain anonymous, and it seems hardly fair to overwhelm them with still more Americans.

1. Introduction

I did not choose to study Delhi for reasons connected to some broad theoretical framework, or even as some sort of limiting case (to test generalizations about Indian party competition in this two-party arena, for instance). The study is a "political ethnography." It describes and analyzes the way municipal government in Delhi works, particularly at the ward level, within a system of decentralized administration.

I believe that the way municipal government in Delhi operates is comparable to the way it operates in other Indian cities, particularly those with a corporation form of government, and to the way it operates in cities in other democratic systems. To the extent that there is a "theory" of urban politics, some of my conclusions are relevant. But these theoretical implications were not arrived at as a result of a priori conceptualization and operationalization of ideas derived from a theoretical framework. Rather, they emerge inductively out of my observation and analysis of one instance of municipal government and only then are they related to extant "theories." Their proper place, then, is in the conclusions of the study, although some of them will be found in the body of the study as well.

Underlying this study is one "thesis" which, in a sense, I am attempting to "prove." It is that an urban politics not only can exist in India, but that it is also a significant part of Indian democracy. This is not, as it appears on the surface, a

trivial question. There are many cities in India
which have been governed for considerable periods
without democratic participation, administered by
the state government. There are many in India who
believe that "politics" has no place in municipal
government. And the focus of studies of politics
in India has been on national and state arenas in
part because it has been assumed, I think, that
the significance of politics is determined by the
"importance" of the issues with which it deals.
National defense and national integration are more
significant for some than the placement of a new
sewer line or the improvement of slum housing. But
it is not self-evident that the typical politician
in the national or state arena is involved in more
"significant" or valid politics than the municipal
councilor. Certainly there is a sense in which
municipal politics can be far more relevant to the
city citizen than national politics; his involvement is more immediate and usually more intense.
Voting turnout in local elections in India is consistently as high as that for national and state
elections. Local politics is very much a part of
Indian life and culture, and Delhi is no exception.
     There is one conclusion that is worth antici-
pating, because it is implied in the organization
of the analysis. Municipal politics in India
generally, and in Delhi in particular, concerns
itself almost entirely with the implementation of
policy and the distribution of benefits to the
citizenry. The councilor is not, on the whole,
involved in policy formation or the mobilization
of resources; that has been largely determined by
the chartering Act of the Municipal Corporation
(promulgated by Parliament in the case of Delhi),
which in turn is a product of a long development
of local self-government in the British Raj. Most
of what political actors in Delhi's municipal
arena do is circumscribed and directed by governmental structure, and not by ideology, socio-
economic "understructure," party competition, or
whatever.

I find that governmental structures--the
arrangement of government authority, especially
its division between elected official and admin-
istrator--is the single most important determinant
of political behavior in Delhi. These structures
have been instituted from "above" by the national
government, using previously existent examples.
There is some debate on this issue by councilors
and other politicians in Delhi--on the question
of "statehood" for Delhi, or on a proposed "cabinet system" of municipal government--but, despite
the near unanimity of political opinion on the
question, there is no indication that the national
government will in any way accommodate it. Indeed,
the Corporation was under pressure to abolish a
significant institutional innovation, the "constituency fund" (in 1969-70, an annual appropri-
ation of Rs 50,000 for projects of ward improvement, which the councilor assigned to specific
locales and to specific projects [e.g., the
installation of new street lights]; see below,
p. 72, n. 2).

   This study is thus organized in accordance
with governmental configurations and roles in
Delhi: the municipal ward, the zone (a group of
wards), and the Municipal Corporation as a whole;
the councilor, the administrator, and the citizen,
at all three levels.

   At this point it would be well to discuss
briefly the actors and institutions with which I
will be dealing. The Delhi Union Territory (its
present name) has an area of 573 square miles of
which 447 square miles are rural (with some 300
villages) and a population, in 1971, of about four
million. The entire area, except for the Delhi
Cantonment, is covered by the authority of the
Delhi Administration, which functions something
like a state government elsewhere in India, con-
trolling the police, higher education, etc., but
which is largely under the more or less direct
control of the central government. The Delhi
Administration has associated with it a popularly

elected but comparatively powerless body, the Delhi
Metropolitan Council. The entire area of the Territory, rural and urban, with the exception of the
Delhi Cantonment (army base) and the New Delhi
Municipal Committee[1] (NDMC) area, is also under
the authority of the Delhi Municipal Corporation
(see Fig. 1). The division of powers between the
various bodies is discussed in detail in Chapter 8.
     The Delhi Municipal Corporation is the govern-
mental body with which this study is concerned.
The corporation form of local government has a long
history in India,[2] and the Delhi Corporation fits
the pattern. There are two "wings" of the Corporation: an "executive wing" headed in Delhi by an
official called the Municipal Commissioner, and a
"deliberative wing," composed of 100 councilors
elected from single-member constituencies (the
municipal wards) plus six aldermen elected by the
councilors. The term of the Corporation is four
years. Meetings of the councilors (these are
called "meetings of the Corporation") are presided
over by a mayor who is also the ceremonial head of
the city, and whose role in Delhi government is thus
a mixture of constitutional monarch and (English)
Speaker of the House. Councilors are elected to the
various committees of the Corporation, most of which
deal with specific subjects such as education
or works, but the most important committee, the
Standing Committee, deals with all subjects, and
most importantly screens the budget proposals after
they are presented by the municipal commissioner.
The entire set-up is not unlike the council-manager
form of municipal government.
     The Corporation since 1963 has been divided
into a number of zones. (The details of the arrangement can be found in Chapter 6.) Each zone is a
grouping of a number of wards, and each zone has
a zonal office in which administrative officers
dealing with public health, works, electricity, and
other subjects sit. The councilors of the wards in
the zone (averaging twelve or so) constitute a
zonal committee, which passes on the expenditure of

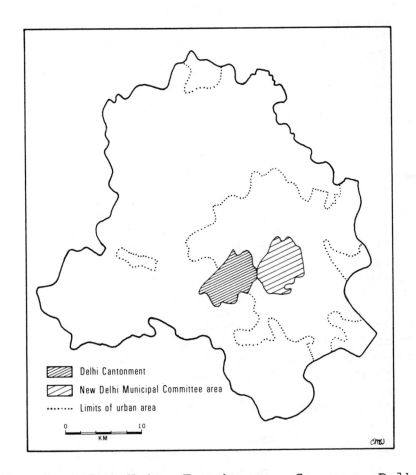

Delhi Cantonment
New Delhi Municipal Committee area
Limits of urban area

Fig. 1 Delhi Union Territory. Source: Delhi
District Census Handbook, 1971, Parts A & B,
frontispiece.

a certain level and discusses questions such as the
effectiveness of the collection of property tax.
The committee keeps minutes of its resolutions.
Administrative officers sitting in the zone may
have subordinates (this is not true of several
departments) who are assigned, as Works Section
Officers are for example, to individual municipal
wards. The supervising administrative officers of
the zone, like the councilors, operate in all three
arenas: they meet the councilor and the citizen in
the ward, and they are closely tied to their
superiors in Town Hall.

AN OUTLINE OF THE STUDY

A major difficulty in organizing the presentation of this study arises from the fact that the
basis of many of my conclusions about government at
the level of the zone and of the Corporation as a
whole is my findings about government and politics
at the ward level, findings in which I have a great
deal of confidence. And yet, politics and government within the ward clearly depend on their configurations in the city and in the Corporation--e.g.,
it is important that the overall party system is a
two-party one, with the Congress and the Jana Sangh
competing almost by themselves. My solution is to
break up my discussion of the all-city level of
Delhi government into two parts: the first, which
is a sketchy treatment of the physical, social,
economic, and historical "settings" of the city,
is the second part of this Introduction; the
second, consisting mainly of a discussion of how
the Corporation operates at the all-city level, is
placed after my discussion of the ward and of the
zone, in Chapter 8.
At the outset of my discussion of each system-
level of Delhi government, I deal with the physical,
social, economic, and historical parameters (not all
of which are relevant at each level) of the political arena. In the discussion of the ward (Chapter

2), I set out the physical "questions" of sanitation
and high-density housing; the social "questions" of
caste, class, and communal (Hindu, Muslim) cleavages; the economic "questions" of the pattern of
occupation of residents of the ward, and the distribution of industrial establishments; and other
material taken largely from the 1971 census. At
the level of the zone, in Chapter 5, I consider the
historical unit of Shahjahanabad and again discuss
socio-economic factors. The parallel discussions of
Delhi as a whole begins at the end of this chapter
and continues in Chapter 8 with an outline of the
history of municipal government in Delhi. These
are the various "settings" of politics at each
level.

　　　Chapters 2, 3, and 4 deal with the ward which
I have called "Kucha Khirkiwala"; Chapters 5, 6,
and 7 deal with the City Zone (one of whose wards
is Kucha Khirkiwala). In each of these groupings,
after I have discussed the setting, I move to a
delineation of the three "interfaces" of councilor
and administrator, councilor and citizen, and
citizen and administrator. These interfaces vary
in prominence with each system-level. Chapter 3,
dealing with the ward, focuses on the councilor,
and particularly on his regular "rounds" of his
ward; the emphasis is on the councilor-administrator and councilor-citizen interfaces. Chapter 4
examines a crucial part of the latter interface in
a discussion of elections and election campaigns in
the ward.

　　　At the zonal level, the three interfaces are
more institutionally defined: the administrators
sit in offices where they have hours for meeting
the public and where complaint books are available;
councilors meet, with administrative officers in
attendance, as a zonal committee, and councilors,
acting in an "omsbudsman's" role, "get things done"
for their constituents. The citizenry, however,
recedes into the background at this level (which I
discuss in Chapter 6) and the councilor-administrator interface increases in importance. The

special case of the councilor-citizen interface, the
election, is discussed in Chapter 7. At the all-
city level, the interface of councilor and administrator is again the most significant of the three,
but at that level the importance of the interfaces
themselves declines. There the more important
question is probably the councilors' relationships
with each other as they meet to consider resolutions.
I discuss this aspect of Delhi government in the
middle part of Chapter 8.

At the end of each grouping of chapters (plus
Chapter 8, which is internally like the groups of
three chapters on the ward and the zone), I attempt
a more general analysis of political patterns at
each level. At the ward and zonal level these
appear as extensions of the electoral analysis (in
Chapters 4 and 7), as I consider the mesh of socio-
economic and historical patterns with electoral outcomes. At the all-Delhi level, electoral patterns
are also important, but I am able to treat them
only sketchily. I concentrate on some facets of
system-level interaction, in this case between
committees of the Corporation (including zonal committees), the Corporation, "superior" authorities--
the Delhi Administration, the Metropolitan Council,
and the national government--and the autonomous
authorities such as the Delhi Development Authority.
These are discussed in the latter part of Chapter 8.

METHODOLOGY

For various reasons (outlined at the beginning
of Chapter 2), I have chosen to give the ward I
studied in detail a pseudonym. I am therefore unable
to give in precise detail my reasons for choosing it
over others. My original intention was to study
several wards, but this plan succumbed to a lack of
means. To a certain extent the absence of comparative experience is overcome by material obtained in
my interviews with all 18 councilors of the City
Zone. One of the major criteria for choosing the

City Zone, and "Kucha Khirkiwala," was, in a sense,
extraneous to the research design: I wanted to be
in an area where almost all the population spoke
Hindi or Urdu (there are large areas of Delhi
where Punjabi is spoken) so that I could dispense
with an interpreter. My ability in Hindi/Urdu not
only permitted me to conduct some interviews in it,
but, more importantly, allowed me to listen in on
innumerable conversations--in the offices of councilors and administrators, in the streets of the
ward, at political meetings, and elsewhere. These
turned out to be some of my most valuable data
sources.

Although I carried on my studies at all three
levels of Delhi government simultaneously, it will
perhaps be easier to detail my methodology level by
level. In the ward the most important thing I did
was to join myself to the "round group" of the
councilor (scheduled once a week, rounds took place
roughly two-thirds of the time) over a year's
period. I did not take notes while on the round,
except for an occasional key word jotted down on a
scrap of paper, but wrote up a description immediately afterwards. While on the round, I listened
in on virtually every conversation the councilor
had. I amalgamated some data from other wards into
my account of "Kucha Khirkiwala" and I went on a
number of rounds with the councilor of the neighboring ward and on a few rounds with councilors of
two or three other wards. I use the responses of
some of the other City Zone councilors as responses
of the "Kucha Khirkiwala" councilor.

I interviewed all the defeated candidates of
the previous two elections in the ward, plus four
"political workers." I obtained, after a six
months' period of near daily visits to one of the
offices of the zone (during which I learned a great
deal about administrative operations), a map of the
ward, and I covered the ward systematically, putting
house numbers on the map. A long-lasting attempt to
get my own copy of a voters list of the ward failed,
and so I used the office copy of the Chief Election

Officer (Delhi) to count the number of voters living
at each house number, along with noting whether they
were Hindu or Muslim. I made copies of political
posters that appeared in the ward from time to time,
and I went there fairly often to meet friends, get
books bound, or simply to wander around. My aim was
to observe as much of the political interactions
that took place in the ward as I could without
living there. (I tried to find a place to live in
Kucha Khirkiwala, but was unsuccessful.)

I had expected to find a well-articulated
social structure in Kucha Khirkiwala, in part
because physically it seemed "made for it."[3]
Adrian C. Mayer, in a series of articles, argues
for the analysis of political networks centered on
the candidate at the time of election, and implies
that the "quasi-groups" so formed have at least a
more than transitory existence.[4] Others have
described the role of vote "broker" in India.[5]
My expectation thus was to discover a network of
intermediaries between councilor and citizen, a
network reaching "down" from the councilor via
political workers, and "up" from the citizen via
caste association, mohalla (neighborhood) committees,
sports clubs, cooperative societies, etc. This
pattern has indeed been found in other large Indian
cities.[6] But I did not find it in Kucha Khirkiwala.
That part of my research design which called for the
interviewing of ward "notables" or "influentials"
had to be scrapped.

I discovered the existence of the zonal system
in Delhi only after I arrived, but it not only
seemed significant, it also allowed me to limit my
research task to a logical unit, instead of choosing
a series of wards for less intensive study as I had
originally intended. I interviewed all 18 councilors of the City Zone, and almost all the Class II
Officers--the senior administrative officials in the
zone. Here the focus was more "governmental"--I
asked how the zonal system worked administratively,
and what the relationship between councilor and
administrator was--but I also attempted to discover

how the citizen interacted with officials at this
level. There is a fair amount of literature relevant here, though little of it deals directly with
a system of zonal decentralization.[7] In the course
of setting up interviews--which on occasion took
many visits to home and office--I was able to
observe the workings of the zonal office in my role
as an office-sitter, waiting my turn to speak to
the officer (waiting typically occurs inside the
office, so that all those waiting get to hear the
"cases" of all those who precede them). The zonal
committee keeps minutes of its proceedings, and I
was able to examine these for a number of years,
and I copied those for 1969-70. A few of the newspaper cuttings I collected pertained to the zone.

In studying the city arena, I relied mainly on
secondary data:[*] newspaper accounts of Corporation
affairs (I read four newspapers daily), reports
written in the Corporation on its activities, the
minutes of the year 1969-70 (running to many thousand pages), including the budget for that year. I
also observed a few meetings of the Corporation, and
visited several offices--the election office, for
example--fairly regularly. At this level also I
made use of informants: several former zonal
officers, newspaper reporters who covered the
Corporation, local party officials, a professor
of political science whose father had been a
municipal councilor, and several others.

After I left India, I made use of a large
number of printed sources. The single most important of these were the several volumes of the Delhi
Census for 1961, and particularly the District
Census Handbook.[8] This volume has data which is,

---

[*] I had intended to interview elected and
administrative officials, in particular the nine
Metropolitan Councilors of the City Zone area, but
my experience in the zone, where it took me four
months to arrange and conduct just over fifty interviews discouraged me from attempting interviewing on
a larger scale.

as far as I know, more detailed than that for any
other Indian city: the units (census blocks) for
which data on literates, the number of scheduled
caste people, workers in nine census categories,
etc., averaged less than a thousand people. Data
on type and number of industrial establishments is
also given by census block. This enabled me to plot
this data on maps, and to compare it with electoral
data (see the analysis in Chapter 2 and 4). For the
revised version of the study, I have substituted
data from the 1971 census in most of the analysis.[9]

The keynote of my method was participant
observation. I attempted to avoid the pitfalls
of drafting a reliable survey instrument, and the
well-known phenomenon of interviewees attempting
to answer as they believe the interviewer wishes
(in this case, in order to be courteous to the
foreigner), by spending as much time as I could
actually observing interactions between councilors,
administrators, and citizens. Indeed, I used those
observations during my interviews--which were open-
ended, with a few leading questions only written
out--to challenge and probe the answers I received.
Similarly, I pursued reluctant officials (one councilor and one administrator in particular) for interviews so that I could have a complete set of interviews for the City Zone, thus eliminating non-
response bias, and, indeed, the two reluctant interviewees were significantly different from their
fellows. I believe that I was able to spend enough
time, especially with the councilor of Kucha
Khirkiwala, so that my "sample" of experience was
representative, and I believe that I was "in and
around" the ward long enough so that despite my skin
color I no longer intruded and biased interactions
by my presence. Delhi is indeed a cosmopolitan city,
and I was constantly surprised, given my experiences
elsewhere in India, how little notice I received,
even when, say, I was standing in the middle of a
busy bazar copying down a political poster. At the
zonal level as well I attempted to find out, as best
I could, what was "really" going on, not opinions

about it.   I flatter myself that on the whole I
succeeded.

A DELHI SKETCH

Delhi not only is a capital city today, as it
has been often in the past, it also looks like one.*
There are grand and imposing monuments, as well as
ruins, some of which are many hundreds of years old.
The spacious New Delhi government area (a small part
of the New Delhi Municipal Committee area) is
sparsely populated, yet there is a daily influx of
thousands of people from the surrounding residential
areas, from the old city and from the post-Independence, peripheral housing colonies.   Delhi has
been growing at a rapid rate, and as one moves about
in Old Delhi and New Delhi, one seems to feel the
city growing.
      The setting of Delhi politics consists of its
physical attributes (it is not accidental that the
civic receptions given to visiting dignitaries by
the Corporation are held in the Red Fort, the palace
of the later Moghul Emperors), its geographically
differentiated social and economic character, and
its political history.   These elements not only
define the boundaries of the political arena of the
city, as a wall defines the boundaries of the sports
arena, they also interact with the politics.   The
setting is in a sense also an actor.

---

*I follow the Indian practice of implying
"New Delhi" in saying "Delhi."   The new city, built
next to the old one, has, in that sense at least,
been swallowed up by it.   For a brief description
of Delhi in morphological terms, see Gerald Breese,
Urbanization in Newly Developing Countries
(Englewood Cliffs, N.J.:   Prentice-Hall Inc., 1966),
pp. 63-69.

Physical, Social, and Economic Features

Delhi is not so much a city, historically, as a
city site. The Indraprastha of the Pandavas is traditionally located within the walls of the palace-
fort of the sixth city of Delhi (by the most popular
numeration--the fourteenth in another).[10] What is
left of most of these "Delhis" are mainly mosques,
tombs, and palace walls. The excavations of the
mound within the Purana Qila have yielded the
Painted Grey Ware, which dates from 1050 to 450
B.C.,[11] and have revealed a more or less continuous
sequence of habitation from then to the present
(the Purana Qila having been used as a refugee camp-
site for a while after 1947).[12] But there are few
houses--as opposed to palaces--in Delhi that are
more than a hundred years old, for it wasn't until
the British came that constructing houses "built to
last" became important.[13] And so the houses of poor
quality brick or of mud (including some of the
palaces of Shahjahan's Queens) tend to fall down
or wash away. The oldest part of the city (the
"Seventh City of Delhi," built by Shahjahan, starting
in 1638) contains the houses, few of them more than
a hundred years old, least likely to last much
longer (for a detailed history of Shahjahanabad,
see Chapter 5, below).

There are many explanations for Delhi's
popularity as a city site, and even more important,
as a capital city. Its situation astride the trade
routes eastward to Bengal and southward to Gujarat,
although varying in importance over time as the
center of gravity of Indian empires shifted and as
the threat of invasion from the northwest waxed and
waned, is one. Indraprastha was one of several
capital cities of the age of the Mahabharata
(c. 700 B.C.). For more than 1,500 years (until
around 1000 A.D.) Delhi ceased to be a capital, or
perhaps anything more than a village. A Hindu
Kingdom, which was probably centered in Delhi,
ended with the early Muslim invasions, and the
Delhi Sultanate (1206-1526 A.D.) ushered in the

centuries in which Delhi was often the premier city
of North India. All the Delhis that followed
before the founding of Shahjahanabad exist in
today's Delhi mainly as tourist attractions, pic-
turesque settings for posh residential colonies,
and sources of building materials for some of the
poorer of Delhi's new residents. And even the city
of Shahjahanabad has passed through periods of near
desolation, when the writ of its rulers ran for
only a few miles around. Even its nominal status
as capital was lost for sixty years after 1857;
Calcutta had been the "real" capital for British
rule under the East India Company for the hundred
years previous (after Clive's victory at Plassey in
1757). When the British returned the capital to
Delhi, in 1911, they followed imperial traditions
by moving it to a new city of Delhi, but this new
Delhi has not replaced the old city as previous new
Delhis had done, although it may happen yet.*

The Delhi that exists on the ground today, the
physical Delhi with which city government must concern itself, with its core of the old city of
Shahjahanabad and the later accretions of building
around it, has little to do with the history of the
city before the fourth Moghul emperor. It is important that Delhi was the seat of the later Moghul
emperors, because there is a rich literary tradition
which looks back to that period, especially among
the Muslims of the old city.[14] And this literary
attachment is significant politically, for it makes
for a determination to retain one's life style in
the area of one's roots, no matter what the planners
may think: the residents of the "slum" housing near
the Jama Masjid successfully resisted eviction

---

* Certainly there are some city planners who
would like to see the old dangerous buildings of
the city razed to make way for new housing in a
"modern" planned city; much of the old city wall
has already disappeared, in one area replaced by a
row of multi-storied office buildings.

orders even when they were offered resettlement in
"better" housing. They did not wish to move for a
variety of reasons, including some sound economic
ones, but the sentiment of physical contiguity
with the artifacts of Moghul glory was certainly
one of them.

The Revolt of 1857 resulted not only in the
nominal relocation of the capital when the British
replaced the East India Company with direct rule,
dropping the by then fictional acceptance of the
sovereignty of the Moghul emperor,[15] but also in
physical changes: the residential quarter between
the Jama Masjid and the Red Fort was leveled for
military reasons,[16] and the area has now become
one of the more important parks in the city.

The British, when they began moving back to
Delhi in the late nineteenth century, built houses
in a "civil lines" area (a typical pattern of
British dwelling in India) outside the city walls,
and indeed split part of the city off by putting a
railway line through it around 1870. Already in
Moghul times, settlements outside the city walls,
in Paharganj and Subzi Mandi, had grown up, and
when the architects of New Delhi plotted out their
city, they worked on a "map" which was largely
free from built up areas. As it turned out, they
built their city not as an extension of the civil
lines and Cantonment areas to the north, as they
had originally intended, but put the city to the
south of the old one, partially on the site of the
pre-Moghul Delhi of Sher Shah (the Delhi described
by the first European travellers to India). The
old city is thus bordered on the north as well as
on the south by "newer" Delhis, both with far lower
population densities (and also total population)
than the old city, both with areas of tree-lined
streets with impressive bungalows on large plots.
The northern border of New Delhi--the Connaught
Place region--has become in recent years the commercial center of the city, with modern high-rise
office buildings joining the concentration of
retail stores and the housing of middle-level civil

servants. But the core of New Delhi retains its
imperial character: the buildings of the government have expanded in size and number, but they
are as yet far from crowding the plan of circles
and axes that is Luytens's Delhi.[*]
   To the west of the old city other sorts of
nineteenth- and twentieth-century expansion took
place. Along the railway line, industries grew up
with their associated workers' tenements, and later
on, the first "suburb"--Karol Bagh. With the bur-
geoning of Delhi's population after 1947, brought
on by the influx of refugees and the expansion of
the central government, this expansion westward
increased rapidly, and other colonies were spotted
all around the perimeter of the "newer" Delhi--to
the west mainly, but also north of the civil lines,
south of New Delhi (proper) and east of the old
city, on the eastern bank of the Jumna. Then, as
the central government became more and more important in the 1950s and 1960s, and as Delhi pros-
pered (e.g., new opportunities in medium-size
industry--making such things as electric motors--
opened up), the colonies of the emergent middle
class began to spread, this time largely to the
south of New Delhi, intertwined with the old
refugee camps, encircling villages and monuments
alike. This new middle-class city also spread to
the north (near Delhi University) and west.
   Each of these regions of the city of Delhi
(and some of these regions are also zones of the
Municipal Corporation--see Fig. 2) has distinctive

----

[*] Sir Edwin Lutyens, along with Sir Herbert
Baker, drew up the plan for the new capital and
designed the major buildings. The plan features
broad avenues, intersecting at circles, magnifi-
cently planted and providing grand vistas. Most
of the buildings, other than the Parliament
buildings, the Viceroy's Place, and the Secre-
tariats, were one-storied bungalows set in large,
well planned compounds.

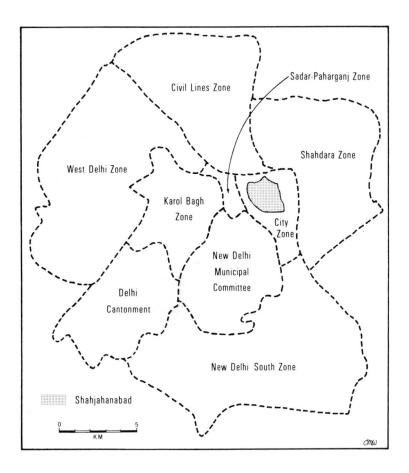

Fig. 2 Zones of the Municipal Corporation of
Delhi, 1969-70.

socio-economic patterns, and thus differing patterns of political and governmental action. (The
following description should not be taken as
definitive; it represents a prevalent conception
of the city's composition.) The walled city of
Shahjahanabad retains its character as a place of
settled residence,[17] with the largest concentration
of Muslims in the city and the core of the wholesale commercial establishment, as well as some
of the more "traditional" craftsmen, such as the
jewelers. The suburbs to the west--Paharganj,
Sadar Bazar, Subzi Mandi and the built-up areas in
the interstices--have a less "aristocratic," more
"lower-class" air. Indeed, many of their inhabitants are workers in industry or in the big lumber
and iron markets of the area. These areas have
had comparatively few immigrants from the Punjab,
though immigrants are a political force in some
wards. Their governmental problems have to do with
intense overcrowding: poor sanitation, dangerous
buildings, inadequate water supply, unauthorized
additions to and alterations of existing buildings,
etc.

     The civil lines area north of the old city is
small; the colonies which surround Delhi Univer-
sity--Roop Nagar, Model Town, Malkaganj, et al.--
probably have many more inhabitants than the civil
lines proper. Here one finds people "in service"
(government employees, teachers, etc.) and Punjabi
entrepreneurs of the first wave of immigrants.
This is now one of the most prosperous parts of the
city, although there is less evidence of luxury
(aside from the fast-spreading forest of television
aerials) than in the posh South Delhi colonies.
Here the problems are not mainly sanitation or construction of buildings but rather those of education, transport, etc.

     There is a major retail market in Karol Bagh,
but the rest of the western colony area is similar
to the northern colonies, except that the people
"in service" work for the central government. But
the number of entrepreneurs is also impressive, and

the area is largely Punjabi. The fringe colonies,
west and south, tend to house the professionals and
those who work for the larger Delhi businesses.
The housing is newer and in a more "modern" style;
the colonies more spacious, and the problems are
those associated with new settlements: expanding
the sanitation system, the water lines, the paved
streets, and getting zoning variances for house
construction. Here and in the trans-Jumna colonies
more particularly one finds the "unauthorized"
colony--houses that have been built on land not
zoned for residential use. It is difficult for the
government to extend municipal services to built-up
areas that are not supposed to exist, but it can be
arranged. These are the areas of most recent immi-
gration into the city and are less homogeneous in
terms of the origin of the inhabitants--many are
Punjabis moving out from the older, more crowded
colonies, but many are from elsewhere in India.
Finally,* there are the rural areas surrounding
the city. Delhi's area is 573 square miles, and
78 percent of that area (447 square miles) is
rural.[18] There are approximately 300 villages
under the jurisdiction of the Corporation, and
clearly their "municipal" problems differ radically
from those of the rest of Delhi. Although Delhi's
villages are prosperous because of their proximity
to an urban market, they are still a "drain" on the
Corporation: more money is spent there (on education, etc.) than is realized in tax revenues.

---

*
    I omit a discussion of the New Delhi Municipal
Committee (NDMC) area and the Cantonment Board area,
since these are not under the jurisdiction of the
Corporation. The Cantonment is an army base, with
barracks and housing for officers, and is under the
direct administration of the army. It has a population (1971) of 57,339. The New Delhi Municipal
Committee area has a population (1971) of 301,801.
(Delhi District Census Handbook 1971, p. 19.) The
NDMC has eleven members, all nominated by the
lieutenant governor.

In particular political terms, the rural areas
are solidly Congress; the Punjabi refugee areas
solidly Jana Sangh.[19] The mixed areas of the older
suburban colonies are divided, with the Punjabi
component tending to provide the Jana Sangh its
support. The situation in the old city is similar:
Punjabis supporting the Jana Sangh, Muslims supporting the Congress, etc. The commercial and
"service" middle class of the city--the "Bania"--
is split. Congress and the Communist Party get
support in the organized trade-union areas. Thus,
although the Corporation is roughly divided in half
between the Congress and the Jana Sangh, the City
Zone (also divided half and half) is not representative of the political profile of Delhi as a
whole--the modal Congress member of the Corporation
is a villager and the modal Jana Sangh a Punjabi
refugee residing in the colonies of the 1950s,
largely in West Delhi. The Congress and the Jana
Sangh are divided evenly in the City Zone as well,
but there the Congressmen are Muslims and/or professionals and/or merchants (typically nonrefugee),
and the Jana Sangh are non-Muslim (in fact, Hindu),
professionals and merchants (again, typically nonrefugee, though some are refugees).

The municipal problems with which the Corporation has to deal vary from zone to zone in a
way that no single zone can be said to be typical.
The City Zone, along with the Sadar-Paharganj Zone,
is an area in which the Corporation is concerned
with high density housing; in the zones of the new
colonies (Karol Bagh Zone, for instance), the Corporation concerns itself with problems associated
with expanding populations--new schools, new roads,
etc.; in the rural areas, the concerns of the Corporation are obviously different. And yet, the
way the Corporation deals with the problems of the
City Zone is in part a function of the problems of
the entire city. An obvious instance would be
deciding on the placement of new water lines or
bus routes. The wholesale markets of the old city
also serve the rest of Delhi, and City Zone

residents work and visit in other areas also.
The physical and social patterns of Delhi are thus
not only a "setting" of the governments of the
entire territory, they are also the "setting" of
government within the City Zone, and, to a degree,
the "setting" of the government in the ward as
well.

Delhi as a Political Unit[20]

The complex of structures which share the job
of governing Delhi has fairly clear historical
roots. After the (symbolic) end of Moghul rule in
1858, Delhi became a district of the Punjab, and
the headquarters of a seven-district division
(the area is now roughly that constituting the
state of Haryana). The decision to shift the
capital of the Government of India from Calcutta to
Delhi (announced in 1911 and implemented in 1912)
was made, in part, to separate the seat of the
central government from the seat of the provincial
government (Calcutta was also the capital of Bengal),
to isolate the imperial capital from its political
surroundings, on the model of the U.S., Canada, and
Australia.[21]
So Delhi became the site of a new city, and
temporary government buildings were put up pending
the completion of Luytens's new Delhi (which was
formally inaugurated in 1931). In 1912 a few
tehsils of Delhi District were made into a Chief
Commissioner's Province, a form of provincial
administration which featured strong control by the
central government. This meant, among other things,
the loss of representation in the central legislature until 1919, when one seat was given to Delhi.
Under the constitution of independent India,
which came into effect on January 26, 1950, Delhi
became a Part C State, i.e., one of several political units that enjoyed the least amount of autonomy
from central control and supervision. And, as the
Report of the States Reorganization Commission
notes:

The present [1955] set-up of Delhi State . . .
is even more anomalous than that of other
Part C States in that, within the narrow
ambit of powers delegated to these States,
the legislative authority of Delhi is subject
to certain special limitations. The subjects
specifically excluded from the purview of the
State Legislature include law and order, local
self-governing institutions, the Improvement
Trust and other statutory boards regulating
certain public utility services in Delhi and
New Delhi.[22]

A legislature and a council of ministers was elected
in Delhi in 1952; the latter was to "aid and advise
the Chief Commissioner [the administrator for the
state appointed by the national government] in the
exercise of his functions in relation to matters in
respect of which the State Assembly was given power
to make laws."[23] The result of this arrangement,
according to the Report of the States Reorganization
Commission was that "it is contended . . . that
there has been a marked deterioration of administrative standards in Delhi since dual control was
introduced in 1951 [sic]."[24] This suggests that
the relationship between the chief commissioner and
the council of ministers was probably not a comfortable one.
    In 1956 States Reorganization abolished Part C
States and Delhi became a Union Territory. One
result was that it lost its legislative assembly and
council of ministers. The reasoning again was based
on the feeling that the capital of the country
should not be a political arena (a popular government was all right for municipal affairs, which were
in theory at least "non-partisan"). The States
Reorganization Commission had argued:

    If it is conceded that the national capital
    has to be under the effective control of the
    national government and both New Delhi and
    Old Delhi have to be treated as a single unit

for administrative purposes, there will be
little scope for difference of opinion on
its future administrative pattern.[25]

And so they recommended the establishment of a
Municipal Corporation. They denied that the abo-
lition of the legislature was a "retrograde step"
because with a Municipal Corporation and parliamentary representation, the people of Delhi would
be in a better position than the residents of the
other federal nations (the United States is particularly noted).[26] For the next ten years the only
popularly elected body in Delhi was the Delhi
Municipal Corporation (after 1958, when it was
formed out of a number of previously existent
local bodies; see Chapter 8, below).
    In 1966, a Metropolitan Council was installed
in Delhi. (An Interim Council was appointed by the
central government; elections were held early in
1967 along with the general election and the Corporation elections.) The Metropolitan Council consists of members elected from 56 wards plus five
who are nominated. Fifty of the elected members
come from the Corporation area (their constituency
is formed by two Corporation wards), five come from
the New Delhi Municipal Committee area, and one
comes from the Delhi Cantonment. Thus, unlike the
Municipal Corporation, it covers the whole of Delhi.
The Council is essentially a forum for debate: it
has no powers of legislation. It tends to meet for
the statutory minimum of two sessions a year, but
it has no power to do anything other than criticize
the Delhi Administration, and its resolutions have
tended to lie unimplemented by the central government.[27]
    Associated with the Metropolitan Council, but
not responsible to it, is the "Executive Council"
consisting of a Chief Executive Councilor and three
Executive Councilors nominated by the president of
India (that is, chosen by the central government).
In practice the central government has nominated
members of the party dominant in the Metropolitan

Council as executive councilors, even though there
is no legal requirement to do so. The executive
councilors are to "assist and advise"[28] the administration, but they have no real power. The
meetings of the Executive Council are presided
over by the Lt. Governor (the head of the Delhi
Administration). The chief executive councilor
especially, but the other executive councilors too,
do manage to wield some influence, largely because
of their ability to command public attention (they
are frequently guests of honor at ceremonies--at
which speeches may be given--for example), and
because of their access to information about, and
some informal penetration into, the administrative
process.

But the real authority in the Delhi Territory
is the latest incarnation of the chief commissioner--
the lieutenant governor. (Indeed, when the Metropolitan Council was set up, the incumbent officer
simply changed his title from Chief Commissioner to
Lt. Governor.) The Metropolitan Council can debate
and the Executive Council "advise and assist" on a
certain list of subjects ("transferred," as in the
old terminology of the "dyarchy" system instituted
by the Montagu-Chelmsford Reforms of 1919), leaving
the lieutenant governor with the "reserved" subjects
--law and order, police, services, nominations to
the New Delhi Municipal Committee, and some other
areas.

The power of zoning has been given to an
autonomous authority--the Delhi Development
Authority (the DDA)--whose membership of eleven
(excluding the chairman (the lieutenant governor)
and the vice-chairman) consists of two members of
Parliament, two municipal councilors, and seven
officers of the central government (attached to the
Delhi Administration, the NDMC, etc.). The DDA has
an Advisory Council made up of ten elected representatives and ten members drawn from social
service organizations or government agencies.

Control over the police is clearly a crucial
subject: when the central government has spoken

about insulating the national capital from political
pressures, it has probably meant that responsibility
for law and order could not be permitted to get into
the hands of a parochial political unit. In short,
the Delhi Administration (and, for all practical
purposes, this means the lieutenant governor) has
most of the executive authority of a state government, with the exception of supervisory powers over
the Municipal Corporation which, in Delhi, is exercised by Parliament.[29] Legislative authority rests
with the central government, and this gives the
lieutenant governor considerable scope for administrative initiative, because Parliament is unlikely
to concern itself with the less visible elements of
Delhi government. The pattern of governmental
authority in Delhi is diagrammed in Fig. 3.

The status of Delhi has been a political issue
since even before independence. A memorandum pre-
senting the "Case for Greater Delhi" to the States
Reorganization Commission traced the beginnings of
the demand for a Delhi State (which would add the
two westernmost divisions of the United Provinces,
Meerut and Agra, to the former Delhi Province, i.e.,
Ambala Division of the Punjab), to a speech by
Pirzada Hussain, chairman of the All-India Reception
Committee of the All-India Muslim League in 1926.[30]
The idea was taken up by the Congress and presented
to various conferences between 1928 and 1932. The
argument was to recognize politically the "natural
boundaries" (my words) of a historic, cultural and
economic region.[31] The question of the national
capital is handled by suggesting that New Delhi be
retained as the (disenfranchised) capital, for which
arrangements for municipal services in common with
Delhi city could be worked out.[32]

The Vishal (Greater) Haryana Party was active
in the late 1960s in pressing (none too successfully)
the demand for a "greater Haryana" which would comprise much of the area of this early proposal, and
would have Delhi as its capital. Recent demands
from Delhi itself--and both major parties have at
one time or the other suggested it--have been for

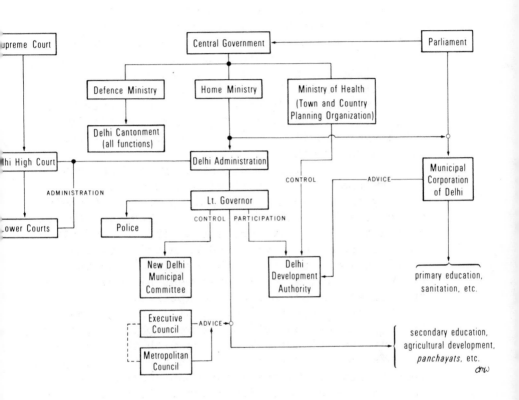

Fig. 3 Major authorities in Delhi.

the restoration of statehood, although this is presented in terms of "restoring the popular will,"
etc., and does not deal with the difficulties of
the national capital location.[33]

The Administrative Reforms Commission, following the suggestion of its study team, has
proposed that the Metropolitan Council be given
de facto status as a state assembly, with the powers
of the (abolished) Municipal Corporation added to
it, with an Executive Coucil responsible to it, but
with stringent safeguards and ultimate central control over its decisions.[34] This recommendation has
not as yet (April, 1975) been acted upon by the
central government.*

The discussion of the history of Delhi government resumes in Chapter 8 with an outline of the
history of the Delhi Municipal Committee (1863-1957)
and of the Corporation (1958-). The configuration
of the zones as they were set up in 1963 and after
was not unconnected with the boundaries of the
previous local bodies of the province, and this
aspect of Delhi's local government history will be
treated at the beginning of Chapter 6.

In this "portrait" of Delhi I have touched
briefly on the connections between physical, social,
economic and historical factors with the day-to-day
concerns of the Corporation. In the three chapters
that follow, I examine these connections in the
setting of Kucha Khirkiwala ward. Here the "vocabulary" and the "idiomatic expressions" of urban
politics in Delhi will be explored in detail if
only to make their more complex usage at the zonal
level and at the all-city level comprehensible. But
Kucha Khirkiwala is also a meaningful political
arena in its own right.

---

*The Corporation was, however, superseded on
March 24, 1975 for the period of one year.
(Hindustan Times, March 25, 1975.)

2. A Portrait of Kucha Khirkiwala Ward

The municipal wards of Delhi are obviously political and administrative units, and they are socio-economic entities as well, each with its own character. They vary from the rural wards, which contain villages and fields, to the densely built-up wards of the old city; from the spacious wards of the civil lines area, with broad avenues and large bungalows, to wards where there are factories, warehouses, and slums. There are wards with a sparse and homogeneous population and wards with very large, heterogeneous populations. One aim of this chapter is to evoke the atmosphere of one of Delhi's wards, and to give meaning to the vocabulary of municipal government at the lowest level, rather than merely to define the terms. Another aim is to present in as much detail as possible the socio-economic background of the ward, minimally to provide the scene for the description of the councilor's activities which follows in Chapter 3, and to test assertions about the relationship of these structures and patterns to ward politics, an attempt made in Chapter 4.

THE PHYSICAL AND SOCIAL PROFILE OF THE WARD

Setting

The one ward of Delhi's 100 wards which I studied intensively is called Kucha Khirkiwala,

after one of its principal <u>mohallas</u>.* The Hindi
names for streets and other physical features are
not easily translated into English equivalents, and
so I shall begin by setting out their meanings and
retain the original Hindi word.

A <u>mohalla</u> refers to a locality. It is a complex of <u>galis</u> (lanes) with one or a number of exits
into a main street. Occasionally <u>mohallas</u> are also
so named, as in "<u>mohalla</u> Shahganj," but more frequently they are given names such as "Kucha Pandit,"
"Chhatta Lal Mian," "Gali School Wali," "Haveli Azam
Khan," "Phatak Ram Kishan Dass," "Chandni Mahal,"
etc. Most of these names refer to structures: a
<u>phatak</u> is a gate and hence any <u>gali</u> with a gate at
its entrance, or with a large house with a gateway
entrance might be named "Phatak." A <u>chhatta</u> is a
set of buildings, where the second story of one
bridges a <u>gali</u>, forming a gateway; a <u>haveli</u> is a
nobleman's or rich man's mansion; a <u>mahal</u> is literally a palace. A <u>katra</u> can be residential or
commercial. The latter has a number of small shops
fronting on a passageway, the former a large number
of separate households sharing a courtyard and a
single entranceway. A <u>basti</u> is often a small scale
village within the city; it indicates a segregated
area of small shacks with its own lane system.

<u>Galis</u> etc. are usually named after persons--
the owners of the most important house, a leading
citizen of the city--but also occasionally after the
occupation or caste of the people who live there
("Gali Sonarwali"), a local monument or historical
event ("Gali Magazine"), or a physical object, for
instance a tree ("Gali Imli"). Often the objects
referred to have long since disappeared. Names do

---

*All the names given to localities and persons
of the ward are pseudonyms; this has been done not
so much to disguise the location of the study as to
underline the fact that I am consolidating observations of many wards and councilors into one ward
and one councilor.

change, however, either by municipal action (many
streets have been renamed after nationalist heroes),
or by a more gradual process. If a local citizen
doesn't know the name of a gali--which is not uncom-
mon--he will invent one for the occasion. When a
school is constructed in a gali formerly named after
a nobleman of 200 years ago, now forgotten, it may
become "Gali School Wali" (the gali where the school
is). The municipal ward is usually an artificial
unit, and can be thought of as a conglomeration
of various mohallas, katras, bastis, and bazars
(streets lined with wholesale or retail shops, often
with vendors on the pavement as well).

Municipal ward Kucha Khirkiwala, then, is just
such a conglomeration, bounded on two sides by two
of the major bazars of Delhi, with a secondary bazar
as its spine, and a number of mohallas, some with
gates that can be shut at night, others simply
neighborhoods with vague boundaries (see Fig. 4).
Although there is heavy traffic on the two main
bazars, and an occasional car down the secondary
bazar as well as cycle rickshaws (pedicabs) and
bullock carts, almost all the traffic in the ward
is foot traffic. Most of the movement of goods
(and there are a number of large godowns [ware-
houses] in the ward) is by handcart (thela) and many
of the largely residential galis are blocked by iron
or concrete pillars, so that goods are carried into
these areas on the heads of laborers. Indeed, due
to the concentration of population and commerce,
walking is a perfectly sensible way of moving about,
quite apart from the vehicular traffic itself
moving at walking pace.

Kucha Khirkiwala is in the center of the two-
square-mile area of the old city of Delhi and is no
more than half an hour's walk from most of the
residents' jobs, amusements, or places of municipal
business. The zonal office, although located outside the site of the old city wall (now replaced by
a wall of commercial buildings), is at most 20
minutes' walk away, and Town Hall is from 10 to 25
minutes away. Even Connaught Place, the commercial

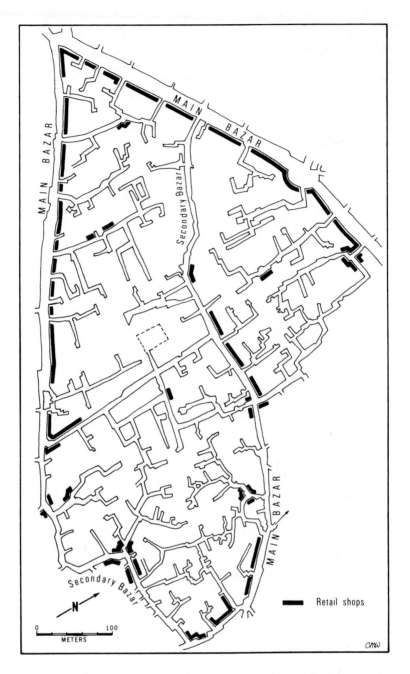

Fig. 4 Kucha Khirkiwala Municipal Ward, showing
the approximate locations of retail shops in
1969-70.

heart of New Delhi, is less than an hour's walk,
and on bicycle, by bus, tonga (horse-drawn car-
riage) or scooter rickshaw (a three-wheeled cab
for two passengers powered by a motor scooter),
it is readily accessible. The ward is almost in
the shadow of the Jama Masjid (the great Friday
Mosque which is one of the architectural gems of
Delhi) and has temples and small mosques scattered
throughout. The impression conveyed to even the
casual visitor is of an area alive with activity
of all kinds, inhabited by people of every degree
of prosperity and poverty, not perhaps a unit in
social terms (or at least not visibly so), but
clearly central to contemporary Delhi's vitality
and meaning.

Rory Fonseca has studied a similar area in
Old Delhi, and presents a view of it opposed to
the conventional Western-oriented condemnation by
city planners as a "slum" for which the only cure
is demolition and reconstruction on the lines of
the colonies which have grown up since Independence
on the outskirts of Delhi.[1] His point of view can
be summarized as follows:

The indigenous city of Delhi presents some
workable alternatives to the present trends
in planning and architecture. . . . Some
of its more significant features [are]:
    1) Land is intensively used and the
occupational pattern thoroughly mixed.
Those who seek the unity and order of a
plan comprehensible at a glance, characterized by neat zones, perceive the city as
congested and unplanned. But we have seen
that there is a definite pattern. A typical
ward breakdown is 15% in streets, lanes and
chowks [square]; 6% in public, religious, and
monument space; 25% in internal courtyards;
54% in structures. . . .
    2) [high densities of population]
    3) Those who see the old city as congested
do not look beyond the narrow streets that

form the interstices between buildings,
yet approximately 25% of the old city
is open space in the form of private
internal courtyards. As the common
space of a house, appropriate to the
climate and the social habits of the
occupants the internal courtyard is a
simple device for maximizing trans-
actions with one's immediate relatives
and family. As a personal space, it
compensates for the anonymity and stress
of urbanism. . . .[2]

Almost the entire area of the walled city has
been declared a slum, and the Delhi Master Plan
suggests a reduction in the population densities.
At least one area has had 48-hour notice of the
demolition of its houses served on its inhabitants
(later withdrawn after a demonstration had been
organized). There is also provision in the Master
Plan for the widening of streets, which would mean
the removal of commercial properties fronting on
the bazar and a realignment of the physical structures of the mohalla. Similarly there are plans
for the segregation of land usage into residential,
commercial, and industrial. All of these are live
political issues in the ward.
The core of Fonseca's argument is that the
indigenous land usage makes sense in terms of
efficiency of transport and services as well as
for a comfortable living area. Although the entire
non-street area is built up, the open space which
the planners seek, is there already as private
courtyards and semi-private roof space (used for
sleeping in the summer, for kite flying and other
games, for drying clothes, etc.). The narrow gali
looked at positively is a device which keeps out the
sun in summer and conserves the heat of the buildings in winter in a way that the broad roads of
the new colonies cannot. Note that in Kucha
Khirkiwala (Fig. 4) the major galis run north-south
(except in the eastern portion where there is a

"hill" perhaps 50 feet high--the galis point to the
summit) so that there is a maximum amount of light
in the winter yet a good deal of shade in the summer when the sun is higher and the three-story
buildings lining the gali block it out. Fonseca
describes the network of primary, secondary, and
tertiary streets not only in economic terms--
"Production accumulates in the courtyards, moves
in accretions down lanes in hand-drawn vehicles or
on the backs of doubled-over men to distribution
centers along secondary streets where it filters
up to the bazars"[3]--but also in terms of the privacy
of the individual who moves in a series of "spatial
envelopes" from private courtyard to mohalla gali
of caste fellows and friends, and finally out into
the urban anonymity of the main bazar. Fonseca
argues that along with this physical organization
there are symbiotic social organizations, formal and
informal, which regulate behavior and insure that
mohallas, and the roof-world which bridges mohallas
(since the houses of mohallas are aligned back to
back, perhaps separated only by a narrow jhot [open
sewer]),are functioning social units, that the
impression of jumbled and decaying housing hides a
powerful underlying social and economic fabric.

Quite apart from the question of the reaction
of local residents to the Master Plan notions of
"proper" city organization, this viable socio-
economic order clothed in degenerating buildings is
clearly the central concern of the municipal government as it penetrates into the ward. Because densities are very high and because houses are decaying,
the demands are for adequate sewer systems and a
vigorous sanitation effort, for permission to recon-
struct or add to cramped housing, for adequate water,
good street lighting, etc. These are, as we shall
see, what the councilor of Kucha Khirkiwala spends
his time (and the money from the zonal budget) on,
and to an extent it is the framework within which
the ward is organized.

The Problem of Sanitation--a Paradigm

> The gutter was wide as a channel. Once in a
> while, especially before the elections, the
> Municipal officials [of Malgudi, a fictional
> South Indian town] came down and walked along
> the edge peering into its dark current and
> saying something among themselves as to its
> being a problem and so on. But there they
> left it until the next election. It was a
> stock cynicism for people to say when they
> saw anyone inspecting the drains: "They are
> only looking for the election votes there!"[4]

The zonal office maintains a register of complaints from the public in which by far the most
frequent complaints have to do with blocked sewer
lines. In an eight-month period of 1967, 54 percent of the complaints were on that, 18 percent on
problems of water supply, and 10 percent on other
insanitary conditions. A blocked sewer in Kucha
Khirkiwala, as in most of the zone, means that an
entire gali may be covered by a sheet of liquid
sewage. The smell is unpleasant and walking through
it even worse. The councilor is so concerned with
this and similar problems that he has the Assistant
Sanitary Inspectors (ASI) of whom there are two in
each ward, report to him daily. The ASI supervises
the sweepers* assigned to the ward, some permanent
and some temporary. The ASI has the power to chalan
landlords (issue summonses) for leaking or nonexistent sewage connections[5] and private sweepers
for dumping nightsoil and rubbish in the gali
instead of carting it to the dalao (a shed which is
the collection point for nightsoil garbage). The
sweepers are unionized and the union is affiliated
with the Congress Party. The problem of sanitation

---

*   These are men, women and children of an untouchable caste who sweep up nightsoil and other
filth in the galis; "private" sweepers clean out
dry latrines in individual houses.

in the ward may thus be used to illustrate how government operates at that level: the citizen com-
plains to the councilor and to higher authorities
(the zone) about the problem; the councilor exercises control (he "orders" the ASI to do certain
things) over the administrative officer concerned;
the councilor is at the same time caught up in the
larger political system (here in his relation to a
Congress union). And the whole issue is involved
with the "policy" question of the implementation of
the Master Plan, since it makes little sense to provide sewer lines for a population whose density is
to be reduced, and for houses which will be
demolished.

In order to understand governmental concern
with sanitation, it will be necessary to elaborate
the purely physical dimensions of the problem.
Kucha Khirkiwala can be divided into two sections:
the "hill" in the east and a gently sloping section to the west. Each gali has gutters, usually on
both sides, which run either into a sewer opening
(there is only one system of sewers, handling both
sewage and rain water) in the gali itself or into
the sewer system of a large gali or the bazar.
House sewer lines connect with the gali sewer lines
or terminate in pipes which end a few inches above
the street surface. These channel rainwater from
the roof, water from floor-washing, and occasionally
urine into the gali gutters. The open drain (jhot),
which separates the backs of the house rows,* is a

---

*
Perhaps it should be made clear here that the
houses of the gali form a solid wall, often without
any setback at all, and the front steps may begin
with a slab of rock set into the base of the house
wall. Although there are occasional trees in the
chowks of the gali and many courtyards with plants
in them, there are no "yards" anywhere in the old
city. Houses apart from those fronting on the main
bazar are two and three stories high. There are also
bastis with one-story housing and katras with shacks
built on their roofs.

fairly common feature. Urinals are put on the main
streets by the Municipal Corporation, but small
children are taught to defecate and urinate directly
into the street gutter until they are old enough to
use the latrine. The municipal sweeper is supposed
to clean each gali twice a day (but usually it is
done only once) by sweeping up the dirt and cleaning
the gutters with a stiff broom made of twigs, while
a stream of water is directed into them by a man
carrying a goatskin water bag. All the galis are
cleaned with water in this fashion. The nightsoil
and garbage collected (it is mixed together) is carried to the dalao in flat metal thelis (which are
like a very shallow, large bowl) or in small hand
carts.

The sweepers tend to work as families; the
Zonal Health Officer estimated that a family could
earn 900 rupees a month (as much as a college lec-
turer, whose wife and children would probably not
be wage-earners). According to the Zonal Assistant
Commissioner of the City Zone, each ward has a
Sanitary Inspector, two Assistant Sanitary Inspectors, and about 100 sweepers. In addition the
sweepers are directly supervised by three daroga
safaiis ("sanitary constables" [supervisors]) and
four "sanitary guides." These are the men who
specialize in unblocking sewer lines (while regular
desilting of sewer lines is the responsibility of
the Water Supply and Sewage Disposal Undertaking
and not of the Health Department), and one man with
a few helpers is responsible for the dalao.

The Sanitary Inspector and the ASIs have
received training in public health. In addition to
supervising the sweepers and "chalaning" offending
landlords and sweepers, they can chalan shopkeepers
for displaying food in an insanitary way. They also
maintain an office for registering births and deaths.
They do not get their hands dirty and are definitely
not sweepers promoted from the ranks; some wear
jackets and ties on the job. In the year of councilor's rounds which I observed in Kucha Khirkiwala,[6]
both ASIs were absent on only one of the 34 rounds

and only on two other rounds was one missing. The
Sanitary Inspector was present on at least two of
these rounds as well.

Not only do the ASIs report to the councilor
every day, he also expects them to report problems
--leaking public water faucets, a pile of malba
(brick rubble) on the road--not related to their
responsibility. Councilors may ask the ASIs to
refrain from yet again chalaning a storekeeper, and
berate them for not chalaning a landlord who refuses
to repair his sewer pipe. On at least one occasion
I heard the ASI ask the councilor "do you want me to
chalan the owner of this house?" and the councilor
replied, "of course." When a marriage is to take
place in the house of a particular gali, the councilor will ask the ASI to see that the area is given
special attention, and might even say to him,
"please do everything [the citizen concerned] tells
you to do." And indeed, special efforts were made,
and the streets were cleaned thoroughly.*

Just before I began studying the ward, and also
six months later, there were sweepers' strikes, the
second one lasting two weeks. Kucha Khirkiwala was
one of the wards hard hit by the strike--other areas
had sizeable numbers of "loyal" sweepers on the job
--and the filth piled up quickly, although the dalao
continued to be emptied, albeit irregularly. For
the first week nothing was done by local people, who
were hoping for an early settlement. In the city as
a whole, the first reports of local residents doing
their own cleaning occurred on the eighth day. The
councilor of Kucha Khirkiwala didn't go on his round

---

*
It should be noted here that despite the
formidable obstacles of an overburdened sewer system,
a propensity to litter by the general public (and an
insufficient number of litter baskets)', an abundance
of stray and working animals, and an often tense
labor situation (the ASIs are often ignored and/or
insulted by chastised sweepers), the ward is kept
remarkably clean; there are many streets in American
cities filthier and fouler-smelling.

on the fifth day of the strike, saying "it would
do no good; it would only make trouble."

A week later on the round, he made it a point
to initiate conversations by apologizing with "how
terrible the filth is," which generally got the
response "it doesn't matter." He encouraged people
to clean their own streets, or pay their private
sweepers to do it, bringing the garbage out to the
main streets where trucks could collect it. By
this time, special groups of "loyal" sweepers had
been organized and removal of collected garbage was
going on. In some areas--and a nearly complete
coverage of the ward was made on this round--resi-
dents were cleaning the galis and carting away the
filth, but in most areas nothing had been done.

People did expect the councilor to do something about the situation--he emphasized that he had
worked to clean his own gali--but the response to
his appeals to citizens to do their own cleaning was
weak. In addition he attempted to deal directly
with some private sweepers in one mohalla, without
result. Indeed, the councilor has very little
influence over the actual sweeper, as is indicated
by the following newspaper report of some two months
before the strike:

> The latest effort [to clean up the area] was
> made by the area councilor. He came along
> with a few sweepers, urging and goading them
> to clean the area. The sweepers told him
> curtly that they were not employed for the
> personal publicity of the councilor; they
> would do their duty in their own way, and
> dropped their brooms and rakes and sat back
> for a smoke.[7]

On numerous occasions during the year, I observed
arguments between councilor and sweeper, and between
sweeper and the ASI, in which it was clear that the
sweepers had no intention of being "ordered" to do
anything. On the other hand, one newspaper report
on the twelfth day of the strike ran:

According to Corporation officials, the reason
more sweepers returned to work was because
they were getting police protection, and
"genuine" support from the residents who in
some areas even helped them to clean the
locality.[8]

Helping sweepers clean was so uncommon that it presumably provided an added inducement to work. Of
course sweeping is not only an unpleasant task, it
is also polluting for Hindus, and thus it is hardly
surprising that the middle-class Hindu residents of
Kucha Khirkiwala would not be anxious to help,
except as a last resort. Still, the stench and
inconvenience after the first few days of the strike
was considerable, and since Gandhi, there is an
available ideology which would permit even Hindus
to "scavenge" with propriety. There were Hindu and
Muslim mohallas in Kucha Khirkiwala which cleaned
their own galis and Hindu and Muslim mohallas which
didn't. Nor was their any connection with mohalla
organizations, few and powerless as they are; in
organized mohallas there was just as little chance
of citizen self-help as in other mohallas. There
was no indication either that Congress Party
workers were taking the lead in clean-up campaigns.
The few of these that happened seemed to arise
spontaneously in random areas.
    Several interviews with opponents of the Kucha
Khirkiwala councilor indicated that his failure to
organize the ward during the sweepers' strike was
something the citizens didn't like, something that
would contribute, these men hoped, to his defeat in
the next election. Sanitation is something that the
government is supposed to provide for, even in the
exceptional circumstances of a sweepers' strike.
    Keeping the neighborhood clean is one of the
major efforts of urban community development projects; it is seen as something which is obviously
of local concern and in which local cooperative
effort would be productive. Marshall Clinard, in
his book on an urban community development pilot

project in Delhi[9] tries to find reasons why Indian
slums are filthier than similar slums in Ceylon,
Thailand, Japan and other countries. He sees it
as a combination of insufficient latrines, garbage
cans, etc.; "indiscriminate" defecation by children;
village practices, religion, the role of the
sweeper, and the keeping of dairy cattle; and, first
on the list, Citizen Apathy:

> If all the people in a slum area, rather than
> an occasional few, fail to cooperate in main-
> taining cleanliness, it is almost impossible
> to deal with the problem; if people do not
> cooperate, the government can do little. . . .
> Most Indian families insist upon cleanliness
> of their own brass cooking utensils, which
> are kept well polished, and often upon the
> cleanliness of their personal living quarters,
> yet they appear to think little of adding to
> the general disorder and filth in the streets
> and alleys.[10]

The pilot project vikas mandals (development councils) attempted various programs to tackle this
problem, providing physical facilities--latrines and
garbage cans--and pressure and permission to change
practices,[11] yet in an evaluation made eight years
after the inception of the project reported that
only a third of the sample interviewed felt sanitary
conditions had improved, and nearly half said that
there had been no change.[12] The study is deficient
in that there was no control group from non-project
areas of the city, and there is no way of saying to
what extent general cleanliness improved (if it did)
due to physical improvements or to a reduction of
citizen apathy. One question on the practice of
defecation (by children) and urinating (by adult
males and children) in public gutters shows the
situation to be worsening.[13]
    Sanitation in the ward is the most salient
problem with which local government has to deal.
Self-help efforts, even in crises such as the

sweepers' strike, have failed, though it is obvious
that local attitudes are significant: two galis in
Kucha Khirkiwala inhabited largely by one organized
Muslim biraadari (literally "brotherhood"; more or
less equivalent to a caste) were without question
the cleanest in the ward, as was pointed out by the
councilor to those who went with him on rounds.

Citizens apparently feel that sanitation is
solely the government's business. Government action
and expenditure--the laying of new sewer lines,
encouraging and/or financing flush latrine installations, building of public urinals, the supervision
and control of public and private sweepers--did have
noticeable effects in Kucha Khirkiwala. The councilor, however, noted that there was no need to ask
citizens about the problem: it was obvious from
just walking through the ward. The councilor maintains his supervision over the ASIs more closely
than that over any other administrative officer.
It was also clear that despite the citizen's recognition of the problems the councilor had to deal
with in getting sweepers to work efficiently, he was
criticized for not doing enough during the sweepers'
strike. The councilor is considered ultimately
responsible for much of what is or is not done to
keep the ward clean.

The problem of sanitation is a representative
problem of municipal government in the ward. The
involvement of the councilor and his relationship
with the administrative officers involved is
typical. The problem itself is also significant
as a marker of the economic and physical condition
of a ward of the old city, and, indirectly, of
social structure, when we look at the absence of
citizen activity during the sweepers' strike.
Finally, this discussion has shown that there is
a sphere of responsibility which citizens assign
to "government." The councilor, in theory concerned only with "policy" matters, is expected,
and himself expects, to be concerned with that
sphere of administrative activity.

Social Structure and the Mohalla

Other problems in the ward have much the same
pattern of actors and action, although usually not
as clearly outlined as in the case of sanitation.
Before we look at the relation of councilor to
administrative officer at this level, the powers of
the councilor (especially over Corporation expenditure), the attitudes of citizens toward government,
and other related issues, let us examine some of the
relevant socio-economic characteristics of the ward.

The brief discussion of community development
in relation to sanitation is indicative of one
feature of Kucha Khirkiwala--the relative powerlessness of local associations. It should be noted at
the outset that despite Clinard's generally optimistic assessment of the community development
pilot project in Delhi, another study[14] came to the
conclusion that the program, and the Department of
Community Development that was set up to insti-
tutionalize it, had been a total failure. I myself
observed a Corporation by-election in one of the
pilot project areas: the vikas mandal office had
become a party office, and no one in the ward,
politician or citizen, so much as mentioned the
project, nor were any of its results visible to
me.[15]

The project did not include Kucha Khirkiwala,
but there are some local associations in the ward.
These typically are mohalla committees whose functions are confined to maintaining a wooden platform
at a central point and subscribing to newspapers
which are placed there; perhaps to hiring a chowkidar
(watchman) to guard the mohalla gate and keep
"troublemakers" out; and to providing a notice
board at a central place in the mohalla. There are
also temple committees which, in addition to seeing
after the maintenance of the small temple, will
often also maintain a dharmshala (hospice) which is
rented out to marriage parties. These associations
are very few in number: they exist in only six of
the mohallas of the ward. Further, these

associations are fragile and short-lived. They not
only keep out of politics, but also out of disputes
between landlords and tenants within the mohalla.
I asked party workers, and candidates for Corporation office, about these and none felt they were
politically significant.

There are, however, less formally organized
forms of neighborhood community solidarity, at least
potentially. For a number of weeks, for example,
the councilor attempted to persuade mohalla citizens
to "get together" and paint all their house fronts
one color for Diwali (a "new year" festival in which
repainting the house is a traditional feature).
Nothing was done, however. Or to take another
instance: one week a few posters of the "Vedwara
Bhaichara Committee" (Vedwara Brotherhood Committee)
appeared, saying:

> Our Goal Is to Serve You
> Friends! Seeing the increasing anarchy in the
> country a few people of Vedwara called a
> meeting and thought it necessary that every
> person in the country . . . has the duty, each
> getting together with others in his own mohalla,
> . . . to help in the reconciliation and to
> share the suffering of his fellow . . . and to
> keep peace in his area. . . .   [We] have estab-
> lished a "Bhaichara Committee" in Vedwara . . .
> [with] the following tasks:
>   1) the Brotherhood Committee will attempt
> to see that no child of the mohalla remains
> illiterate
>   2) to aid the sick and the helpless
>   3) to foster respect of elders and love of
> the young. . . .
> This Brotherhood Committee is not connected
> with any political party nor will there be in
> any way a feeling of difference on the grounds
> of caste or religion. In order to reach these
> goals we pray that all the people of the area
> and fellow youths give us their help in this
> task.[16]

An office address was also given, and there was
much emphasis on the "duty" (kartavya) of the
citizens to help. The emphasis on the lack of
political ties and the generally revivalist tone
is typical of the few other posters of a similar
nature that I saw. This committee turned out to
be simply a group of friends who liked to get
together (according to one informant); its efforts,
as far as I could tell, came to nothing.

On Independence Day (August 15) there were
three flag unfurling ceremonies[17] held in the ward,
sponsored by various kinds of neighborhood groups
(a temple committee which had also sponsored a
local library, etc.). The only other organization
which I came across in the ward was a "young men's
Muslim sporting club" (which had a clubroom in one
mohalla). These youths invited the councilor to
their clubroom in order to ask him for help in
improving the building, and he in turn attempted
to persuade them to affiliate formally with the
Youth Congress. None of these organizations are
numerically significant: the mohalla committee of
Kucha Khirkiwala (the mohalla after which the ward
is named), a mohalla with a population of approximately 6,000, had a membership, according to its
founder and former president, of 60 to 65.
Finally, it should be noted--unfortunately I have
little data--that some caste-homogeneous katras
(with populations of up to 300 people) had a formal
"traditional" structure, with a chaudhari (headman).
In my interviews with ward political activists, in
which I asked about locality leaders of political
significance, only two of these chaudharis were
mentioned, and it is questionable whether their
authority was in any way "traditional." Similarly,
there are Muslim biraadari organizations in the
area which might be politically significant. No one
was willing to come out and say so, however. Kucha
Khirkiwala, despite its physical division into
clearly demarcated mohallas, has few and relatively
insignificant associations corresponding to them.
When in the eighteenth and nineteenth centuries

mohallas had real significance as defensive arrangements against the periodic lootings of Delhi, things
may have been different;[18] I have seen no evidence
which would support this assumption, however. Nevertheless, later analysis will make it clear that
mohallas are relevant units for a political analysis
of the ward.

What I have attempted to indicate here is that
the ward or even the mohalla is not a clearly
visible unit in terms of formal or informal organizations. Indeed, few people identify their home as
"Mohalla X," but rather give their house number.
This is not to say that citizens of the ward do not
belong to "voluntary" or "common interest" organizations. Citizens of the ward are members of
economic interest organizations such as wholesale
merchants' associations, and unions; of religious
organizations which set up a grandstand at the
annual Ram Lila celebrations; of semi-political
organizations such as the RSS (Rastriya Swayamsevak
Sangh); and so on. Owens and Nandy report a situation in which ward-level organizations play important political roles,[19] but in Kucha Khirkiwala
these organizational ties, at least seen from
"below," from the point of view of the average citizen, were not politically significant. Political
workers were members of such organizations, but they
didn't seem to see these ties for political purposes
as a rule.

The Polling Station as a Unit of Analysis

The time of the greatest political activity in
the ward is during municipal elections, and the
socio-economic divisions of the area appear most
clearly at such times.[20] A "polling station" is an
electoral precinct. Party organization at election
time--and consequently post-election analyses and
action is based on polling stations. There are
roughly 15 polling stations in a Delhi ward; Kucha
Khirkiwala has 18. Polling stations are set up to

have approximately equal numbers of voters (700-
1,000) and thus do not necessarily conform to "natural" units: one polling station may encompass many
mohallas (polling station 17 in Kucha Khirkiwala;
see Fig. 5), roughly one mohalla (polling station
2), or a part of a mohalla (polling station 14).
The first situation is the modal one: five of the
eighteen Kucha Khirkiwala polling stations covered
one mohalla, one covered part of a mohalla, and the
remaining twelve covered more than one mohalla.

At election time each candidate will have an
"in-charge" at each polling station who supervises
checking of the electoral roll; distributes party
"identification slips" to voters a day or two before
the polling; introduces the candidate when he is
canvassing in the area; and provides a continuing
account of voting trends in the locality.   The Jana
Sangh organizes its active sthaniya samitis (local
councils) by polling station also.[21]   On the whole,
the political worker sees the ward as a series of
polling stations which can in turn be broken down
(or combined) into mohallas and katras and other
units.

Although I do not intend to assert that polling stations are perceived by citizens as meaningful political units, it is not clear which units,
if any, are politically meaningful to them.   The
common method of giving an address is by house
number (the house numbers in the walled city are
divided into eleven groups reflecting the old
division of the city into eleven administrative
wards, dating from at least 1871; a typical house
number would be VII/1986).   A number of people I
asked had no idea of the name of the mohalla in
which they were living, or that--as was not unusual
--it had changed its name in the recent past.   While
many mohallas are quite clearly set apart, with a
gate at the entrance, or one street, others are
open-ended, with many streets and many entrances,
and their boundaries are not at all clear.   Many
people live on the secondary streets, above the
shops of the bazar, in no mohalla at all.   There are

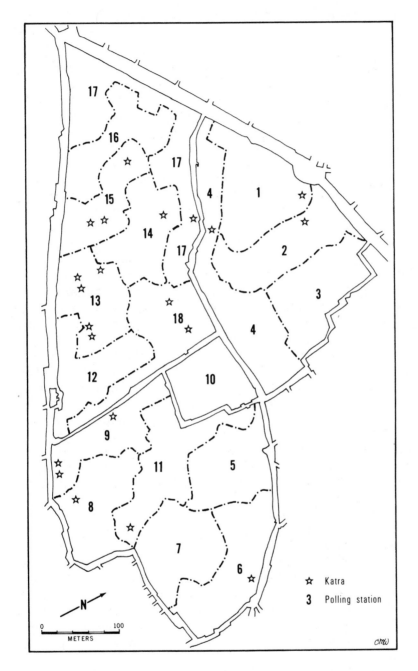

Fig. 5 Polling stations in Kucha Khirkiwala, showing the approximate locations of katras.

also encapsulated residential units--<u>katras</u> and
<u>bastis</u>--within <u>mohallas</u>, so that for the residents,
particularly those that live in a caste-homogeneous
<u>katra</u>, their place of residence is "Katra Ram Lal"
or whatever. Moreover, <u>mohallas</u> can be grouped:
people speak of "the Muslim <u>mohallas</u>," "<u>mohallas</u> X,
Y, and Z where the Jatava live," and so forth.

The polling station is of course a territorial
unit. There are, however, other ways of dividing
up the ward, starting from the perceptions of the
inhabitants. Kin, caste, and religious ties all cut
across these territorial units and indeed usually
cover neighboring wards and often the entire city.
Similarly, economic connections are not confined
to one area, and in political affairs ties extend
beyond the ward: an active Jana Sangh worker, for
example, will tend to go to a nearby Jana Sangh
councilor to get his "work" done rather than to his
own (Congress) councilor.

Any given citizen places himself differently
given different contexts of action or identification:
<u>qua</u> political party worker he is resident in a poll-
ing station, or in a <u>mohalla</u>, or in a <u>katra</u> if he
is out canvassing for votes; <u>qua</u> citizen he resides
in the ward, and in the zone and in Delhi; <u>qua</u>
political party worker also he is a <u>kinsman</u>, a
caste-fellow, a man with ties of religion; he may
be a merchant, or the member of a trade union; and
so on. On one political issue one of these "place-
ments" will be more significant than another. If
the question is the place of Urdu as a language of
administration in the Corporation, then his ties to
his fellow Muslims/Hindus will be of more importance
than the <u>mohalla</u> he lives in. If the issue is the
placement of new street lights, the ties of locality
might well predominate. Obviously, without speci-
fying the context one cannot say that any given unit
of analysis is more "natural" (or, is more appropriate) than another.

It is clear that organization by polling
station is adopted at election time, (with some
important exceptions--"the <u>katras</u>" were an important

unit of political analysis in Kucha Khirkiwala, and
they are widely scattered; see Fig. 5) for the sake
of convenience: the polling lists come printed that
way, and they are at least more or less compact
areas in which some reference is made to the "natural" unit of the mohalla. Special political
workers may be assigned to look after the katras, or
to approach important occupational groupings, but
the basic organization is based on the polling
station. Not surprisingly, this has relevance for
continuing political contact after the election
(which is also the time before the next election),
and although there is no longer the need for pre-
cision (such as calculating just how many Muslim
voters there are in polling station 15) the councilor and other political workers continue to divide
the ward by polling station.

The above discussion is an attempt to justify,
but not validate, my subsequent use of the polling
station as a unit of analysis; it is not entirely an
artificial category. On occasion I shall also use
census blocks, but these units were apparently set
up by an arbitrary division of the sequence of house
numbers and conform to few "natural" territorial
units. I have indicated that the inhabitants of
Kucha Khirkiwala do not "reveal" themselves in
organizational terms, and that the polling station
is a proper unit of analysis. I now move to a
description of the ward drawn from census data,
where the inhabitants and the polling station can be
classified by a series of characteristics.

SOCIO-ECONOMIC DIMENSIONS: THE CENSUS DATA

The area of Kucha Khirkiwala is approximately 50
acres, and its 1971 population was just over 30,000.[*]

---

[*] In 1961, the population was only 1,500 fewer,
so we can say with confidence that the population in
1969-70 was 30,000.

This density is higher than that of the walled city as a whole and about twice as high as it will be if and when the Master Plan suggestions are implemented. The characteristics of the population which can be drawn from the 1971 census are presented, in raw form, in the Appendix, Table 1 (below, p. 356), and in percentages in Tables 1 and 2. The census data does not conveniently arrange itself by polling station (see the note to Table 1 of the Appendix), so the numbers in the various categories (except for the number of Muslims, which comes from the voters list) are likely to be wrong by a small amount. I therefore present the percentages as whole numbers.

Workers, Literacy, and the Hindu-Muslim Cleavage

Tables 1 and 2 reveal several important patterns, and enable us to focus our attention on the more significant population divisions. There are not very many workers in household industry, construction, and transport and communication resident in Kucha Khirkiwala, and almost none in the non-urban occupations. Only three percent of the residents--and no more than 20 percent in any polling station--are of scheduled castes. I shall concentrate my analysis, therefore, on the variations in the number of Muslims, of literates, and of workers in the census classes V(b) (manufacturing), VII (commerce), and IX (services).* Some of these categories are problematic. The number of literates is a poor measure of "literacy" in the sense that children who could not be expected to know how to read and write (say those up to age six) are included in the population; I don't believe that the

---

*This will also minimize the inaccuracy caused by fitting the census data into polling station divisions; see note to Appendix, Table 1.

TABLE 1

KUCHA KHIRKIWALA POPULATION DIVISIONS -- PERCENTAGES

Polling Station	Muslim[a]	Scheduled Caste[b]	Literate[b]	Workers[b]
1	0	7	76	31
2	19	0	50	30
3	41	0	50	29
4	71	1	43	29
5	72	..	51	29
6	95	..	43	27
7	95	..	43	27
8	64	..	40	28
9	0	1	61	28
10	44	0	62	27
11	37	..	57	28
12	0	6	70	27
13	0	6	69	28
14	0	1	69	24
15	0	15	58	28
16	0	..	76	29
17	13	0	68	30
18	25	20	46	30
Kucha Khirkiwala	34	3	56	28

Sources: [a]Voters list of January 1, 1969.

[b]Delhi District Census Handbook 1971; calculations from Appendix, Table 1.

Note: Dots of ellipsis indicate percentages of 0.0; zeros indicate percentages of less than 0.5.

TABLE 2

OCCUPATION OF WORKERS RESIDENT IN KUCHA KHIRKIWALA -- PERCENTAGES

Polling Station	I-IV	V(a)	1971 Census Category V(b)	VI	VII	VIII	IX
1	..	1	22	3	28	5	41
2	..	0	33	2	36	9	20
3	..	1	40	2	33	10	14
4	0	3	51	2	21	4	20
5	..	7	47	3	19	7	19
6	..	11	42	2	23	4	18
7	..	13	48	8	19	2	11
8	2	6	46	4	22	5	16
9	2	1	18	2	42	9	26
10	0	7	26	2	40	2	24
11	0	7	34	1	38	2	18
12	..	1	21	2	40	8	29
13	0	1	21	1	35	7	35
14	..	1	22	14	42	4	17
15	0	1	23	5	47	6	18
16	0	3	14	3	49	5	26
17	0	3	23	3	35	9	27
18	1	1	46	1	32	5	14
Kucha Khirkiwala	0	4	33	3	32	6	21

Source: Delhi District Census Handbook 1971; calculations from Appendix, Table 1.

Note: Zeros indicate percentages of less than 0.5; dots of ellipsis indicate percentages of 0.0.
I-IV = Agriculture, Mining, etc.; V(a) = Household Industry; V(b) = Manufacturing; VI = Construction; VII = Trade and Commerce VIII = Transport and Communication; IX = Other Services (for full description, see Ibid.)

TABLE 3

SPEARMAN'S R FOR VARIOUS PAIRINGS OF SOCIO-ECONOMIC PATTERNS,
KUCHA KHIRKIWALA

	Percent Literate	Workers in Manufacturing [V(b)]	Workers in Commerce [VII]	Workers in Services [IX]
Percent Muslim[1]	-.575	+.675	-.693	-.405
Literate		-.864	+.645	+.729
Workers in Manufacturing			-.804	-.671
Workers in Commerce				+.322

[1]Ranks were computed for the other categories for only those eleven polling stations in which there were Muslims.

number of children in that age group varies much between polling stations, so the comparisons will still hold. Census class IX (services) is another problem: it includes a range of people from "peons" (men in offices whose main job is to carry files from one desk to another) to clerks to professionals such as teachers. Thus polling stations 4 and 17, which rank fourth and ninth in the number of workers in category IX, are almost entirely "lower class" areas, while the polling stations which rank first and second (numbers 1 and 13) have a mixture of "lower" and "middle" classes, and the third ranked polling station (number 12) is almost entirely "middle class."

I ranked the polling stations in terms of percentage Muslim, percentage literates, and percentage of workers in manufacture (category V(b)), commerce (category VII), and services (category IX), and computed Spearman's R for the various pairs of rankings (see Table 3). As one would expect, literacy is highly correlated with the three major census classes; that it is marginally less correlated with workers in services (category IX) than with workers in commerce (category VII) is due, I would imagine, to the inclusion of non-white-collar workers in the former category.

The correlations of category V(b) with categories VII and IX can be interpreted to mean: workers in commerce and services tend to live apart from workers in industry. The association would seem less between the number of workers in commerce and the number of workers in services. Again, I would argue that workers in white-collar service occupations would live in areas where people in commerce do; it is the "lower class" service workers who live in separate areas. I say "living apart" in a relative sense only: the ward's pattern of residence is highly mixed: looking at the absolute numbers, it must be noted that no polling station has fewer than 14 percent of its workers in manufacturing (or more than 51 percent); the range for category VII (commerce) is 19 to 49 percent; and for category IX (services) from 11 to 41 percent.

Let us turn to the pairings of ranks of all these categories with the percentage of Muslims in polling stations (applicable to eleven of the eighteen only). The greater percentage of Muslims in a polling station, the lower the percentage of literates and the lower the number of workers engaged in trade and commerce, but the greater the number of workers in industrial occupations. These correlations are underlined by the data as presented in Table 4 in which the 11 census blocks having 80 percent or more Muslim voters are set against the 23 census blocks having 80 percent or more non-Muslim voters. The mean percentage of Muslim voters in the former is 95, and the mean percentage of non-Muslim* voters in the latter is 99. For literacy and industrial occupation, the differences are startling, and the differences in the other categories are significant.

Inferring from this to the ward as a whole, we can say that Muslims have a literacy rate less

---

* Called "Hindu" because the category would include only a few Jains, Sikhs, and Christians.

TABLE 4

"MUSLIM" AND "HINDU" CENSUS BLOCKS, KUCHA KHIRKIWALA, PERCENTAGES

	Popu-lation(N)	Workers	Literates	Occupational Categories V(b)	VII	IX
"Muslim" Census Blocks (N=11)	6,925	27.5	41.1	49.4	18.9	12.7
"Hindu" Census Blocks (N=23)	13,775	29.3	67.7	20.8	39.0	25.4

than two-thirds that of Hindus; that about half
the number of Muslim workers are in industrial
occupations, while less than a quarter of Hindu
workers are; that about twice as many Hindu
workers as Muslim workers are in commerce; and
about twice as many Hindu workers as Muslim
workers are in services. Fig. 6 shows these
patterns "on the ground"--note particularly the
concentration of Muslims in the south end of the
ward, where the bulk of census blocks with low
percentages of literates are, and in which workers
in manufacturing are the largest category. The
congruence of census blocks which are "Hindu,"
which have a high percentage of literates, and
which have workers in commerce as a modal category is also very clear.

In short, Hindus are (for whatever reason)
more literate and probably better off than Muslims,
a conclusion in line with what people in the ward
said, and with my own observations. It is impossible to discover from this data why Muslims have
fewer literates, so few workers in commerce, etc.
I was told that Muslims give less importance to
educating their daughters than Hindus do. But
while the women in both "Hindu" and "Muslim"
census blocks are 46 percent of the population,
38 percent of the literates in the "Muslim" census

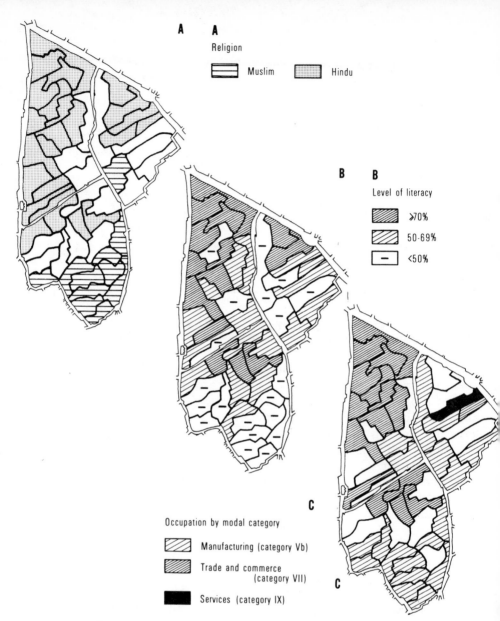

Fig. 6 Patterns of residence in Kucha Khirkiwala
(a): by religion; (b): by literacy; (c): by
occupation.

Note: the divisions shown are census blocks.
A "Muslim" census block is one in which 80
per cent or more of the voters are Muslim; a
"Hindu" census block is one in which 80 per
cent of the voters are non-Muslim (Source:
voters' list of January 1, 1969). A census
category is called "modal" only if there is
a difference of ten per cent or more between
it and the next largest category.

blocks are women and 41 percent of the literates in
the "Hindu" census blocks are women--not a very
significant difference. Lower levels of literacy
presumably are related to the relatively large
number of Muslims in manufacturing. But whether
the widespread poverty implied by the large number
of "blue collar" workers "causes" the low level
of literacy, or vice versa, remains to be seen.

Industrial Establishments and
Other Economic Institutions

The census categories I have been discussing
refer of course to the occupation of enumerated
residents. The "character" of a given area is,
however, not simply determined by the kinds of
people who live there, but also by the kinds of
activities that go on. Building uses in Kucha
Khirkiwala are mixed, as has been said before:
a small industrial establishment, a shop, and
residential quarters may be all in the same
building. The Delhi District Census Handbook 1961
unfortunately can provide evidence of only one
kind of usage--industrial establishments--and even
that, if the impression that such usage is a
rapidly expanding one in the ward can be trusted,
is seriously out of date (and the 1971 figures
are not available). But the amount and pattern
of small-scale industrial activity in 1961 is of
sufficient interest to be worth examining in some
detail.

Most industrial establishments in Kucha
Khirkiwala are set up in one room (a small room,
at that) but some are surprisingly large. Toward
the end of my stay I was invited into one workshop containing five or six large drill presses
and lathes located behind a wall in what I had
thought (and I had passed by many times) was a
purely residential area. "Industrial establishments" range from artisans manufacturing musical
instruments, to book binderies employing 20 workers,

to flour milling establishments, to workshops turning out "antiques" for the tourist trade. The <u>Delhi District Census Handbook 1961</u> presents data on industrial establishments by census block, and following the Indian Standard Industrial Classification (ISIC). The ISIC has some 200 "minor groups" in its Divisions 2 and 3 (manufacturing), which comprise rather specific types (e.g., code number 278, the manufacture of umbrellas). I have condensed this classification into nine major categories (the short form, to be used below, is given in parentheses):

TABLE 5

CATEGORIZATION OF INDUSTRIAL ESTABLISHMENTS

Category Number	Description	ISIC Code Numbers
1	Processing of foodstuffs (Food)	200-226
2	Textile and garment manufacture (Textiles)	230-279
3	Wood and paper product manufacture (Paper)	280-292
4	Printing and publishing (Printing)	300-303
5	Manufacture of leather, rubber, chemical, cement, clay, stone, and glass products (Leather, etc.)	310-357
6	Smelting, rolling, etc. of basic metals (iron, steel, etc.) (Metals)	360-369
7	Manufacture of machinery (Machinery)	370-389
8	Jewelry manufacture (Jewelry)	393
9	Other: manufacture of scientific equipment, matches, pencils, etc. (Other)	390-399 (except 3

In 1961, there were 43 census blocks in Kucha Khirkiwala. Only nine had no industrial establishments at all, 19 had from one to four establishments, six had from five to nine, and nine had 10 or more, ranging up to 24 establishments. The distribution by category is given in Table 6. Printing and publishing is clearly the most significant industry--Kucha Khirkiwala had nearly 25

TABLE 6

INDUSTRIAL ESTABLISHMENTS IN KUCHA KHIRKIWALA, 1961

Category	N	Percent
1 Food	9	3.8
2 Textiles	13	5.4
3 Paper	29	12.1
4 Printing	99	41.4
5 Leather, etc.	9	3.8
6 Metals	43	18.0
7 Machinery	16	6.7
8 Jewelry	8	3.3
9 Other	13	5.4
Total	239	99.9

percent of the total in Shahjahanabad in 1961--
and these print shops are located largely in one
area of the ward (polling stations 1-4). In that
area, and indeed elsewhere in the ward, one feels
that one is in an "industrial" area, but if we
make a (high) estimate of 10 workers per establishment, and compare it to the ward's population,
the economic impact is hardly overwhelming.

Industrial establishments are invariably in
the basement of a building or on the ground floor,
and there are few workshops in the ward which
didn't have residences above them. These establishments don't seem to have much impact on the
politics of the ward, if that can be measured by
salience during the rounds of the councilor.
There were some complaints about the noise and
traffic nuisance of the carts which serviced the
workshops, but the councilor almost never had
anything to say to the owners or workers of the
establishments, many of whom are not voters in
the ward.

Retail shops are, of course, far more visible
to the councilor and citizen. Fig. 4 (above,
p. 32) shows the approximate location of retail
shops in the ward. Those along the major bazars,
which border the ward, are intermixed with wholesale shops, and one bazar is the site of a daily
pavement vegetable market in the morning. The
shops of the "interior" are small food shops,
shops for cigarettes, paan (the ubiquitous Indian
eatable), string and other odds and ends, tailors,
barber shops, bicycle repair shops, kite shops,
etc., etc. It must not be thought that the
people of Kucha Khirkiwala do most of their
shopping within the ward, however; Chandni Chowk
and the other major retail bazars of the city
are within easy walking distance and most of
the shops in Kucha Khirkiwala (apart from a few
on the main bazars) are of minor importance.
Shopkeepers do, however, have to deal with the
Municipal Corporation, particularly in the
matter of licenses, control of food purity, and
encroachments on the pavement (which are either
illegal or for which a special tax [teh bazari]
is paid). I observed the councilor while on a
round ask a shopkeeper who had recently opened
his shop whether he had a license, and then urge
him to get one quickly. On another occasion a
shopkeeper complained about the number of chalans
he was getting, and the councilor said he would
put a stop to it. In some wards there are whole
markets of unauthorized shops, and the councilor
may organize demonstrations and put pressure on
the administration to prevent their demolition,
and ultimately have them regularized. On the
whole, the councilor of Kucha Khirkiwala paid
little attention to shops on the main bazars,
but some attention to the smaller establishments
in residential areas; one or two of these shopkeepers were political workers, or at least
important men of the neighborhood.

Many a paan shop provides the focal point
of a chowk of a mohalla. A chowk is a "square"

(literally, but also in the same sense as the
Western "town/village square") where people meet
and stand around and talk. Chowks are not entirely
a physical feature; although they tend to be
broader areas of a gali, not all broadenings of
a gali are chowks, and sometimes the chowk is nar-
rower than the nearby gali. Chowks are to be
found where main galis meet (these are the ones
that are focused on a paan shop or a food "stand").
These are typically filled with movement and with
knots of people standing around in front of the
shops. There are three chowks of this kind in
Kucha Khirkiwala. More numerous are the chowks
within mohallas, perhaps located next to a tree
or a well. These chowks often feature a wooden
platform on which newspapers subscribed to by a
mohalla committee are put. Groups of men sit and
stand in these quiet chowks; children play in them
and occasionally meetings will be held in them.
I suspect that certain men are "regulars" at these
mohalla chowks, spending an hour or half-hour
there each evening in discussion with friends.
These gatherings are clearly important to the
political workers, and the councilor on rounds
would always stop and talk with the men at a
chowk. The councilor of a neighboring ward in
fact has his "office" on the chabutra (low wall)
next to a major chowk of his ward. Political
workers gathered in the chowk not only discuss
politics with their neighbors, but they can also
observe and be observed by their busier neighbors
as they move through the galis.
     One aspect of life in the ward which should
at least be noted is the "nuisance" of stray cattle
and other animals, and the place of animals generally. There is one gali which has stables for
tonga horses, and a number of individuals keep
horses and donkeys to draw other carts. Cows and
buffaloes are present in surprising profusion.
There is one dairy with 15 or 20 animals in a
cramped courtyard almost exactly in the center
of the ward, and there are many "stray" (some are

owned and are let out to forage) cows wandering
about, particularly in the <u>galis</u> near the bazar
where the morning vegetable market is held.
Cows also eat green garbage deposited in the
<u>galis</u> for them. These cattle are usually ill-fed
and ill-tempered; a cow can effectively block
many <u>galis</u> of the ward and squeezing past the
swinging horns is not pleasant. And of course
there are the ever-present droppings which clog
drains and trap the unwary in badly lit <u>galis</u>.

   This "cattle nuisance" is endemic to the
whole of Delhi, and the Corporation has periodic
campaigns of rounding up cattle and bringing
them to a pound where they can be claimed on
payment of a fine or be put out to pasture in a
<u>goshala</u> (a farm for cows maintained by a religious
institution or a religiously-minded individual).
But the problem has not been solved, for the reason
neatly put by one councilor: "I went to one councilor, before I was elected and asked him why are
all these stray cattle roaming about, making a
mess? He said, 'Are you a fool?' I said, 'What?'
He said, 'Are you a fool? Those are not stray
cattle, those are my voters.'" Many Jana Sangh
councilors felt that the anti-cow slaughter
agitation of 1966-67 had been an important factor
in their success (although this was an election
in which many anti-Congress parties and coalitions
won in other states, without the issue of "cow"),
and the importance of the cow--and other religious
symbols--in the politics even of the ward cannot
be underestimated. There is no question of cow
slaughter, but there is the difficulty of denying
people the merit of owning and feeding cattle,
and of encountering auspicious signs at crucial
times.

   Some of the cattle contribute to the economy
of the ward, but most do not; their scavenging
function is offset by the nuisance of their droppings. A few horses, goats, and donkeys are kept
for domestic use. Pigeons are kept for sport
(see Ahmad Ali's <u>Twilight in Delhi</u> for a classic

description of pigeon flying). There are no dogs
and cats kept as pets; indeed, they are barely
tolerated nuisances. The ubiquitous crow and
an occasional troop of monkeys are a combination
of trouble and entertainment. The keeping of
animals is not forbidden in the city, and the
Corporation has a minimal program of rat elimi-
nation--they collect rat traps in which people
have put the rats they do not wish to kill--but
on the whole, animals are not much of a concern
to city government.

The Katra

The katra is an important sociological
unit in Kucha Khirkiwala, and particularly since
katra improvement became something of an issue
in Delhi in 1969-70, it merits our attention.
Fig. 5 (p. 49) shows how katras are scattered
throughout the ward. Katras are usually one or
two storied buildings, with a large courtyard
in which cows may be kept, or charpois (cots)
set up for sleeping in the summer. Each katra
will have one water tap, and often a tree in
the courtyard. The courtyard is surrounded by
a building divided into "apartments" of one
room and a front area for cooking, cleaning
pots, etc. Most katras in Kucha Khirkiwala are
converted large houses, and many have impressive
gateway entrances. Others are closer to a basti
style: shacks put up in a cleared area, which in
some cases is what is left (along with a gateway)
of the palace of a nobleman of the Mughal era.

On a number of occasions, political workers of
the ward analyzed its voters for me, and one category which was almost invariably used was "the 42
katras." The figure 42, as we shall see below,
seems arbitrary. One Congress worker estimated that
the "katra vote" was about 2,500. Administrative
officers concerned with the ward did not seem to
know which 42 katras were meant. For the purpose of

Corporation payments for improvements, a _katra_
is defined as a building (one house number) with
either ten families (operationally, ten ration
cards) or 50 people living in it. Using the
rule of thumb ratio of two people for each vote,[22]
I have computed the number of _katras_ by taking
house numbers with 25 or more voters listed. In
this computation, Kucha Khirkiwala has 78 _katras_,
with a total of 3,360 voters. The largest _katra_
of the ward, which covers three house numbers but
is considered one _katra_, has 170 voters in it, and
there are others with 136, 124, 94, and 92 voters.
I am not sure that there is such a thing as a
"Muslim _katra_" in ordinary speech: that is,
katras are not simply descriptive of the type of
living quarters but also of the type of people
living in them. The implication of "_katra_ dweller"
is usually "low-caste" Hindu. Not that this is
clear: one of the larger _katras_ is more than half
Muslim, and although some _katras_ are named by
caste ("the Dhobi [washermen] _katra_," etc.), others
have proper names ("Katra Ram Lal") or are named
by location ("Katra Ischoolwali" [the _katra_ by the
school]). There are 14 _katras_, defined by the 25-
voters-or-more criterion, inhabited by Muslims, with
627 voters. Only three _katras_ are inhabited by
both Muslims and Hindus; aside from the one large
one mentioned above, the other two have two or
three Muslims and 90-odd Hindus living in them.[23]
Some of these concentrations of Muslims are in
large, old houses which have not been divided up
katra style and so should not be considered _katras_,
but which these are I am unable to say. There is
no break between the size of the forty-second
largest _katra_ and the forty-third largest, as they
are listed in Table 7.

The largest 42 _katras_ have fewer than 2,500
votes and all 78 have fewer than 5,000. The "_katra_
vote" is an important category of political analysis
for political workers in the ward because it is considered a bloc vote. Opinions differed as to
whether it was still being bought (with cash and

TABLE 7

KATRAS IN KUCHA KHIRKIWALA

Number of Voters	Number of Katras	Total Voters	Cumulative No. Katras	Cumulative Tot. Voters	Cumulative Mean (Vtrs.)
100+	3	430	3	430	143
90-99	2	186	5	616	123
80-89	1	80	6	696	116
70-79	1	74	7	770	110
60-69	5	325	12	1,095	91
50-59	6	331	18	1,426	79
40-49	10	443	28	1,869	67
35-39	6	225	34	2,094	62
34	3	102	37	2,196	59
33	3	99	40	2,295	57
32	3	96	43	2,391	56
31	3	93	46	2,484	54
30	2	60	48	2,544	53
29	6	174	54	2,718	50
28	10	280	64	2,998	47
27	3	81	67	3,079	46
26	6	156	73	3,235	44
25	5	125	78	3,360	43

liquor); most said that in early elections it was
purchased, and if the katra or its chaudhari took
money, then it was "honorable" and voted as it was
paid to. Then, these informants continue, after
some elections in which people took money from both
sides and voted as they pleased, the parties have
downgraded the importance of the practice.* Katras
are also important--and there I am talking about
"true" katras (those with large numbers of people
living around one courtyard)--because large concentrations of voters simplify electioneering. As one
political worker put it:

_____

*I have witnessed a bottle of liquor being
given to a voter (during the Basti Julahan by-
election) and heard a man bargaining with a party
official to "sell" a bloc of votes (the party
official wasn't buying), so the practice is not
terribly well hidden. But with the secret ballot,
"buying" votes is recognized as the most hazardous
method of securing them.

> The candidate must go to the <u>katras</u> daily,
> and in the last two or three days of the
> campaign, two or three times daily. If he
> should miss, particularly in the last week,
> then he won't get their votes. . . . You
> go to the <u>katras</u> and the people stand
> around. . . . This is an advantage over
> going house to house. Say the workers come
> to a house like this [a large, modern, one-
> family house]. Well, we ring the bell, then
> the servant will come to ask what we want,
> and will go upstairs, then the man will say,
> "I am taking tea, please wait." So fifteen
> minutes are wasted. And then he will say,
> "Oh yes, I will vote for you." With the
> educated, you can't judge how he will vote.
> In the <u>katras</u> they will tell you straight
> out, "I am going to vote for you" or "Get
> out, I won't vote for you."

The mean size of the 42 largest katras is over 50
votes and so this analysis makes a good deal of
sense: not only are there invariably many voters
standing around, but also there is no question of
spending too much time in waiting for hospitality
(in the form of tea or Coca-Cola), which is often
offered in the "better" houses. As the next
election began to draw near, the councilor concentrated a great deal of effort on the <u>katras</u> (I will
discuss this in the next chapter).
    The <u>katras</u> are scattered throughout Kucha
Khirkiwala, although in other wards they may be
grouped together. Often they occupy open spaces
between the back walls of houses facing two
parallel <u>galis</u>. Most are owned by private land-
lords--who get little in the way of rent--but many
are owned by the Corporation, and at least one was
a squatters <u>katra</u> (the residents paid rent to no
one). There were only five <u>katras</u>--and the councilor on his rounds visited the major <u>katras</u> at
least once--in which I remember anyone being
addressed as <u>chaudhariji</u>." One of these was a

Dhobi katra, another housed tonga drivers, and
the others were inhabited by distinct caste groups
(but of uncertain occupation). There were perhaps
another five large katras which seemed to have
some internal structure (along caste lines or
extended kin lines, probably), but most katras are
simply residential conglomerates. As in the
mohalla, leadership, if it exists, is as likely
to be on a "modern" basis (the leader of the
largest katra was a teacher) as on some "traditional" basis such as caste. The role of women
in the katra should be noted. Although the
younger women tended to "keep purdah" (they covered
their faces) while talking, both they and the older
women (faces uncovered) seemed to me to be more
outspoken in the katras than women in other houses.
In one katra, an elderly woman was the spokesman--
the chaudhari of the katra was simply greeted by
the councilor, not listened to.

The explanation of why political workers in
Kucha Khirkiwala place so much emphasis on "the
katras" as a class of voters, whatever their true
number may be, lies in the ease of access to a
large audience, and in the possibility, at least,
of the use of an indigenous social structure
headed up by men who might be vote brokers. The
upshot, in political terms, is that the "lowest"
strata in the ward get considerable attention from
the councilor, and thus at least a fair share of
municipal benefits (we will explore this in the
next chapter). Numbers offset lack of education
and economic clout; in Kucha Khirkiwala benefits
flow to where the votes are.

SUMMARY

This then is the physical and socio-economic
context of government in one ward of the old city
of Delhi: densely populated, with mixed commercial,
residential, and "industrial" areas; mixed also in
terms of caste and class, though there is a division

between Hindu and Muslim; a "slum" area requiring
much in the way of municipal services. I have
already outlined some of the administrative apparatus which penetrates the ward, and have also suggested that the councilor is a key figure politically, insofar as these services are concerned.
In the following chapter, I shall therefore
concentrate on the councilor, in his day-to-day
work, and at election time.

3. The Councilor of Kucha Khirkiwala

The Delhi councilor is concerned, in the
arena of the ward, with the administrative process
directly and, indeed, operates in a close relationship with specific administrators. He is in theory
a member of the "deliberative wing" of the Corporation, a man concerned with policy matters only.
But it is not just in Delhi that his role in the
administrative process is a very significant, if not
the most significant, part of his job, both as he
conceives it and as his day-to-day activities
indicate. Roderick Church writes of the Lucknow
councilor:

Councillors are essentially intermediaries
between the public and the municipality in
routine administrative matters. . . . Although city councillors and legislators
everywhere spend some of their time doing
these things, virtually the entire job of
the Indian city councillor revolves around
administration. In describing their jobs
councillors usually show little concern with
policy, general issues or matters that do
not concern the immediate allocation of
municipal services. Instead, they are out-
put oriented and concerned with administrative
demands and the outcomes of administrative
decisions.[1]

In Los Angeles, where the system of regional city
offices is the closest approximation in the U.S.
of the zonal system in Delhi,   each city council-
man works, in part, as an ombudsman.[2] Instances
of councilmen seeking to influence the processes
of municipal administration, even where this sort
of contact is not formally permitted, are an
obvious feature of American city government.[3]

The Delhi councilor, because of the "constituency fund,"* can do a fair amount for his
constituents in terms of material benefits as well
as in terms of access and influence in the bureaucratic system. Councilors do tend to find themselves in a position of asserting their importance
and competence to a skeptical audience; their
position is almost exactly like that of their
counterparts in England:

> The local councillor does not usually per-
> form his public duties in the spotlight of
> publicity; nor are councilors, as a group,
> regarded with any particular respect by the
> general public. The individual councillor
> may be treated with some deference, espe-
> cially if he achieves a year of office as
> mayor, but he will practice his political
> skills against a chorus deploring the low
> calibre of local political representatives.[4]

---

*Fifty thousand rupees per year of the zonal
budget is reserved for projects designated by the
councilor. These must be approved by the administrative officers (and projects with large budgets
by the zonal committee) and so cannot be things
like repairing the councilor's home. But the councilor can designate specific galis for improvement
(new paving, a sewer line, etc.) as well as deter-
mining which projects should be done first (one
year concentrating on installing new street lights,
the next year adding more public urinals, for
example).

The councilor is thus not only trying to enhance
his own personal position qua councilor, but also
has to change the notion of what a councilor should
properly do: otherwise, if he "gets things done"
for his constituents he is "improperly interfering"
in administration.

In the ward, the councilor is the pivotal
person in council-citizen interaction.   It is
at this level that the citizen has the greatest
access to the governmental process, but largely
because the councilor brings the government to
the citizen in the form of himself and ward-level
administrators, on regular "rounds" of the constituency. The "round group" has a structure of
deference patterns and implied authority, and the
relations between councilor and citizen and between
administrator and citizen are complex, consisting
of mutual deference, mixed formality and informality, etc. These relationships, as they appear
in the context of the round, and in the setting of
Kucha Khirkiwala, are the subject of this chapter.

The councilor indeed has some power over
administrative officers, power not derived from
legitimate lines of command (except insofar as the
councilor can determine administrative actions by
the assignment of constituency fund projects). The
basis of the power he holds is threefold: the
councilor's expertise, his influence over transfers
and promotions of officers, and his ability to
"expose" or slander the officer.

Since the councilor frequently is at least as
familiar with the rules and regulations of the
Corporation as the officer, he can tell the officer
what he is "required" to do; the councilor keeps the
officer up to the administrative mark. An officer
can generally be transferred out of a ward at the
instance of a councilor, either by direct request
or through influencing the officer's superiors, perhaps via the party leadership. Conversely, a councilor's commendation of officers for work well done,
particularly if the councilor is influential or
seems to have a bright future, is very important.

Transfers are themselves a form of promotion or
demotion, depending on the location of the new
ward, the new position in the administrative
hierarchy, etc. Finally, the councilor can de-
nounce the officer for being, say, "insensitive
to citizen complaints," a charge which is difficult to disprove and which constitutes a black
mark on the officer's record. A threatened
denunciation in the presence of the officer's
superior can be quite effective. (This theme of
the councilor's power over the officer reappears
in our discussion of the zone, in Chapter 6.)

    Rather than plunge directly into a generalized
description of the three interfaces in the ward, I
present first a continuation of the presentation
of a feature of the ward described in the previous
chapter: the katra. Here I shall describe what
might be called "the politics and government" of
the katra; this should be a useful introduction to
a description of the contact of a councilor with
his constituency.

THE COUNCILOR AND THE KATRAS

    A not untypical example of the contact of the
councilor with his constituency concerns the largest
katra of Kucha Khirkiwala. This katra is built on
the land formerly occupied by a palace; indeed, the
arched gateway of the palace still remains. The
land apparently belongs to the Delhi Administration,
and in the Master Plan it is slated to become a
park. The councilor nevertheless had a sewer line
laid into the katra, and was going to have the
central gali paved, but the Delhi Administration
got a court order to prevent the completion of the
project. One political worker said before the court
order, "We can't permit the park until the Administration has resettled the people living here, and
that may take five, ten, twenty years. In the meantime, people must have amenities." The sewer line
was completed before work was stopped, and when

later the residents asked the councilor when the
related work would be completed, he said that the
only way was to get a petition signed by the members
of the katra placed before the court. It was
clearly against the regulations, if not exactly
illegal, to have the katra improved when it was
scheduled for demolition, yet there were powerful
political compulsions to do so: other katras were
being improved, and the blame for the stoppage of
the project could be placed at the door of the
Delhi Administration, and, by implication, on Jana
Sangh policy.*

The "beautification of Delhi" was very much a
political issue at this time, and, seemingly, both
parties wanted to have their cake and eat it. In
the Basti Julahan by-election, for instance, there
were a number of speeches by the Jana Sangh claiming
credit for the creation of parks where slum hutments
had been, while the Congress charged that this
beautification had been made "over the corpses of
the poor." The Jana Sangh conceded that the slum
dwellers had to be moved, but insisted that all this
was in the provisions of the Master Plan, which had
been drawn up during the Congress regime. The Congress pointed out that the credit for beautification
should not go to the Jana Sangh but to the Delhi
Development Authority (the executive authority of
the Master Plan), which was set up by the Congress.
In this confusion, it was generally agreed that the
hutment dwellers were overwhelmingly Congress voters,
and that their removal had definite political outcomes: one Congress councilor went to jail in an
effort to prevent the relocation of his constituents. Basti Julahan had had 1,500 voters removed
between 1967 (when the Congress won) and 1969 (when
the Jana Sangh won), but the ward returned to the
Congress in 1971 by a larger margin than that of

---

*The councilor of Kucha Khirkiwala belongs to
Congress.

1967, although the Jana Sangh improved its position slightly citywide. By 1970 the Jana Sangh had moved to counter charges of insensitivity to slum dwellers by its campaign to improve the katras, highlighted by the padyatra (foot pilgrimage) of the Chief Executive Councilor to various katras (see below, pp. 324-26).

The core of the katra improvement campaign was the commitment of the Corporation to finance the repair of the central courtyard, the installation of flush latrines, the provision of a water tap and an electric light, and a few other specific repairs, in katras having ten families or 50 people living in them. These repairs were carried out irrespective of what the landlord might have to say. "Irrespective" because it is not true that landlords in Delhi always favored the repair of their property. The Rent Control Act has fixed rents at an artificially low level, so that all agreed (tenants and councilors as well) that repairs would cost the landlord more than he could ever hope to recover in rent. And even repairs carried out at no cost to the landlord may not be welcomed by him, because he may want to use the land to put up shops, or rent the building to a new tenant (having made repairs) for which he could get a sizeable pugree payment.* Once a tenant has occupied a house, it is practically impossible to remove him, and so a landlord may not be unhappy to see a house fall down about the tenants' ears. In the course of one round, a tenant approached the

---

*Pugree (literally: turban) is an extremely important institution in Delhi. It is the initial payment a prospective tenant must make to be allowed to rent a building or apartment. I was told that the pugree for shops in prime locations in the old city ran into the hundreds of thousands of rupees. The landlord of a one-room apartment, which I knew about, with a rent of 20 or 30 rupees a month, was asking a pugree of 4,000 rupees.

councilor complaining that the landlord had
brought suit to halt the repairs that the tenant
was making. It is not obvious, therefore, that
the landlord is happy about the finance of katra
repair by the Corporation. In a list of private
katras slated for improvement, I found the
notation "[funds] allotted; no work done as
owner did not allow." Landlords can be fined
for keeping a house in dangerous condition, but
as the councilor pointed out on one round, the
fines are so low and the time it takes to
enforce the law so long that there is no effective legal remedy.

The councilor made a point of asking in
large houses how many people resided there, and
then carefully explained the criteria of a
"katra." He would promise to send an officer to
collect the information formally if it appeared
that they qualified for Corporation-financed
repairs. But he spent much more time inspecting
the work in progress in the larger (i.e., obvious)
katras and the similar repair work being done in
the Corporation (slum) properties. The Slum
Department of the Corporation was administratively
separate from the Corporation before 1962 and even
now, according to a section officer of the department, it is funded by the central government. The
properties for which it is responsible are largely
confined to the old city, and most of them are
properties of people who left for Pakistan, whose
title initially was in the hands of the Custodian
of Evacuee Property. There is an average of one
section officer of the Slum Department (with
three or four assistants) for every two wards
of the old city, but he does not sit in the zonal
offices. His job is mainly to let contracts to
private contractors--having prepared an estimate
of the costs--and then supervise the completion
of the repairs. At the end of fiscal year 1969
(in April, 1970), there were 67 private katras
and Corporation houses in Kucha Khirkiwala for
which the Slum Department had completed repairs,

had allotted a contract, had a contract under
tender, or had work in progress (see Table 8).
The table shows that there is roughly four times
the per capita expenditure on the Corporation
houses than on private katras (since private
katras are subject to the "ten families or 50
persons" rule, while Corporation houses are not).
By the time I left, most of the work on private
katras had been completed, and work on Corporation
houses was beginning in earnest.

In the year August, 1969 to July, 1970 the
councilor of Kucha Khirkiwala went on 34 regularly
scheduled "rounds" of the ward. On four of these
the Slum Department section officer was present
and on one more his superior officer in the department. On these five occasions (and on one other
when two contractors doing work on the katras were
present) the round consisted essentially of visiting
ten or so katras to inspect work completed, about to
be done, and in progress. In addition, there were
few occasions on which the councilor passed a katra

TABLE 8

SLUM DEPARTMENT REPAIR WORK, KUCHA KHIRKIWALA

	Number	Cost (Rs)	Voters
Private katras			
Work allotted	9	24,450	200
Work in progress	1	3,380	26
Work completed	16	62,680	985
Subtotal	26	90,510	1,211
Corporation houses			
Work under tender	3	15,730	42
Work allotted	25	130,634	348
Work in progress	1	3,400	7
Work completed	12	65,944	274
Subtotal	41	215,708	671
Total	67	306,218	1,882

Source: A list supplied by the section officer, Slum Department.
There are a number of inconsistencies and obvious in-
accuracies in the list supplied, which I have attempted
to eliminate as best I can; I am confident that the gross
figures are nearly correct.

by on a regular round. On the first such "katra"
round (in November, 1969), the councilor was
effusive in his praise of the section officer,
though he did say to the katra residents, "Don't
say now that after being made councilor I did
nothing." On a number of occasions the councilor
asked the section officer to stretch the rules
about what could be repaired, to put up a brick
wall on the roof to prevent children from falling
into the courtyard, for example. There was only
one instance where this could be interpreted as
an attempt to get something done for a party fol-
lower. The section officer tended to insist on
doing only what he was permitted to do. By May,
with the election to be held the next February,
partisan considerations were creeping in. The
councilor explained to the section officer before
one round that his election strategy involved
getting katra votes (which he computed to be 4,000),
and when he met political workers on the street,
the councilor would ask, "Are there any of our
people in Corporation houses, for whom we can get
things done around here?" At one house of a political worker (a Corporation house) the councilor
ordered the section officer to "get their needs
seen to on an urgent basis. This is my house, he
[the tenant] is my elder. [Jokingly.] If you
don't get it done within fifteen days, he will
murder me. . . ." On another round, later, the
councilor accused the section officer of "being the
man" of a neighboring (opposition) councilor; the
section officer countered by saying that it was
the contractor who was that councilor's "man" and
that he (the section officer) was "powerless."
(I gathered that special favors were being done--
with Corporation cement, etc.--for opposition party
supporters.) At one point there was a long discussion, held in the house of the opposition party's
candidate in the 1969 election, in which one man
accused the section officer of taking bribes. The
section officer defended himself by trying to
explain that he could not do any repair he wished,

that there were restraints of policy and law. The
councilor, when he took part in the discussion,
supported the section officer.

A month and a half after this round in which
the section officer had been accused of corruption
and favoritism, the councilor had the section
officer's superior along (without the section
officer), and the theme of the round, as it were,
was the shoddiness of the work on the katras and
the implied incompetence of the section officer.
(I might add that some of the work was indeed
shoddy: cracks were beginning to appear, etc.)
My field notes read, in part:

> Most katra dwellers blamed the contractor
> (although the Slum Department, as the
> councilor said, is responsible for super-
> vising them), and one man claimed to have
> seen a contractor selling five bags of
> cement. . . . The councilor's complaint
> was that the section officer had promised
> to get things done, this and that repaired,
> had written it down four and five months
> ago, and nothing was done. The councilor
> introduced the superior officer as "the
> officer bigger than X (the section officer)"
> and on a number of occasions the councilor
> said to the katra dwellers: "Don't talk to
> me, tell him (the officer) straight, let him
> hear." [One old lady] persisted in saying,
> "oh no, I am complaining about you (the
> councilor); it's your responsibility."

The councilor also complained that the section
officer, in concert with the neighboring councilor,
was maligning him. At one point the councilor succeeded in getting the officer to make a note to get
something done which was strictly speaking not
allowed, but at another point, the officer flatly
refused to have an unallowable repair made.

Quite apart from the importance of the katras
per se (as indicated by all this attention--the

councilor never asked the people concerned with the
schools to come on a round, for example), what is
worthy of note here is the relation of the councilor
to the administrative officer. The councilor on the
whole identified himself with the officer's work,
praising him on occasion, helping explain to citizens why certain things could or could not be done.
Some citizens had an unclear idea of what "policy"
and "rules and regulations" might mean, and
believed that the councilor and the officer could
do pretty much as they pleased. This may of course
have been a tactic on the part of the citizens to
try and force a little rule bending (i.e., in
order to prompt the officers to think: "They just
don't understand, so let's try and accommodate
them . . .") and certainly both the councilor and
to a lesser extent the officers were willing to
go out on a limb in a good cause.

The real conflict between councilor and
officer is on the question of partisanship, the
accusation that the officer is "so and so's man"
or "a Jana Sanghi." This sort of accusation is
made at all levels of the Corporation, leveled at
officers from the commissioner on down. The
officers tended to resent the implication that
"following the orders of the democratic representative" (particularly just before an election) could
get them labeled as partisan. Nonetheless, I for
one could see little evidence that decisions on
katra repair were made in a partisan manner;
certainly the styles of operation of the two councilors of opposing parties that I saw on "katra"
rounds were remarkably similar. Both seemed bent
on doing as much for katra dwellers as they could,
with the idea of getting their votes, to be sure,
but also, it seemed to me, with a real commitment
to social welfare goals.

The section officer of the Slum Department has
a greater degree of independence than other officers
concerned with the ward. He does not sit in the
zonal offices and is thus not even in theory
directly responsible to the councilors of the zone,

individually or as a body. His department is
situated in Town Hall but is not financed by the
Corporation (although the repairs he supervises
are), and his job is quite clearly defined.
Therefore, it is particularly significant that
he deferred to the councilor in manner and often
in deed (he respectfully received "orders" and
criticism; he came along on rounds--held at 7 A.M.
on Sundays--when "called" by the councilor, etc.).
It is indicative of the extent to which the councilor influences the administrative process.

THE COUNCILOR'S ROUND

I have been talking about the councilor's
rounds in a number of connections, and it is time
that the scope and importance of the round be
examined in detail. Virtually all the councilors
of the City Zone cited the round as one of their
prime contacts with the people of their constituency. One claimed to go on rounds daily; another
said twice a week; and a few said they go only
occasionally (or didn't mention rounds in their
answer to the general question about contact with
their constituency). The councilor of Kucha
Khirkiwala has a schedule of going once a week, but
due to rain, political gatherings, etc., in the
year 1969-70, he went on rounds 34 times. I would
imagine that this is a typical pattern.
A round is not necessarily a complete tour of
the constituency, but is rather a systematic coverage of a given area. The councilor once claimed
to a citizen that he aimed to systematically cover
the entire ward over a given period; my observation
was that this was not so. Not only was there no
record kept of where the previous rounds had gone,
there were often days on which the councilor was
undecided about where he should go, even as he was
setting out. Further, there were galis in the ward
into which he never went that year, and others into
which he went only once or twice, while other areas

and _galis_ were visited ten or fifteen times (see
Fig. 7 below, p. 88). These "neglected" areas
were relatively insignificant (in terms of number
of residents), and most of the ward got a fairly
even coverage. In addition to the regular round,
there are special rounds, held at the councilor's
request, and of course the councilor moves through
the ward many times a week on his own, when he can
observe conditions and receive complaints.

Each councilor has a different style of
going on a round, yet the activity is a widely
recognized one (the English word "round" is used
in Hindi speech). The councilor may take a round
by geographic area, noting complaints and issuing
"orders" to the accompanying officers, or he may
do a "subject" round, looking at drains, for
example. He may walk quickly from place to place,
or stop to pass the time of day with people, or
go systematically from house to house. I accompanied the councilor on seven house-to-house
rounds (he was planning to cover the entire ward
in daily rounds in a one-month period), in which
he not only entered every house, but also asked to
make sure that he had spoken to someone from every
family living in the house. I asked him whether
he had done this before--and he replied that before
there was no need: the things that had to be done,
such as road repair and the installation of water
lines, were obvious to him; he had no need to ask.
In answer to residents' criticisms that now
("before the election") he was coming around, he
would say, "It is not my custom when I come and
see the _gali_--and I have come here many times--
to make a noise and call out. I look quietly and
get the needful done." Indeed, a common theme is
that the councilor is constantly keeping his ward
under close supervision.

The crucial aspect of the round is the
presence of the officers. I have noted above that
the Assistant Sanitary Inspectors (ASIs) are expected to report to the councilor daily as well as
to accompany him on rounds. The councilor sometimes

asks them to report things to be done which are not
their responsibility. In some instances, councilors told me that they expect their party workers
to act as "inspectors" of a given area, and, indeed,
a party worker is often present on a round to introduce the councilor to the resident. On many occasions I have seen party workers come also to the
house of the councilor with complaints. Still the
"core" of the rounds group is the councilor, the
ASIs, and the occasional specialized officer
(Drainage Department section officer, etc.). They
are the "core" in the sense that most of the time
of the round is spent in the dialogue of the councilor and some officer or other--the councilor
telling the officer to repair a sewer quickly,
prepare an estimate of road repair costs, etc., the
officer explaining why the delay in desilting the
drains has occurred, and so on. I have no way of
judging whether the "round group" of the Kucha
Khirkiwala councilor was typical, but I believe
that it was, at least, not unusual.

There were five people who, with very few
absences, were present on every round: the councilor, the two ASIs, the chief political worker
(and personal friend) of the councilor, and the
councilor's secretary ("P.A."--personal assistant)
whose job it was to keep the book in which complaints and observations were entered. In addition,
the Works Department section officer was present on
six rounds of 34: in August, November, February,
March, April, and June; the Slum Department section
officer on four (November, March [twice], May); the
Drainage Department section officer on three
(November and March); the Water Department section
officer on one; and two more senior officers on
three rounds. (Some of the section officers of
various departments were present on the same rounds.)
Other political workers came along on four rounds
during the year, and only in one case by arrange-
ment--in the other three, they happened to meet the
group and joined it for the remainder of the round.

The "inspection" is a sort of "super round" on

which the most senior officers of the zone are
called and which usually attempts to cover the
entire ward. The effort is to make a general
assessment of the condition of the ward and
decide what can be done. The inspection, unlike
the round, has a sizeable political component:
it is considered part of the councilor's pre-
rogative to be able to "call" the officers (from
the Zonal Assistant Commissioner on down) and to
display them, as it were, in his ward.* The
Zonal Assistant Commissioner (ZAC) told me that
a proposal of his to reduce the numbers of allowed
inspections was resisted by the councilors. A
councilor can in theory call an officer on a round
once a month, and some officers insisted that they
were called to each councilor that frequently. A
few councilors said they went on frequent inspections (say, six times a year or more), but
most claimed to go on three or four a year. A
few said that they rarely went on inspections. A
former ZAC told me that each councilor has at most
two inspections a year, and that more would make
no sense. The councilor of Kucha Khirkiwala had
had one inspection shortly after his election and
none since. Both councilor and officer probably
exaggerate the number of inspections made, because
frequent inspections, as the former ZAC said, don't
make sense: the amount of work that requires the
personal visit of all the officers, including the
ZAC, to the site is so small that it makes far more
sense to have the specific officer concerned with a
specific project come individually, and this of
course happens.

---

*
This was the impression I got from my interviews and from the criticisms of the one or two
councilors who didn't believe in inspections. On
the one inspection I was able to observe, however,
there was no effort made to "play to the gallery"
and indeed, the people in the ward paid relatively
little attention to the large ensemble of officers.

The "round group" of councilor, political
worker, and low-level officers has a certain structure and cohesiveness, unlike the inspection group,
which is amorphous. Leaving aside the councilor's
P.A., who played a purely subordinate role (although
this may have been a function of the particular
incumbent of the office when I was there), the
councilor treated the rest, especially in private,
as part of his team, people with whom he was working
to get things done. The councilor asked for and
listened to the expert advice (not simply whether
or not a certain structure could be built, but also
on administrative rules and regulations) of the
section officers and the ASIs; he also interpreted
this advice to citizens who were standing around.
At the same time he issued "orders" to the officers
which, strictly speaking, he is not entitled to do,
since they are not subordinate to him, but to their
superior officer. The councilor also criticized
the officer in public for doing a poor job. The
political worker on occasion "ordered" the officer
to do something, but he mainly operated as the councilor's aide in the discussion with constituents,
explaining the citizen's complaint to the councilor
and interpreting the councilor's reply, when necessary. All the members of the group deferred to the
councilor, in speech forms, in seating patterns
(when the group was invited into a house for tea,
for instance), and in walking. He was always
addressed as "councilor sahib" or "member sahib";
he was given the best seat (in the city this is
rarely the head of the charpoi (rope cot) but
rather, in the realm of the "sofa set," the seat
on the couch next to the host); while walking, the
councilor would go with the chief political worker
at his shoulder, occasionally a section officer
with whom he was on good terms also at his shoulder,
and with the ASIs, the P.A., and other officers a
few steps behind him. On one round the councilor
had praised the work of one of the ASIs and so when
the group was invited into a house for tea, the ASI
was asked to sit in a good chair and was offered the

first cup of tea. But the ASI resisted the honor
strenuously and, indeed, the banter and exaggerated
pressing of the deference on him suggested that it
was highly irregular. On another occasion, the
councilor handed the ASI a cigarette before leaving
on the round, saying, "Here [in the councilor's
office] we are friends; outside it is something
different." The round group thus has both a
spatial structure, in various settings, and a
"structure" of deference and implied hierarchy;
the councilor is unquestionably its leader.

The areas of the ward covered by the rounds
are shown in Fig. 7. _Galis_ which have no numbers
near them were visited once or twice, and of course
many of the main roads were covered on virtually
every round. The numbers refer to fairly lengthy
visits of at least 15 or 20 minutes; many areas were
visited quickly or were simply the neighborhood of
a _katra_ or a house that the councilor wanted to
inspect. What is significant is the evenness of
the coverage--there were relatively few areas
missed entirely, and only one of these was in a
sense "enemy" territory (the neighborhood of the
houses of prominent opposition party members). I
got the feeling that the councilor tended to avoid
one strongly opposition _mohalla,_ but I don't think
that was terribly significant: it is also one of
the better-off _mohallas_ and therefore there was
less to be seen and done in it. Rounds took place
on Sunday mornings, as good a time as any for having
a maximum population in the area. There were occasional complaints that "the councilor never comes to
this _mohalla,_" but the councilor's defense that he
came without being seen, or when the complainant was
away, is on the whole, a valid one. The councilor
is consistently visible.

What is true of the area covered is true also
of the length of the round and of its regularity:
there is a remarkably even spread. The 34 rounds
I observed averaged just under two hours each and
varied from one fifteen-minute round (the next
shortest being three one-hour ones) to three three-

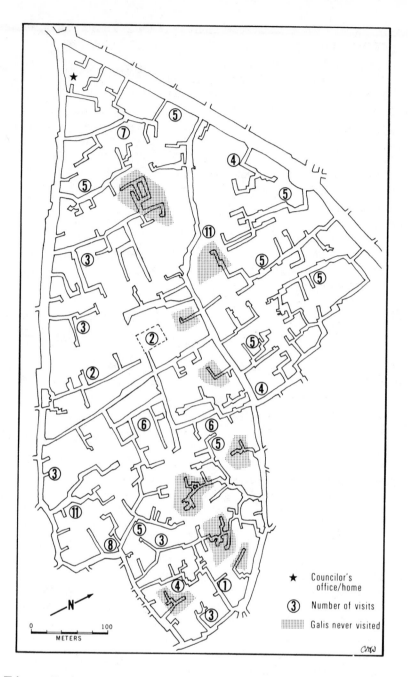

Fig. 7 Areas visited on rounds, July 1969–
July 1970.

hour ones. The councilor planned to go every week, and thus "missed" 18 rounds in 1969-70. One was cancelled because of rain; another because a relative had arrived suddenly; a third because the sweepers' strike was on; others because the councilor was attending national meetings of the party; and so on. Over the year, rounds occurred as follows:

TABLE 9

DATES OF THE KUCHA KHIRKIWALA COUNCILOR'S ROUNDS, 1969-70

July				27	
August		10			31
September	7	14	21	28	
October		12			
November	2		16		30
December	7	14			
October		11	18		
February	1	8	15	22	
March		8	15		29
April	5		19	26	
May	3	10	17		31
June	7		21		
July	5	12	19		

Three Sundays were missed in August (rain), three in October (Diwali and Dusshera holidays), and three in December-January (party meetings plus a vacation). Although the rounds could thus not be said to be "weekly" in practice (as opposed to in intent), they were certainly regular--it was rare to have two in a row missed. Coupled with the councilor's trips through the ward on business and on occasions when he was specially called, the round must give him a good continuing idea of how the ward is faring. In addition, of course, he meets the ASIs daily and the section officer (Works) frequently.

No round can be said to be typical, particularly since the area of concern varied over the year's span. By the beginning of 1970, for example, the constituency fund had run out, so that all that

could be done in the way of projects was to inspect
areas for possible ones for the next year. From
April on there was a great emphasis on the katras,
while in the fall there had been more concern with
street repairing. The councilor's style also varied
somewhat; one week he would be concerned with lis-
tening to the complaints of citizens, and the next
would be more interested in keeping the officers up
to the mark.

But some of the elements of the round were
repeated frequently enough that a composite portrait is possible. We (the round group) would
start from the councilor's home and go quickly
down the main bazars to the area of the round's
concentration. Occasionally, the councilor would
stop to greet people, asking after their health,
etc. Once at the mohalla, the councilor would look
at the public urinal to see if it was working. If
the road were being repaved, the councilor would
talk to the section officer about it, or explain to
people why the work was being delayed. In these
localities the councilor would greet people he
didn't know, and ask specifically if there were any
complaints, always indicating a great willingness
to help (except in "police matters"); he would
explain his practice of noting down the complaint
with the date and then the date of the action taken
(in the ledger kept by the P.A.). Citizens would
gather around the group--particularly when we were
in katras--and there was no indication of shyness
in bringing forward complaints. Blockages of the
drainage gutters would be noted and orders given to
the ASI to have them cleared. Usually there was a
sweeper working near enough to accomplish this immediately. Politics, even after the Congress split,
was rarely discussed, although there was an occasional remark on every round. We often stopped for
up to half an hour at the house of political workers
or prominent citizens, to have a cup of tea or a
Coca-Cola. This was usually a purely social occasion.

Piles of malba (broken brick and earth) on the

street, blocked sewer lines, leaking sewer/drain
pipes on house walls, missing sewer gratings,
and other more major problems were the occasion
for a lecture to the concerned officers, often
coupled with profuse apologies to the nearby
citizens. Political workers might accompany us
on short tours of their neighborhoods, but only
a few workers were systematically visited when we
were in their locality. Once in a mohalla, we
would move at a slow pace, stopping every 50 feet
or so, for some reason or other. The groups of
citizens that gathered around the councilor varied
in size from three to thirty (not counting children). The round would finish at almost any point
in the ward, at which time the officers would be
told they could leave, and, typically, the councilor and his chief political worker would get a
cycle rickshaw (pedicab) and go off to some
meeting.

The councilor undoubtedly felt that going on
rounds was not only necessary ("nursing the constituency") but also a duty. He was fond of
pointing out to people that on Sundays, when other
people slept late or went on picnics, he was out
on rounds. On the first round I observed, the
councilor asked me how I liked his technique and
said that he enjoyed helping the people, and that's
why he spent his Sunday holiday doing it. On the
second round I observed he told me that he can do
nothing for citizens but that "sympathy eases the
pain." Later on in the year, he complained to me
that doing all this inspection work wasn't his
proper job--the officers should do it--and it left
little time for considering policy matters. But
he clearly did enjoy talking with people, pro-
jecting an image of serious concern, and probably
also accomplishing things. Indeed, this was true
of every councilor I had the opportunity to observe:
they clearly took pleasure not only in being a councilor (i.e., status rewards) but also in "con-
tacting" the people. I would guess that in this,
the Indian politician is no different from politicians elsewhere.

On a few occasions the councilor was asked to
mediate a dispute while on a round; one of these
is worth describing in detail. The following are
my notes of that round:*

Two more people on rounds today (friends?
workers?). Went straight to a <u>katra</u> where
two nights ago a fight had taken place.
The councilor went off to one corner to
talk, and a couple of old women approached
me and others (saying "Member Sahib" to us)
telling about bruised (?) bones, etc.,
which at the time puzzled me. A little
talking later, people were discussing the
stoppage of water and the building of a
flush latrine, at this point the [landlord]
came and then he mentioned the fight (there
had also been more buzzing and an inordinate
amount of excitement). He has, I gather,
filed a suit; the whole thing is in the
hands of the police. After telling his side
of the story he left (he had been much inter-
rupted by emotional shouting: not only [the
chief political worker] but also [one of the
ASIs] took part in asking people to wait
their turn, shoving away curious children,
etc.). Then the councilor (he had heard
about the fight) sat down and had some of
the participants tell the story. With many
interruptions (there was also some general
talk of "goondas" [toughs], "sharab" [liquor],
etc.)--I gather that a son of the <u>katra</u> <u>choud-
hury</u> is involved. It didn't seem to be a poor
<u>katra</u>; one "panditji" (he was so addressed)
was a principal, others were well-dressed.

---

*
    These notes will also give, I hope, something
of the "flavor" of a round. All the conversation
reported was in Hindi, and the question marks in parentheses represent my various puzzlements. The
names of the participants appear in my notes; I have
replaced them with descriptions, in brackets.

The councilor kept saying that he was going
to sit and settle the dispute, and threatened to leave several times when things got
out of hand. The cause of the dispute was
essentially over where the charpois were to
be placed (there was also something about a
bamboo rod which was holding up a tarp, but
that seemed to be settled with ease); as
[the chief political worker] said to me
"simply a matter of overcrowding." The
councilor had the people bring the charpois
out, moved into position. He then had the
position changed to settle things, and had
someone mark the spot with tar. All this
with assorted alarms and excursions. At
the end of it he asked then "haath joRkar
praathana kartaa hun" ["with hands folded
I beseech you"] that if there is some more
difficulty to come to him first before
fighting. He had also said that he could
do nothing about the court case. The councilor had said "here is my decision"
[faislaa]. Said at one point there was no
question of who did or did not give him
votes. Others had spoken--carefully, so as
not to reflect on [the councilor]--with "in
the time of [the previous councilor] . . . "
["X kee zamaanee main . . ."]. The councilor had said, "Please don't do these things
because it reflects on me and my area." The
ASI complained to [the chief political worker]
about being asked to spend time while disputes
were being solved. We continued on the round,
but an hour and a half having been spent, and
the rain beginning, the round was cut short.

Although the councilor played the role of mediator
in this particular dispute, the role is not a common one; he is not like the caste chaudhari or even
the village sarpanch (elected headman). On another
occasion, in an equally stormy argument between a
landlord and a tenant with an added component of a

communal clash (one party being Hindu and the other Muslim), the councilor quickly moved away with the argument in full cry. People whom I asked about disputes said that they could be solved informally-- by the mohalla committee, by a group of respected men--but that often the parties went to court, and that no one could intervene between landlord and tenant. It was clear that the councilor had no desire to get involved in that sort of dispute, even when he was asked to help.

On a number of rounds, specifically "polit- ical"* things were done. The new Congress Party Block chairman was introduced to the local polit- ical workers, invitations to civic receptions were passed out, etc. Certain rounds concentrated on specific areas, especially the katras. A round might also include a stop off for a ceremony (the opening of a new shop, for instance), and on August 15 (Independence Day), the councilor attended three or four flag unfurling ceremonies in his ward and the neighboring ward. Two of these were organized by Congress groups, another by a neighborhood organization, and both the councilor and the Metropolitan Councilor of the area, a member of the Jana Sangh, were present.

I have mentioned that political partisanship was not very prominent on rounds. I would like to describe its extent in a little more detail now. Although the Congress party split occurred midway through my study, and toward the end of the study (July-August, 1970) the next Corporation election was on the horizon and a general election was rumored, there were only 20 occasions on all the rounds in which politics per se were mentioned in a sentence or more. Some of these were in fact asides, as when someone asked the councilor which

---

*In Indian usage "political" usually means "partisan" and so in order to be consistent with my informants' usage (in quoted interviews, for example) I will use it with quotation marks.

"side" he was on and he replied "Indira's" (that is,
the "New" Congress led by Mrs. Gandhi). Some
referred specifically to the Jana Sangh being in
power in Delhi, to explain why something couldn't
be done, saying that it was "Jana Sangh policy not
to sanction new public water taps, so what can we
do?" A few discussions of local and national
politics occurred on rounds, but even these lasted
for only a few minutes. Viewed against the time
spent in conversations on rounds, this degree of
political partisanship is trivial; indeed, the
councilor objected when citizens alleged he was
doing things for "political" reasons. On occasion,
people from "opposition" wards (with a non-Congress
councilor) would come to the councilor--one suspects that "strong" party workers would do this--
and other councilors agreed that this was not uncommon. On the other hand, the councilor encountered
several of his former electoral opponents on rounds,
and was extremely friendly with them. There is no
doubt in my mind that the councilor did not dis-
criminate against voters or even party workers of
the opposition (while remembering that those he
might have discriminated against may well have gone
to a fellow party councilor to get their help and
favors done), though he probably did make extra
efforts on behalf of his strong supporters.

                    COUNCILOR AND CITIZEN

     Turning to the more specific aspects of the
round, let us examine the interaction of councilor
with citizen. Most contacts were initiated by the
councilor, in the sense that he would approach a
group of men standing by the roadside or in a katra,
and ask them (if there was a clearly defined leader,
or a special friend present, he would be approached
first), "How are things? Any difficulties?" or
"Of what service [seva, khidmat] can I be?" Occasionally he had to introduce himself--this was
particularly true when he covered the galis door to

door--but usually people knew who he was. He was
careful to define the nature of what he could do,
specifically excluding "police matters" from the
troubles he was willing to deal with[5] and sometimes saying "What can you or I do--it's what the
law says." When the councilor asked generally in
this fashion, he was sure to get a number of complaints. Although the councilor made it contin-
uously clear that he was a councilor--and never
more pointedly than when he said to a constituent,
as he often did, "Member Sahib, give me your
orders; I am only your worker"--an elected official
with certain powers which he could and would use,
still I never saw him speak with a constituent with
other than attention and respect.

    Contacts were also of course initiated by
citizens. Most commonly this would occur when
the councilor was inspecting, say, a broken drain
cover, and people would come and say how long it
had been broken, when they had made a complaint,
and bring up other complaints. Sometimes citizens
would come to the councilor's home before the
round--or would come during the week and be told
that he would see to it on the day of the round--
to bring him to the locale of the problem. Once
discussion began, contacts initiated by either
side were indistinguishable. On the whole, I
would describe these contacts as informal (the
councilor was fond of draping his arm over the
shoulders of the men he was talking to), with
mutual deference, usually short, and content
specific (a complaint, or whatever).

    As a contrast, let me describe in some detail
the most acrimonious interaction, one of a very
few, that I observed. From my field notes:

   [The chief political worker] had gone ahead,
   and the next thing to be heard was one man
   shouting "Yes, I have complaints--the cleaning
   of the gali. Today the inspector has come
   because you are here, but otherwise never.
   The election is coming, so you come." The

councilor, when he came up, immediately
went up the steps, although we were not
invited in right away, and said, "There
is no need to shout and make the whole
area think there is some dispute [there
were a number of people watching]. I
have come to listen." There was an
"avoidance of eyes convention": The two
of them were standing shoulder to shoulder,
and both addressed the onlookers in front
of them.

This encounter continued on as a peaceable discussion. The "avoidance of eyes convention" is
one I observed on a number of occasions of verbal
conflict. The two arguing parties would address
their remarks to a third, though they would mix
the second person address in with third person
description. The chosen "auditor" would usually
nod his head and say, "Ah, yes" or something. As
long as the argument was heated and personal, they
would not look at each other; even gestures would
be confined to a vague arm movement in the opponent's direction. Some feeling of two parties
appealing to a judge was created, thus obviating
the necessity of direct accusation.[6]
    Almost all interactions between councilor and
citizen seemed to be "instrumental" in the sense
that one party or the other was attempting to get
something very specific done; contacts did not
seem to be "for show." Nonetheless, I do not think
that the presentation or non-presentation of complaints is necessarily an index of the substance
of the councilor-citizen interface. For one thing,
it is not the people who would seem to have most
to complain about (at least from my "outsider's"
point of view), the katra dwellers, who in fact do
the most complaining. The councilor once remarked
to me, when he had received no response to his
usual "any difficulties?" in one katra, "Look at
these people--so poor, and yet no complaints, while
people in the big houses [sentence left uncompleted].

And these people are happy also." There are any
number of quite plausible reasons for this, ranging
from the hesitancy of the "oppressed" to try to deal
with the government or their social "superiors" to
the "resignation of the downtrodden" to the fact
that one water connection, for instance, may make a
tremendous difference in the life of the katra
dweller and a marginal difference to a person with
a higher standard of living (i.e., equal outlays
on services may be differentially appreciated
depending on their relative impact).

The attitude of the councilor toward the constituent was also somewhat ambivalent. Most often
he clearly enjoyed the contact and believed in his
ability to accomplish things and solve problems,
but occasionally--in asides to me--he would express
his disillusionment, saying things like "People
only want sweet words or that the worker should
show himself." And to one complainant he said,
after justifying his actions, "Please explain to
people that I am doing my best, that the sincerity
is there." In other words, it is the councilor's
duty to demonstrate--by exposing himself to public
contact--his sincerity and desire to get things
done, and this excuses to some extent any failure.
There is definitely a "darshan" (literally: a
"seeing"; one "takes darshan" paradigmatically of
a god, but also of persons of high status) element
to the rounds: the Member Sahib "shows" himself
to the people who then make requests and complaints
not so much out of the expectation that they will
be acceded to or dealt with, but because they feel
it is expected of them. I think that this is only
a part, and a small part at that, of the interaction, but it is definitely there.

OFFICER AND CITIZEN

The interactions of officers with citizens
while on rounds were usually mediated by the councilor; even in the instances of discussions (or

accusations of incompetence, or whatever) the
councilor was at least initially an interested
observer, someone to refer to for an opinion,
although he might continue to deal with other
complaints. The ASIs, since they did cover the
ward daily, were well known to the people, as
was the works section officer. When not involved
directly in what the councilor was doing, the
officers tended to converse among themselves
(this was facilitated by the fact that almost
all of them spoke Punjabi) or acted as "aides"
of the councilor. For example, they would
shoo away the innumerable small children who
would inevitably crowd in underfoot when the
councilor was talking. Or they would ask someone with a complaint to wait until the previous
complainant was finished. Twice, when the
argument between two men got really heated,
they physically restrained the angry disputants.
In more informal situations, when the group was
invited for tea, or when the discussion shifted
to general political matters, they would take
part, as any interested and informed citizen
might.

     But the substance of the officers'
relationship with citizens on rounds was
shaped by the councilor. Most typically, he
would ask the officer to treat a given citizen
as if he were the councilor: one ASI was
asked to "take orders" from the "chaudhari
sahib" of one katra in which a wedding was to
take place that evening; in other words, see
to it that the gali was extra clean and get
the approval of the chaudhari. These requests
seemed to be accepted by the officers, at least
formally, but it was clear that, as in other
instances, it was the councilor who would see
to it that the officers did the job. The
councilor once jokingly told some people who
were complaining about insanitary conditions,
"the first time it happens [the filth not
being removed] inform me; the second time

gherao* the ASI, and I will call the press and
have photos taken." There were instances in
which the responsibility of overseeing the
officer by the councilor was made explicit by
the citizen (cf. above, the insistence of the
old lady in a katra on fastening responsibility
on the councilor and not on the Slum Department
superior officer). The councilor's presence
insured that he was party to any officer-citizen
interaction.

The situation is somewhat different when
the officer is not on rounds. My data on this
aspect of the interaction is less complete. I
did spend long hours sitting in the office of
the works section officer (about two hours a
week for the twelve-month period), and only once
did someone from the ward come in to see him
about a problem. Even though the office of the
ASIs was quite near the ward, my impression is
that few people went there either. Both the ASIs
and the works section officer spent a good deal
of time in the ward; but their contact with
citizens there is minimal. They concentrate
on telling their subordinates (sweepers, laborers)
what to do. When they did converse with people,
they were polite, explaining why the inconvenience
--for example, a street being torn up in order
to put in a new water line--was necessary and
how long it would last. "We have to be patient
with people and explain to them what we are
doing," was how the works section officer put it.
This willingness to accommodate may go so far as
to include negotiations on an administrative
action; I recorded one instance in my field
notes:

---

*
  A technique of labor or political action
in which someone (a plant manager, a University
Vice-Chancellor) is surrounded and prevented from
leaving until he accedes to a request.

Went and saw [X]. While there two men came
to cut the water connection because of non-
payment of bills. They agreed not to do it
if [X] would write that he was coming to
the office to settle them today or tomorrow.
[X] suggested next week, and they agreed on
the day after tomorrow. This was written on
the back of the notice to cut the line. The
officer said that he had come from cutting
two other connections and was doing this
because of [X's] "sharafat" [roughly, "good
name"]. He said also that [X] didn't have
to pay the whole amount [Rs. 700] at that
time, say half.

Ten days later, the bills still unpaid, the water
connection was cut. On other occasions similar
results might be obtained through bribery. Finally,
officers may see themselves as quasi workers of the
councilor. One officer told me, "When I go into an
area to do work, I say to the people there, 'The
councilor is getting this work done.'"
    Clearly, the core of "ward government" is in
the relationship of councilor to officer. On rounds
the councilor is the "superior officer" of the ASIs
and the section officers. He gives them orders--
chalan this person, don't chalan that person--as
well as deciding on how to do a specific job,
although he does defer to the officers' expertise.
Some of this is "legitimate," in the sense that it
follows from the councilor's authority to allocate
priorities in projects from his funds, some stems
from the councilor's knowledge of the appropriate
rules, but much seems to be derived quite explicitly
from the councilor's power to injure or advance the
position of low-level officers.
    Officers at the ward level as well as those at
higher levels find themselves in the bind of having
to obey the orders of the "ruling" councilors, who
also determine where the dividing line between
legitimate and illegitimate orders lies. Thus, one
section officer who completed a construction job in

record time in the weeks before the election was
threatened with transfer (on the gounds that he
was "a Congress man") when the Jana Sangh councilor won. He claims he asked the councilor to
please wait six months, "so people will not think
I have been transferred for political reasons,"
and the councilor agreed (and indeed retained him
when he proved he could work as well for the new
man). Some months before the elections of spring,
1971, all transfers at all levels in the Corporation were halted. But usually ward level officers
can be transferred out on the request of the councilor.

    I have noted above that the deference patterns
of councilor and officer vary in public and private.
I might add that in private, while in seating patterns, e.g., the councilor retains the preeminent
role, still there is a great deal of informality
(joking, etc.) between councilor, political worker,
and officers. All aspects of politics are discussed, with all joining in; to be sure, the
officers tend to agree with the councilor, but they
don't hesitate to be "partisan."* Outside, on
rounds, the officers were less likely to become
involved in such discussions. There the initiative
is unquestionably with the councilors, most particularly when he has "called" a specific officer to
be present on the round. Officers did not hesitate
to protest when they felt they were unjustly
accused of negligence by the councilor, though one
officer told me (and his colleagues) "It's best not
to argue," just make a note and swallow the insult.

    Most interactions, and particularly those with
more senior officers, are in the nature of con-
sultations: How shall we solve this problem of
standing water? How much will such and such
cost, and how soon could we get it done? On some

---

    *
    Government officers in India are not per-
mitted to take part in any political activity.

occasions there were jurisdictional disputes between officers, each claiming that a given job was in his colleague's department; both the councilor and his chief political worker were of course well informed about the rules and regulations and entered into these discussions. Indeed, the councilor tended to have the last word. On some rounds, when specific projects were being looked at, the councilor might take the role of privileged visitor, to whom what was being done was explained, to show that it was in accord with the rules, or project plans, or what- ever. The councilor would never order an officer to do something irregular, but rather would make a request in a weak form, "Just look at it and see what you can do. . . ." In these cases, it seemed to me that the officer relied (probably justifiably) on the councilor's taking respon- sibility for the action should it be questioned.

Apart from the election campaign, the round is the most significant part of the councilor- citizen interface and also is the modal type of councilor-officer interaction in the ward. Citizens come to the councilor to get papers notarized, to get specific things done outside the ward, to talk politics, etc., but the coun- cilor goes to the citizen, frequently and con- scientiously, on the round. The councilor thus presents himself primarily as an actor in the administrative process, a presentation underlined by the presence of subordinate officers on the round. If the councilor's role were one primarily of policy maker, a participant in the "deliberative wing" of the Corporation, as in theory he "ought" to be, then one would expect, perhaps, his contacts with citizens to be in the nature of reports to his constituency, given in the form of speeches or posters or flyers. This style of contact was never in evidence except when the candidate in an election was pointing out the achievements of his party, or the perfidious politics of the opposition. But just as often, he was outlining what he could do

for the ward if elected, in terms of drains and
street repair. The councilor's style of action
changes in the context of the zone and of the city
as a whole, but the core of his responsibilities
as an elected member, as perceived by him and as
shown in the time and effort invested in it, lies
in his ward and in the process of day-to-day
administration affecting it.

From the point of view of the citizen, the
councilor takes on a different aspect. He is a
representative of only one part of the government;
the bulk of the citizen's participation in government (aside from elections) occurs, I suspect,
elsewhere, in various offices of the Corporation,
and involves filling out forms and waiting in
queues. A citizen is likely to see a councilor
once or twice a year when he comes through on a
round or when he notarizes a document for him; and
perhaps the citizen will hear him give a ceremonial speech. It will be most unlikely that the
councilor's name will appear in the newspaper.
The majority of voters, let alone citizens,
probably never have spoken with the councilor,
and since the presence of the city government in
the ward is hardly noticeable--or rather, particularly noticeable only by its absence, as in the
sweepers' strike--the councilor as a constant
"fact of life" would seem to be an overstatement.

Nonetheless, when questions of access and
effectiveness of interaction in the governmental
process are considered, the citizens' eye-view of
the councilor changes: he is nearby, accessible,
deferential to requests, and, on the whole, an
effective intercessor if needed. It is known to
the citizen that the councilor is supposed to be
keeping his eye on how the ward is faring, when he
goes on rounds. If he sees the councilor on rounds
--or, I would imagine, if his relatives, neighbors
or friends see the councilor and tells him about
it--he is being given proof of the councilor's
continuing concern (unfortunately, I was unable to
ask the citizen about this in any structured way,

and I am forced to rely essentially on the councilor's perception of what the citizen wants). The
councilor is not, therefore, simply some kind of
artifact of the governmental system, but rather a
figure of importance, possibly the only one, in
his constituency.*

SUMMARY

This chapter has focused on the councilor in
his role as mediator in the administrative process,
both as "custodian" and as a man directly involved
in the delivery of services, the "superior officer"
of the ward-level administrative officers. This
role is, of course, intimately connected with the
politics of the ward: it constitutes one part of
"nursing" the constituency. In the next chapter,
I turn to the broader frame of politics in Kucha
Khirkiwala: elections and the "fit" of electoral
patterns with socio-economic patterns.

---

*
The position of the Metropolitan Councilor
forms a contrast. This man represents a constituency of two Corporation wards in a Council
which is administratively powerless. He is consequently a person of little importance in his
constituency, except on ceremonial occasions.

4. Kucha Khirkiwala Politics and Elections

I don't say, now the elections are over,
I'll talk to you after five years.
Every day I fight like the election were
tomorrow.[1]

Kucha Khirkiwala is only tenuously a geographical and socio-economic unit, as we have seen
in Chapter 2. It is, however, a significant unit
of municipal government, having, in a sense, a
staff of administrators concerned almost exclusively
with it, and an active councilor to oversee them,
as we have seen in the previous chapter. It is also
an electoral arena. The remark of the Punjab M.L.A.
underlines the implications of part of what we have
discussed: the councilor sees his "governmental"
role to be intimately tied to his "electoral" role,
to his success or failure as a political figure.
    The councilor of Kucha Khirkiwala was fond of
saying "Don't say I didn't try to fulfill my election promises," by which he meant, in part, don't
hold my unfulfilled promises against me in the next
election. Fully a year before the coming municipal
election (which was postponed by two months subsequently), the "tempo" of councilor activity had
increased, and this was seen to be directed at the
up-coming election not only by the press, but also
by the citizens of the ward. Elections and electoral results would thus seem to be an easy starting
point for the study of politics in the ward.

The politics of Kucha Khirkiwala is not confined to elections and electoral strategy, of
course. Although there is no evidence of a "power
elite" or dominant caste/class in the ward as a
whole (there may be something on this order at the
mohalla level), there is a ward-defined political
structure, centered on the municipal arena, but not
confined to it, since the ward is used by Delhi
politicians as a unit of analysis, of support, and
of organization for Metropolitan Council and Lok
Sabha elections. I shall explore some of these
latter dimensions in Chapter 7. What is missing
from this chapter, however, is a detailed analysis
of ongoing party structure between elections, and
the mesh of socio-economic factors with it. The
obstacles to getting this data are considerable,
and I did not have the time to attempt to surmount
them. I present a brief sketch of politics in
these terms at the end of the chapter. But elections remain the centerpiece of ward politics, and
it is to elections that I now turn.

THE CAMPAIGN AND THE VOTE*

Since 1967, elections to state legislatures
in India, in contrast to the first 15 years of
electoral politics, have tended to occur more frequently than the usual, statutory maximum of every
five years. Municipalities, on the other hand,
right from the time of Independence, have frequently had their terms extended by one or more
years. The Delhi Municipal Corporation, with a life
of four years, nonetheless had its elections in 1967
along with the "state" (in Delhi, this was the

---

*This section is based on three sources:
press reports of elections, interviews with councilors and candidates, and, most important, my
intensive observation of the Basti Julahan bye-
election in April-May, 1969.[2]

Metropolitan Council election) and national elections, five years after the last election. Even
after the date for an election is announced (by
the lieutenant governor of Delhi), it can be
fairly easily postponed. This general uncertainty about the precise date of the poll means
that a low-key campaign begins quite early, but
continues quite close to the polling date, since
no one can be sure that a high-pitch campaign
won't have to be started all over again. Campaigning begins in earnest one month to six
weeks before election day. The process of
selection of candidates has been described
elsewhere.[3] In Kucha Khirkiwala, as might be
expected, persons denied Congress tickets have
fought elections against the Congress, as
Independents, been re-admitted into Congress,
etc., etc. Alternate candidates are selected
along with the prime candidates to insure that
the party will have a contestant if the nom-
ination papers of the prime candidate should
be rejected; these alternates will withdraw,
sometimes after the last date for official
withdrawal (i.e., their names will remain on
the ballot). Except in a few cases, one of
which proved significant in one Kucha Khirkiwala
election, candidates who have withdrawn but whose
name remains on the ballot receive only a handful
of votes per polling station: voters apparently
know who the real candidates are.

    Each party may field one or more "dummy"
candidates, in order to "cut" votes from the
opposition by splitting the votes of their strong
supporters, usually defined in ascriptive terms
(in Delhi, especially, Muslim, "Bania," etc.).
Thus, the Jana Sangh may set up a Muslim Independent to "cut" Congress votes--almost no Muslim
votes for the Jana Sangh--or the Congress may try
to split the Jana Sangh's "Punjabi" vote by supporting a Punjabi Independent. My impression is
that this is not a common technique in Delhi,
perhaps because the provenance of "dummy"

candidates is either known or strongly rumored,
and voters will resist being manipulated. More
common, perhaps,* are the political entrepreneurs
who file their own names and then approach the
party whose vote they might "cut" with a proposal
to withdraw for a consideration, which might not
be money, but, say, a promise of the party ticket
in the next election. One would assume that in
close elections--and withdrawals occur on the last
day of the campaign--these offers may be considered.

There are three major elements of a councilor's
campaign: door-to-door canvassing, corner meetings,
and public meetings. Canvassing is unquestionably
the most important.** Usually this means canvassing by the candidate himself, though party workers
also go door-to-door. Typically, the candidate
spends three or more hours every morning and/or
evening (and longer on Sunday) visiting the house
of every voter, starting a month or more before
the poll date. The candidate is surrounded by a
few party workers, including the man in charge of
that particular polling station, and, in important
elections (like the Basti Julahan by-election),
often also important party figures, such as the
local member of Parliament. The candidate may
introduce himself to the voter or he may be introduced by a party worker; he may admire the children
and bend a sympathetic ear to problems; in short,
depending on the candidate's personality (and
possibly on party policy) almost any mode of contact can occur. Candidates will canvass everyone,

---

*This remains a twilight realm of charge and
counter-charge, often of corruption, since "dummy"
candidates tend to be paid candidates (or candidates paid to withdraw).

**I am basing this description on responses
to the question I asked 18 councilors of the City
Zone: "Will you please tell me how the election
campaign was run."

including known opposition supporters, though not
active opposition party workers. The families of
opposition candidates and workers are not exempt,
however; one important Congress worker told me.

> In the 1967 election, my own sister's son
> was contesting on the Jana Sangh ticket.
> He came to my house in my absence and said
> to my wife, "I know your husband is working
> for [the Congress candidate] but you can
> vote for me." My wife said, "If [the
> Congress candidate] loses, my husband's
> prestige will go down, and therefore mine
> will go down also."

This same man also told me,

> In 1958, my wife was saying that, "On the
> one hand [the Jana Sangh candidate] is our
> uncle and on the other you are working for
> [the Congress candidate], so I will vote for
> both" [this was at the time a double-member
> constituency]. I said to her, "All right,
> I am asking you to cast both your votes for
> Congress, but it is all right."

Approaches, of course, vary with the preferences of
the voter being approached. All the contacts I saw
were models of courtesy on both sides, and voters
seemed genuinely pleased to have been personally
contacted by the candidates.

   Personal canvassing by the candidate seems to
be less a technique for gaining votes than it is
insurance against losing them. Since voters expect
to be contacted, they will view non-contact as
evidence that the candidate has no concern and will
vote against him. The councilor of Kucha Khirkiwala
says that he probably saw every voter in his campaign; judging from the time spent, this does not
seem to be unreasonable for a constituency of 15,000
voters. One candidate, who is a doctor, claimed

that his profession gave him an edge because he
could walk into a house and talk to the women,
which other male candidates could not do.*   He
would call the women "behnji" (sister) or "amma"
(mother), both terms of respect in general usage,
in a semi-literal way: "I am your brother, I am
your son." Often the action would be suited to the
words, with the candidate making the gesture of
touching the feet (a gesture made with out-reaching
hands and bowed body, with the hands brought
together at the chest in the gesture of respect
to gods, and, by extension, a way of greeting
elders in India), and receive in return the
gesture of blessing (aashirvaad), having one's
head touched. One canvasser made jocular use of
this practice, saying to the woman whose feet he
had "touched," "I don't want your blessing; just
give me your vote." Even more than the councilor
on rounds, the candidate defers to the voter, in
speech and in posture, "against" hierarchy in all
its dimensions. I saw one high-caste councilor,
while canvassing in Basti Julahan, make a nearly
complete touching of feet gesture (he all but
actually touched the feet) to an untouchable
woman, and then sit and fan another woman while
she was cooking, as he asked for their votes.

    Along with personal canvassing by the can-
didate, there are those who canvass on the candidate's behalf, typically men of respect in a
mohalla. One councilor described his method:

    Before the campaign, I gathered the workers
    of the area and the best, the influential
    people of the area. We had an informal
    meeting, and I told them what I had done
    in the last four-five years; streets,

---

    *
    On the other hand, one woman candidate
did not feel that being a woman was a particular
advantage in canvassing, even with women.

schools, health centers, lighting, cleanliness. Then the workers go to the people
and tell them about it.

Similarly, another councilor said, "Most importantly, in each polling unit we had selected four
or five more dependable, reliable, influential
persons, and they were in charge of getting out
voters for us." These important local men may
simply canvass door-to-door in a manner similar to
the candidate's, but probably more often they are
doing something more specific: on the day before
polling, they hand out voter identification slips
(which are used by the party workers and government
officials at the polling booth to check their names
on the voters' lists), for example. But almost as
soon as the campaign begins, and later on during it
as well, they check the accuracy of the voters'
lists, getting new residents registered, possibly
preparing challenges of names no longer valid.
     Voters' lists are prepared by the state elec-
tion officials--the actual enumerators are government employees, ranging from senior-level clerks to
school teachers--as near to the polling date as
practicable, by going door-to-door listing new
voters and eliminating voters who have died, moved
away, etc. These lists tend to have errors which
can be converted into "bogus" voters, and each
party tries to discover which opposition voters no
longer exist (so that their possible substitutes
can be challenged at the polling booth) and which
of their own voters need to be added. It is of
course possible to discover also how many bogus
voters (looking now from the point of view of the
"unscrupulous" party worker) need be alerted to
vote the names of the deceased or departed. But
despite the frequent charges of the prevalence of
these practices, my impression is that the importance of these techniques is minimal: in one by-
election there were 100 bogus voters caught (out of
12,000 voters), and in Basti Julahan there were
only a handful of "tendered" votes, votes made by

bona fide voters who had arrived to find that their
name had already been used.[4]
     The voters' list itself provides some infor-
mation of use to the campaign strategist; for
example, Muslims can be picked out by their names,
and the relationship between members of a household can be figured out, so one can tell whether
there is likely to be a "patriarch" there. More
important, probable voting patterns are marked on
the list as the polling station area is canvassed:
strong supporters are marked, areas of weakness
noted, etc. On polling day, special efforts are
made to make sure that one's voters have in fact
voted; the names of those voting are checked off
the list and the remaining people are contacted,
reminded and often escorted to the polling booth.
(Which is, of course, very much what the precinct
captain does in the United States.) The polling
station "in-charge" is responsible for the checking
of voting lists and for understanding the shape of
the preferences of the voters of his area so that
various strategies can be decided on. Polling
station in-charges have party workers under their
command. In an important by-election such as Basti
Julahan, the in-charge would stick to the polling
station party office (a shopkeeper's storeroom or
an extra room of a residence rented or borrowed for
the duration of the campaign) or "take a round" of
his area, leaving the actual door-to-door checking
to other workers.
     The in-charge tends to be a local man, although
experienced party workers from other areas in the
ward may be put in charge, especially if they have
kin or caste ties with the inhabitants of a polling
station area. In Basti Julahan (again, an especially important contest), many of the polling
station in-charges were sitting municipal councilors,
some of them party leaders and all-Delhi figures.
The polling station in-charges are one level of
intermediaries in the councilor's campaign organization. Below them are the ordinary workers,
above them are a few specialists on the candidate's

staff: someone in charge of posters and literature,
perhaps, and a co-ordinating in-charge.

It is at this upper level that there is a
significant difference between Congress and Jana
Sangh organizations in Delhi. Although both
parties have ward organizations on paper, the
Jana Sangh bodies (the mandal) actually exist;
indeed, many polling stations have functioning
sub-groups called sthaniya samitis. In Kucha
Khirkiwala, according to one Jana Sangh candidate,
there are seven sthaniya samitis. These groups
meet regularly (optimally, once a month) to discuss
problems of the ward as well as arrange for more
general Jana Sangh activities--participation in an
anti-cow-slaughter demonstration, for instance.
The sitting Jana Sangh councilor may be invited
to these but he will not be an officer of the
mandal.

During the election campaign, it is the Jana
Sangh mandal that is in charge: they appoint the
polling station in-charges, determine strategy,
and even arrange the candidate's schedule. In
some instances, higher levels of the party may
perform these functions. Several Jana Sangh councilors said that they had a say in strategy and
day-to-day organization, and one Congress councilor
said that he had nothing to do with the campaign,
that it was all run by his workers. But typically
the Congress candidate was in command of his own
campaign. If he had a separate in-charge, it would
be a close friend or old party comrade. A number
of the Jana Sangh candidates had been mandal
officers and were thus probably not excluded from
campaign decision-making. In the 1967 election,
the Jana Sangh gave tickets to men who were not
strong party members (more importantly, perhaps,
who were not members of the RSS[5]) but who were local
influentials--the secretary of a spice merchants'
association, for example. These men as well
reported that the organization of the campaign was
left in the party's hands, although the participation of friends and relatives who were not party

members was reported by most candidates. In the
course of the three-week Basti Julahan by-election,
I visited the Jana Sangh campaign headquarters at
least once a day at varying times. There were
frequently two or three of the most influential
Jana Sangh leaders in Delhi present--but I never
saw the Jana Sangh candidate there.

Andersen and Saini confirm this impression:
"The Jana Sangh candidate and the campaign workers
were linked by the election-in-charge and planning
was apparently done without much consultation with
the candidate. The candidate himself admits to
meeting only infrequently with the Jana Sangh's
organizational men during the campaign."[6] By way
of contrast, I saw the Congress candidate in his
campaign headquarters quite often, discussing his
program and prospects with important party leaders,
even though the organizational responsibility was
not in his hands.

There are also contrasts in the kinds of
workers of the two major Delhi parties. From the
point of view of one Jana Sangh councilor:

> Congress workers are 75% paid. Jana Sangh
> workers pay for everything themselves. . . .
> Today in Delhi the Jana Sangh has a shakha
> [branch] in every gali. Workers are mostly
> 16 to 50 years old. Congress workers are 50
> and over. They don't welcome new blood.
> Then there is the RSS, a social organization,
> which is at the back of the Jana Sangh.
> There are people who are unmarried who are
> responsible for running the organization.
> Workers go to every house and try to mold
> the character of the children so they will
> be good. And so the children's families
> come to Jana Sangh and the children become
> Jana Sangh workers.

Jana Sangh candidates insisted that the Congress
paid its workers and that no Jana Sangh worker was

paid; indeed, it is a rule, I was told, that
every Jana Sangh councilor must have a source
of income other than his councilor's salary.
The Congress does employ some staff workers,
and a few Congressmen admitted that party jobs
are found for workers who could not otherwise
afford to devote their time to the campaign
(and there are few people other than students
who can afford to spend three weeks on political
activity). And there are also Congress workers
who have an ideological commitment to the party,
despite its organizational disarray in Delhi.
Almost all councilors claim to have a range of
types of workers, young and old, male and female,
but they tended to emphasize youth. Most would
also probably agree with a Congress official who
said "Workers are not from the privileged class,
in either party. They do not bother much about
politics, but bother about their works [getting
jobs done]. They--the businessmen--try to win
over the successful candidate, but they don't
produce workers." The polling station in-charges
tend to be older and more experienced, of course,
but campaign participation does range from the
very old and respected to bands of small children
(five years and older) who parade through the
galis chanting slogans and carrying the party
flag.

     A feature of Indian politics in general
which comes to the fore in elections is the
presence of "brokers" who control "vote banks."[7]
In rural areas particularly these are generally
leaders of caste or religious groups. In Basti
Julahan there were blocs of votes defined in
these terms--Muslims, Jatava, etc.--but there
were few mentions of local influentials. I have
discussed the situation in the katras of Kucha
Khirkiwala, and noted the extent to which the
councilor seeks out direct contact with citizens,
rejecting intermediaries. I was able to interview five unsuccessful candidates from Kucha
Khirkiwala (three of the Jana Sangh, one of the

Republican Party of India (RPI), one Independent),
and one question I asked was, "Who are the important men (baRee aadmii) of the area?" I also asked
the same question of two of the more important campaign workers of the ward (both Congress). One of
the candidates insisted that "there is no one with
influence." The other four candidates named 52
men. One worker named 62 men, the other 16. I
specifically asked for the names of important men
of all parties.

The lack of overlap, of multiple namings, is
the most striking result: there was no man who
was mentioned by all four candidates; only one man
mentioned by three; nine mentioned by two; and the
remaining 42 mentioned only once. If we add the
number of times the two campaign workers named men
on the candidates' lists, the result does not
change much; out of six possible "nominations,"
no one was mentioned five or six times; five men
got four nominations; another five got three nominations; eight got two mentions; and the remaining
34 were named only once. Only 14 of the 62 names
given by the one worker appeared on the lists of
the four candidates. Each candidate's list is
restricted geographically and ethnically. The
Muslim candidates named no Hindus; only a few
Muslims were named by the Hindu candidates. Candidates who could give me the house numbers of
important men in their mohalla had to search for
names of men further off, and most didn't name
anyone in large areas of the ward, even when I
prompted with the names of specific mohallas.
These men were mentioned as being "important";
I got no indication that they "controlled" blocs
of votes, but rather that they had some kind of
influence. If they did "control" votes, the
number would not be above 100. Since the number
of "influentials" was so small, I did not explore
their role further. That there were at most ten
and possibly only four or five such "influentials"
in this ward of 15,000 voters suggests that the
"broker" is not the important actor in old Delhi

that he apparently is in rural areas and small
towns.

In addition to the various kinds of canvassing done during a campaign, the candidate
participates in "corner" meetings and "public"
meetings. Corner meetings are held in the
evening in the various mohallas--sometimes
there are two or three in an evening--toward
the end of the campaign. They may be held out-
doors in a chowk or on a large rooftop, or
inside in a large room. They are not scheduled
too far in advance, perhaps in the morning, and
neighbors are told about it by the local workers;
the speakers may have to wait while an audience
is rounded up. In addition to the candidate and
his chief workers, there will be one or two
notables asked to speak and answer questions.
The Basti Julahan campaign featured the Chief
Executive Councilor of the Delhi Metropolitan
Council and the leader of the Congress in the
Metropolitan Council, and men of like stature at
these meetings--an ordinary campaign might bring
in the occasional all-city figure. "Public"
meetings, held in large open areas with loud-
speaker systems and announced by posters days
beforehand, feature, in Delhi, important national
leaders as well as the member of Parliament for
the area. Depending on his speaking ability,
the candidate may only be introduced at these
meetings, leaving the speeches to others, who
will touch on the more general issues of city
and national policies. General elections for
Parliament were held at the same time as the
Corporation election in 1962 and 1967 (and elections for the newly-formed Delhi Metropolitan
Council also, in the latter year), so that these
public meetings served as platforms for parliamentary electioneering as well.* Similarly, some

---

*In the opinion of one informant, the "coat"
is worn by the municipal candidate, and the parliamentary candidate holds the "tails."

posters were printed with general messages,
or simply "Vote Congress," while others had
a space for the candidate for the Corporation
to put his name. And of course the local
candidate can produce his own posters. There
is some literature passed out, but most
"written" campaigning is done with posters.
    The first "poster" to make its appear-
ance is a simple message containing the name
of the candidate, his party, and its symbol
which is stenciled, using a metal stencil and
paint, on house walls throughout the ward.
Printed posters can be designed, printed
and pasted up overnight (they are put up
between midnight and dawn by a contractor).
There is thus scope for posters answering
the opposition posters in addition to those
announcing public meetings and the straightforward one with a picture of the candidate.
In the Basti Julahan campaign the following
posters appeared successively:

Poster No. 1:   (Congress) "Ahmedabad
                has shown the way [an
                election had just been
                held there]--Congress
                62, Jana Sangh 3," etc.

Poster No. 2:   (Jana Sangh) "This is
                Delhi, not Ahmedabad,"
                etc.

Poster No. 3:   (Congress) "To those who
                make a distinction between
                Delhi and Ahmedabad [we say]:
                All India is One. . . .
                And in the whole of India a
                whirlwind is blowing to
                extinguish your lamp [the
                lamp is the Jana Sangh
                symbol]," etc.

Poster No. 4:   (Jana Sangh) [You people
                talking about Indian unity
                --who divided Punjab,
                Assam. . . ?]*

These sorts of posters become more common as the
"tempo" of the campaign increases, and almost all
available space is covered with posters in the
two weeks before polling day, at least in important elections. To bring the "tempo"** to its
correct pitch, a procession may be held, in which
the candidate and as many of his supporters as
can be gathered from the ward and from the city
will march, snaking their way through the major
galis, carrying placards and chanting slogans.
The placards and the slogans, at least in Basti
Julahan, were usually two lines, with a leader
chanting the first and everyone coming in on the
second. Children go around in bands shouting
these slogans at all times of day and night. Here
is a sample of these (in the form: leader/
response):

(Congress slogans)
     Vote for / Congress!
     Put the seal / On the bullocks [the
               Congress symbol]
     Put out the lamp [the Jana Sangh symbol]
          / Save Democracy

----

*
 These posters were written in both Devanagari
and Perso-Arabic (Urdu) script. I have made summary translations, in the main, because much of the
impact came from the posters' design. These four
posters appeared within a week's time.

**
 The English word is used, as it was in the
election observed by Adrian Mayer ("Municipal
Elections").

(Jana Sangh slogans)
    Bharatiya Jana Sangh / Victory!
    It'll win, Brothers, it'll win /
        the lamp [party] will win
    What did Bapuji [Gandhi] say? / Break
        up Congress[8]

The effort is to time the crescendo correctly, so
that in the last few days the supporters will be
kept firm, and the waverers will be persuaded by
the surge of enthusiasm to climb on the bandwagon.
A correct tempo is also considered important to
get the maximum number of active workers.
    The strategies of the candidates and/or their
parties is, in its particulars, very much a secret.
No one in Basti Julahan volunteered the typologies
of "hard" and "soft" campaigns that Mayer describes
for the Dewas election, although one campaign worker,
when asked, said that they did go to the katras the
opposition had visited an hour after they had left
to check on what had happened. Judging from the
Basti Julahan election, there is a generally festive
spirit and cordial relations between the parties:
when canvassing groups met in a gali they would
shake hands all round, ask after each other's
health, and possibly make mild, half-joking, remarks
on the other's style of campaign. Most people
agreed that up to 80 percent of the voters were
committed to one party or the other, and I got the
impression that election campaigns were designed to
keep party supporters firm and get them out to
vote. There are of course "sub-themes" of the
reputed buying of votes, mix-ups in party symbols,
etc., etc. It is clear that unlike the small city
situation, there are few local structures and
leaders that a campaign strategy can be built
around.
    The financing of the campaign proved vir-
tually impossible to investigate. Expenses include
posters, literature, sound and light systems for
public meetings, party flags, and other parapher-
nalia. In addition, at least the food (and these

days, Coca-Cola), consumed by the party workers
and handed around in great amount during canvassing and after, probably comes out of some
campaign fund. Some money comes from general
party funds, but most comes from donations by
specific people, and in many cases, largely from
the candidate himself. Whether a man has money
to spend on his campaign is an important factor
in whether or not he gets the ticket, according
to one party official I spoke to. The estimates
of the total cost of a campaign are obscured in
charge and counter-charge (there is a legal
maximum which is almost certainly exceeded by
every major candidate), but it is undoubtedly in
the thousands of rupees and probably in the tens
of thousands. Independent candidates and candidates of small parties often simply cannot afford
a full campaign.

The campaign ends by law 24 hours before the
opening of the polls. On the polling day (usually
booths are open 8:00 A.M. to 5:00 P.M.; recent
elections in Delhi have been on Sundays), the
workers of each candidate set up a table--putting
it the legal distance away from the polling booth--
where voters can have their "identification slips,"
which have been issued to them by both parties two
days before, checked or new ones issued. The party
workers check off the name of their supporter as he
goes in to vote (the idea being that voters will
bring the "identification slip"--which contains
all the information on the voters' list and thus
facilitates the checking of the voter's name by
polling officials--to the workers of the party
they intend to vote for). People who haven't
voted will be contacted in the afternoon. Voters
who are unable to walk to the polling booth will
be carried there. In the exceptional case of the
Basti Julahan election, there was an estimated one
party worker for every voter, so that the galis
were jammed with bands of workers seeking out voters
to bring to the polls. When the voter enters the
polling station (located in a school or other large

public building, or in a large tent (<u>shamiana</u>)
pitched in an open area), the first people he
sees are the official party poll watchers, who
are permitted to challenge any prospective voter
(for a small charge which is returned if the
challenge is successful). A voter so challenged
is asked to go with a policeman to retrieve proof
of identity and residence--usually a ration-card,
but a well-known resident can be heard as a
witness. If the voter is found to be "bogus,"
he is kept in custody. As noted above, I was
told that in one by-election, 100 or so bogus
voters were caught, but were simply released at
the end of the day because prosecuting them would
have been too long and too tedious a process.

The voter then moves to a government official
who checks off his name on the voters' lists and
then to another who marks his hand with indelible
ink and hands him a ballot paper. He then goes to
a screened-off booth to mark the paper by stamping
the candidate's name or party symbol with the
"seal" (it is a rubber stamp with an "X" mark).
Having folded the paper correctly--incorrect
foldings which result in the still wet mark making
a second impression elsewhere on the ballot are
the most common cause of invalid ballots--he
deposits it in the ballot box under the eye of
yet another official. At the end of the day
everything--ballot box, voters' lists, tendered
ballots, challenges--are sealed separately. In
the case of the ballot box, seals are put on both
the lock and the burlap sack the box is put in.
The polling station officer and each representative
of the candidate puts on a separate wax seal (with
a distinctive marking), and the ballot boxes are
moved, under police guard, to the site of counting,
usually a courthouse. The counting is done,
beginning the next morning, by officials watched
by representatives of the candidates; the results
are recorded and tabulated on the spot--by hand--
by the election officer, who is usually a senior
official, a Class II Officer. At least one

magistrate is present on the polling day and the
counting day to deal with bogus voters and legal
challenges. The victorious candidate is taken
out in a procession through the ward.

Promises are made in speeches during the
campaign, of course, but they tend to be fairly
general: "I will see that the ward is kept properly clean, that it has sufficient water," etc.
More important, voters are urged to elect a party
into office, because it is party policy which is
seen to be significant, for everything from more
schools to less filth. During the campaign, as has
been noted above, there is a general suspension of
the enforcement of municipal regulations--unauthor-
ized construction is rampant. Sitting councilors
drive officials to complete works in record time.
Election time also provides an opportunity for
citizens to get fast action on problems. I was
present in Basti Julahan when a Congress worker
arranged to have some people accompany a woman to
a court appearance, even though she told the
Congress worker that she was supporting the Jana
Sangh candidate. (Indeed she lived across the
street from him, and the entire street was saffron
with Jana Sangh flags.) The arrangements made,
another Congress worker said, in slogan style,
"Don't worry, and vote Congress," and was promptly
silenced by his leader, who said, "This is not a
matter of getting a vote. If someone is in
trouble, then. . . ." Presumably applications
for water connections, problems with licenses, etc.
are all dealt with expeditiously at election time.

But the most significant aspect of the campaign is the emphasis on the direct personal
contact of candidate with voter, and that contact
is put in terms of the servant (the candidate) and
master (the voter). If a councilor is high-handed
with his constituents (and I never observed an
instance, although I heard about some), he can't
have that appearance at election time. It is this
image of a "servant of the people," close to the
people, which, I think, the candidate tries to

cultivate; an image consonant with his role as a
link between citizen and administrator in city
government.

ELECTION RESULTS AND ELECTION ANALYSES

One of the questions I asked of the 18 councilors of the City Zone was "with regard to the last
election, can you tell me why you think you were
successful?" Few answered that socio-economic or
political bases of support were important. Only
three gave answers such as this one: "Fifty percent
of the population are people of my trade, and the
area is a Jana Sangh stronghold [garh]." Most
emphasized their long practice of social service in
the area and the quality of their personal relationship with voters. For instance, "I've had 22 years
of medical practice right here in the center of this
ward. I've done a great deal of good here. So the
people give their love to me." Other reasons were:
the general ideological issues of the 1967 campaign, particularly cow slaughter; rhetorical
ability; a father prominent in politics, and
superior party organization. There were in addition a few implied generalities of voting behavior:
Muslims would not vote for the Jana Sangh, the Jana
Sangh had a superior apparatus for getting out the
vote, etc.
The picture which emerges from my interviews
with defeated candidates and party workers in
Kucha Khirkiwala is somewhat different. One of the
latter said, "Not even one percent of the voters are
not committed to one party or the other. Caste
system plays a great part. Although the area is
dominated by Banias, X [the non-Bania ex-councilor]
won, using the vote of the katras. . . . The whole
election depends on the votes of the katras. The
maximum vote the Congress has gotten from the Muslim
areas is 700 to 800." Another Congress worker made
a similar analysis, beginning with the ties of the
candidate to the workers:

> Most workers in the old city operate on
> personal relationships, even solid workers.
> For example, in 1962 the Jana Sangh can-
> didate was an Agarwal, and our workers who
> were Agarwals, even the most solid, didn't
> work for us. About 50 percent didn't work
> for him either, but stayed out of the
> contest. . . . Not more than 30 percent
> of the workers vote on the basis of ide-
> ology in municipal elections; the rest on
> community and personal relationships. . . .
> The educated voters will vote for the
> educated and able man, regardless of
> party.

The defeated candidates, Independents and Jana
Sangh, spoke of the solid Muslim antagonism to the
Jana Sangh. One said that no Muslim could ever win
in Kucha Khirkiwala because the area is 75 percent
Hindu, and a few charged that the Congress had
bought votes or engaged in "illegal practices."
Most mentioned an array of reasons for defeat; for
instance:

1) Of the 14,000 votes, 5,000 are Muslim,
   who are generally with the Congress.
   That was a great handicap.
2) The sitting member was a strong candidate. He had been a member for 20
   years and had developed contacts.
3) The workers on our side were slightly
   nervous because of past defeats of
   even stronger candidates.

And one argued that he lost because voters made a
mistake in marking their ballot papers.
    This last instance is an interesting case, if
somewhat unusual, but it is worth going into because
it throws some light on the "mechanics" of voting
behavior in the ward. In his interview the candidate had said, "I had the scales as a symbol and
[X], a Lok Sabha candidate, also had that symbol.

He withdrew before the election* but still people
were confused, and votes that were to go to me
went to him. In that way 950 votes of mine were
destroyed." The votes in the Corporation and Lok
Sabha elections are shown in Table 10.

There appears to be little relationship
between these two columns: the Lok Sabha candidate did not get more votes in the areas where the
Corporation candidate was strongest, and the total
of 533 votes is considerably less than the 950
allegedly "destroyed" votes.** But those 533 votes

TABLE 10

"SCALES SYMBOL" CANDIDATES' VOTE TOTALS, CORPORATION AND
LOK SABHA ELECTIONS, 1967

Polling Station	Corporation	Lok Sabha	Polling Station	Corporation	Lok Sabha
1	101	26	10	98	24
2	71	28	11	305	40
3	44	14	12	139	21
4	31	14	13	172	70
5	86	10	14	213	44
6	66	9	15	130	51
7	278	19	16	124	38
8	263	45	17	62	9
9	72	33	18	73	38
		Total		2,328	533

*But after the last day of official withdrawal,
so his name remained on the ballot.

**An interesting feature of the political life
of Delhi is how little the councilor knows of the
"statistics" of his ward. Few councilors retain
records of the results of past elections by polling
station, and many had wildly wrong estimates of,
say, the number of residents of the ward.

in 18 polling stations compare to 926 in the 219
polling stations of the entire constituency. With
an average of just over four votes per polling station, the Lok Sabha candidate "should" have received
75 votes or so in Kucha Khirkiwala (presumably from
people who had not heard he had withdrawn). Thus
the local candidate probably did lose 450 votes from
the confusion of symbols, assuming that voters did
not vote for both "scales symbol" candidates, but
only for one, as they had been told to do. This
incident underlines the fact that there are numbers
of people who vote by symbol rather than by name.
While this is the only case of losing votes in this
fashion that I encountered, the possibility of other
or similar aberrations should not be discounted in
analyzing election returns; in conjunction with
"bogus voting," dummy candidates, and other "marginal" aspects of the voting process, they can add
up to decisive portions of the total vote.

The analysis of elections provided by the few
participants I was able to interview is too sketchy
to permit any judgment of its depth and accuracy.
My impression from even less formal materials--dis-
cussions with staff members of the municipal election office, my observation of the Basti Julahan
election, etc.--is that politicians in Delhi analyze
vote preferences both at a very gross level ("Muslims will not vote for the Jana Sangh") and at the
level of the individual voter (workers should know
which man in his mohalla can be counted on, etc.).
There is some awareness of "middle-range" units,
such as the mohalla or the gali ("This gali is so
strong for me that they wouldn't even let the opposition party workers in during the election"), but
on the whole activists are unaware of the voting
patterns of polling stations. One candidate I
interviewed didn't know how many polling stations
there were in the ward.

THREE ELECTIONS IN KUCHA KHIRKIWALA

The voters of Kucha Khirkiwala have voted in
three elections since the current delimitation of
the ward was made in 1967. I did not obtain polling station delimitations for earlier elections,
so my analysis will be confined to these three.
In 1967, elections to the Corporation and to the
Lok Sabha were held on the same day. A by-election
was held in the ward two years later. The initial
description here will be of the voting patterns by
polling station, as seen in these three elections,
and it will outline the areas of Jana Sangh,
Congress, and Independent candidates' strength. I
will then attempt to correlate those patterns with
the socio-economic profile presented in Chapter 2.

There were nine candidates for the Chandni
Chowk Lok Sabha seat in 1967. There were 11,318
votes cast in the 18 polling stations of Kucha
Khirkiwala and 783 were rejected as invalid. Table
11 presents the results by party.

TABLE 11

1967 LOK SABHA VOTE IN KUCHA KHIRKIWALA

Party	Votes	Percentage
Jana Sangh	3,972	37.7
Congress	2,943	27.9
Independent 1 (Muslim)	2,322	22.0
Independent 2 (Hindu)	533	5.1
Independent 3	521	5.0
Independent 4	110	1.0
Independent 5	63	0.6
Independent 6	60	0.6
Independent 7	11	0.1
Totals	10,535	100.0

Independent 2 is the "Scales Symbol" candidate discussed earlier; Independent 4 had some support elsewhere in the Lok Sabha constituency, but on the
whole the number of votes the Independents received
in Kucha Khirkiwala is an accurate reflection of how
well they did in the larger constituencies: most
had probably withdrawn or had not really waged a
campaign. Since most informants spoke of the
"Muslim" vote, in the subsequent analysis I shall
separate Muslim Independents from Hindu Independents.* The results of the Kucha Khirkiwala Corporation elections are shown in Table 12; the results
of the 1969 Corporation by-election are shown in
Table 13; and the results in percentages, by polling
station, are shown in the Appendix, Table 2. The
results by polling station are presented in Fig. 8
and 9, pp. 132-134 It might be well to note here
that in 1967, concurrent with a wave of anti-Congress voting throughout India, the Jana Sangh
surprised observers by beating the Congress in
Delhi, winning six of the seven parliamentary
seats and gaining a majority in the Corporation.

TABLE 12

1967 CORPORATION ELECTION, KUCHA KHIRKIWALA

Party	Votes	Percentage
Congress	3,278	30.1
Jana Sangh	2,858	26.2
Independent 1 (Hindu)	2,328	21.4
Independent 2 (Muslim)	2,196	20.2
S.S.P.	155	1.4
Independent 3	80	0.7
Totals	10,895	100.0

*In 1969 the R.P.I. candidate was a Muslim
whose party affiliation was tenuous; I have counted
him as the year's Muslim Independent. In 1969 there
was no Hindu Independent who received a significant
vote.

TABLE 13

1969 CORPORATION ELECTION, KUCHA KHIRKIWALA

Party	Votes	Percentage
Congress	5,694	49.7
Jana Sangh	3,683	32.2
R.P.I.	1,709	14.9
S.S.P.	226	2.0
Independent 1	43	0.4
Hindu Mahasabha	32	0.3
Independent 2	23	0.2
Independent 3	16	0.1
Independent 4	14	0.1
Independent 5	7	0.1
Independent 6	3	0.0
Totals	11,450	100.0

Fig. 8 and 9 represent a "profile" of party
strength in Kucha Khirkiwala. Although these
figures are plotted as line graphs, the horizontal
axis has only an arbitrary order: the polling stations are ordered by the percent of the vote received in the 1967 Lok Sabha election (that election
was chosen arbitrarily), from the polling station in
which the highest percent of the vote was received,
to the polling station where the lowest percent was
received. Where there were ties, the polling stations were put in numerical order. The solid line
on the graph thus "descends" by definition; the
figures, to repeat, are "profiles."
     The pattern of the Congress vote (Fig. 8a)
indicates first, by the "slow" rate of descent of
all three lines, the support of the Congress
throughout the ward (the range is from 14 to 59
percent); second, by the close relationship of the
lines of the two 1967 elections, a clear tendency
for straight ticket voting; and third, by the total

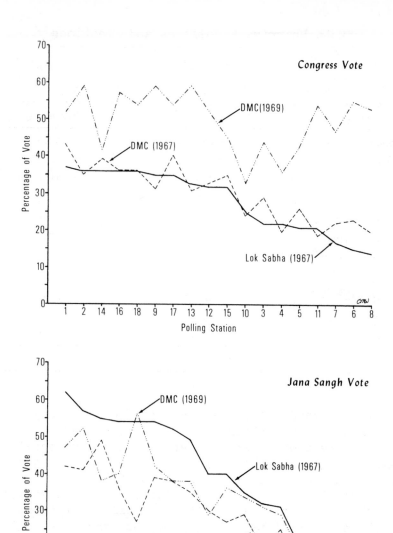

Fig. 8 Congress and Jana Sangh vote in Kucha Khirkiwala.

separation of the 1969 election line, and by its
many peaks and valleys, that the 1969 election was
very different from the other two.

Fig. 8b suggests that Jana Sangh supporters not
only voted a straight ticket in 1967 (and note, too,
that the Lok Sabha candidate ran ahead of his Corporation ticket-mate--the line of the former is above
that of the latter), but also continued to support
the Jana Sangh in 1969. The "rapid" "rate of
descent" of all three lines shows clearly defined
areas of Jana Sangh support, ranging from very high
to very low.

Muslim Independents too, as we can see from
Fig. 9a, draw supporters from only certain polling
stations. Note also the generally close relationship of the lines for the two Corporation elections,
in 1967 and 1969: support for Muslim Independents
persists in local elections, while support for a
Muslim candidate for the national election has only
some similarity in pattern (on the graph, there is
a rough "descent" of all three lines, but the two
Corporation election lines, which tend to run
together, form peaks and valleys in relation to the
Lok Sabha election line).

The "profile" of the Hindu Independent vote
(Fig. 9b) suggests that the Congress attracted supporters of the 1967 Hindu Independent in the 1969
Corporation election (since Jana Sangh and Muslim
Independent vote patterns continue in 1969).
Indeed, the 1967 Hindu Independent was a Congress
"rebel," a man who had been denied the Congress
ticket, so it is not surprising that his votes
became Congress votes two years later. It is also
clear, however, that the line of 1969 Jana Sangh
vote is consistently, though only slightly, higher
than the line for the 1967 Corporation election,
suggesting that a few of the Hindu Independent's
1967 supporters may have voted for the Jana Sangh
two years later.

If we treat each polling station as if it were
a separate constituency, then over three elections
there were 54 electoral contests in Kucha Khirkiwala.

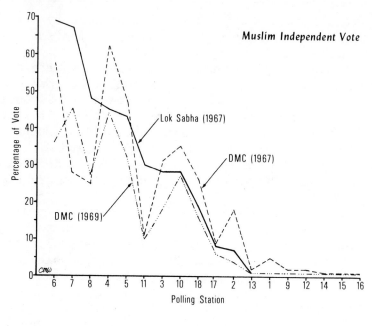

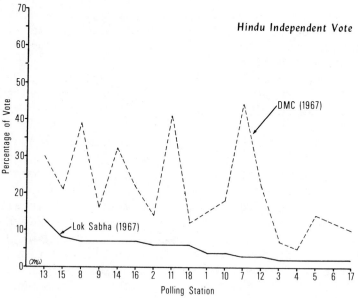

Fig. 9 Muslim Independent and Hindu Independent
vote in Kucha Khirkiwala. See Note to Figure 8

The results tabulated in Table 2 of the Appendix
can be rearranged into Table 14:

TABLE 14

"ELECTION CONTESTS" IN KUCHA KHIRKIWALA POLLING STATIONS

Party	1 No. Contests Won	2 No. Contests Runner-up	3 "In the Money" (Col. 1 plus Col. 2)
Congress	21	28	49
Jana Sangh	19	18	37
Muslim Ind.	11	7	18
Hindu Ind.	3	1	4
Totals	54	54	108

Polling stations in which the Congress candidate
had a plurality are counted as a "win." The runner-
up position is also tabulated, since one would
expect consistent strength to show up in some
measure of "in the money" finishes. The Congress
finished "in the money" in 91 percent of the 54
contests, the Jana Sangh in 69 percent, Muslim
Independents in 33 percent, and Hindu Independents
in 11 percent (of 36 contests).[*] The picture that
emerges is that of a Congress strength distributed
throughout the ward, with the Jana Sangh strength
noticeably less well distributed. If we look at
the 36 "contests" which took place in the Corporation elections (Table 15), we get a similar
pattern. The Congress was "in the money" in 91
percent of its contests; the Jana Sangh, in 61
percent; Muslim Independents, in 36 percent;
Hindu Independents, involved in 18 contests, in
6 percent. The breakdown into individual elections
is also revealing: in 1967, the Congress, the Jana
Sangh, and the Muslim Independent each "won" five

---

[*] Note that a party could "win" a majority of
polling stations and still lose the ward as a whole,
if its "wins" were by narrow margins and its
"losses" by large ones.

TABLE 15

THIRTY-SIX "CONTESTS" IN CORPORATION ELECTIONS

Party	No. Contests Won		No. Contests Runner-up		No. Contests "In the Money"	
	1967	1969	1967	1969	1967	1969
Congress	5	15	10	3	15	18
Jana Sangh	5	2	4	11	9	13
Muslim Inds.	5	1	3	4	8	5
Hindu Inds.	3	..	1	..	4	..
Totals	18	18	18	18	36	36

polling stations and by 1969, with no Hindu Independent in the field, the Congress "won" 15 of the
18 contests.

I have plotted these patterns of polling station strength on a map (Fig. 10) using the summary
table, Table 16. The table is read (taking the
first line, for example): there was one polling
station in Kucha Khirkiwala where the Congress got a
plurality of the vote in all three elections, and in
two polling stations the Congress candidate was the
runner-up in three elections. The Muslim and Hindu
Independents are tabulated together here; I shall
look at the separate patterns later. Note that
there is, on the whole, a pattern of preponderance:
there are only three polling stations where the Congress candidate won once, the Jana Sangh candidate
won once, and an Independent won once. On the other
"extreme," there are only three polling stations
where each of these "parties" won in all three elections, and then no "party" won three times in more
than one polling station. Twelve polling stations
have a "preponderance" pattern, where one "party"
or the other won in two of the three elections.
The pattern of "runner-up" finishes is almost the
same.

Fig. 10a shows that the polling stations can
be grouped into larger areas by party "preponderance": the Independent winners plus the evenly

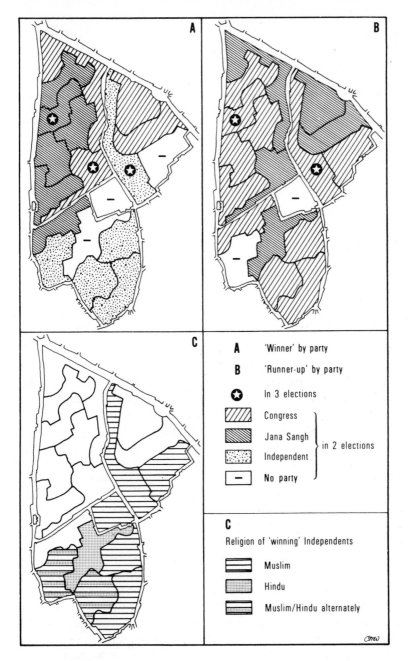

Fig. 10   Patterns of electoral strength in
Kucha Khirkiwala, Lok Sabha election of 1967
and Corporation elections of 1967 and 1969:
    a: Polling stations by party of "winner"
    b: Polling stations by party of "runner-
        up"
    c: Polling stations by religion of "win-
        ning" Independent

TABLE 16

POLLING STATION "CONTESTS," KUCHA KHIRKIWALA: FREQUENCY OF
VARIOUS PATTERNS

Pattern	Winner	Runner-up
Congress candidate three times	1	2
Jana Sangh candidate three times	1	0
Independent candidate three times	1	0
Congress candidate twice, Jana Sangh once	3	6
Congress candidate twice, Independent once	0	3
Jana Sangh candidate twice, Congress once	5	3
Jana Sangh candidate twice, Independent once	0	2
Independent candidate twice, Congress once	4	0
Independent candidate twice, Jana Sangh once	0	1
Congress candidate once, Jana Sangh once, Independent once	3	1
Totals	18	18

balanced polling stations are all contiguous and
compact, and a comparison with Fig. 6a (showing the
distribution of Muslim voters) on page 58 above will
indicate that this is almost exactly the Muslim area
of the ward. Jana Sangh winners are concentrated
together also, in six of the seven polling stations
in which there are no Muslim voters at all. The
Congress polling stations--if I can so characterize
them--are less clearly patterned, but are also
largely contiguous (the long "tail" of the polling
station in which Independents won three times has a
different character from the thicker end, and may
well be a Congress area).

Fig. 10b, the portrayal of the "runner-up" tabulation, makes the spread of the Congress evident:
its candidates were runners-up in both Jana Sangh
and Independent areas. The Jana Sangh, on the other
hand, is "runner-up" largely in the Congress polling
stations (and in one of the "Independent" polling
stations). That is, we can divide the ward in two,
on religious lines: the Congress and the Jana Sangh
are the contestants in the Hindu area, and the Congress and the Independents are the contestants in
the Muslim area. What has to be done now is to
separate the Independents. Consider Fig. 10c. The

first thing to notice is that the Jana Sangh was
"runner-up" in the polling station where Hindu
Independents won; we can say with some confidence
that the Jana Sangh has no support among Muslims.
But we cannot say that Muslims will not vote for a
Hindu Independent, for there are two polling stations (one 64 percent, the other 95 percent Muslim)
which "elected" a Hindu Independent once. This
should alert us to the fact that there are probably
distinguishable "sub-regions" within the Muslim
area. The Hindu Independent candidate who "won" in
fact lives in the polling station which is 95 percent Muslim and is respected for having stayed there
during the stress of the 1947 riots. He is also
closely allied with a major Muslim leader of the
area. Clearly he received support from his neighborhood.

Having made these first geographical distinctions on the basis of a religious community, let us
turn to the other socio-economic patterns we have
plotted earlier. Fig. 6b indicates that the "Jana
Sangh" polling stations are those with high literacy rates; these are also polling stations with
few industrial establishments. The Jana Sangh area
is thus a more thoroughly residential area in which
better educated Hindus live. Fig. 6c would suggest
that this is an area where workers in business and
the services (most probably Class III Officers and
above) live; these are the Banias in class terms,
and in caste terms as well, in all probability.
Note, however (compare Fig. 5), that there are a
sizeable number of katras in these polling stations
as well. On the interpretation that the katra vote
is more likely to be Congress than Jana Sangh, the
presumption that the Jana Sangh vote in Kucha
Khirkiwala is a "Bania" vote is strengthened. The
Congress area cannot be neatly characterized, in
that the Congress runs well in the rest of the ward.
The three polling stations where the Congress was
"out of the money" (looking again at Figs. 10a and
10b) are in no way alike, even though they are
contiguous.

I have gone into some detail in describing a
municipal election campaign in the Delhi ward in
order to indicate the complexity of the modes of
contact political activists, and candidates in particular, make with the electorate. One does get a
summary impression of an election campaign in which
politicians must run very hard to stay in the same
place. The analyses of Kucha Khirkiwala elections
made by the activists, and that which emerges from
a tabulation of the results, suggests that voters'
support is remarkably stable over time. A comparison with socio-economic data permits us to have some
confidence in some of the generalizations about differing bases of party support in Delhi. Reliable
survey data would help extend the scope of these
data, which are in one sense more valuable because
they concern actions, and do not rely on the
opinions, attitudes, or even reporting of facts
("whom I voted for," for example), which are far too
frequently biased.[9]

The stability of voter support may be explained
in part (i.e., not discounting factors of ideological commitment, political socialization, etc.) by
the success of the councilor in delivering services
to voters on an equitable basis, given the fact that
he seeks to maximize his vote, and our observation
(Chapter 3) that no area of the ward seemed to be
denied municipal benefits or the councilor's attention. Where there are no "active" cleavages (so
that one faction wishes to benefit at the expense
of the other), where voters who support and oppose
occupy all neighborhoods, albeit in differing proportion, the councilor's strategy apparently is to
distribute more benefits to areas where the larger
numbers of voters live. One might say, "one man,
one vote, one 'benefit quantum.'" This again is a
case of the councilor running hard to stay in the
same place, as all benefits being equal, voters
will tend to vote, presumably, as they have before,
in accordance with their beliefs and upbringing.[10]

AFTER THE ELECTION

Once elected, the councilor does not continue his partisan role vis-à-vis his constituents, as we have seen in Chapter 3. With the exception of strong supporters and associates of defeated candidates, who will tend to go to a neighboring councilor of their party to "get their work done," the councilor "de-politicizes" his contact with the citizens of the ward.

The councilor does, however, participate in on-going party activities. As was mentioned above (pp. 86-87), in reference to the election campaign, the Jana Sangh in Delhi has a well-articulated ward and polling station level political organization, while the Congress does not.*   One Jana Sangh councilor said that he attended mandal (ward-level party body) meetings "in order to ascertain their [the workers'] views, keep them in touch, keep them equipped with the knowledge of our achievements."

The councilor meets his workers regularly to receive complaints transmitted by them from their neighbors; the following are some of the representative statements by councilors:

---

*Studying these organizational patterns is difficult, in part because the Jana Sangh has a tendency to keep its organization (or rather, what the organization is doing and discussing) under wraps, and its discipline is such that members are not forthcoming to the foreign researcher. I did ask questions of the 18 City Zone councilors ("After the election, do you still have contact with your workers? How many of them; how frequently, and for what reasons?") which permitted me to probe on-going party activity. What follows is derived from those answers. One problem here is that in several interviews political workers were present.

> I go to the constituency daily and meet
> people only through the workers. Other-
> wise they will feel I am thinking I can to
> without them.

> They report complaints--they have a round of
> the area assigned to them. I have to depend
> on them.

> One to three workers come to me in a day.
> They are responsible for the area where they
> live.

> One must keep up connections with one's
> workers. They bring the public's work to
> me. . . . If the workers didn't bring the
> complaints, then in the next election, then
> what? Therefore it has to be done.

These responses suggest that the role of political
worker vis-à-vis the councilor that I observed in
Kucha Khirkiwala is typical of other wards of
Shahjahanabad. The councilor must defer, at least
in manner, to his strong supporters (one councilor
objected to calling them "my workers"; the implication of his extended comment was that he was their
"worker"). Requests to a worker to look out for his
area, though undoubtedly helpful for the neighborhood, are also aimed at keeping the worker involved--
and the next election is always on the horizon.
But the negative evidence here (i.e., what the
councilors did not mention) is that there is little
active political structure--workers meeting together
regularly, coordination of activity, etc.--on
municipal matters. There is no suggestion that
workers go out and organize their neighborhoods
(though a few may already be local leaders), and
the fact that no "worker mobilization" occurred in
the sweepers' strike in Kucha Khirkiwala would
indicate that such action would be unusual.
    Both Jana Sangh and Congress have active Lok
Sabha constituency level organizations, as well as
Delhi-wide organizations, in which councilors participate (the Delhi Youth Congress, for instance).

But one can readily assert that the focus of a
councilor's political network, insofar as his
municipal role is concerned, is not the larger
party structure. Still, as I have mentioned
above, the round of the Kucha Khirkiwala councilor frequently ended with him and his chief
political workers leaving to attend some political
meeting or the other; these meetings were usually
of Delhi-wide bodies.

The councilor-citizen interface presents its
political aspect most sharply at the time of an
election. At other times, the councilor may
indeed avoid what political activity does occur;
the Kucha Khirkiwala councilor told me, "Every
area has its politics, but as much as possible
I try to stay out of them; I have no political
hates." The Jana Sangh does have on-going party
activity, but the evidence I have suggests that
meetings are not about municipal issues or problems,
but about national issues and Delhi-wide activities
(a demonstration in favor of Hindi, for instance).

The councilor, in his participation in the
administrative activity concerning his ward, is
also "nursing the constituency." Some councilors
undoubtedly wish to move up politically, to run
for Parliament, and certainly an impressive
victory in a Corporation election would be an
asset. Others seem to be concerned only about
their continuing tenure in the Corporation; there
are many councilors who have had long careers in
the Municipal Committee and then the Corporation.[*]
For most councilors, the job is one that brings
prestige, and for others, certainly, it is a job
which brings in money. There are other motives
for seeking to continue as councilor. One is the

---

[*] These generalizations are drawn from answers
to a question asked of the 18 City Zone councilors ("Please tell me something of your career
in political life") in which I probed for future
plans.

"intoxication" of politics. This was expressed as
follows by three councilors:

> Political power is just like gambling. . . .
> a form of recreation.

> [I have made] no decision to give [my seat]
> up; the intoxication [nashaa] of doing the
> work has started.

> Of course I enjoy politics . . . it is
> hypocrisy to say that you don't like
> politics [if you are a politician].

The desire "to serve the people" was the most frequently mentioned motive for contesting elections,
and it is one that should not be discounted. As
one councilor said:

> [After my first election] my interest in
> municipal politics developed. I found the
> work very interesting. Of course, everyone
> says they want to perform a service, but it
> is true that a man can be helpful to many
> persons in this capacity.

The councilor can thus obtain satisfaction from
service, money, and/or status rewards, a boost in
his political ambitions, or simply the pleasure of
political action. But as long as these are pursued via the path of getting as much as possible
done for the citizens, Kucha Khirkiwala and other
wards like it surely benefit.

Most of these themes will reappear in our
discussion of Shahjahanabad and the City Zone in
the next three chapters. Indeed, many of the
inferences about socio-economic and electoral
patterns are grounded in the more solid data
obtained in Kucha Khirkiwala. This next section
repeats the scheme of these last three chapters:
I begin with the geographical, historical and
socio-economic setting (Chapter 5), move on to
a discussion of the three interfaces at the

zonal level, and conclude (Chapter 7) with an
analysis of electoral patterns.

5. Shahjahanabad and the City Zone:
An Historical and Socio-Economic Portrait

The 100 wards of Delhi have been organized into
zones (the details are given briefly below, and more
fully at the beginning of Chapter 6), and whatever
the reasons for the specific inclusion or exclusion
of a ward--they turn out to be largely political--
some of the zones are "real" entities, in that in
addition to an administrative structure, they also
have a history and an economic and demographic
character. Kucha Khirkiwala is included in the City
Zone (in 1969-70), the zone which covers, roughly,
the old walled city of Delhi, which was known as
Shahjahanabad.

Shahjahanabad is thus the setting of zonal
government of the City Zone, and the following
detailed analysis of its socio-economic characteristics is directly relevant to the concerns and
patterns of zonal administration (presented in
Chapter 6) and to the politics of the area (Chapter
7). As we have seen in the comparable chapter on
Kucha Khirkiwala (Chapter 2), the high density of
population, the mix of building usage (residential,
commercial, industrial), the division between Hindu
and Muslim, the position of the scheduled castes,
and similar characteristics set the parameters of
the problems of municipal government in the area
(some would say some of these constitute the problems). These patterns are those that are found
in Kucha Khirkiwala and, in a sense, can be "generalized" up to a larger unit, and, it is hoped, the
ties to government and politics can be similarly

generalized. To continue the metaphor used earlier,
the "vocabulary" learned in Kucha Khirkiwala will be
expanded and combined to be used in the complex
phrases and sentences which "are" the governmental
dimension of the City Zone and Shahjahanabad.
Finally, I hope to present the old city to the
reader to convey a sense of the individuals about
whom these generalizations are being made; I wish to
portray something of the atmosphere of the old city.
    It is with this latter point in mind that I
begin the chapter, after a brief discussion of
precisely what area of Delhi is included in the
analysis, with a historical sketch followed by
more impressionistic data. "Impressionistic"
because, although I am dealing with numbers as
much as I can, the significance of those numbers
(the population of Muslims, the location of scheduled caste residence, for example) is dependent on
what I have gathered from talking with many of the
inhabitants of the area, usually not in an interview situation or even in conversations memorable
enough to find their way into my field notes. My
data source here is also, to an extent, works which
are best called "literary."
    The socio-economic data presented in the
latter part of the chapter are derived largely from
the 1961 and 1971 censuses. To supplement these
sources, I believe I have assembled virtually all
the relevant data available, but the socio-economic
"portrait" that emerges is limited by those sources:
I have not been able to decide beforehand what
factors and characteristics would be important, and
then set out to analyze them. It would be nice to
know, for instance, where the owners of the commercial and industrial establishments of Shahjahanabad
live, in addition to knowing how many of the residents of Shahjahanabad work in commerce and industry;
but those data are not available. These data are
important, not only for the discussion of how
"typical" Kucha Khirkiwala is, but also, more
directly, for the discussion of electoral patterns
which I present in Chapter 7.

Although I believe that Shahjahanabad has a
certain cultural unity, I have found no evidence
that it has a structure other than the administrative set-up which is the City Zone. There are
associations of wholesale merchants in a given
trade (spices, for example) whose businesses are
centered in Shahjahanabad, certainly, but these
cover a small part of the walled city's populace,
and I have seen no indication that they have
engaged in coordinated activity: there is no
"Shahjahanabad Chamber of Commerce." There is no
economic elite of Shahjahanabad who exercise considerable economic power. Similarly, there is no
social or status elite of the walled city, no set
of "first families"; the only person who could be
identified as such, perhaps, would be the member
of Parliament from Chandni Chowk constituency.
(The incumbent at the time of my study was very
much in the background: I do not recall ever
seeing his name in print or having it mentioned
to me in a conversation.) The 18 councilors of
the City Zone, in the interviews I had with them,
did not project a sense of dealing with the zone
as a community, a city within a city. Their
concern was mainly with their own wards (themselves something of an artificial unit, as we
have seen).

SHAHJAHANABAD AND THE CITY ZONE: THE
PROBLEM OF THE UNIT OF ANALYSIS

The Delhi Municipal Corporation Act has a
section (40-3,4) providing for the establishment of
ward committees for each ward or for a group of
wards. In addition to the councilors, provision is
made for the co-optation of three ward residents to
the committee. Committees in a single ward have not
been set up, but in 1963, acting on the report of a
special committee, the Corporation established a
zonal system, in which the 80 wards of that time
were grouped into ten zones.

Initially there were two zones covering the walled city of Delhi. Since the zones are technically ad hoc committees, they must be formally reconstituted at the start of each "municipal" year (which begins on April 1). There have been frequent changes in the number of zones and in the wards assigned to a given zone; one of these changes, occurring in 1967, was to amalgamate the old City North Zone (minus the two northernmost wards) with the City South Zone to make a new City Zone. The City Zone is the Chandni Chowk Lok Sabha (Parliamentary) constituency plus two wards adjacent to it on the south. These two wards are large and sparsely populated. Since 1967, they have lost population as jhuggi-jhompri (hutment) dwellers were resettled, and the old government servants' quarters in ward 1 (Minto Road) were demolished. Neither ward has much in common with the rest of the City Zone; they were included in it for convenience: the zonal office is in fact located in one of them.

The main part of the City Zone is the old walled city south of the railway line (thus excluding the wards of Mori Gate and Kashmiri Gate), and the names of the old bazars and localities are preserved in some of the ward names: Chandni Chowk, Kalan Masjid, Dariba, Matia Mahal, etc. (see Fig. 11). The City Zone's history is that of Shahjahanabad, the walled city built by the Moghul Emperor Shahjahan (1627-1658) in 1648. Shahjahanabad and not the "Old Delhi" of common usage (i.e., as contrasted to "New" Delhi) because "Old Delhi" includes the thickly settled suburbs of Sadar, Paharganj, and Subzimandi.

Although almost all the city wall has been demolished, the city is bounded on the west by railroad lines and on the south by the wall of commercial buildings developed by the Delhi Improvement Trust in the late 1940s and early 1950s. Parks separate Shahjahanabad from other built-up areas on three sides. The main park to the south is the Ram Lila ground; there are several parks beyond the

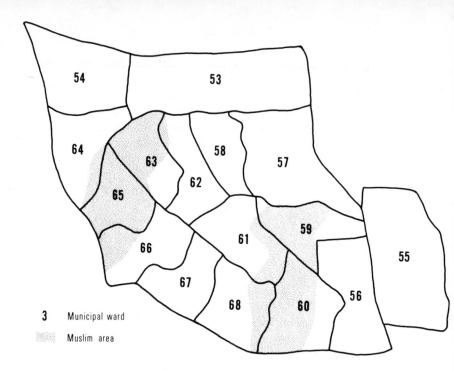

Fig. 11 Municipal wards of the City Zone, showing major concentrations of Muslims.

Ward No.	Name
1	Minto Road
2	Purana Qila
53	Chandni Chowk
54	Shardhanand Bazar
55	Darya Ganj (the dotted line indicates the builtup area)
56	Chhatta Lal Mian
57	Dariba
58	Maliwara
59	Matia Mahal
60	Suiwalan
61	Lal Darwaza
62	Charkhewalan
63	Ballimaran
64	Naya Bans
65	Farashkhana
66	Ajmeri Gate
67	Kucha Pati Ram
68	Kalan Masjid

Note: The location of Muslim residences is based on personal observation, not census or survey data.

city's north wall (much of which survives); and
the "Champs de Mars" area between the Red Fort
and the Jama Masjid is a large park on the city's
eastern side. Beyond the east wall of the city
are the fields in the old bed of the Jumna River
and the memorial parks surrounding the spots where
Gandhi, Nehru, and Prime Minister Shastri were
cremated.

THE HISTORY OF SHAHJAHANABAD

   Whatever number of cities of Delhi there may
have been (traditionally, seven; most probably, 15
or 16), Shahjahanabad is the latest "old" Delhi,
and one, like some others, built on the ruins, and
with the building stones, of its predecessors.
Within the walls of the city there remains the
Kalan Masjid, built during the Tughlaq period,
possibly in 1387.[1] In 1857, during the Mutiny and
Revolt which shook British rule in North India,
Rai Bahadur Jeevan Lal, a prominent citizen and
employee of the British, took refuge in his cellar
which was made with stones from the nearby Ferozehah
Kotla, a palace-fort built by Ferozshah, Tughlaq
ruler of North India, in 1354 A.D.[2]   The city wall
itself was improved by the British in 1804 during
the Maratha Wars.[3] Only short stretches remain
standing today. The walls of the Red Fort and some
of the buildings inside it date from the time of
Shahjahan, as does the Jama Masjid. The various
mahals (palaces) built for members of the royal
family during the Mughal reign survive only as
gates (if they indeed do survive), often as not
leading into the worst katras. There are a scattered few mosques, an occasional ruined tomb, and
a few houses which may be over a century old. But
on the whole Shahjahanabad today is an old city on
an ancient site with buildings that are relatively
new (50 to 100 years old) but often on the point
of collapse.

Still, Shahjahanabad has an atmosphere more of
the old than of the decrepit, because the house
styles and the street patterns have tended to be preserved. The major bazars--Lal Kuan, Chitli Qabar,
Chandni Chowk, Faiz Bazar, etc.--retain their align-
ments, if not their original character. Part of Lal
Kuan is now the wholesale hardwares market, and
Chandni Chowk, originally a square with a pool in
the center in front of the site of the present Town
Hall, has come to mean the retail bazar, shorn of
its arcades, its canal, and its trees, stretching
from the Fatehpuri Mosque to the Red Fort.[4] Feeding
into these main bazars are secondary bazars which
are devoted to one trade (Dariba for jewellers, etc.)
or commercial katras--cul de sac alleyways in which
15 or 20 tiny shops abut--for wholesale cloth merchants. There are also specialty retail bazars
(book shops on Nai Sarak, for example). And the
residential areas which are "contained" by the bazar
streets--the maze of galis, mohallas, katras, etc.--
at least seem to date from the city's founding.

Shahjahanabad began as the city of the Emperor
and economically it was bound to the court.[5] After
the Revolt of 1857, as the Punjab developed, Delhi
regained its position as a crossroads, now economically rather than militarily significant.[6] The
railway line was put through the center of the city,
parallel to Chandni Chowk. Old gates of the city
were demolished to make way for it, and the line
passes through the fort of Salimgarh on its way
across the Jumna River. This breach of the city's
defenses so soon after they had been stormed after
a four-month siege (and about 60 years after the
British had repaired them for military reasons) sym-
bolized the changed character of Shahjahanabad.
Delhi today is of course once again a "court" city,
whose economic life is centered on the national
government to a significant extent. But Shahjahanabad is not as directly involved with the new
"court" as is the rest of the city. Since 1947
Delhi's growth has been phenomenal, but while there
has been some influx of refugees into the old city,

occupying houses abandoned by those who left for
Pakistan, the center of "Punjabi" economic activity
is outside Shahjahanabad.[7]

SHAHJAHANABAD: ISLAMIC CULTURE AND
MUSLIM AND HINDU SOCIAL PATTERNS[*]

The "Islamic City"

Shahjahanabad is an Islamic city.[**] This is
not entirely an historical assertion (nor is it,
obviously, a demographic one, since Muslims formed
a small minority of about 12 percent of the population in 1961), but rather a description of its
physical and cultural character. Xavier de Planhol,
relying on a discussion of Islam in Europe and the
Near East,[8] argues that Islam has an urban ideal
implicit in it--as a religion it encourages the
foundation of towns. It is a congregational
religion requiring a permanent Friday mosque, and

---

[*] The following analysis is not grounded in
"hard" data. I am constrained to make it in part
because it covers much that is crucial to understanding the character of Shahjahanabad: the
relations of Hindus with Muslims, caste and class
factors, etc. And to pass that aspect of the city
by without mention would falsify any subsequent
generalizations. But I do have confidence in the
"soft" data I present in the following pages; I must
rely on words such as "some" or "most," but within
the limits imposed by that kind of terminology, I
believe that my characterizations are accurate.

[**] Blake argues persuasively (see especially
pp. 17-19) that Shahjahanabad at its height, before
1740, decidedly does not fit the "Islamic City"
model. Still, he implies that after the sack of
Delhi by Nadir Shah in 1740, some "Islamic City"
features may have developed.

"city life. . . is equally indispensable to the
dignity of life which Islam demands. The true
Moslem must lead a middle-class life. . . .
By virtue of its social constraints as well as
its spiritual demands Islam is a city religion."[9]
De Planhol points out that despite the urbanism
of Islam, the Islamic city, in contrast to its
European counterparts, has "no separate municipal
life. . . . The price paid for the predominance
of religious conceptions in Islamic social organization is the absence of any political interest
in the community as such."[10]
     These facts have consequences for the
physical aspects of the city:

> These two facts, the urban ideal implicit
> in Islamic religion and the absence of
> municipal organization in Islamic coun-
> tries, go far toward accounting for the
> form and appearances of the cities. From
> the first influence derives the strong,
> strict framing of the towns, their general
> appearance of having been established in
> consequence of rigid principles. From
> the second influence derives the extra-
> ordinary anarchy of detail, which conceals
> the basic skeleton beneath a proliferation
> of parasitic influences.[11]

Chief of the planned features is the "central position of the chief mosque. It is the heart of the
whole complex. . . ."[12] In the area of the mosque
there are bazars and the public baths; the seat of
government is on the outskirts, for defense against
popular uprisings; there is a concentric ring of
residential quarters, then semi-urban districts and
finally the cemeteries before the fields begin.[13]
     The second fundamental characteristic of the
Islamic town, de Planhol argues, is "the ordering of
different trades into a hierarchy, with most of them
physically separated from other trades and concentrated among their own kind."[14] From the Great

Mosque outwards there are the sellers of candles,
incense and perfumes; the booksellers and bookbinders; wholesale textile shops; workmen in
leather, the makers of slippers; the tailors, the
rug and tapestry salesmen, the jewelers; the food-
sellers and butchers; the carpenters, locksmiths
and coppersmiths; and blacksmiths and potters at
the city gates.[15] Other trades--and some of these
also--may be scattered throughout the city.

> The third characteristic of Islamic towns
> is segregation into districts of different
> ethnic and religious groups. Everywhere
> the residential districts are divided into
> closed units, consisting of internal court-
> yards and alleys leading off a main street,
> which can be closed at either end by great
> gates.[16]

Although the Islamic city can have, and has had,
planned street systems, especially the towns founded
by Princes, the plan quickly becomes obscured by
intricate narrow alleyways, de Planhol notes; he
suggests a partial explanation lies in Islamic
notions of rights over public land, and the lack
of municipal regulation.
     The house in the Islamic city has special char-
acteristics: "Islam is fundamentally hostile . . .
to luxurious dwellings, and above all to lofty ones,
which are symbols of pride and arrogance . . . the
low built house is characteristic of Islam . . . ."[17]
Further, "Islam has also encouraged the use of
fragile and perishable materials";[18] ". . . the use
of fragile materials is a token of the insubstantiality of material things and the unimportance of
the individual."[19] De Planhol notes that despite
the difficulty of segregating the women in a courtyard house, this Greek-derived layout has persisted,
encouraged by "the prescription against height and
the use of fragile materials."[20]
     With this structure of the Islamic city in
mind, let us look at Shahjahanabad. As noted above

(p. 151), except for the Jama Masjid (the central
mosque, situated on a hill and clearly the centerpiece of the city), the Red Fort (the seat of
government on the eastern edge of the city), a few
city gates, themselves not very old, a sprinkling
of mosques (including the Kalan Masjid), and a few
other structures are the only buildings which are
more than 100 to 150 years old. This "transience"
of buildings is more strikingly evident when one
looks at the Islamic Delhis which preceded
Shahjahanabad: one can see the remnants of an
earthen or stone city wall, a fortress-palace,
mosques, and tombs, but no houses. The latter were
made, as are those of Shahjahanabad (until recently)
of poor quality brick and mud mortar and have long
since washed away. And of course the courtyard
house is universal, in Muslim and Hindu localities.[21]

    There is no question that Shahjahanabad is a
maze of narrow, twisting alleyways: from the top
of the minars of the Jama Masjid I was hard put to
make out the course of even the largest bazars.
And the planned form is there as well--the great
boulevards of Chandni Chowk and Faiz Bazar, the
major arteries leading to the various city gates,
the placement of the Jama Masjid and the Red Fort.
The residential area to the east of the Jama Masjid
(between it and the Red Fort) was cleared after the
1857 Revolt and the area to the west and north is
almost entirely Hindu, so the concentric pattern
of land use does not hold. But in the area to the
south of the mosque, which remains largely a Muslim
area right up to the site of the city walls, the
"hierarchy" of occupations is still apparent--the
booksellers of Urdu Bazar next to the mosque, the
bookbinders of Chitla Darwaza, the shoemakers in
Jootewalan and behind the Victoria Zenana Hospital;
the tailors, embroiderers and jewelers of Bazar
Pahari Bhojla and Bulbuli Khana; and the semi-
urban area of Suiwalan (I have listed these
localities in order of their distance from the
Jama Masjid) conform, to a certain extent, to
the pattern outlined by de Planhol.

The residential segregation which de Planhol discusses in terms of Jewish and Christian quarters, etc., applies in Shahjahanabad analogously to caste "quarters"--Kayastha, Jain, and Bania mohallas. It is suggestive that patterns of residential and occupational segregation of castes which are found in (Hindu) villages "fit" neatly with the Islamic city pattern, for from the beginning Shajahanabad was a city of mixed communities, at least in the lower strata of society.

The Muslims

Until 1857, Muslims ruled in Delhi, and yet Hindus shared not only in supporting the economic base of the court, but also in the regime itself, as soldiers and administrators. The population of Hindus and Muslims has remained remarkably stable over time (see Table 17).[22] Aside from the loss of Muslim population in the Revolt of 1857, the most noteworthy change in the distribution is the decrease of Muslim population between 1941 and 1951, when, in one estimate, 100,000 Muslims left Delhi,* in a migration to Pakistan. Most of the Muslims of Delhi live in Shahjahanabad: in 1961 approximately 82 percent lived in Census Zone II, and although there are concentrations of Muslims in Qasabpura and other areas near the Idgah (a mile or two west of the walled city), the over-whelming majority of the Muslims of Zone II live in the walled city. One index of this is the fact that in 1969-70, five of the six Muslim municipal councilors came from Shahjahanabad; the sixth was from Qasabpura. Muslims constituted about 18

---

* Ashok Mitra, Delhi: Capital City (New Delhi: Thomson Press (India) Ltd., 1970), p. 17. Note, however, that the Muslim population of Delhi Territory dropped from 304,971 in 1941 to 99,501 in 1951 (cf. Table 17).

TABLE 17

RELIGIOUS COMPOSITION OF DELHI CITY[a], 1847-1961

Year	Number of Hindus (%)	Number of Muslims (%)	Others (%)	Total
1847	87,145 (54)	72,807 (45)	327 (0)	160,279
1853				152,426
1864	83,346 (59)	56,808 (40)	1,554 (1)	141,708
1868				154,417
1875				160,553
1881	99,046 (57)	72,519 (42)	1,828 (1)	173,393
1891	108,041 (56)	79,238 (41)	5,300 (3)	192,579
1901	114,417 (55)	88,460 (42)	5,698 (3)	208,575
1911	121,735 (52)	102,476 (44)	8,626 (4)	232,837
1921	147,169 (55)	107,006 (40)	12,517 (5)	266,692
1931	188,232 (51)	162,696 (45)	14,599 (4)	365,527
1941	277,169 (51)	239,561 (44)	26,254 (5)	542,984
1951[b]				1,008,985
1961	846,794 (79)	131,476 (12)	99,470 (9)	1,077,740

[a]The area referred to as "Delhi City" has not remained the same over time. The areas referred to are as follows:
    1847-1881--The walled city, Pahari Dhiraj (i.e., Sadar), Paharganj, Subzimandi, Civil Lines, and other suburbs.
    1891-1941--The Delhi Municipality, Civil Lines, and the Delhi Cantonment area.
    1951-   --Old Delhi (Municipality?), Civil Lines, Red Fort.
    1961-   --Census Zones II and IV: City Sadar-Paharganj, Civil Lines-Subzimandi.
The 1961 figure omits some of the area (part of Karol Bagh Zone in Census Zone II) included in previous definitions of Delhi City, but may add some area (not, however, densely populated) to the north of the city. Unfortunately, I could find no map showing the boundaries of the Delhi Municipality, Civil Lines Notified Area Committee, etc.

[b]The 1951 census does not give a breakdown by religion for units other than Delhi State.

Sources

1847-1881: Gazeteer of the Delhi District, 1883-4 (Punjab Government: no further publication data), p. 207.
1891: Census of India 1891, Vol. 20, Part II, Table V, pp. 8-9 [International Documentation Company, Microprint ed., Box 24B, fiche 1010].
1901: Census of India 1901, Vol. 17-A, Part II, Table V, pp. V-ii, V-iii. [IDC ed., Box 40, fiche 1776].
1911: Census of India 1911, Vol. 14, Part II, pp. 19-20 [IDC ed., Box 40, fiche 2343].
1921: Census of India 1921, Vol. 15, Part II, Table V, pp. 26-27 [IDC ed., Box 62, fiche 2750].
1931: Census of India 1931, Vol. 16, Part II, Table V, p. ix [IDC ed., Box 73, fiche 3220].
1941: Census of India 1941, Vol. 16, Tables, p. 18 [IDC ed., Box 81, fiche 3565].
1951: Census of India 1951, Vol. 8, Part II-A, Table D-II, p. 298 [IDC ed., Box 93, fiche 4146].
1961: Census of India 1961, Vol. 19, Part II-C, pp. 194-95.

percent of Zone II; I estimate that they constitute
at least a quarter of Shahjahanabad--perhaps a
population of 100,000 in the total of 400,000.

The Hindu-Muslim cleavage, as has been suggested by the data from Kucha Khirkiwala, has
social and political significance--there are indeed
two "communities" in Delhi. During the Revolt of
1857, when the city was in the hands of troops
nominally under the command of the Mughal Emperor
Bahadur Shah, there was a spirit of cooperation
between Hindu and Muslim inhabitants of the city.[23]
But when the British regained control, their wrath
and revenge was directed more strongly against the
Muslims. All the inhabitants of Delhi were
expelled from their homes (which were then thoroughly looted), but after some months Hindus were
permitted to reenter, and then some months later,
Muslims. There was a serious suggestion to
demolish the Jama Masjid; it was not handed back
to the Muslim community until 1862.[24] Bahadur Shah
was tried for treason and exiled to Rangoon,[25]
where he died shortly after. The adjustment of
the Delhi Muslim to the loss of even the pretense
of imperial glory was painful.[26]

Once past the high water mark of Hindu-Muslim
unity in the Khilafat movement[27]--during which
Swami Shardhanand (later assassinated by a Muslim
because of his alleged anti-Muslim actions) addressed a gathering in the Jama Masjid--Delhi too
had its communal riots,[28] and was swept up in the
general political developments which culminated in
Partition. Within the Congress, of course, Muslims
continued to hold prominent positions while the
membership fell off, but the synthesis of Hindu and
Muslim culture of North India, with Delhi holding a
central position, became less important than the
division between the communities.

The Muslims of Shahjahanabad, like those of
Kucha Khirkiwala, tend to live contiguously. There
are two main concentrations, one extending southward from the Jama Masjid into Suiwalan and up to
the Turkaman Gate, the other extending from Chandni

Chowk and Ballimaran westwards through the area
south of the Fatehpuri Mosque to Farashkhana and
Kucha Pandit (see Fig. 11, above, p. 150). These
areas of residence have remained roughly the same
despite the precipitous decline in the Muslim
population of Delhi as a whole. The tendency was
for some members of a family to emigrate to
Pakistan, leaving others in possession of the
family property. Other Muslims from elsewhere in
Delhi may have then moved in. When entire families
left, their property was given to refugees from
Pakistan. One of my informants estimated that
before Partition, Farashkhana was 85 percent Muslim
and is now 50 percent Muslim and 25 percent refugee.
Another ward, Kucha Pandit, also has had a considerable shift on this pattern, but it has been
less in other wards. For example, only one of the
mohallas of Kucha Khirkiwala now has a significant
mix of Muslims and refugees.

There are important cleavages within the
Muslim community also. In Delhi sectarian divisions among Muslims (Shia, Sunni, Ismaili, etc.)
are not as important as they are elsewhere in India.
Donald Ferrell divides the Muslim community of 1911
into "sharif" and "non-sharif," a status differ-
entiation which in itself does not show a structural
division.* The 1931 census lists seven purely
Muslim "castes" in Delhi city: Arain (1,528
persons), Faqir (386), Meo (2,636), Moghul (5,955),
Pathan (21,913), Sheikh (106,454), and Sayyad
(14,924). In addition, nine predominantly Hindu
castes had Muslim members.[29]

According to one of my informants, there are
five main Muslim "biraadaris" (which are endogamous
units) in Delhi: Attar, Hakim, Punjabi, Jootewala
(Siddiqi), and Kasai. Another source lists six
"famous" biraadaris: Punjabi, Attar, Parachi,
Chandiwali, Qureshi, and Delhi Sidiqqi.[30] Some

---

*"Sharif" means "noble," "cultured"; Ferrell
uses it to mean elite status.

of these are located in specific areas of the
city--the Jootewala near Churiwalan and the
Punjabi in Ballimaran, for example--but members
are scattered throughout the city. These
biraadaris are associated with a "traditional"
occupation and at least two have organized
"panchayats"--organizations with office-bearers.
Informants were reluctant to discuss these divisions, which are contrary to a strict interpretation of Islamic thought, so I am unable to
give any further details on what is clearly a
significant, probably semi-structured cleavage.*
There is no hard data on the economic position
of Muslims. The most that can be said is that
the Punjabis and Hakims of Ballimaran seem
to be the most prosperous and the workers of
Farashkhana and Suiwalan the least.

An estimate of the number of Muslims who
have received advanced education can be made by
applying a chain of inference to the 1961 census
data, as follows: It is probably true that virtually all those entering Urdu as a mother tongue
are Muslim; the number of Urdu speakers who know
English as a second language is about 4 percent,
compared to 14 and 15 percent for Hindi and
Punjabi speakers, respectively; knowledge of
English is probably a fair index of the degree
of higher education (secondary school and above).[31]
The number of Muslims who pursue an Islamic higher
education (in Arabic medium) must be very small.
But all that can be inferred from this is that
Muslims are less well educated than Hindus. There
is nothing to indicate that religion is the

---

*Another cleavage which I heard mention of is
the one between "Delhiwalas" and "foreign" Muslims
(those who immigrated into the city from western
U.P.). The major problem in attempting to assess
the significance of these divisions is their extent
in the Muslim community--how many people are in the
five or six well-known biraadaris, for instance.

TABLE 18

BILINGUALISM IN DELHI, 1961
(in percentages)

| Mother Tongue | Zone II | | | | Delhi |
| | Second Language | | | | |
	Hindi	Urdu	Punjabi	English	English
Hindi (N=524,241)	...	1.8	1.1	13.8	14.7
Urdu (N=128,402)	3.5	...	trace	3.7	5.3
Punjabi (N=48,929)	24.5	5.0	...	14.6	19.4
All languages				12.1	15.6

Source: Census of India 1961, XIX, Part II-C, pp. 163-66.

Note: Hindi, Urdu, and Punjabi speakers total 701,572 of the
         715,564 persons of Zone II.

independent variable; indeed, economic position is
a more likely candidate. Muslims are poor. (But,
of course, they might be poor because of religious
discrimination by Hindu employers, as some Muslim
activists suggest.) The figure for Muslims literate
in English in 1941 (7 percent) would support the
impression of informants that the better-educated
Muslims left for Pakistan.[32]

The Hindus

Data on "the Hindus" of Shahjahanabad is as
suspect as that on the Muslims, in that caste data
is of 1931 vintage and in the cosmopolitan atmosphere of Delhi, very difficult to update. Since
they demonstrate that no caste was even close to
being numerically "dominant," the 1931 caste data
are presented in Table 19. These data are for
the whole of Delhi city and presumably the proportions in Shahjahanabad would be different: I
would estimate, for instance, that there were
proportionately more Kayasthas. Clearly, no caste
even predominates, and when one takes note of

intra-caste cleavages (not only gotra distinctions,
say, but also distinctions between "locals" and
"foreigners"), the ethnic fabric of the city seems
very complex indeed.

The caste breakdown of the 1931 census is not
what one finds to be relevant for political mobilization or even analysis some forty years later.
After people separate out the Muslim, they talk
about "Banias," "Harijans," and, by implication,
the others in between. I don't recall anyone
talking about the "Rajput" vote, for example. In
interviews I tried to break down at least the
"Bania" category, but got no reliable data. "Bania"
is a particularly slippery term because it is in
Delhi a word used for an economic class as well
as for a caste grouping, and one is never quite
sure which is meant. Indeed, Banias (the caste
group) tend to be a class as well (merchants,
small factory owners, landlord). The same is true
of "Harijan." It was rarely true that this sort of

TABLE 19

MAJOR HINDU CASTES IN DELHI CITY, 1931

Caste	N	Percentage of Total Hindu Population[a]
Brahmin	24,389	13.0
Aggarwal	20,031	10.6
Rajput	18,501	9.8
Chamar	13,884	7.4
Khatri	10,974	5.8
Jhinwar	9,702	5.2
Kayastha	7,887	4.2
Chuhra	7,163	3.8
Rahgar	7,137	3.8
Julaha	7,009	3.7
Total	126,677	67.3

Source: Census of India 1931, XVI, lviii.

[a]That is, not a percentage of the population of the castes listed;
these 10 castes contain 67 percent of the total Hindu population
of 188,232.

broad caste label was self-applied ("we
Banias . . ."). There are one or two caste
associations--the Kayasthas have one--but
there is no evidence of how widespread the
membership is, nor did they show up as political activists in the year of my observation.
My inclination is thus to avoid putting much
weight on caste divisions in an analysis of
politics and government in Shahjahanabad.[33]

The important political division within
the Hindu community at the all-city level--that
between "Punjabi" and local--is present in the
City Zone to a certain extent. Two of the
councilors were refugees and there are sizeable
concentrations of "Punjabi" citizens.[34]

A further major grouping of Hindus is the
scheduled castes. In the 1971 census, 27 of the
623 census blocks in Shahjahanabad* have "high"
scheduled caste populations; that is, more than
half scheduled caste. These 27 census blocks
contain about 40 percent of Shahjahanabad's
scheduled caste population. Table 20 presents
the census figures, with the details of the
seven "scheduled caste" census blocks (i.e.,
those with more than 80 percent of the population
scheduled caste; cf. "Muslim" and "Hindu" census
blocks in Kucha Khirkiwala).

The comparison of these two categories of
census blocks with the Shahjahanabad figures is

---

*
Here and in the following section, I am
shifting my use of the name "Shahjahanabad" to
include Mori Gate and Kashmiri Gate wards; it
thus differs from the portion of the walled city
within the City Zone, for which I have been using
the name Shahjahanabad, but is, of course, the
proper use of the name. As it happens, the 1971
Census (unlike the 1961 Census) uses "charges"
(groups of census blocks) which force the change.
(Compare Fig. 11, p. 150, above with Fig. 12,
below, p. 171.)

TABLE 20

"SCHEDULED CASTE" CENSUS BLOCKS IN SHAHJAHANABAD, 1971

		Percent of the Population		Percent of workers in categories						
		Scheduled Caste	Literate	I-IV	V(a)	V(b)	VI	VII	VIII	IX
census block[a]	A	98	40	..	46	23	2	5	3	22
	B	87	38	..	52	24	2	7	5	11
	C	100	46	0	1	11	15	36	21	16
	D	100	34	..	7	31	3	14	6	40
	E	100	38	..	..	10	..	4	..	87
	F	100	27	..	33	38	3	13	2	12
	G	100	41	..	..	55	4	19	6	16
	an:	98	38	0	20	27	4	14	6	29
caste population census blocks[b]	Mean:	72	40	0	13	26	3	20	11	28
	Range:	51-100%	23-58%	0-1%	0-52%	9-55%	0-16%	4-50%	0-28%	8-87%
	(N=27)									
	hjahanabad	8	56	0	5	25	3	34	8	26

urce: Delhi District Census Handbook 1971, Part X-B, pp. 74-104.

ocks where more than 80 percent of the population is scheduled caste.

ocks where more than 50 percent of the population is scheduled caste.

:e: I-IV = Agriculture, etc.; V(a) = Household Industry; V(b) = Manufacturing;
VI = Construction; VII = Trade and Commerce; VIII = Transport and Communication;
IX = Other Services. Zeros indicate figures less than 0.5; dots of elision
indicate figures of 0.0.

very suggestive: scheduled caste people are much
less likely to be workers in trade and commerce
and more likely to be workers in household industry.
They also have a significantly lower literacy rate.
The tremendous variation in the "profile" of the
"scheduled caste" census blocks--87 percent in
services in one, 52 percent in household industry
in another, etc.--is a warning that the figures
must be interpreted with extreme caution. (Note
also the range of values in the census blocks with
"high" proportions of scheduled caste.) A more
detailed occupational breakdown--one that distinguished between the wholesale cloth merchant and
the sidewalk fruit seller, and between the Municipal
Health Officer and the ordinary sweeper--would
certainly give us a far better picture of scheduled
caste occupations. Overall, it should be noted that
scheduled castes do not bulk large in Shahjahanabad
as a whole; with only a few exceptions, specific
scheduled castes did not figure in political
analyses presented to me.

OCCUPATIONS, INDUSTRIES, AND POPULATION:
THE CENSUS DATA

Let us now turn from the examination of the
ethnic composition of Shahjahanabad, and the
general culture of the city, to a profile of its
economy and population. Shahjahanabad* has had its
share of Delhi's economic growth since Independence.
There has been an expansion in small-scale industry
and commercial establishments within the walled
city. There is no simple way to document this
change, although to a certain extent the expansion
in the municipal budget (see Chapter 8, below) is
indicative. (What follows here is obviously not a

---

*
   Again, I shall be dealing with the entire
walled city, including the area north of the railway
line.

summary of the current economic position of Shahjahanabad, but rather it is more an attempt to indicate some of the magnitudes involved, and a rough categorization of the kinds of visible economic activity.)

Occupations

The major source of economic data on Shahjahanabad is the 1971 Census (figures from other sources are usually not broken down by geographical areas within Delhi); see Appendix, Table 3. Before the 1971 Census there was no easy way to determine the demographic character-istics of Shahjahanabad. The 1971 Census was divided into "Zones", and "Zone II" (City-Sadar-Paharganj) is roughly equivalent to the area covered by the old Delhi Municipality, the unit of computation in earlier censuses (see the note to Table 22, below). The population of Shahjahana-bad in 1971--413,073--therefore cannot be compared with earlier decades, although the slow growth of Kucha Khirkiwala's population in the 1961-71 decade (see above, p. 51) points to a similar rate in the walled city.

    Delhi has prospered in recent years. For instance, the employment in registered factories (in the entire Union Territory) had increased by about 35 percent between 1961 and 1965[35] and despite a period of recession afterwards I would guess that industrial expansion in Delhi since 1965 has been even more rapid. An increase in factory employment is not, of course, an index of the expansion of the economy of Shahjahanabad, but the walled city has visibly benefited along with the rest of the territory.

    Let us begin with the data on the occupations of the residents of the city of Delhi as a whole; those data are presented in Table 21.[36] The first thing to be noted is the steep decline in the pro-portion of agricultural workers: from 21 percent

TABLE 21

WORKERS IN THE TERRITORY/STATE/PROVINCE OF DELHI

Year	1971 Census Categories[a]							
	I-IV	V(a)	V(b)	VI	VII	VIII	IX	Total
1941[b]	59,442 (20.8%)	102,857 (36.0%)			56,023 (19.6%)	21,197 (7.4%)	46,257 (16.2%)	285,776 (100.0%)
1951[c]	65,025 (10.2%)	117,724 (18.5%)	59,497 (9.4%)		133,227 (21.0%)	39,143 (6.2%)	220,762 (34.8%)	635,378 (100.0%)
		177,221 (27.9%)						
1961[d]	71,449 (8.4%)	16,710 (2.0%)	170,324 (19.9%)	35,360 (4.1%)	146,727 (17.2%)	49,569 (5.8%)	364,312 (42.6%)	854,451 (100.0%)
		222,394 (26.0%)						
1971[e]	60,856 (5.0%)	27,930 (2.3%)	263,655 (21.5%)	65,138 (5.3%)	244,597 (19.9%)	114,976 (9.4%)	451,245 (36.7%)	1,228,397 (100.0%)
		356,723 (29.0%)						

[a] I-IV = Agriculture, Mining, etc.; V(a) = Household Industry; V(b) = Manufacturing, VI = Construction; VII = Trade and Commerce; VIII = Transport and Communication; IX = Other Services.

[b] Census of India 1941, XVI, 39-65, passim.

[c] Adapted from M. D. Chaudhury and Bert Hoselitz, "State Income of Delhi State, 1951-52 and 1955-56," Economic Development and Cultural Change, XI, No. 3, Part II (April, 1963), p. 19.

[d] Delhi District Census Handbook 1961, pp. 262-65.

[e] Delhi District Census Handbook 1971, Part X-B, pp. 4-5.

in 1941 to 5 percent in 1971. The category which
has expanded over those 30 years has been services,
from 16 percent in 1941 to 43 percent in 1961.
But note the decline (to 37 percent) in 1971, as
the industrial categories expand. "Blue collar"
workers (categories V(a), V(b), VI, and VIII)
declined from 43 percent of the total in 1941 to
32 percent in 1961, then rose significantly to
39 percent in 1971. Finally, trade and commerce
has retained a proportion of about 20 percent in
all four years.

Looking at the actual number of workers in
the 1941-71 period, one sees that there are virtually the same number of workers in agriculture
in 1971 as there were in 1941. The number of
"blue collar" workers has nearly quadrupled; so
has the number of workers in trade and commerce.
And the number of workers in services was nearly
ten times the 1941 figure in 1971. (Of course,
both the total number of workers and the population of Delhi in these three decades also
quadrupled.) Government employment has grown
about as fast as employment in private sector
establishments (with 10 or more workers) between
1961 and 1970, according to one set of figures.[37]
Central government employees constituted about
half the total of public sector employees in 1970,
compared to two-thirds in 1961,[38] so the expansion
in the service workers in the 1951-61 decade may
well have been due to the expansion of central
government employment.

Let us now look at how Shahjahanabad compares
with this all-city pattern (Table 22). (Caveat:
the 1941 and 1971 figures are not, strictly
speaking equivalent; see the note to the table.)
Unsurprisingly, agricultural workers do not live
in Old Delhi, nor did they thirty years ago. The
proportion of "blue collar" workers has declined
and that of service workers increased. This
mirrors the all-Delhi picture.

There is a larger proportion of workers in
commerce in Old Delhi than in Delhi as a whole, and

TABLE 22

WORKERS IN "OLD DELHI" -- PERCENTAGES

Year	1971 Census Categories[a]				
	I-IV	V(a)-VI	VII	VIII	IX
1941[b]	2.2	45.6	30.9	9.8	11.4
1971[c]	0.4	32.1	33.5	8.4	25.6

[a]See Table 21, above.

[b]"Delhi Municipality"; Census of India 1941, XVI, pp. 39-65.

[c]"Shahjahanabad"; Delhi District Census Handbook 1971, Pt. X-B, pp. 74-104.

Note: The two sets of figures presented here are, strictly
speaking, not comparable. The "Delhi Municipality"
included, as far as I can determine in the absence of
maps or accurate descriptions of boundaries, Subzimandi
(containing a number of large industrial establishments
and workers' housing), Karol Bagh (government servant
residences) and other areas along the railway lines, in
addition to Shahjahanabad. Shahjahanabad would, however,
be a large part of the 1941 Delhi Municipality, in population if not in area, but just how large is hard to say--
my estimate would be no less than half, and perhaps as
much as three-fourths.

a smaller proportion of service workers, in 1971
as in 1941. There was about the same proportion
of "blue collar" workers in Old Delhi as in all
of Delhi in 1971, and, indeed, if we look only
at the non-agricultural workers in 1941, this was
true then, too (they formed 54.8% of the non-
agricultural workforce).

The "balance" between the three major occupational categories changes when one takes into
account areas within Shahjahanabad. Figure 12
(based on data in Appendix Table 3) shows the
modal category for each of the 10 census "charges"
in Shahjahanabad. (A category is called "modal"
when the difference between it and the next
largest category is 10 percent or more; bi-modal
and tri-modal charges are shown with bar graph
representations of the categories.) The predominance of residents who work in trade and

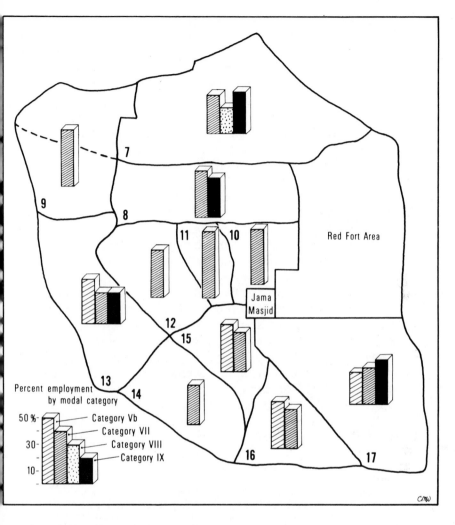

Fig. 12   Patterns of residence by occupation
in Shahjahanaband, 1971.
Note: "modal" categories are those which are
greater by 10 per cent or more than the next
largest category; where this does not obtain,
the two or three largest categories are shown
as bar graphs. "Shahjahanabad" here includes
Mori Gate and Kashmiri Gate areas. The
boundaries shown are of administrative wards
(which correspond to the "Charge Numbers" of
the 1971 census), as they appear in a map in
the 1891 census (vol. 20, Part II). These
ward boundaries have remained unchanged to the
best of my knowledge.

commerce in most of the city is clear, and if we
consider a "white collar" category (combining
categories VII and IX), all but charges 13, 15,
and 16 would be "white collar." Note also that
"blue collar" workers live in the southern section
of Shahjahanabad, and the workers in trade and
commerce in charge 14 may well include hawkers,
pavement merchants and others who would be
closer in life style to "blue collar" workers
than to, say, the wholesale cloth merchants of
Chandni Chowk.

As in the Kucha Khirkiwala data, we are
examining here the patterns of residence, not
patterns of work performed in Shahjahanabad.
Patterns of residence are, however, not unrelated
to the kind of work performed in the city, since
most people in Shahjahanabad live very near their
work, so in a sense most live and work "in the
same place." (See Table 23.) The average
distance from place of work in these wards is
1.7 miles;[39] for Daryaganj, the most prosperous
area of the walled city, it is 2.1 miles.[40] The
dimensions of Shahjahanabad are roughly two miles
long by one mile wide, and so it is not unlikely
that at least half of the workers resident in the

TABLE 23

DISTANCE FROM PLACE OF WORK: KUCHA PATI RAM/SUIWALAN AREA[a]

Miles	Percentage of Earners	Cumulative Percentage of Earners
nil	10.5	10.5
0-1	29.0	39.5
1-2	15.2	54.7
2-4	16.5	71.2
4+	7.3	78.5
variable	21.5	100.0

Source: Delhi Development Authority, Master Plan for Delhi
(Delhi: Delhi Development Authority, 1962), II, p. 128.

[a]These wards are on the southern periphery of Shahjahanabad and
are almost entirely "slum."

old city also work there. The occupational pattern
of the residents thus probably reflects the overall economic character of the city, with the
exception noted that most service workers probably
work outside Shahjahanabad.

Let us add one more dimension to the
comparison: the Kucha Khirkiwala data (Table 24),
and in addition remove most agricultural workers
from consideration by presenting the figures for
"Delhi (Urban)."

The major contrast between Shahjahanabad
and urban Delhi is the greater proportion of
service workers in urban Delhi and the greater
proportion of workers in trade and commerce in
Shahjahanabad. Kucha Khirkiwala is quite similar
to Shahjahanabad, and differs from urban Delhi,
in those respects. All three units have about
the same proportion of workers in "blue collar"
occupations: 46 percent for Kucha Khirkiwala,
41 percent for Shahjahanabad, and 40 percent for
urban Delhi. Shahjahanabad, with 11 percent of
the total population of urban Delhi, also has 11
percent of the workers in "blue collar" occupations,

TABLE 24

WORKERS RESIDENT IN KUCHA KHIRKIWALA, SHAHJAHANABAD, AND
URBAN DELHI, 1971 -- PERCENTAGE OF TOTAL NUMBER OF WORKERS

	I-IV	V(a)	V(b)	VI	VII	VIII	IX
Kucha Khirkiwala[b]	0	4	33	3	32	6	21
Shahjahanabad[c]	0	5	25	3	34	8	26
Delhi (Urban)[d]	2	2	22	6	22	10	38

Census Categories[a]

See Table 21, above.

See Table 2, above.

See Table 3, Appendix.

Delhi District Census Handbook 1971, X-B, pp. 4-5.

only 7 percent of those in services and 17 percent
of the total number in trade and commerce. These
differences are not enough to stamp a "character"
on parts of Delhi like Shahjahanabad--"government"
town versus "businessman's" city, for instance.
Shahjahanabad, to look at the data from another
angle, has significant numbers of workers in all
three major areas. The mix in building uses--
residential, commercial, and industrial--which
I described in the Kucha Khirkiwala chapters is
repeated throughout Shahjahanabad. And one would
expect that problems of municipal government are
similar throughout the walled city, and also
similar to those of Kucha Khirkiwala.

Industry and Business

The industrial establishments* of Shahjahanabad
totaled approximately 2,640 in 1961.**[41] The largest

---

* The "number of industrial establishments,"
with no indication of their scale (measured in terms
of working capital, gross income, employment, or
however) is hardly an adequate index of "industrial-
ization." Indeed, I would imagine that establishments in Shahjahanabad are smaller in all respects
than their counterparts elsewhere in the city,
especially in those categories (machinery manufacture, for example) where large-scale factories
are almost a necessity. There are, I believe, no
"factories" in the American sense of the term within
the city walls, although there are many very large
workshops. (I should add that there are few
"factories" in the whole of Delhi; most industry
is carried on in workshops.)

** The categories used in the following discus-
sion ("Food," "Textiles," etc.) are the summary categories presented in Table 5, p. 60. Except for Fig.
13, "Shahjahanabad" in this section includes Mori
Gate and Kashmiri Gate wards.

number of establishments is in the "Metals" category (23 percent), followed by "Printing" (18 percent) and "Machinery" (11 percent). All other
categories have less than 10 percent of the establishments, but none has less than five percent.

If one computes various measures of the
geographical distribution of establishments in
the walled city,[42] the spread is striking: only
one of the 18 municipal wards has more than 10
percent of the total number of establishments
(and the figure for that ward is 13 percent).
The "density" of industrial establishments in a
ward ranges from about two per 1,000 persons to
14 per 1,000 persons, with most wards clustered
around the mean of about seven per 1,000 persons.
As in Kucha Khirkiwala (see above, p. 61), this
does not seem to suggest an "industrialized"
area.

There are, however, significant concentrations
of industrial activity which cross ward boundaries
(see Fig. 13). The east-west band of "industriali-
zation" follows the line of the major wholesale
markets for those products. In those areas, and
in Dariba, where jewelry manufacture is tied closely
to the jewelers' bazar, the impact of a given
industry on the economic life of its neighborhood
is probably considerable.

It should be emphasized at this point that
the data on industrial establishments dates from
1961, and that there has been a great deal of
economic expansion in Delhi since then. It is
unlikely that the general proportions of various
categories of industrial establishments has changed
much, though their numbers have probably increased
tremendously. However, when we compare the number
of industrial establishments in Shahjahanabad to
the total number in Delhi, this caveat gains
force: Shahjahanabad's percentage of industrial
establishments has most certainly decreased since
1961. (Still, fully one-third of the industrial
establishments in urban Delhi were in Shahjahanabad
then.) Given the rapid growth of Delhi as a whole,

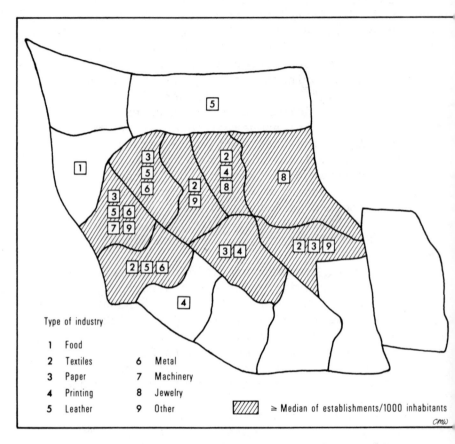

Type of industry

1	Food		
2	Textiles	6	Metal
3	Paper	7	Machinery
4	Printing	8	Jewelry
5	Leather	9	Other

▨▨▨ ≧ Median of establishments/1000 inhabitants

Fig. 13 Industrial establishments in Shahja-hanaband, 1971, showing the "industrialized" area and locations of establishments by general category (Table 5).

this decrease may be quite large. Shahjahanabad
probably still has the majority of jewelry establishments, though less than the 80 percent of the
total as in 1961 (a minor industry in terms of
capitalization, employment, etc., obviously), and
the number of printing and publishing establishments is undoubtedly less than the 54 percent of
1961. These two industries are the only ones
in which Shahjahanabad contained a number of
establishments disproportionate to its share of
the total number.

The data on wholesale and retail business
within the walled city are both outdated and
incomplete. A survey made in 1957 by the
National Council of Applied Economic Research[43]
dealt with five major commodities: textiles,
bicycles, fuels, iron and steel, and food grains.
For textiles, the survey suggests that most of
the 1,300 to 1,500 wholesalers of cotton goods
were located in and around Chandni Chowk and they
did a 700 to 800 million rupee a year business.[44]
The cloth trade accounted for almost 20 percent
of the commercial activity of Delhi.[45] The wholesale bicycle market for Delhi was located entirely
along one road near the Jama Masjid; since then
it has spread out to other areas. At the time
the NCAER survey was made, the Ajmeri Gate-Hauz
Qazi iron and steel market was already waning in
importance, although it still had a sizeable
portion of the trade.[46] Food grains wholesalers
were also located largely in Shahjahanabad (in
ward 64).[47] In the cases of all these industries,
manufacturing units were located mainly outside
Shahjahanabad, and retail outlets were distributed,
sometimes evenly, sometimes in a few locations,
throughout Delhi. Shahjahanabad is not only the
traditional commercial nucleus of Delhi, but also
is bounded on two sides by railway yards. It also
lies on the main truck route from newly industrialized towns on the east bank of the Jumna
(Shahdara, Ghaziabad). Its prominence in whole-
saling is therefore not surprising.

The NCAER data are 20 years old. The relative importance of Shahjahanabad has undoubtedly
declined. Nevertheless, the food grain and
textile markets, as well as lesser ones--paper,
hardware, spices, and others--are still very much
in evidence, and certainly doing as much business
or more business now as before.

Population

In 1971 the population of Shahjahanabad was
413,073.[48] Some of the data which can be found
in the census (apart from the data on workers)
are presented in Table 3 of the Appendix, in Table
25 in summary form, and in Figure 14.[49] I do not
have the maps necessary for calculating the population densities of the wards of the city, but
they are certainly very high; Kucha Khirkiwala
(see above, p. 51) would be typical. In 1951,
gross densities (population divided by total area)
ranged from 101 to 493 persons per acre, and net
densities (population divided by built-up area)
from 159 to 1,128 persons per acre, for wards
which have since disappeared as new boundaries
were drawn.[50] For the walled city as a whole,
the mean gross density was 319 persons per acre
and the mean net density 482. These data are
presented fully in the Appendix, Table 4. Population densities have increased since 1951, of
course, but in comparison with the 133 percent
increase in population of Delhi from 1951 to
1971, the approximately 9 percent increase for
Shahjahanabad is a very modest one. Present net
densities are probably not far from 500 persons
per acre.[51] Densities of 1,500 persons per acre
in purely residential areas are probably not
uncommon.
An examination of Fig. 14 discloses a distribution of high rates of literacy[52] in the
northern wards in which commercial establishments and the "better" residences are located,

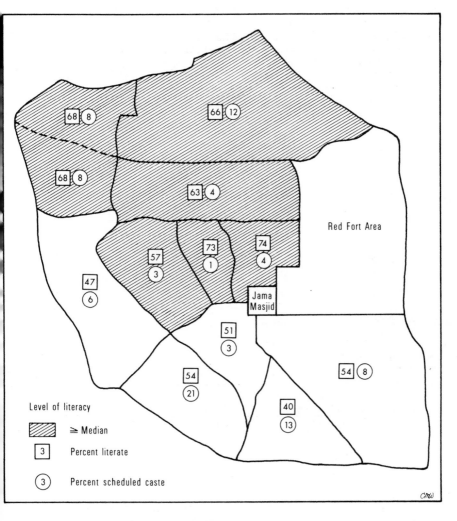

Fig 14 Percentages of literates and Scheduled
Caste, Shahjahanabad, 1971. See Note to Fig.
12 on "Shahjahanabad."

TABLE 25

POPULATION, LITERATES, AND SCHEDULED CASTE, SHAHJAHANABAD, 1971

Census Charge No.	Population	Percent Literate	Percent Scheduled Caste
7	17,609	66	12
8	25,975	63	4
9	34,721	68	8
10	22,938	74	4
11	21,605	73	1
12	52,552	57	3
13	54,185	47	6
14	46,561	54	21
15	42,497	51	3
16	34,212	40	13
17	60,218	54	8
Totals	413,073	56	8
Delhi (Urban)	3,647,023	59	15
Delhi Union Territory	4,065,698	57	16

Source: Delhi District Census Handbook, Part X-B, passim; my
         calculations. Cf. Appendix, Table 3.

and the lower rates in those wards which are
poorer, wards that house workers in "blue collar"
jobs or menial service jobs. In short, the poor
are less educated than the rich. A comparison
of the two sets of numbers in Fig. 14 suggests
that a low literacy rate is associated with a
high percentage of scheduled caste residency,
but there is not necessarily a direct relation
involved: the scheduled castes live in the
poor areas. Or perhaps, it is only the poor
who will live in areas where scheduled caste

people live. What is more, data previously presented (above, p. 57) suggests that the crucial
factor may be Muslim population--all four of the
wards with the lowest literacy rates are "Muslim"
wards.* In literacy, Shahjahanabad is typical of
the rest of Delhi (Table 25, above).

The percentage of scheduled castes within the
walled city is lower than that for Delhi as a whole.
The scheduled castes, whose major castes in Census
Zone II in 1961 were Chamars (20,877 of the total of
67,724 scheduled caste members, or 31 percent) and
various sweeper castes (approximately 10,000)[53]
and other castes (Dhobis, for example) whose traditional work (leather tanning, washing clothes,
etc.) has meant location in open spaces at the
periphery of areas occupied by "clean" castes.
Originally there were some areas open just behind
the city wall on the south side of the city; and
this is where these castes are still located.
Indeed, an examination of the "scheduled caste"
census blocks (cf.above, p. 165) in wards 67, 68,
and 60 reveals that within these wards, the scheduled caste persons live at the southern extrem-
ities, just behind where the city wall used to
be.**

---

*
There is no data on religion detailed enough
for comparing individual ward percentages. I base
this assertion on the estimates of religious background of constituents that I asked for in my
interviews with councilors and on my own observations (looking at the dress of the residents,
the language of the shop signboards, etc.).

**
This is not precise: the map on which this
assertion is based--the election office map of
Chandni Chowk Parliamentary constituency, which
shows the location of house numbers--is somewhat
inaccurate, in addition to being really only a
rough sketch.

As one would expect from noting the expansion
of the old city in recent decades, in 1961 only
half the population was born in the place of enumeration (i.e., at that house address), and many
would have been young children--nearly 30 percent
of the population of Zone II was under ten years
of age.[54]   In 1961, 53.1 percent of the people of
Zone II were born in Delhi, 17.2 percent were born
in U.P., 8.4 percent in Punjab, 5.3 percent in
other states of India, and 15.3 percent in what is
now Pakistan. Probably half of the adults of
Shahjahanabad are "immigrants" (or at least "non-
local"), and this clearly has implications for any
development of "civic pride": It may also be a
partial explanation for not finding the vigorous
"traditional" social structure in the mohallas that
one might expect from the historical and physical
background.

SUMMARY AND IMPLICATIONS

The census data on occupation, industries,
and population are not easily summarized. The
1971 data indicate that Shahjahanabad differs
little from Delhi as a whole in the proportion of
workers in "blue collar" jobs, when compared to
the proportions of those working in commerce and
in services. The data over time (Table 22) suggests that the trends are the same in both areas:
more and more people in services, fewer in "blue
collar" jobs, and about the same proportion in
trade and commerce. Along with the mix of building
usage in Shahjahanabad--and this is not common in
most of the rest of Delhi, where the small workshops in the basement of Old Delhi give way to
large factories on industrial estates--there is a
comparatively even distribution of workers in the
three major categories living there.
Industrial establishments are scattered
throughout the walled city, though there is something of an "industrial belt," and there are a few

wards in which particular industries are concentrated. The data on Kucha Khirkiwala suggest that
there can be considerable concentration of industrial establishments in certain areas of the ward:
I believe that Kucha Khirkiwala is typical of
Shahjahanabad in this respect. While there is in
a sense a surprising amount and variety of industrial activity occurring in Shahjahanabad, still
these workshops are not as conspicuous as commercial establishments, especially wholesale
shops. And Shahjahanabad has a "white collar"
character when one looks at the modal occupations
of its residents.

The data from the census must be supplemented
by the "soft" data presented in the first part of
this chapter. The entire walled city has what can
only be called incredible population densities.
The wards differ widely in terms of literacy, and
there are probably wide intra ward variations, as
there are in Kucha Khirkiwala. The scheduled
caste population, while relatively small, is also
concentrated in certain areas of the walled city;
again intra ward patterns are also important.
Finally, a very large proportion of the residents
of the walled city were not "born and bred" there.
It has been suggested above that the Muslims of
the walled city, however, are more likely to be
"old residents" than their Hindu neighbors. In
that sense, the Islamic city of Shahjahanabad is
losing its Islamic "stamp" not only in physical
terms, but also in cultural terms, as the Muslims
become a smaller minority.

Before I examine the implications of these
patterns for municipal government in the City Zone,
let me briefly compare Shahjahanabad's economic,
demographic, and cultural portrait with cities
elsewhere in India and the world. Delhi has a
geography similar to many other Indian cities: an
old city, separated from a "civil lines" area built
by the British by a railway line, surrounded by
post-Independence suburbs. Delhi has had the
greatest growth in the 1951-61 decade of all the

major cities in India--64.2 percent (i.e., 6.4
percent average annual growth); Calcutta grew by
8.5 percent, Bombay by 38.7 percent, and Madras
by 22.1 percent.[55] The eight largest cities in
India have very similar patterns of the division
of work: workers in manufacturing (1961 census
category V), in trade and commerce (category VII),
and in services (category IX) are the most numerous
in all eight cities. The modal top ranked occupation category (in number of workers), in five
of eight cities, is services; the modal second
ranked occupation category, in four of eight
cities, is manufacturing; the modal third ranked
occupation category, in seven of eight cities, is
commerce.[56]

Delhi ranks second to Hyderabad in the
proportion of workers in services, and second to
Calcutta in the proportion of workers in commerce.
All the cities except Hyderabad have a greater
proportion of workers in manufacturing.[57] Thus
Delhi, and Shahjahanabad, are similar to the other
metropolitan cities of India in the composition of
the work force, given the gross categorization of
the census, but differ in the "weightage": Delhi
is one of the least industrialized cities, and
one of the cities more centered on commerce and
services.

The 1961 literacy rates in the eight largest
cities range from 46.7 percent of the population
(Kanpur) to 59.3 percent (Madras); Delhi, with its
rate of 56.2 percent, ranks fourth. Delhi has
become "more educated" over time: in 1901, the
city ranked seventh of the seven largest cities
in India in literacy, and sixth in 1931.[58] In
1951, of the four Indian great cities, Bombay had
the largest number of in-migrants in its population
--72 percent--and Madras the lowest number--41 percent; the figure for Delhi was 59 percent.[59] The
percentage of the population of these four cities
which was scheduled caste in 1961 was: Bombay--3
percent; Calcutta--4 percent; Madras--12 percent;
and Delhi--12 percent. Here again we see Delhi as

a typical large city in India, if there is such a
thing. From a "political" point of view, of course,
each city would have a different set of significant
demographic factors: for instance, one would want
to look at the number of "South Indians" in Bombay,
since the Shiv Sena Party there has made an issue
of non-Maharashtrians "taking" jobs which "belong"
to Maharashtrians.

How does Delhi compare to cities elsewhere in
the "Third World" and in the "developed world"?
The answer must of necessity be brief. Comparable
statistics on cities elsewhere in the world are
difficult to find. The emphasis here is on the
word "comparable." In a sense the "pariah" communities (Fred Riggs' term), e.g., the Chinese in
Thailand, may have a comparable significance, in
terms of their political powerlessness, to the
original "pariahs"--actually one caste of South
India, but more generally, the scheduled castes--but
I am doubtful. Literacy can be measured but its
significance depends, I would argue, on the availability of media other than newspapers, magazines,
etc.

Delhi, with an annual average rate of population growth of 6.4 percent in the 1950s (and
5.3 percent in the 60s), is growing faster than
some other "world" cities (selected because data
were available for them): Berlin--0.4 percent;
Buenos Aires--1.9 percent; London--minus 0.6 percent; Mexico (City)--4.6 percent; Rio de Janiero--
3.5 percent--Tokyo--5.4 percent.[60] There are
figures, for various dates, on occupation reported
in Table 26. (The categories given in the source
are strikingly similar to the categories of the
1961 Indian census, so I have adopted the Indian
census roman numerals in the table; the list of
what the numerals mean comes from the source.)

Leaving aside the difficulty of a large "other"
category in three of the cities, some tentative comparisons can be made from these figures: Delhi is
most like Cairo, with some 40 percent plus people
in services, although unlike Cairo in the large

TABLE 26

PROPORTION OF THE WORKFORCE, IN PERCENTAGES, IN NINE
OCCUPATION CATEGORIES, FOR SELECTED CITIES

City	Date of Survey	I-III	V	VI	VII	VIII	IX	Other
Delhi	1961	8.4	19.9	4.1	17.2	5.8	42.6	2.0
Delhi Zone II	1961	0.4	25.8	2.7	29.1	7.5	31.4	3.2
Berlin	1957	2.3	38.4	9.4	15.5	26.3	8.0	...
Buenos Aires	1947	0.7	34.6	4.9	19.9	8.5	13.3	18.0
Cairo	1947	1.5	11.2	2.1	8.6	12.3	46.6	17.8
London	1955	0.2	34.0	5.8	22.7	16.6	10.1	10.5
Tokyo	1955	4.2	31.8	5.5	27.9	6.6	24.1	...

Sources: For the Delhi figures: Delhi District Census Handbook 1961
For the other cities: Tokyo Metropolitan Government, Com-
parative Statistical Table of World Large City 1961 (Tokyo:
Tokyo Metropolitan Government, 1961), pp. 18-19.

[a]I-III: Agriculture, Forestry, Fishing, Mining; V: Manufacturing;
VI: Construction; VII: Wholesale and Retail Trade, Finance, In-
surance, Real Estate; VIII: Transportation, Communication, and
Other Public Utilities; IX: Services.

proportion of workers in manufacturing and commerce, and the smaller proportion in transport.
Note, however, that Zone II, Old Delhi, looks like
the "developed" cities, especially Tokyo, with an
even balance between manufacturing, commerce, and
services (which is a nice irony, given the contrast
of "old" and "new" Delhi). This data should be
extended to include a time dimension,[61] but that
clearly would go beyond the scope of this study.
Perhaps the most important figure is the relatively larger proportion of the work force in
services in the Third World cities (and the downward trend in Tokyo), for it is relevant to the
issue of "over-bureaucratization" and political
development.

Let us turn to the implications of these
demographic patterns for the political life of
the city. One argument has to do with "over-
bureaucratization," or the "excessive" development of administration, as opposed to political
development. In the words of Fred Riggs, who

is writing here of national systems:

> In transitional societies . . . the relative
> weakness of political organs means that the
> political function tends to be appropriated,
> in considerable measure, by bureaucrats.
> Intra-bureaucratic struggles become a pri-
> mary force of politics. But when the
> political arena is shifted to bureaucracies
> --a shift marked by the growing power of
> military officers in conflict with civilian
> officials--the consequences are usually
> ominous for political stability, economic
> growth, administrative effectiveness, and
> democratic values.[62]

It is difficult to close the gap between this sort
of generalization and the figures showing a far
larger percentage of the work force in services--
and it is a fair assumption that government service
bulks large in this total--in cities of the "Third
World" as opposed to "developed" world cities.
Clearly, there is no "critical" figure which would
indicate that an urban system, or, for that matter,
a national system, is "over-bureaucratized." Still,
it is a question which gains relevance in our examination of the relationship between councilor and
administrator in the Delhi zone, in the next
chapter.
    Rates of literacy are significant for theories
which, to phrase the proposition in non-causal
terms, see a clustering of high literacy rates,
high levels of urbanization, etc., and "moderni-
zation."[63] It is also presumably relevant for
theories of government which emphasize communication.
The Delhi material I have assembled does not bear
on these theories directly, but a clear implication
of the data on the municipal election, and the Kucha
Khirkiwala data, is that political activists "get
around" the lack of literacy: campaigning is oral
and direct; it consists of canvassing and speeches,
not leaflets (and only secondarily of posters).

The scheduled caste proportion of the
population, as such, is obviously relevant only
in intra-India comparisons. But if we broaden
"scheduled caste," if not into "pariah communities," then into (to use a cumbersome phrase)
ethnically defined lowest strata peoples, such
as blacks in the United States, then comparisons
can be made.[64] Questions of relative depri-
vation, urban unrest, etc., become relevant. I
do not have the space to explore these implications further, and I am setting aside the
problem of converting these factors into "the
proportion of the population who are X." Here,
as with other demographic factors, a negative
formulation might be more accurate: there are
some indications that scheduled caste proportion
(or literacy, etc.) is not unrelated to political
actions.

Finally, there is the issue of the "sense of
community," or "civic sense" (broadly interpreted),
of a city's citizenry. Lapidus poses the issue
with respect to the Muslim city (as a sub-category
of the "oriental" city): "Students have stressed
the physical formlessness of Muslim towns as an
expression of communal lifelessness and lack of
public spirit."[65] And he concludes that this was
not the case in the medieval period, although he
argues that European and Muslim cities can be
contrasted, if not precisely, as "commune vs.
bureaucracy": the more segmented European city
"required formal agencies for the defense of
special interests or the co-ordination of diverse
interests within the towns."[66] But:

In the fluid situation of Muslim towns,
public or political life was no more differentiated from the mass of religious,
economic, familial and communal concerns
than were any of the other functions from
each other. Public affairs fit into the
comprehensive structure of these overwhelming solidarity and functional ties.

They were carried on by the part-time
initiative of the society as a whole,
and by its notables in particular.[67]

I have suggested that Shahjahanabad physically
is an "Islamic" city, but there is no evidence
to support the view that its political culture
is somehow "Muslim" (and one doubts that medieval Muslim political culture carries over into
the current Muslim city, even in West Asia).
    Nor indeed is there any evidence that
Shahjahanabad's political culture (and I am using
the term loosely) is in any way "Hindu"--so that,
for example, it would be "proper" for a Kshatriya
caste to govern. Shahjahanabad is a city area
that has a commercial flavor, with a literate population and a disappearing "Islamic" stamp to its
geography and high culture. The demographic and
cultural patterns I have been dealing with are
only sketched out in the Shahjahanabad data, and
even then I am limited, essentially, to what the
compilers of the census considered important. The
comparisons with cities elsewhere, and the political
implications I have touched upon, are intended to
suggest possibilities, not exhaust their range.
    My argument will be that these factors, these
demographic and cultural patterns, are not deter-
minants of political action, but rather set the
parameters of municipal government in Delhi. This
argument is made in a somewhat roundabout fashion
in the discussion in the next chapter, in which
the zonal system in Delhi is analyzed: I believe
the institutional arrangements of zonal decentralization, coupled with the councilor's concern with
his ward (again, strengthened by the institutional
innovation of the constituency fund) are virtually
all that is necessary to explain the dimensions of
municipal politics in Shahjahanabad. The implication of this view is that there is a lack of
civic sense--if the evidence is the lack of active
voluntary or ethnic group organization advancing
their interests--not because that would be contrary

to the political culture of the people of
Shahjahanabad, but because the way municipal
government is set up at once discourages such
pressure (the input side is protected from
pressure by ideology/ethic and the insulation
of the decision makers from day-to-day politics)
and obviates the need for it, by being responsive to citizens' demands, as channelled through
the councilor.

6. Councilor and Administrator in the City Zone

The City Zone is an administrative unit with a political body, the zonal committee, associated with it. The administrative unit covers 18 wards, 16 of them in the old city of Shahjahanabad, and the zonal committee consists of the 18 councilors from those wards. The primary interface at this level is the one between councilor and administrator, and I shall introduce the discussion of the City Zone with an analysis of the councilor-administrator interface, set in the context of the relationship of administrator and elected official in India generally. We will see that the Delhi pattern is similar to the general Indian one. I will then discuss the operation of the zone, and the zonal committee in particular, in some detail. It will become clear that the committee deals with the entire range of municipal problems, and deals with them in considerable detail. The councilors in their "zonal" role, moreover, tend to be "non-partisan" actors, not bargaining for benefits along party lines. At this level of government, the institutional arrangement of a decentralized administration coupled with a body of elected representatives, seems to provide the major framework of government in Shahjahanabad and the City Zone area, at least between elections. From the point of view of the councilor, government in the zone consists of zonal administration actively supervised by himself, an efficient administration whose purpose is to see that his ward is well serviced.

COUNCILOR AND OFFICER; ELECTED OFFICIAL
AND ADMINISTRATOR

The interface between elected official and administrator exists at all levels of government in India: ministers of the central government hold portfolios of departments headed by career civil servants; ministers at the state level are in the same position; the system of panchayati raj (usually a three-tiered system of rural local government, with village units [panchayats], tehsil or taluka units, and a district unit)[1] provides for elected officials and administrators to sit together on bodies which plan and administer development programs; and so on. Contact exists in informal ways as well, as the Member of the (state) Legislative Assembly (the MLA) seeks to nurse his constituency by influencing the administrative action that takes place there. The brief overview of the literature and the examination of the councilor-officer interface in the Delhi zone, which follows below, suggest that the interaction results in effective working relationships, even if they are somewhat abrasive.

The Interface in Arenas Other than Delhi

Let us first examine the interaction at the state level. Richard Taub writes of the state government in Orissa that:

The Collector, whom officers imagine once to have been "King of the district," must now share his kingdom with political agents.
. . . [An] informant explained the new situation . . . succinctly: "Today there is political interference with government. A member of the legislative assembly can go to a Collector and say, you do this and this. And the Collector does it, because he is afraid of a phone call from the minister." The work of the Collector is no longer the

path defined by an abstract call to a
clearly-defined duty, but rather one of
conciliation and maneuver.[2]

Taub is talking about the all-India civil service,
the Indian Administrative Service. A former member
of that service writes:

It is now twenty years since the political
leaders and the administrative personnel
came together to achieve the object of
establishing a progressive and prosperous
nation. Over this long period, the want
of understanding and trust between the
political party and the Civil Services,
which was inevitable under the circumstances in which the transfer of power
took place, should have disappeared, any
rough edges in mutual relationship smoothened
out and a harmonious and an efficient team-
work should have developed between the two
wings. Unfortunately this has not been so.[3]

And Rao goes on to list some of the reasons for the
continuing conflict, which include the following:

Many a civil servant has tended to be
rigid and not sufficiently appreciative
of the problems facing ministers and the
environment in which they worked. Some
even resented the new arrangement which
vested powers at their expense in individuals about whose intellectual capacity,
and often of character, they had a poor
opinion. The inexperience of many ministers
and the consequent mistakes committed by
them in the initial stages on assuming
office exacerbated the situation.[4]

Taub and Rao are talking about the conflict of
bureaucrat and politician (civil servant and democratic representative) at the highest level of

government. The civil service draws on a heritage of British style administrative impartiality, and, to a degree, on a British heritage of administrative autonomy. The politician is often a product of a nationalist movement which denounced Indians who joined the civil service as traitors, while relying on the stability of administration they provided after Independence. These traditions exist at the municipal level as well, particularly in Delhi, where some senior officers are members of the IAS and of the Provincial Civil Service, and many politicians were active participants in the nationalist movement.

Ramashray Roy and Shanti Kothari conducted a survey focusing on the district, and the conclusions of their study note that "the interactions between administrators and political leaders is likely to be characterized by tensions and conflicts,"[5] not only because of these traditions and beliefs of the actors, but also because of differential perceptions of where the boundary between "politics" and "administration" lies. As they put it:

> Our discussion emphatically indicates that the conventional notion of a clear-cut and clean division of function between administrators and political leaders does not operate in practice. According to the conventional notion, leaders are exclusively responsible for determining policies whereas administrators should concern themselves with the implementation of policies once they have been finally formulated. In practice, however, as our respondents testify administrators claim responsibility in formulation of policies while leaders would not like to be excluded from influencing the course of administration.[6]

It should be added here that the idea of a boundary between politics and administration finds

institutional form in the "deliberative" and
"executive" "wings" of the Corporation (in Delhi,
and throughout India), and the counterpart institutions at the zonal level in Delhi. Again, the
dispute is not so much about the propriety of the
division of the two "realms"--Delhi councilors,
at least, seem to believe they ought to be
separate--but about whether a given action is
part of the executive function or the deliberative
function, particularly since the deliberative
function would include the supervision of
executive action as well.[7]

Roy and Kothari discuss the administrators'
"strong sense of upward deference"--to their
superiors[8]--and state "the importance of contact
between administrators and political leaders is
perceived largely by the latter.[9] This suggests
that there is not only a boundary dispute involved
but also a notion that the boundary ought to be
impermeable to lateral entry; in short, everything
should go "through channels," which are in theory
well defined. The administrators see contact as
being legitimate only at the highest level and in
written form; the politicians see it as proper at
all levels and often in oral form.

The Interface in Delhi

Let us now turn to the interaction in the
arena of the Delhi zone. The councilor and officer
are brought in contact during the meetings of the
zonal committee. Typically, the councilor will
meet with particular officers just before or just
after the meeting; they may meet at the councilor's
"call" in the committee room or the councilor may
go to the officer's office. Officers are called to
the ward on inspections and for discussions of
special projects. They will call on the councilor
when they are in the ward, especially if they are
there to inspect a project. And the councilor will
phone the officer as needs arise.

The Officers' Attitude

When I asked officers about their contact with councilors ("Do you meet with the councilor? How often? On what occasion?") almost all replied that they had little contact, and the occasions that were mentioned were the weekly zonal committee meetings and inspections.* A few mentioned receiving phone calls. I think this represents not so much a judgment of the actual situation, for I saw officers at this level frequently in contact with councilors, as it represents the officer's perception of his position vis-à-vis the councilor. This perception was underlined in the answer to the question on "political interference" (see below, p. 198). My feeling is that the officer sees himself as a technical man whose expertise is questioned unjustifiably by the councilor, and yet he is forced to defer to the councilor; his reaction is to minimize the extent of that contact, or even to put the councilor in a subordinate role. In one interview, when I had suggested that the councilor might serve a function in helping administrators explain rules and regulations to the citizen, the officer replied

---

*   It was difficult to induce administrators to give me candid answers to some of my questions. I had submitted a list of six broad questions to the Municipal Commissioner for approval; his letter was countersigned by the Zonal Assistant Commissioner. I usually gave the letter and the approved list of questions to the officer being interviewed. I assured him that I was there to learn, and I took no notes during the interview. (I jotted down a summary as soon after the interview as I could.) Despite all this, I had the feeling that many of the answers I received were less than candid. All the interviews with officers were in English. As a consequence of this procedure, the quotations that I give are usually paraphrases, though I put them in quotation marks when I am confident that they are almost exactly the words used.

"the councilors are sort of our unpaid helpers.
They provide the link with the people and enable
us to keep informed about every corner of the
constituency." But the recognition of the power
relationship of councilor over officer is also
there: one officer claimed that all councilors
(he meant all 106 of the Corporation) were concerned with getting illegal things done, and that
to a certain extent, the officer must comply.

A number of the officers felt that having
councilors was an unnecessary luxury, but some
admitted (after I pressed them) that perhaps they
could serve a "supervisory" role. One pointed
out that councilors in Delhi--as opposed to what
he saw in Lucknow when he went there on a visit--
are very active in getting things done. "They
pull the officers up and keep them working."
One section officer said,

> If everyone were literate, there would be
> no need for the councilor, because we
> could show [the citizen] the rules and
> regulations, and he will understand them.
> But then the councilors ask us' to do some-
> thing which is against the rules. Then we
> ask for it in writing and recommend it to
> the Executive Engineer, because we have to
> please [the councilor] and then [the coun-
> cilor] says, "Why did you send it to your
> officer?"

Most officers implied that the majority of councilors were interested in getting illegal things
done (the only difference, one said, is that some
are polite about it), though a few councilors will
accept no explanation of why doing something is
against the rules. And one officer described the
interaction of councilor and officer as "a process
of accommodation, a continuing one . . . each
learning what the other can or cannot do."

The Councilors' Attitude

The councilor's perception of the role of the officer is of course totally different, and there is a surprising degree of agreement between councilors: it doesn't seem to matter if they are Congress or Jana Sangh, young or old, experienced or inexperienced.* The first point of agreement was that if councilors did not exist to "pull up" the officer, then the latter would not do his job. Here are some representative remarks, each by a different councilor:

> The councilor is the link between the administration and the public. If the link is broken, the administrators won't do their work.

> If there were no Corporation, no councilor, then, I tell you, thousands of Delhi-ites would die just then. By themselves, the officers would not perform their duties.

-----

*The material from my interviews with councilors is very rich on this subject--they reacted very strongly and eloquently on the question of their self-abolition. (One of my questions was: "Some people say that there is no need for democracy on the municipal level; that administration doesn't function well because of political interference. What is your opinion?") These remarks on administrators were also made in the context of their judgment of the effectiveness of the zonal system, see below, p. 212 ff.

Interviews with councilors were slightly longer than those with administrators. I asked councilors if I could take notes and only one objected (and that was mid-way in the interview). My impression was of getting candid responses to almost every question. About half the interviews were conducted in English and the other half in Hindi or Urdu (in the latter instances, I wrote my notes directly in English).

The councilor is the Corporation custodian and the advocate of the public.
He approaches the officer to explain
that here is what the public wants, and
this is what the Corporation is supposed
to do. Otherwise nothing would operate. . . .
If you leave it to the officers, they won't
do it.

Without councilors, no work can go on.
Otherwise the administrative wing will
make trouble for the public. Without
elected members, officers would spend
all the money on their own bungalows and
on big roads. . . .

And one political worker, in answer to the same
question, said:

In the absence of a democratic setup, the
official machinery is not going to be
much responsive [sic] to the public in
solving their problems. Officials will
only take up general problems. He will
only bother with the individual who is
accompanied by the municipal councilor.

There is a very clear implication of the assertion
of authority by the councilor in these quotations.
It was an assertion of authority that I observed
frequently, as councilors "ordered" officers to do
things which the officers felt could only be
"ordered" by their superiors.

This assumed authority and even threat to the
officer was not denied by the councilor. The modal
response to my question, "How well do you feel the
officers in the zone are doing their work? Do you
get cooperation from them?" was "They do their work;
they have to give me cooperation" (with this latter
portion often only implied); for example:

> The officers work satisfactorily. They
> are cooperative. If there is some dif-
> ficulty, then we go to their superior.
>
> No senior officer is unreasonable if you
> don't ask him to do something out of the
> way. . . . Officers are ever so nice,
> [and] do the maximum for me.
>
> We get the work done. Sometimes they won't
> listen to me, but I can always call their
> superior. In the end, I get the work done.
>
> They work.

This sort of response was given by about half of
the 18 councilors of the zone. Others made their
position of authority more explicit:

> The officers are always found around the
> man of highest rank in the party, and
> one who has the language to abuse him. . . .
> They have to be cooperative.
>
> Cooperative--yes. They have to be. . . .
> They are too small not to be cooperative.
>
> If a decision is made and the officer
> doesn't follow it, it is necessary to
> pressure him and make him do it.
>
> Our municipal officers are doing better
> work than [officers] in several departments
> of [the central] government. . . . Some
> members interfere [with administration];
> I have never done it. [A bystander said,
> "Sometimes it may be necessary."] Yes,
> sometimes it is necessary, and the officer
> has to be threatened also, sometimes.

And a few councilors distinguish some officers from
others; for example, "All kinds of mentality are

there--some cooperative, some not.   Usually they
accept what I say."
      Some councilors, in reply to my probes, were
willing to discuss the kinds of sanctions (apart
from going to the officers' superior) they might
use against him:

      The officers are cautious because they
      know that maybe the person will go to the
      councilor [and complain about not getting
      cooperation] and then their promotion or
      increment might be stopped.

      Because the House [the Corporation] promotes
      officers, therefore they favor the party in
      power, no matter how legal-minded they may
      be, or honest.

      In the Corporation, officials have the
      feeling that they can be charge-sheeted
      if they don't cooperate with the councilor.

Or they told me by implication: when I asked about
getting officers to do illegal works, one councilor
said, "If the officer is an honest man, he will not
obey the councilor's threats because he will suffer
if his superior should check."
      Other councilors emphasized that the key to
cooperation with officials was their mode of contact
with them.   Only one seemed to favor the abrupt
style:

      I called the ZAC [right after the election]
      and I said "Hello, I am [X], newly elected
      member, and I want my work to get done; this
      is the first and last warning."

Most favored more accommodating modes, relying on
what one councilor called "mutual give and take."
For instance:

      Sometimes I feel that officers do not attend

to the councilor properly. My personal
observation is that to some extent in that
case our councilors are also responsible.
It depends on your behavior with the staff.
If you behave like a king and treat the
officers like a pupil, then cooperation is
less. For example, don't criticize them
in public--he cannot exchange words with
us, being a Corporation employee.

We [councilors] are to be blamed if the
officers are not working properly. It
depends on how you treat them--if you give
them due respect and don't ask them to do
illegal things.

At least two councilors mentioned methods of playing
the bureaucratic game:

If you know the [Corporation] Act, then you
can come to the officers and tell them "this
man has a right to this" or "you have a duty
to do that," and if some other councilor,
who can't quote the section, does the same,
then the officer thinks it is interference.

I take benefit from the disputes among
officers for promotions. I have made most
use of money [i.e., had more expenditures
sanctioned] of any councilor, because I have
a file of loopholes, for each department,
and I have sources [of information] in every
department.

And two councilors charged that some other councilors got cooperation from officers by going into
"partnership" with them:

If the officers are filling their own
pockets, okay. But they won't do things
on our say so. No officer will do it.
Of course, some councilors are partners

of the officers and get a small per-
centage--councilors of either party.
If their work is then done by the
officers, it's not on the say so of the
councilor, but on his partner's say so.

One other councilor said to me, "What
is this, why don't you ever come to the
officer?" He is slipping people something to get his work done.

It is clear that officers are forced to keep
their political fences mended, and at least one
councilor suggested that in return for cooperation,
he "fought for" his officers. One officer, respond-
ing to the question of "political interference in
administration" said, "The executive is also to
blame for interference: we go to the councilors
to get things done also." Many of the officers
have developed ties to important party leaders
(of both parties) with the idea of having someone
to go to if they should be "persecuted" by a less
important councilor. Officers can reply to the
threat of sanctions by demanding that (irregular)
orders be written down, or by referring the matter
to their superior. This "escalation" can occur on
both sides, if the councilor tries to bring pressure on the superior officer by working through
his party leaders. Officials at the highest levels
of the Corporation are largely immune to this kind
of party pressure, and if the officer succeeds in
getting the conflict resolved in that arena, his
chances of success are far better (but he also
runs the risk of antagonizing the councilor, who
will then "punish" him in some other matter,
perhaps). Officers also have recourse to the time-
honored technique of stonewalling--forcing the
councilor to ask repeatedly to get something done,
if he should remember to ask again at all.

Conflicts and Ties

The following diagrams, which set out a few
of the "paths" of administrative decision, may make
this clearer. Figs. 15a and 15b show cases in
which the councilor, having requested an action and
having it implemented (in the longer run in Fig.
15b) would presumably be satisfied. The councilor
might accept the denial of his request (Fig. 15c),
or he might proceed as shown in Fig. 15d or 15e,
and appeal the denial to a "leading councilor,"
usually of his own party, but perhaps of the
opposition, if it was the ruling party.

It is obvious that even within these diagrams
I have omitted arrows, particularly those showing
the conveyance of information. They are all sim-
plified to show a singular "administrative superior"
(there is, of course, a long chain of command), and
a singular "leading councilor" (which represents
the upper-level political structure, including
cross-party linkages).[10] Depending on his connections, the councilor might make a direct appeal
to the administrative superior, and so on. These
diagrams show some paths beginning with the initiative of the councilor, but similar diagrams could
be drawn showing an administrative decision as the
initiator of action.

Summary

The potential for conflict between elected
representatives and administrative officials exists
at every level of government in India, even if the
various factors of Civil Service Tradition vs.
Nationalist Critiques, of differential perceptions
of the boundary between policy and administration,
and other issues vary in importance. The tactics
pursued by the participants also are similar: one
finds the attempt of the administrator to insulate
himself from what he perceives as improper "political interference" by denying the legitimacy of
direct contact with elected representatives on

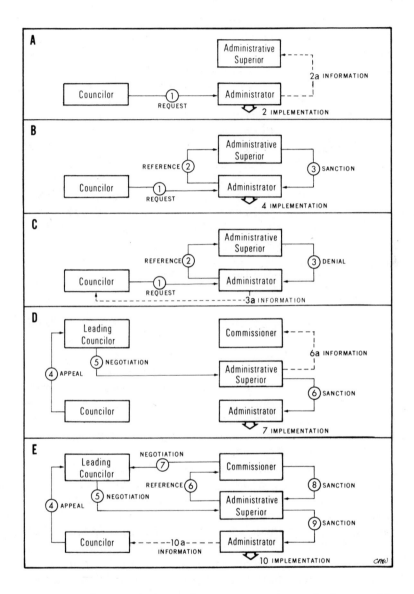

Fig. 15 Five possible patterns of Councilor-
Administrator interaction.

specific administrative issues, by insisting on
keeping his (written) responsibilities, by
"escalating" the problem upwards to his superiors
who are less susceptible to pressure. The politician on the other hand insists on his duty to
make an (enforceable) judgment as to whether an
administrator is making a decision in line with
some policy directive, and meets the administrators' "escalation" with an "escalation" of his own
to more powerful political leaders. In Delhi the
zonal system and the constituency fund make it
possible to extend the legitimate interface "down"
further into the polity than in other cities in
India (although not in the countryside, where the
system of panchayati raj has brought it to the
village level), but the contact and the conflict
is by no means peculiar to Delhi.

THE ZONAL SYSTEM OF DELHI--HISTORY AND RATIONALE

The councilor and administrator in Delhi operate, at the zonal level, in an arena which has a
history. Although the zonal system was inaugurated
in 1963, and although the boundaries of each zone--
i.e., which wards are to be included, and in how
many zones--are set each year by the Corporation
(see the discussion below, p. 214), the zones correspond roughly to the "natural" divisions of the
city, not only in geographic terms, but also in
socio-economic and historical ones. In a minute
appended to the report of the Delhi Municipal Organization Enquiry Committee of 1948, Sir Arthur Deans,
Mr. V. S. Mathur, and Mrs. Hannah Sen argue for a
two-tier authority for Delhi, with eight municipalities of around 200,000 people each and an indirectly elected city council which would deal with
water supply, electricity, education, and other
city-wide functions. Six of the eight proposed
municipalities correspond almost exactly to the
zones as they were originally set up; West Delhi
(at that time an unsettled area) and the rural areas

are not included, while the New Delhi Municipal
Committee area is.[11] One Municipal Committee--
Shahdara--already existed in 1948 (in addition
to the Delhi Municipal Committee, which in the
plan would be divided into four parts). The
South Delhi Municipal Committee was created in
1954 and the West Delhi Municipal Committee in
1955.[12] When these bodies and the five Notified
Area Committees of the area were merged into the
Delhi Municipal Corporation in 1957, they "continued to keep up their de facto existence as
zonal and sub-zonal offices of the Corporation."[13]
These zonal offices (and one which was established
later in Karol Bagh) performed limited functions--
collection of taxes, etc.--but most municipal
functions were centralized, including securing of
water connections, passing of building plans, etc.
Four years after its inception, in June 1962, the
Corporation appointed a distinguished committee
of its members to examine the possibilities of
decentralization, and within six months its report,
recommending the establishment of zones with
greatly increased functions and a committee of
councilors associated with it, had been approved.
The system went into operation a few months later.

As we shall see later, the major rationale for
decentralization into zones was one of "administrative efficiency" and "convenience to the public"
--a method to relieve the bottlenecks of Town Hall.
Today also similar "administrative" reasons are
seen as most important. Nevertheless, the "political" reasoning which argues that decentralization
is part and parcel of democracy is also present.
This is clear as early as the Delhi Municipal
Organization Enquiry Committee Report. The pro-
posers of the two-tier system argued:

What we want is a system which would have all
the advantages of a Corporation without its
defects. It is obviously desirable that the
administrative unit for subjects of common
concern should be large enough to enable the

service rendered to be efficient and econom-
ical. At the same time, it is also essential
that the common man should be able to exercise control in respect of local matters,
through his own representatives. The unit
should be of such a size as to permit true
democracy, rule not merely for but by the
people, a chance to assert itself.[14]

Their proposal differs from the zonal system later
adopted in that they saw the lower tier (the municipalities) as the basic one, on democratic grounds,
and the upper tier, the city council, as a matter
of administrative convenience. The zonal system
is a devolution of power from the Corporation, and,
invariably, the main reason given is one of administrative efficiency.[15]
    It is clear that the reasoning for a two-tier
system either formed from previously autonomous
units or by devolving powers from a larger unit, has
much in common with that for "metropolitan" governments the world over, and this appears in the literature dealing with "decentralization."[16] The Rural-
Urban Committee (whose three-volume report is a
benchmark of India's central government thinking on
municipal government) discusses metropolitan government in Toronto and Tokyo immediately after its
"need for decentralization in larger cities"
section.[17] But aside from the Calcutta region,
there are few areas in India for which a "metropolitan" government has been suggested. The two-
tier system has been usually discussed as being
effected by the devolution of power.[18]
    B. D. Sanwal, Commissioner of Agra Division of
the State of Uttar Pradesh, writing in 1958 on
citizen participation in municipal government,
argues for the creation of "blocks" similar to rural
community development blocks (with a population of
10,000) with each block having an elected committee
and a chief executive who "should have more or less
the same relationship with the block sub-committee
as the Municipal Commissioner has with the Standing

Committee."[19] After noting systems of decentralization in India and abroad, the Rural-Urban Relationship Committee made the following recommendations:

> The committee recommend that the Corporations
> and the larger cities with a population of 5
> lakhs [500,000] and over should be divided
> into a number of circles or zones so that
> each circle or zone covers on an average a
> population ranging from 50,000 to 200,000
> according to the population of the city.
> Each circle or zone should be further divided
> into 5 to 10 wards, each one of which elect
> one or two members for the Corporation Council.
> The councilors belonging to a particular
> circle/zone shall constitute the Circle/Zonal
> Committee. The Zonal or Circle Committee
> should maintain its own zonal office with
> separate administrative and technical staff
> and get allocation of sufficient funds from
> the City Council to meet the cost of local
> works. . . . The Committee feel confident
> that such decentralization effected through
> the Functional and Zonal Committees would
> improve the implementation of local works and
> bring the local people closer to the Municipal
> administration.[20]

This recommendation is essentially a summation of
the system current (in 1966) in Delhi and Madras.
Mohit Bhattacharya adds Calcutta to the list of
Corporations which have similar patterns of decentralization, and notes further that Bombay and
Hyderabad have set up "local area offices" (similar
to the Delhi "zonal" offices before 1962).[21]
     To return to Delhi. A Municipal Commissioner
of Delhi, K. L. Rathee, wrote in his introduction to
a report on the zonal system: "The primary and most
important idea under-lying decentralization was to
take the civic administration as close to the
citizen as possible--indeed to their very door-
steps."[22] In describing the functions of the Zonal

Assistant Commissioner, who was to be the administrative head of the government in the zone, the
committee whose report resulted in the establishment of the zonal system note:

> The first and foremost responsibility of
> the Assistant Commissioner shall be to
> ensure clean and efficient administration
> in the zone and to see that no officer or
> other employee attached to the Zonal Office
> indulges in any sort of corrupt practice
> or is discourteous to members of the
> Corporation or the public.[23]

One concern here is with an efficient administrator
responsive to its political authority: for "is
discourteous to members of the Corporation" we can
probably read "does not display due regard to the
wishes of the Corporation" or perhaps the stronger
"refuses to carry out the legitimate demands of the
members of the Corporation." The two themes of decentralization occur again--efficiency in administration and a logical extension of democracy. These
themes came up again and again in the seminar on
decentralization sponsored by the Corporation in
March 1969 and in the interviews I conducted with
councilors and administrators in the zone. Before
moving to the routine but necessary task of reporting the functions, powers, etc. of the zone, I would
like therefore to present the results of these
interviews as they relate to the zonal system
itself.

"The Administrator must make it his creed to
serve the public without appearing to govern."[24]
This delightfully ambiguous statement represents
the core of the ambivalent attitude of the administrator. The system's transition (although most of
the officers are young, they are well socialized)
from a service of the state to an organization of
"public servants" is summed up in this view that
the administrator must govern--and governing is the
province of the expert--while appearing to be

responsive to the demands of the public. For the
administrator, the zonal system has meant that
"legitimate" contact with the public and the councilor has become more frequent and more direct:
not only are there weekly zonal committee meetings
during which officers answer councilors' questions
and (often) accusations, but also meeting the
public--officers are required to keep regular
visiting hours--means meeting the councilor as
the public's representative. I suspect that before
the zonal system was instituted, and the officers
sat in Town Hall, a councilor would contact those
officers connected with his ward directly, instead
of going through the chain of command (councilor--
Standing Committee--Commissioner--subordinate
officer--concerned officer) but probably he could
not do so with the ease and regularity (and justi-
fication) that he can when the officers sit in a
separate, convenient building, with a duty to meet
the public spelled out. In the zonal system the
officer is less insulated; i.e., he is more exposed
and accessible.

 There was no specific question in my interview
which dealt with "decentralization" as such, but
the subject did arise. Attitudes toward the system
emerged to a certain extent in the responses by
officers to the question "Some people say that
there is no need for democracy at the municipal
level; that administration doesn't function well
because of political interference. What is your
opinion?" Four of the 14 officers interviewed
agreed emphatically with this; two disagreed; two
said decentralization was good administratively;
three were ambivalent ("If it worked well, democracy
would be good thing") and three didn't answer.
Officers who agreed with what "some people say"
tended to do so because of the part on councilor
interference ("interference" for all officers was
"wrong") and those who disagreed or were ambivalent
were those who had less contact with councilors.
No one volunteered anything favorable about the
role of councilors in the zone, but when I pressed

them--or presented a devil's advocate argument--
a few agreed that the councilor can be useful as
a link to the people. Four officers said specifically that decentralization was a good thing
administratively: one said some red tape had been
eliminated; another noted that teachers now get
paid on time; a third said that decentralization
is good because people are spared the trouble of
going to Town Hall "from Mehrauli" (i.e., from far
away); and one was particularly emphatic: "Decentralization is a very good thing, although the
people at the center [Town Hall] don't like losing
their power. I have seen the Delhi Municipal Committee [pre-1958] as well as the Corporation before
1963 and after decentralization. This is the
better system."

The administrators' attitude toward the system
is obviously tied up with how he has found it to
work. Few of the officers had had experience of
the pre-1963 system, and so had no standard of comparison. Minimally it can be said that they accepted the system as a matter of administrative
convenience (although in practice there is still
considerable centralization), but were ambivalent
or hostile to easier political access to administration. One said that councilors should confine
themselves to policy making in the Standing Committee and in the Corporation (meeting as a whole),
that councilors could convey complaints privately
and that there was no need to have a zonal committee
meeting for that purpose. But certainly there is
also the negative evidence that no administrator
complained about the system as such, although some,
in the descriptions of the lines of command, etc.,
made it clear that they considered themselves not
so much as "zonal officers" as "ambassadors" of
their Town Hall department; an officer sees himself
as an engineer of the electricity department posted
in the zone, not an engineer of the zone concerned
with electricity.

The 18 councilors of the City Zone were
unanimous in supporting the zonal system (the

question I asked was: "How well is the zonal
system working?"), and only one (who was the one
councilor who missed a large number of zonal committee meetings) felt that in practice it had
become weak:

> It is not efficient nowadays, because of
> too much centralization, which leaders of
> the Jana Sangh want: they don't permit the
> zones to work effectively and independently.
> The zones now come to be simple payment
> offices. The zonal committee meetings are
> simply futile--either scrap the useless
> discussion or the zonal discussion should
> be given due weight.

Those who criticized the system as practiced agreed
that the committee needs more powers, not less:
"works [i.e., the operations of the Corporation]
have been decentralized, but not the powers, as
they should be." Half of the 18 councilors felt
that the zonal committee should be given more
power (a separate budget, a Zonal Assistant Commissioner of higher status and greater administrative discretion, etc.); two said explicitly that
the committee had enough power, and the remaining
seven simply expressed satisfaction with the working
of the system. Eleven councilors pointed out that
the zonal system made things easier for the citizen
(one said, "for the councilor also") but none
mentioned that the zonal system improved administrative efficiency, although that could be implied
from some remarks.
      Councilors, then, with different grounds for
their authority, responsibilities and a different
sense of accountability, have a positive attitude
toward the zonal system in its entirety, while
some administrators have reservations about the
"political" half. Needless to say, these attitudes
are related to the way in which each group "works"
the system: the administrator is responsive to the
councilor yet tries to preserve his freedom of

action by recourse to his technical judgment, and
the decisions of his superiors in Town Hall, and
the councilor tries to expand the powers of the
committee and thus his influences over administrative matters, particularly those which relate
directly to the voters and interests of his ward.

The Structure of the Zone

I have suggested above, and by implication in
Chapter 5, that the City Zone is to some extent a
unit with "natural" boundaries. However, the City
Zone and the other zones are technically only ad hoc
committees of the Corporation, and are thus formally
reconstituted at the beginning of each year; the
zonal system is not part of the Corporation Act.
Most of my informants agreed that zonal boundaries
are adjusted (one or two wards added or subtracted)
on "political" grounds, to ensure that the ruling
party of the Corporation (in 1969-70, the Jana Sangh)
can elect as many chairmen and deputy chairmen of
zones as possible. The six aldermen are assigned
to particular zones by the mayor, and the assignments are made to insure the same "political"
result. Thus in 1969-70, the Jana Sangh, with 57
members of the 106-member Corporation, elected
Jana Sangh chairmen in six of the eight zones.
In 1970-71, the Jana Sangh's strength had been
reduced to parity with the opposition in two of the
zones where it had won the chairmanship before, but
by shifting two aldermen and altering the composition of one zone, the Jana Sangh did not lose
the chairmanship of those two zones and retained
control of the other four zones it had held. Once
this election has been held, however, party activity
and party-determined decisions seem to disappear
from the zonal committee, as we shall see.
The zone has two "wings"; the administrative
wing is presided over by the Zonal Assistant Commissioner and includes about 15 class II officers.[25]
In the City Zone there are nine engineers: four

for works, one each for water, electricity,
drainage, buildings, and dangerous buildings.
Other officers include an Assistant Education
Officer, the Zonal Health Officer, and Assistant
Assessor and Collector, an Assistant Superin-
tendent of Gardens, and a Zonal Superintendent
(who is in charge of matters such as issuing
licenses to hawkers and maintaining records),
a Senior School Inspector, and an Assistant
Chief Accountant. The Zonal Engineer (Dangerous
Buildings) exists only in the City Zone, where
buildings frequently collapse during the monsoon
rains. Other zones may have an Assistant Public
Relations Officer, an Assistant Labor Welfare
Officer, or, in one instance, an Assistant
Engineer (Planning). The 1969-70 Members' Guide
of the Corporation--not very reliable, unfor-
tunately--lists some 111 officers in the eight
zones (an average of 14 each). Most of these
officers has a staff under him, varying from a
handful of skilled electricians, for example, to
hundreds of sweepers under the Zonal Health
Officer.

The job of most of these officers is evident
from their titles: the Assistant Assessor and
Collector ("assistant" because of his relation to
the Town Hall department) assesses property values
and collects the consequent taxes; the Assistant
Education Officer supervises all the schools of
the zone, and so on. The duties of the various
engineers may be less obvious. The Zonal Engineer
(Buildings) sanctions plans for building repair
and construction and is responsible for demolishing
unauthorized constructions. The Zonal Engineer
(Works), is responsible for four or five wards,
supervises construction and repair of Corporation
buildings, roads, and other works projects (a
garden fence, a drainage tank). Some of the works
are done "departmentally" by the staff, consisting
of a section officer (per ward) who is a graduate
(B.E.) or diploma holder in engineering and ten or
so "permanent labor" (i.e., workers) and up to one

hundred "temporary labor" per ward. Or the work
is let out on contract, in which case the zonal
engineer posts the terms of the contract, accepts
the bids, and supervises the work. Construction
work, health care, education, etc., are on the
whole carried out, if not with the highest efficiency, at least with energy, if my impressions
are accurate. That is, when a job was being done--
at least a visible one like road repair--it was
done with dispatch, and indeed both councilors and
administrators seemed satisfied with the quality
and pace of work performed. We can take the
"routine" performance of work as a given, then,
and proceed to an analysis of how the work situation
is structured, administratively and politically.

All the officers considered themselves in
some degree "technical" men, whose supervisors had
offices in Town Hall or somewhere else outside the
zone. When I asked "Who is your supervisor?"--
they almost invariably answered "In technical
matters it is X and in administrative matters the
ZAC (Zonal Assistant Commissioner)," adding however that they had very little to do with the ZAC,
who was considered to be a "glorified clerk." In
my probing I tried to discover whether there were
any disputes between the ZAC and the "technical"
superiors, at least over which matters could be
considered "technical" and which "administrative,"
but apparently these do not occur. No officer
mentioned an instance. My impression was that
officers considered their technical superiors their
"real" superiors (who could deal with matters such
as the payroll, sanctioning of the hiring of temporary workers, etc., as well as purely technical
advice) and that the ZAC, although he had to be
deferred to, had little relation to them. One
engineer said that the ZAC is in there in name
only--he has little to do. The position of the
non-engineer class II officers is much the same.

The other "wing" of the zone is the "political"
one--the zonal committee of all the councilors of
the wards of the zone. This body elects a chairman

(who typically has a separate office) and a deputy
chairman; it meets in a special chamber once a
week for two or more hours, passing resolutions
(and keeping minutes). The members are often to
be found at the zonal office dealing with administration officers; a councilor may call an officer
to him (in the chairman's office, frequently) or
go to the administrator's office.

The powers of the committee are limited in
their formal formulation; the main one is "to
sanction estimates and plans for works to be
carried out in the zone . . . up to Rs 50,000
provided that specific provision exists in the
budget sanctioned by the Corporation."[26] Other
powers are essentially those of enquiry into administration: the councilors of the committee are
"to consider . . . and make recommendations" on
matters ranging from "quarterly progress collection
statements of revenue"[27] to virtually all the works
functions (street paving and repair, drainage,
street lighting, dispensaries, etc.), which are the
obligatory duties of the Corporation and many of
the discretionary functions as well.[28]

The phrase "to consider" suggests that the committee is comparatively powerless, limited to
reacting to what the Zonal Assistant Commissioner
presents to it and having final decisions on few
matters. The ZAC does have considerable powers, not
the least of which is the power to delay implementation of a committee decision. For instance, on
being presented with a report of the ZAC indicating
that the Standing Committee had decided that certain
bicycle stands should not be sanctioned (there are
parking lots for bicycles where one pays a fee [ten
paise] for keeping one's cycle; parking elsewhere is
frequently illegal) but instead used as sites for
"rehabilitating" rehriwalas (pushcart peddlars), the
committee, apparently,* disregarding the ZAC's

---

*"Apparently" because my data comes only from
the minutes of the meeting; the ZAC may have had additional (and contradictory) verbal instructions.

advice to auction the site on a monthly basis
until a rehabilitation scheme could be finalized,
directed that a certain site not be auctioned
after January 30, 1970. Two months later, the
committee reversed itself in that it agreed to
the monthly auctions (two of which had already
taken place, the first three days after its
earlier resolution, which was adopted on January
24, 1970), and "resolved further that the ZAC be
asked to allot the site to the rehriwalas as
soon as possible." The ZAC told me in an interview that he had to have the site auctioned
because if it had been left vacant, it would
have been encroached upon (and thus been difficult to clear) and that he had submitted a
minute to the Commissioner to have the decision
of the Standing Committee changed. A senior
colleague of the ZAC with whom I discussed the
matter said "we have to do it; think of how
much revenue the Corporation would lose."

      Or take another instance. An ex-ZAC, in
discussing the regular reports (of each department) that the ZAC is supposed to submit to the
committee (I had noticed that few were in fact
submitted to the City Zone committee), said,
"When I was ZAC there had been no reports for
four years; nor did I get any submitted even
after the matter was raised in the committee."
These are the most direct cases of ZAC resist-
ance to committee decisions that I encountered.
They were possible because of the ZAC's formal
role: he, like the Municipal Commissioner, has
the executive power, and the committee can only
"consider" and not decide. But looking at the
formal structure (function and powers) of the
zonal committee does an injustice to the institution as it operates in practice; it is to
this that I will now turn.

The Zonal Committee in Operation

Meetings

There is no question that the weekly committee meetings are taken seriously by councilors, if attendance figures are any guide.[29] (See Table 27.) The median attendance percentage for the Zone (putting the two parts together in 1967 and 1968) is 80 percent over three years. All the councilors except one ("P," with an attendance of 46 percent over three years) felt that the committee meetings were useful and that there was no "politics" in them—i.e., little in the way of partisan debate and action.

In the minutes I examined there were one or two votes taken each year, at most, and this is probably typical of other zones as well. Since there is a "party whip" system in operation in the Corporation, it may be that votes are seen as useless because there is no uncertainty of the result. But there are numerous zonal committee meetings in which the opposition could vote down the majority party, since all members are present usually at the first meeting of the year only. On the other hand, roll call votes in the Corporation are relatively frequent, even though the ruling party wins them all. The zonal committee meetings differ from the Corporation meetings also in that the former are not characterized by disruptions and heated arguments, walk-outs and name-calling, as are the Corporation meetings (see Chapter 8, below). One reason for this quiet may be that the zonal committee meetings are not open to the public and the press; the councilor need not concern himself with the votes he might receive or lose because of his position on an issue.

Resolutions

I was able to examine eight sets of zonal committee minutes—these mainly report the resolutions adopted—for three committees: the City North Zone of 1963-64, 64-65, 65-66, 66-67, and

TABLE 27

ATTENDANCE IN THE CITY ZONE

Councilor	City South Zone 1967-68		City North Zone 1967-68		City Zone[a] 1968-69		City Zone[a] 1969-70		Three-Year Mean (%)
	Mtgs.	%	Mtgs.	%	Mtgs.	%	Mtgs.	%	
Totals	26	100	26	100	33	100	41	100	
A	24	92			21	64	35	85	80
B	25	96			29	88	35	85	89
C	19	73			26	79	34	83	79
D	24	92			29	88	31	76	84
E	26	100			31	94	39	95	96
F	11	42			11	33	30	73	52
G/H[b]	15	58					32	78	
I	26	100			32	97	38	93	96
J	24	92			26	79	38	93	88
K	25	96			24	73	29	71	78
L[c,d]	1								
M[d]	23	88							
N			22	85	32	97	39	95	93
O			23	88	32	97	23	56	78
P			17	65	12	36	17	41	46
Q			21	81	30	91	38	93	89
R			24	92	30	91	39	95	93
S			22	85	32	97	41	100	95
T			21	81	29	88	37	90	87
U			23	88	30	91	38	93	91
V[d]			20	77					
W[d]			23	88					

[a]The City Zone "brought together" the two halves of the walled city (minus the two northern wards), but the reason for this may have been in part "political" (see above, p. 214).

[b]G died midway in term; H won the by-election.

[c]The mayor; he is disregarded in the calculation of the median.

[d]Councilors whose wards were not included in the new City Zone.

67-68; the City South Zone of 1967-68, and the
City Zone of 1968-69 and 69-70. The average
number of resolutions considered in these eight
"committee-years" was approximately 150, with a
range of 93 to 212. In addition, as we shall
see in the discussion of the 1969-70 City Zone
committee minutes, there were many meetings in
which general discussion took place, without a
resolution being under consideration.

Perhaps the most frequent resolution was
one sanctioning money for street repairs--these
were probably large projects financed out of the
councilors' constituency funds, and passed, I
would guess, with little debate. Over the years,
the number of resolutions dealing with water
supply and street lighting declined, suggesting
that these were first-priority projects. Indeed,
by mid-1970, when I left Delhi, well over half
the streets of the City Zone, I would estimate,
were lit by improved street lighting. Councilors
I interviewed talked about complete coverage of
their wards with new lighting within the year.

Other resolutions--less than 10 a year,
usually--dealt with matters like the construction
of markets, the improvement of parks, the reno-
vation and repair of Corporation offices, repairs
to hospitals, repairs and equipment for schools,
etc. A few more resolutions--10 to 20--dealt
with sanitation (typically, sanctioning expenditure for a sewer line, or a dalao). And a fairly
large number (on the order of 25) were concerned
with setting "policy." The subject tended to
vary from year to year: one year there were tens
of resolutions proposing the closing of streets
to heavy vehicular traffic; the next year saw a
spurt in the number of resolutions proposing
name-changes for streets; and so on. There were
several resolutions each year on matters like
licensing policy. Many of these "policy" resolutions must have sparked considerable debate.

This quick summary of the resolutions considered by the zonal committee is mainly indicative

of the amount of work it does rather than the
exact shape of its concerns. A little more can
be said by examining the minutes of one year in
detail; I chose the year 1969-70. No year is of
course "typical" (the proximity of an election
would be an influence, for example), but 1969-70
is at least not unusual. In the first meeting,
which took place on May 14, 1969, the only
business was the election of a chairman and a
deputy chairman (Resolutions 1 and 2). The last
(and forty-first) meeting of the year took place
on April 4, 1970. A total of 193 resolutions
were considered, plus other business (since three
numbers were missed, and one resolution was withdrawn before consideration, the last resolution
was numbered 197). The forty-one meetings were
spread fairly evenly throughout the year (Table
28). Meetings are ordinarily scheduled for the
first, third, fourth, and fifth week of the month.
Eighteen of the meetings were devoted in whole or
in part to general discussions of various subjects
(see Table 29). The Deputy Commissioners are the
"generalist" heads of the various departments.
In addition to the Deputy Commissioners present,
there were only three men who were not the (technical) head of a Corporation department, and two
of those (the Executive Engineer, Slums, and the
Deputy Municipal Engineer) were the senior subordinates. The range of subjects covered is a
broad one and reflects, in the number of repetitions, the concerns of the councilor: sanitation,
taxation, licensing, and the budget.

    Although there were 193 resolutions con-
sidered (only two of these were rejected) during
the year, some were purely formal, and others
repetitious. In the first type there were four
resolutions expressing condolences on the death
of a prominent public figure of the relative of
a councilor. Repetitions are those pairs of resolutions which, typically, ask the ZAC to report on
a proposition and then the acceptance (usually) of
his report. These are resolutions dealing with

the closing of streets to heavy vehicular traffic,
for instance, which have to be submitted to the
Superintendent of Police for Traffic, as well as
items which need expenditure estimates prepared.
There were 24 pairs of these resolutions submitted
to the ZAC and then reported on. The mean time
between each pair's submission and adoption was 13
weeks, and the time ranged from one week (the next
shortest gap being four weeks) to 26 weeks; the
median was 12.5 weeks. There were 32 resolutions
not yet reported on by the end of the committee's
term. On October 4, 1969 (i.e., some six months
into the year) the ZAC reported that there were 12
resolutions still pending from the previous year
(1968-69); four of these were disposed of later on
in 1969-70. One can safely assume that some of
those resolutions will be kept pending forever.[30]

TABLE 28

MEETINGS OF THE CITY ZONE COMMITTEE, 1969-70

Year	Month	Week (numbers are the dates)				
		One	Two	Three	Four	Five
1969	May			14 17		31
	June	5				
	July			19	26	
	August	2	8	16	20 23	30
	September		12	16 20	27	
	October	4		15 18	25	31
	November	1		15	21	28 29
	December	6		20	26	
1970	January	3	6 7	17	19 24	
	February		13			
	March			21	27 28	
	April	4				

TABLE 29

GENERAL DISCUSSIONS, CITY ZONE, 1969-70

Date	Subject	Senior Officers Present
5/31/69	Factory licensing department	Deputy Commissioner
6/ 5/69	Licensing (hawkers et al.)	Deputy Commissioner
7/26/69	Slum department	Executive Engineer, Slums
8/8 /69[a]	Sanitary condition of the zone	Municipal Health Officer
8/20/69[a]	Engineering works in the zone	Deputy Municipal Engineer
9/16/69[a]	Education department	Deputy Commissioner (Education); Education Officer
10/15/69[a]	Sanitation drive	Municipal Health Officer
10/31/69[a]	Taxation	Assessor and Collector; Terminal Tax Officer
11/28/69[a]	Sanitation drive	Municipal Health Officer
12/20/69	Drainage department; street lighting	Supt. Engineer, Drainage, DWSSDU[b]; Assistant Engineer, DESU[c]
12/26/69[a]	Gardens department	Deputy Commissioner; Supt. Gardens
1/ 6/70[a]	Budget	None
1/ 7/70[a]	Budget	None
1/19/70[a]	Budget	None
1/17/70	Factory licensing department	Deputy Commissioner; Licensing Officer (Factories)
1/24/70	Sweepers' strike	None
2/13/70	Community Services Department	Director, Community Services Department
3/27/70[a]	Taxation (property tax)	Assessor and Collector

[a]Entire meeting devoted to the subject.

[b]Delhi Water Supply and Sewage Disposal Undertaking.

[c]Delhi Electric Supply Undertaking.

Of the 197 "cases"[*] (which is how the resolution is proposed) 122, or 62 percent, were
disposed of by the committee. These were the
sanctioning of estimates, the "formal" resolutions,
etc. Thirty-two (16 percent) were pending as ZAC
reports and twenty (10 percent) were resolutions
that either required the approval of statutory
committees of the Corporation (for permission to
close streets to heavy vehicular traffic, for
example) or were other references of the "cases"
to a superior authority. The summary of these
types of resolutions is given in Table 30. This
table needs to be explained, but a further compli-
cation must be dealt with first. There were eight
resolutions which consisted of a decision of some
kind plus an order to the ZAC to "report further"
or to prepare related reports on other subjects, or

TABLE 30

CITY ZONE RESOLUTIONS, 1969-70, BY TYPE

Type	N	Percentage
"Formal"	4	2
Estimates sanctioned		
Constituency fund (estimate)	14	7
Other	41	21
Submitted to superior authority	20	10
Various final decisions	28	14
Recording of reports, etc.	35	18
To ZAC for report	49	25
Unclassifiable and missing numbers	6	3
Total	197	100

[*] I am including the missing numbers and the
withdrawn resolution since perhaps what was missed
was the recording of the resolution in the minutes.

other further actions. Three of these "additional"
resolutions (i.e., the second part of the resolution
could stand on its own as a separate resolution)
were requests to superior authorities; for example,
resolution 90 of September 27, 1969, resolved that
the information in the ZAC's letter regarding the
provisions of a cycle stand near Gauri Shankar
Temple "be recorded" and resolved that (as an
alternative to the Gauri Shankar Temple site,
which had not been approved) the Commissioner be
requested to earmark part of the parking sites on
the south side of Lajpat Rai Market for a free
cycle stand.* I decided to count the final decision
in these cases for the tabulation of Table 30, and
to disregard, for the moment, the "additional"
resolutions.

It has been pointed out above (p. 217) that
the main power of the zonal committee is to sanction estimates for works to be carried out in the
zone. The category is further divided into those
resolutions which deal with the constituency fund
and "other."[31] The estimates can be roughly
classified as shown in Table 31. Constituency fund
expenditure would also be found, I assume, in the
"general road repair" and "new works" categories.
Note that only ten wards are covered in the "constituency fund" category; that is, only ten councilors suggested works of a magnitude (over Rs.
10,000), which necessitated sanctioning by the
committee. It is safe to assume that all the
councilors used up their fund (this would total
Rs. 900,000 for the zone), and what appears here
(Rs. 314,640, or roughly one-third) simply indicates
that most constituency fund expenditures are in

---

*I had neither the time (nor the inclination)
to copy each resolution verbatim, since they are
full of reference numbers and stilted language; I
did copy all relevant information, retaining whole
phrases (as in this example) or significant quotations (which will be set off with quotation marks).

TABLE 31

"ESTIMATES SANCTIONED" RESOLUTIONS, CITY ZONE, 1969-70

Category		Amount (Rs.)
Constituency Fund (ten wards only)		314,640
General road repair and improvement		267,648
Annual repair and maintenance (buildings). .		107,715
Special repairs (buildings).		147,745
Alterations (buildings).		111,220
New works		
in parks.	95,215	
schools	91,220	
other	107,157	
Subtotal for new works		293,592
Grand Total		1,242,560

small amounts which don't need the committee's
sanction. I suspect that many of the "estimates
sanctioned" resolutions passed without much
discussion. But others did generate debate:
resolution 183 (of March 28, 1970) sanctioned the
revised estimates of Rs. 24,695 for the repair of
the electric crematorium furnace; and resolved
further that the ZAC be asked to put up in the
next meeting a report regarding the number of
bodies cremated daily during the current year and
the income received from this source. And, in
another instance, on November 15, 1969, the committee rejected the ZAC's proposal that the
intersection of Chandni Chowk with Nai Sarak be
"improved" (an estimate had been framed in line
with the scheme of the beautification of Chandni
Chowk approved by the Standing Committee) "since
the point of view of the committee is that a
clocktower should be built on that spot."[32]
But on January 3, 1970, they sanctioned Rs. 43,200
for the improvements. One can assume that there
was some debate when the ZAC's proposal was

réjected initially, and at the time when the committee reversed itself and approved it.

The general road repair and improvement category covers work on the main arteries of the city.
The annual repair and maintenance (of buildings)--
and again it should be noted that only estimates
of Rs. 10,000 and above have to be sanctioned by
the committee--is straightforward: the largest
amount is for Town Hall, then the Victoria Zenana
[women's] Hospital. These two buildings account
for much of the "alterations" category. Similarly,
few of the "new works" are in any way out of the
ordinary. These might include a new dalao (garbage/
night soil collection structure) or the fence
around a park or whatever.

The amount of money expended on "works"--
construction jobs--is significant for the administrative officer because he gets a "commission" on
it, and so the sanctioning of some expenditure
items undoubtedly has some "partisan" significance.
Works done within a given ward are usually done
under the supervision of the section officer of that
ward and his superior zonal engineer. The supervision of the repair and improvement of the large
roads (which are often boundary lines between wards)
is assigned to various officers. According to one
of my informants, assignments in the "non-Shahja-
hanabad" wards of the zone--where few people live
but where there are many roads--are coveted, because
the section officer and other officers get a 1.5-2.0
percent commission on the value of the contract.
If we take an expenditure of Rs. 25,000, which is
not unusual, there would be a commission of Rs. 500,
which might be divided as follows: Rs. 250 to the
section officer; Rs. 125 to his zonal engineer (who
gets a "cut" from the four or five section officers
he supervises); and Rs. 125 to the accountants who
process the payment to the contractor. These payments are not insignificant; they may be as much as
a month's salary.[33]

This commission means that the administrator,
and the section officer in particular, would like

to avoid antagonizing the councilor, since the
councilor could have him transferred out of his
"lucrative" ward, or denied the supervision of
the large road and other "at large" contracts.
These "at large" contracts are let by the zonal
committee, and the distribution of the supervisory duties (and the commission that goes with
it) would depend, at least in part, on political
bargaining within the zonal committee: the chairman might, for instance, get the contract supervision assigned to the section officer of his
ward. It is generally agreed that the powerful
councilors of the ruling party can get these
larger projects for their wards--the main artery
which borders their ward would get repaved first,
for example. Working "under" these councilors
would get an officer more money, but would mean
a loss of independent action.

Returning to Table 30 (the summary of
resolutions, p. 225), the category "various final
decisions" includes resolutions ranging from
procedural (the election of the chairman, for
example) to the declaration of certain streets
as public (usually on petition from the inhabitants, who want the extension of municipal
services, notably lighting and sanitation, to
their area) to the resolution approving the budget
estimates. The only recorded vote--aside from the
election of the chairman and deputy chairman--took
place on a resolution in this category: one
member wanted a road renamed, and his resolution
was defeated. There were, however, a number of
resolutions rejecting proposals of the ZAC, some
of which were later reversed (as in the clocktower
case). A few resolutions specified goods and
services to be provided (earthenware pitchers in
the schools, additional telephone lines for the
zonal office, etc.); others dealt with the application of general policy to a specific case, and a
few were more general policy decisions:

No. 145. "This meeting of the . . .

committee feels highly satisfied on the new
explanations and provisions introduced in
the building by-laws . . ." [and resolves]
that technical staff be appointed immediately
in the building department and all the
pending cases be disposed of immediately.

No. 150. [Resolved] that the Zonal Health
officer should supervise sanitation work in
latrines and urinals of schools. [Explana-
tion]: although he should now be doing it,
it is being done by the head of the
institutions.

I imagine that some of these "final decisions" are
routine and are approved without discussion, while
it is clear that others may take a considerable time
to resolve.
    Resolutions in the category "recording of
reports" read "resolved that the ZAC report concerning X be recorded"; in some instances, further
action--usually another report--was demanded in
addition. These "cases" vary in type also. Some
are routine reports (the number of complaints from
the public received in months A, B, etc.); others
are simple (lists of municipal properties declared
"dangerous," for example); some "cases" are general
reports (on water supply in the zone); still others
are reports on specific projects.
    The question of how routine the routine reports
are is an interesting one. Five weekly reports on
well-cleaning were recorded, as well as two months
of statements of complaints, one (monthly) report of
the building department and one "monthly progress
report" of the health department. I discovered that
there were indeed forms on which every department
was to submit regular reports, but none of these
did so unless a specific request was made, and sometimes not even then. And this is despite the statutory functions of the zonal committee, which
consists largely of "considering" progress reports
(some monthly but most quarterly) on "the working

of the licensing department," the maintenance of
water supply installations, etc. Officers with
whom I spoke seemed to feel that writing so many
reports would be a waste of time, and no councilor (when asked, "How well is the zonal system
working?") mentioned the lack of regular reporting.
Forty-nine "cases," 25 percent of those
considered, were referred to the ZAC for report.
As noted above, 32 of these were still pending when
the committee ended its 1969-70 term. These 49
"cases" can be further broken down as shown in
Table 32. The following are sample resolutions
for each category identified in the table:

   1.--No. 17. "resolved, that the gali . . .
      inside Kucha Khan Chand, Nai Sarak,
      be acquired and civic amenities be
      provided."

   2.--No. 131. proposing the introduction
      of flush system latrines in the Chandni
      Chowk area [the Corporation would con-
      struct them and recover the cost from
      the landlords through the house tax].

      No. 83. to provide for a labor room
      in the Aryuvedic Hospital, Ballimaran.

   3.--No. 173. on the installation of a
      statue of Smt. Kamala Nehru in Queen's
      Garden.

   4.--No. 88. case concerning construction
      of the underground dalao near Bagh Diwar,
      Queen's Garden, be "referred back to the
      ZAC for examination of the following
      points. . . ."

These resolutions cover virtually all the subjects
with which the committee deals. That there is a
large number of reports--which are very detailed, I
might add--suggests that the committee is able to

TABLE 32

"CASES" "TO ZAC FOR REPORT," CITY ZONE, 1969-70

Category	Subject	N
1.	Closing of streets to heavy vehicular traffic, and declaring streets public	9
2.	"Betterment" proposals	22
3.	"Ornamentation".	5
4.	Further reports[a]	13
	Total	49

[a]There were an additional five resolutions which had as a second part the referral of a matter to the ZAC for report; e.g., No. 77: resolved that the information in the ZAC's letter regarding replacement of small water mains in Charkhewalan constituency be recorded and that reports be prepared for other constituencies also.

make informed decisions on the entire range of subjects it deals with. The facts are certainly made available.

There were 18 cases in which the ZAC was asked to make a further report, and a number of these had specific instructions attached:

No. 176: resolved that the case concerning the provision of a cycle stand at the Zonal Office be referred back to the ZAC for marking the specific site and resolved that the policy of the Standing Committee regarding auction be followed.

There were a number of similarly worded resolutions suggesting a directive to the ZAC, and one or two included a deadline for submitting the report (which was in fact disregarded).

Finally (referring again to Table 30, p. 225, above), there are the resolutions which refer cases to superior authorities in the Corporation. These

were: the Works Committee (9 cases), Standing
Committee (5 cases), the Delhi Development
Authority (1 case), the Chairman of the Committee
(1 case), and Commissioner (1 case). The Works
Committee has jurisdiction over closing streets
to heavy vehicular traffic and these resolutions
were submitted for "approval" as was one resolution referred to the Water Supply Sewage
Disposal Committee. Other resolutions "recommend"
action. Still others informed the superior
authority of the committee's feeling on a given
matter (on a zonal development plan, for example).
And lastly, there were one or two "requests."
Again, it is clear from the text of the resolution
that in many of these cases there was considerable
discussion in the committee, and in a few instances
there was an effort to have policy already set by
the superior authorities altered. There were no
votes on these resolutions--the committee was
apparently acting together in these few cases, the
Jana Sangh members of the committee joining in
the challenge of the policy of a Corporation committee controlled by party superiors.[34]

SUMMARY AND CONCLUSIONS

There is no question that the zonal committee
is an active political institution in Delhi. The
evidence of its smooth functioning lies in the
attention councilors pay to it with hardly a "partisan" stir, in the replies to my questions on how
well it worked by councilors and administrators
alike, and in my observations of the day-to-day
operations of the Municipal Corporation in the City
Zone. At least in 1969-70, as far as I could tell,
the "politics" of the zone took up less time and
energy of the councilor than the affairs of the
zonal committee; I shall return to this subject in
the next chapter. The committee considers the
subjects which, as we have seen in the discussion
of the Kucha Khirkiwala data, are of particular

concern to the councilor in his ward. Indeed, the
system of zonal decentralization, which permits
the councilor, or the councilors acting together,
a legitimate and close supervisory role vis-à-vis
the administrative "wing," coupled with the use
of the constituency fund, allows the councilor to
"service" his ward well, and, not incidentally,
"nurse" his constituency.

In most states of India, the power over
municipal administration is delegated to local
elected bodies, but with close control by the
state government. Municipal government in India
has been seen primarily as a device to enhance the
effectiveness of local administration, by involving
local citizens in the decisions that affect them.[35]
Municipal government was not developed because a
system of democratic representation was somehow
"natural" for all governmental arenas. The zonal
system in Delhi has a similar foundation: the
Corporation was too large for effective administration of certain functions, so it had to be
divided up to shorten the administrative lines of
command, make it easier for citizens to transact
their business with the municipal government, etc.
The administrative officers of the City Zone, and
to a certain extent the councilors also, believe
that the zonal system continues to be an administrative device, not a political one. But the
system does not operate by the book: the zonal
committee plays a more important role in the "zonal
government" than the rules suggest and than the
administrators might wish. The councilors of the
zone, on the other hand, feel that it is their
activity which keeps the administrative "wing"
working well, and, indeed, they tend to believe
that their powers qua zonal committee should be
expanded. (In the Corporation as a whole, the
councilors would like to see the institution of a
"cabinet system" of municipal government, where
councilors would act, like central government
ministers, as the executive heads of municipal
departments.)[36]

This development of the relationship between
the "wings" of the zone has implications for the
relationship between individual councilor and
individual administrator. The latter feels that
his legitimate area of competence is being encroached upon by the councilor, while the councilor feels it necessary to oversee and criticize
the working of the administrator, in order to see
that "policy" decisions are indeed implemented.
The quality of the relationship in the Delhi zone
is remarkably similar to that between elected
official and administrator in other governmental
arenas in India. In the Delhi zone the tensions
inherent in this relationship and in the fact that
it is a changing one seem to be well managed,
permitting an effective municipal administration
at that level.

7. Councilor and Citizen in the City Zone

The "politics" of the Delhi ward, as we have
seen in Chapter 4, is centered on the councilor,
who acts in an ombudsman's role, working as an
intermediary between the citizen and his municipal
government, and directly in the administrative
process, seeing that services are provided to his
constituency. "Interest group" politics, whether
based on economic groupings such as merchants'
associations, on caste or other ethnic groupings,
or on geographical divisions such as the mohalla,
are noticeable by their absence.

Much the same is true of "partisan" activity:
the councilor in the ward seems to play down his
political party affiliation, treating the citizens
of his ward as "my constituents" rather than dividing them up into "my supporters" and "the opposition." In the Corporation arena, where broader
issues are important, partisan activity is indeed
very visible.

In both "interest group" politics and partisan
activity, the "politics" of the zone is more akin
to the ward arena than to the all-city arena of the
Corporation. The councilors acting as the zonal
committee are concerned with "government" as opposed
to "politics," as we have seen in Chapter 6; they
are interested in an effective administration to
see that their wards receive the benefits of good
municipal services. There is little "partisan"
activity in the zone, either on the part of councilors in the zonal committee, or of the zone-level

party organization (these are the units of the
Jana Sangh and the Congress, primarily, which
cover the Chandni Chowk Parliamentary constituency) with regard to zonal matters, or of organizations of the citizenry, however based, who
might be concerned with municipal government.

The councilor-citizen interface at the level
of the zone is not confined to administrative
matters--the councilor has a political role as
well. This is particularly true of his interaction with those of his constituents who were
his "workers" in his election campaign and constitute his "supporters" thereafter; I begin this
chapter with a discussion of this interaction.
My data permit an analysis of the councilor's
perception of his political role (as opposed to
his administrative one) vis-à-vis his constituency.
The analysis of the councilor's political role
does not relate to the zone qua zone, but I place
it at this point because the data base is the
interviews I conducted with the 18 councilors of
the zone; the City Zone is, in that sense, Kucha
Khirkiwala writ large.

The councilors of the City Zone can be
grouped into parties, mainly Jana Sangh and
Congress,[1] and although the councilors do not
act, in the zone, as a "Congressman" or a "Jana
Sanghi," it is possible to analyze the simi-
larities and differences of councilors who are
members of the Jana Sangh as opposed to those
who are members of Congress. These variations
are probably a function of the organization and
political style of these parties in the all-Delhi
arena, but the small number of councilors in the
City Zone make it a convenient locale to high-
light them. Indeed, I was unable to obtain
similar data at the all-Delhi level, so in this
sense, the City Zone is the Delhi Corporation
writ small. The detailed discussion of elections
in Shahjahanabad, which forms the bulk of this
chapter, serves the same purpose: not to suggest
that there are things like voting patterns and

bases of support (in terms of economic classes
of ethnic groupings, for example) that are unique
to Shahjahanabad--though I will argue that there
are a few--but that the City Zone, like Kucha
Khirkiwala, is a useful unit in which to see patterns which are probably Delhi-wide and perhaps
extend to much of North India.

This chapter, then, examines two facets of
the "politics" of the zone (it should be clear
now why I use quotation marks for "politics" here:
these are largely the politics which take place in
the zone, not the politics of the zone qua governmental unit): the councilor's political role
vis-à-vis his constituents and the patterns of
political party activity in the zone. It has been
suggested that the major contrast with respect to
the latter point is between the Jana Sangh and
Congress, although the minor parties (the Republican Party of India, the Communist Party of India,
et al.) and the Independents are significant.

THE CONTACT OF COUNCILOR AND CITIZEN

The "partisan" activities of the councilor--
his interaction with political workers, the election
campaign, the election itself--are, in a sense,
special cases of the councilor-citizen interface.
Before I begin the discussion of those "cases," let
me set out the results of my interviews with the 18
City Zone councilors on their contact with their
constituents.

When I conducted the interviews with councilors, I had observed the councilor of Kucha
Khirkiwala in action for some four months, and I
did not hesitate to probe if I felt a councilor was
exaggerating one aspect of his citizen contact. In
addition, I was often able to observe other councilors in action, usually quite fortuitously: I
had to set up interviews by going to a councilor's
home at the times he designated for seeing the
public; I interviewed the councilor often during

such a "darbar" (public audience) hour; and on
a few occasions I was given a conducted tour of
the councilor's ward, during which citizens would
approach him. As a result of these contacts, I
had a good basis for judging how accurate the
councilors' assertions on these subjects were.

Two questions in my interview were directed
at discovering the extent and quality of councilor-
citizen contact: "Do you meet with people from
your area? How often and on what occasions?" and
"Do you feel you can help the people of your area?"
All but three of the councilors either mentioned
going on regular rounds or said something like "I
go into the galis every day to see the problems"
in answer to the first question. Four of them
took me on extended tours of their wards. All
but one of the councilors either had daily office
hours for the public, either in a room in their
home or at some chowk (usually for one or two
hours), or claimed that they were available to
citizens 24 hours a day. The exception lived a
number of miles away from the ward and did not
maintain an office there, but rather met with
people before the Saturday zonal committee meeting.

Councilors, like other incumbents of public
office in India, act as notaries public, putting
their signature (and a rubber stamp imprint of
name and title) on documents which may be simply
a "true copy" of another (typically a school transcript), or may be testimonials of good character
of an applicant to a school, or for a passport, or
whatever. Councilors almost never stop signing
their names during their office hours and will
usually sign what is presented without question,
often without knowing the person presenting it.
One councilor whom I asked about this said that
"we have to trust the people." And one refused
to make wholesale attestations, saying: "I don't
do this attestation without looking, like the
other councilors do. Unless you follow it up, it
has no effect. Tell me genuine demands, and I
will look into it personally." Most councilors

who gave figures for the number of people coming
for signatures estimated between 25 and 50 per
day (which coincides with my observations), and
one said that at school admission time 400 to 500
people come daily.

Citizens do come with more weighty problems,
of course. One councilor said, "Most councilors
feel that the more people that come to them, to
their house, the better; but I don't. If I know
someone who needs admission [to a school or a col-
lege], I will go all out for him. But I will not
work because some private sweeper has not come [to
his work]--that's not my job." The other councilors
did indeed picture themselves as open to all complaints and willing to expend effort on almost all
of them, some saying that they would help in police
matters and even domestic disputes. (Recall that
the Kucha Khirkiwala councilor said specifically
that he would not involve himself in these cases,
so I am unable even to speculate on how the councilor manages to operate in these extremely delicate
areas.) The most detailed breakdown was given in
answer to the first question:

Fifty, sixty, seventy, a hundred [citizens]
come [daily] in connection with three or
four works: 1) most important--they repair
a building and get a notice [that it is] an
unauthorized construction; 2) roads are bad,
water not there, electricity out, getting
children into schools. I write a letter on
their behalf. 3) attestations. For people
going to Pakistan, entering schools, etc.
4) People also come for work connected with
central and state government. I deal, for
example, with the passport office, the Home
Ministry, the Labor Ministry, the Railways,
etc. I telephone ministers or write a letter.
Then the answer will come via this office. . . .
One councilor does as much work as an MLA
[Member of the Legislative Assembly] and an
MP put together, indeed more. . . . The

Corporation has new housing schemes and
people come to see about repairs in these
also.[2]

These are the kinds of problems other councilors
mentioned. The numbers of people coming daily
varied from two to four to 250 (which can be discounted). Judging from the responses taken as a
whole coupled with my own observations, I would
say that about 10 to 20 people meet the councilor
daily with complaints or requests for getting
things done (other than attestations).

A number of the councilors said that they
met people at social or religious functions, and
many remarked that as they walked through the
ward, people would stop them with complaints. A
few said they relied on political workers to convey complaints to them from specific mohallas,
and one or two mentioned that they would go and
inspect something that was causing difficulties
(say a leaking sewer line) if citizens asked them
to come and see it. My second question (on what
can the councilor do) elicited few detailed
responses.

The answers to these questions underline the
importance of the councilor as ombudsman, and also
as a man who intervenes actively in the administrative process. They gain meaning, moreover,
when viewed against the background of the analysis
of the councilor of Kucha Khirkiwala's contacts
with his constituents, because they suggest that
his experience is typical of most of the City Zone.
There is a great deal of face-to-face contact of
councilor and citizen, almost non-stop, and the
councilor keeps himself open to it. And most
councilors work very hard at that portion of
their job.

THE POLITICAL ROLE OF THE COUNCILOR

As I have suggested in Chapter 4, much of
the political role of the councilor is focused
on the coming election. In this, his political
"workers" play the most significant part, and
after a look at the councilor's motives for
fighting the election and the party organization
(again, this extends the discussion of Chapter 4),
I will analyze the relationship of the councilor
and his workers.

The account of the election campaign in a
municipal ward, presented in Chapter 4, was based
on the interviews with the City Zone councilors
and my observations of the Basti Julahan by-
election. Two broad aspects of standing for
election were not discussed in detail there: why
a councilor contests an election, and the details
of his campaign staff. Because data here come
from the interviews, I cannot discuss the first
aspect with complete confidence. What the councilor felt was proper to reveal to a foreign interviewer may have been less than his own self-aware-
ness and understanding would provide.

Councilors enter politics and contest elections for a variety of reasons, ranging from the
desire for a good supplementary income to wanting
a career in politics in which the first step is to
be a councilor; to needing the satisfaction of
being in the limelight; to being a "good soldier"
asked to do battle by a party to which he is
ideologically committed; to a desire for doing
public service; and so on (and, of course, not
necessarily in that order). Some of these motives
appear in answers to my questions "Why did you
stand for election?", "Please tell me something of
your career in political life." There was considerably more frankness about the style of the
campaign and the councilor's relationship to the
political workers, although here also I sensed
occasionally some inclination to exaggerate contacts and the magnitude of active support. (My

questions were: "[In the past election] how many
workers did you have with you?   What are they
like (that is, are they young, in business, etc.)?"
and "After the election, do you still have contact
with your workers?   How many of them, how frequently, and for what reasons?")

A party worker active in Delhi politics
answered my question on why councilors contest
with "[they have] a lust for power and prestige--
and there is much power and prestige for the area
councilor."   One councilor suggested another
reason: "Political power is just like gambling
. . . a form of recreation.   For me also."   Three
other councilors spoke of their personal interest
in politics ("I always had a mind to contest an
election . . . "), in one instance derived from a
father prominent in politics.   Three others stressed
their commitment to social service, and two mentioned decisive personal incidents which forced
them to interest themselves in municipal affairs:
one was nettled by the previous councilor who had
told him "you will never be successful in an
election."   And seven spoke of being forced to
contest by the circumstance of there being no one
else willing to contest, or because of a party
command.   An example of the latter is the following:
"I am a swayamsevak [member of the Rashtriya
Swayamsevak Sangh] and we in the Jana Sangh do our
duty--if the order comes to fight the election,
then we fight the election.   It is the party's command, there is no personal decision."   And another
version of this theme:

When I fought my first election, in 1962,
I was not in politics.   I was sincerely
working with the down-trodden in slum
areas.   When the ticket was offered to me
they--the slum dwellers--forced me to fight
the election "in our behalf."

Another councilor, a lawyer, answered:

Anyone with intellectual leanings, who
believes in the dignity of the individual,
should not stand for election, because the
standard of the voters is so low and it is
an indignity to present oneself to people
who are not prepared to appreciate your
capacity. On the other hand, a deficient
human being is still a human being and we
like to be of service. Therefore, fighting
an election gives us a forum for service.
For me, the choice was very difficult, and
it was made against myself and in favor of
the people.

This theme of the man forced reluctantly into the
political arena is perhaps the most common among
the councilors.[3] Judging from the enjoyment many
of these men seemed to derive from their job, it
can be taken with a grain of salt. One councilor
in fact said in answer to my question about his
political future, "[I have made] no decision to
leave [the Corporation]--the intoxication [nashaa]
of doing the work has started." One important
note about Jana Sangh councilors can be made here:
of the nine councilors who emphasized their long
and devoted service to their party as a part of
their "career in political life," seven belonged
to the Jana Sangh. The Jana Sangh is known for its
party discipline and the expressions used by its
councilors (of the "I am a soldier of the party"
variety) seemed to underline this.

However a man arrives at the position of being
a candidate, once the campaign begins he must rely
heavily on his staff--his workers. Candidates make
a staff/line distinction within this large group,
and their staff, their "strong" (Thos) workers,
with whom they map strategy, number from two to 25
or 30. The modal number of workers which the councilors claimed to have, was 200, and the numbers
ranged from 30-40 (in one of the low population
constituencies) to 500, at least on polling day.
Because of the way my question was phrased,

virtually all the councilors, when they were not
saying that they attracted "every type" of worker
insisted that their workers (unlike their opponent's) were young. There were few who specifically mentioned businessmen as their workers, and
a couple who said that they didn't have businessmen as workers. Councilors whose constituencies
included large numbers of government servants, who
are not permitted by law to participate in politics
beyond voting, said that some of their workers were
government servants who participated in less formal
ways. Other responses on this part of the question
covered all manner of description--"ladies,"
"middle-class," "staff from the [business] office,"
personal friends, party members, "working people,"
"students," etc. Many of these designations can
apply to the same person, obviously, and the
question clearly didn't work well. The councilors' implication that they attracted workers
of all types can, I think, be accepted.

I asked the question about post-election
contact with workers with the expectation that it
would continue; this turns out to be so. I also
expected to find that political workers would be
the links between councilors and citizens; the
data on the Kucha Khirkiwala councilor suggests
that this may not be so, that direct links were
emphasized. A typical response to my question was
"one must keep up connections with one's workers.
They bring the public's work to me." Almost all
councilors said they met with their workers "daily"
or "constantly." There were only two who said
"occasionally." The estimates of numbers of
workers contacted varied widely, from one to three
per day to 50 per day. Almost all the Jana Sangh
councilors and only one of the Congress councilors
mentioned formal, regularly scheduled meetings with
workers. For the Jana Sangh councilors there were
the mandal (ward) and sthaniya samiti ("local
gathering," the lowest unit of Jana Sangh organization) meetings. The agendas of these meetings
are probably not confined to Corporation matters.

One Jana Sangh councilor said:

> Whenever there is a mandal meeting, I make it
> a point to attend, though I am no longer
> convenor or anything. [I do so] in order
> to ascertain their views, keep them in
> touch, keep them equipped with the knowledge
> of our [the party's] achievements. [There
> is] at least one meeting a month; also, as
> and when the necessity arises. For example,
> to organize a campaign against the govern-
> ment against All-India Radio policy, etc.

One councilor objected to calling these people "my
workers" but said rather "my supporters" and that
is a view which has much merit in it--even if during
the campaign these are "workers" under the "command"
of the candidate or the party, after the election
this man becomes a "supporter" for whom favors are
done, etc. Certainly I saw many people sitting in
the offices of councilors who were probably "workers" at election time but did not seem to see themselves as such after the election.

There were a few councilors, however, who said
that workers had a responsibility to bring the problems to the attention of the councilor ("because,"
as one councilor said, "I can't meet everyone
directly"). Seven of the 18 councilors mentioned
that workers were expected to "bring the public's
work." I frequently saw political workers meeting
with councilors on behalf of a citizen--a neighbor,
a kinsman, or whomever--who typically sat by
silently while the worker explained the difficulty
to the councilor. Workers thus do act as intermediaries between the councilor and his constituency, but they have a great measure of autonomy,
even when they take part in organized party activity.
The role is that of someone who conveys requests,
usually from the citizen to the councilor, and not
that of someone who is either "commanded" or who,
by virtue of a position of power in his area,
"commands" the councilor.

The councilors of the City Zone thus have a
wide range of contacts with their citizens, both
as "government servant," concerned with administrative matters, and, particularly when the citizens we are considering are political workers from
the last campaign, as a politician. The classification of citizen as political "worker" is a
function of electoral campaigns; I came across
no political worker who was not also an election
campaign worker, and I suspect that almost all
become political workers by working in the campaign. Let us turn, then, to a discussion of the
patterns and bases of electoral support in
Shahjahanabad.

ELECTIONS IN SHAHJAHANABAD

There have been six city-wide municipal elections in Shahjahanabad since Independence, three for
the Delhi Municipal Committee and three for the
Corporation.[4] These elections have been on the
basis of adult franchise and two of them (1962 and
1967) were held on the same day as the national
general election. The Jana Sangh, founded shortly
before the 1951 election, has contested all six
elections, although until recently not every seat.
And indeed the current pattern of a two-party
system in Delhi--Contress vs. Jana Sangh--begins
with the first election: other parties--the Com-
munists, the Hindu Mahasabha, the Republican Party
of India (RPI) et al.--have had little electoral
strength. The 1958 election (the initial one of
the newly formed Corporation) used double-member
constituencies, but in all the other elections
single-member constituencies were used. It is here
that one difficulty in comparing election results
over time arises: the constituencies have changed
their number and their boundaries. Table 33 indicates what these changes have meant in Shahjahanabad. Note that the traditional names persist (and
the names of the areas which were wards in 1951 and

TABLE 33

MUNICIPAL WARDS IN SHAHJAHANABAD, 1951–1971

	1951, 1954		1958		1962		1967, 1971
Ward No.	Ward Name	Ward No.	Ward Name	Ward No.	Ward Name	Ward No.	Ward Name
3	Chandni Chowk	4	Daryaganj-Chandni Chowk	7	Chandni Chowk	54	Chandni Chowk
4	Katra Neel						
5	Shardhanand Bazar	5	Shardhanand Bazar-Mori Gate	10	Shardhanand Bazar	53	Shardhanand Bazar
6	Jama Masjid-Dariba	8	Dariba-Maliwara			57	Dariba
7	Maliwara					58	Maliwara
8	Charkhewalan	7	Ballimaran-Charkhewalan	14	Charkhewalan	62	Charkhewalan
9	Ballimaran			?	Ballimaran	63	Ballimaran
10	Naya Bans	6	Naya Bans-Kucha Pandit	11	Naya Bans	64	Naya Bans
11	Farashkhana					65	Farashkhana[a] Kucha Pandit[b]
12	Kucha Pandit			12	Kucha Pandit	66	Ajmeri Gate
13	Kucha Pati Ram	11	Kucha Pati Ram-Kalan Masjid	?	Kucha Pati Ram	67	Kucha Pati Ram
14	Kalan Masjid			22	Kalan Masjid	68	Kalan Masjid
15	Lal Darwaza	10	Lal Darwaza-Suiwalan	19	Lal Darwaza	61	Lal Darwaza
16	Churiwalan						
17	Matia Mahal	9	Matia Mahal-Chatta Lal Mian	17	Matia Mahal	59	Matia Mahal
18	Daryaganj	[4, above]		8	Daryaganj	55	Daryaganj
19	Chhatta Lal Mian					56	Chhatta Lal Mian
20	Suiwalan	[10, above]		?	Suiwalan	60	Suiwalan

1954 persist in "street-level" usage). Unfortunately, the joining of the names does not indicate that the two old wards were simply combined,
except in a few instances.⁵ Fig. 16 superimposes
the 1951 and 1954 delimitation on the 1967-71
one (cf. Fig. 11, p. 150 above). I will be forced
to make comparison not between numbered wards of
exactly the same boundaries, as I would have liked
to do, but rather between "natural areas" to which
various wards in various years correspond. I will
be able to compare the 1967 and 1971 elections
more precisely, of course. For similar reasons,
I am confining myself to the Shahjahanabad part
of the City Zone.

The turnout in municipal elections has been
consistently high: in 16 wards in 1967 the mean
percentage was 73 and the range from 62 to 82 per-
cent.⁶ Some votes--on the order of 3 to 8 percent
of the total cast--are rejected as invalid. There
is no indication, either from the tabulations themselves or from anything that any political activist
or election official told me, that there was any
pattern to this, no charges that one party or the
other "stole" an election by getting votes invali-
dated. Votes are declared invalid at the time of
counting, when there are party observers present.
The number of contestants for office in all the
elections is fewer than in other municipal elections
in India, I think: 86 candidates for 18 seats in
1954; 49 for 16 seats in 1958; 43 for 12 seats in
1962; 69 for 16 seats in 1967; and 74 for 16 seats
in 1971. The average thus ranges from three candidates per seat to five.⁷ Many of these candidates
were probably non-candidates by polling day: these
are the ones who receive 10 or 15 votes.

The Congress contested every seat in each of
the six elections. The Jana Sangh contested all
but one seat in the three Corporation elections
and about two-thirds of the seats in the three
Municipal Committee elections. The minor parties
tended to contest only in a few wards in each
election. The pattern of contesting, over time,

is presented in Table 34. The competition is
between the Congress and the Jana Sangh. Of the
96 winners, only 16 (13 Independents, 2 Communist
Party of India [CPI], 1 RPI) were neither Jana
Sangh nor Congress, and only 22 non-Jana Sangh,
non-Congress candidates were runners-up. Moreover, the non-Jana Sangh, non-Congress winners
tend to be less successful in the later elections.
Congress strength in Shahjahanabad has clearly
declined, as it has in Delhi as a whole, and the
Jana Sangh has been picking up what the Congress
has lost. Note that the Jana Sangh when it did
not contest all the seats chose well: it had the
winner or the runner-up in eleven of eleven contests in 1951, ten of twelve in 1956, and nine of
nine in 1958. When it first contested all the
seats, in 1962, the Jana Sangh was "in the money"
in only seven of twelve, but in 1967 and 1971 it
ran first or second in all but one of the contests.

The summary measures of the vote percentages
of the Congress and the Jana Sangh are presented
in Table 35. The relatively low vote percentage
that the Jana Sangh received in 1951 reflects its
position as a new party and the position of the
Congress as the party "which won freedom," and the
dip in the Jana Sangh's vote in 1962 occurred when
it expanded the number of seats it contested.[8]
But the decline in the Congress vote is clear,
though it is not so dramatic a fall as it is in
the number of seats won. And the Jana Sangh and
the Congress between them share some 80 percent of
the vote consistently; by 1971 it is getting close
to 90 percent. In certain wards, of course, Independents and members of other parties have won, so
that the measures of average vote suggest that in
most wards, these contestants get very little of
the vote indeed. The number of wards in which
Congress received an absolute majority has declined,
and the number of Jana Sangh majority wards has
risen (see Table 36).

Turning from parties to people, as it were,
let us examine the patterns of repetitive contesting

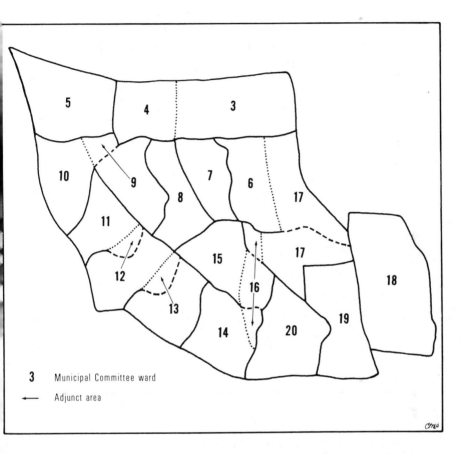

Fig. 16 Delhi Municipal Committee Wards, 1951
and 1954, showing their relationship to current
ward boundaries. Drawn after a map in Rajdhani,
Annual Number, Vol. 6, No. 1 (January 1955).

TABLE 34

SIX MUNICIPAL ELECTIONS IN SHAHJAHANABAD: NUMBER OF SEATS
CONTESTED, NUMBER OF SEATS WON, NUMBER OF CANDIDATES
WHO FINISHED SECOND, BY PARTY

Year		Congress[a]	Jana Sangh	Other Parties	Independents
1951	Contested	18	11	..[b]	..[b]
(18	Winners	15	0	0	3
seats)	Runners-up	2	11	3[c]	2
1954	Contested	18	12	..	..
(18	Winners	8	4	1[d]	5
seats)	Runners-up	9	6	0	2
1958	Contested	16	9	..	..
(16	Winners	8	4	1[d]	3
seats)	Runners-up	7	5	0	4
1962	Contested	12	12	..	..
(12	Winners	11	1	0	0
seats)	Runners-up	1	6	1[d]	4
1967	Contested	16	16	..	..
(16	Winners	6	9	1[e]	0
seats)	Runners-up	8	6	2[f]	0
1971	Contested	16	15	..	..
(16	Winners	4	10	0	2
seats)	Runners-up	8	4	3[g]	1
Totals	Contested	96	75	..	..
(96 con-	Winners	52	28	3	13
tests)[h]	Runners-up	35	38	9	13

[a] In 1971, Congress = Congress(R).

[b] Some party or other was contesting in most constituencies, and many
independents were: figures for number of seats contested would have
little significance.

[c] Two United Progressive Block, one Ram Rajya Parishad.

[d] CPI.

[e] RPI.

[f] One CPI, one RPI.

[g] Congress(O).

[h] One winner was unopposed.

TABLE 35

SIX MUNICIPAL ELECTIONS IN SHAHJAHANABAD: SUMMARY MEASURES OF
VOTE PERCENTAGE, CONGRESS AND JANA SANGH

Year	Party	Mean		Median		Range	
		(C)	(JS)	(C)	(JS)	(C)	(JS)
1951	Congress	48		46		22-77	
	Jana Sangh		29		28		18-43
1954	Congress	46		48		13-63	
	Jana Sangh		40		44		13-53
1958[a]	Congress	45[23]		43.5[21.5]		34-62[16-34]	
	Jana Sangh		[22]		[21]		[17-28]
1962	Congress	45		45.5		35-55	
	Jana Sangh		29		28		13-57
1967	Congress	41		40.5		26-60	
	Jana Sangh		39		41.5		14-59
1971	Congress[b]	38		42.5		13-69	
	Jana Sangh		43		44		17-62

[a]Since there were double-member constituencies in 1958, measures
comparable to other years can only be used for the Congress, which
contested all 16 seats; the percentage of the vote obtained by the
two Congress candidates was simply added. The figures in brackets
are the measures of the vote percentage for individual candidates.

[b]Congress(R).

and incumbency. There were 96 winning candidates
over the six elections, and 55 councilors (again,
by-elections are disregarded) as best as I can
tell. This last caveat because the names of candidates are listed differently in different
elections, and I have had to guess whether differing names apply to the same person. For
example, I have assumed that the "Kundan Lal"
who contested in Chandni Chowk in 1962 is the
"K. L. Sharma" who contested there in the previous
three elections. Or, in a more complicated case,
I have counted Imdad Sabri as contesting four
elections: in 1958 in Lal Darwaza ("Imdad Rashid
Sabri"), in 1962 in Matia Mahal ("Imdad ul
Rashid"), in 1967 in Lal Darwaza ("Imdad Sabri")
and in 1971 in Matia Mahal "Imdad Sabri"), on the
basis of his label (Independent) and sizeable
vote, and an interview with a man from the area.

TABLE 36

SIX ELECTIONS IN SHAHJAHANABAD: NUMBER OF WARDS IN WHICH AN
ABSOLUTE MAJORITY WAS ACHIEVED

Year	Congress	Jana Sangh
1951	6	0
1954	7	2
1958	[3][a]	[1][a]
1962	5	1
1967	3	2
1971	3	6

[a]The vote for the two candidates in the double-member constituencies
has been added.

Candidates with slightly differing names, and some
with the same names (especially very common ones),
if they received a small vote in different constituencies or in the same constituencies but with a
large gap in time, were not counted as repeating
contestants, although they may well have been.
These candidates were, to be sure, a very small
number. By this reckoning, there were 49 candidates who contested more than once, and 235 who
contested only once. Only 15 of these 235 won;
the 49 "repeaters" won 81 of the 96 contests.   In
other words, those who lose tend not to contest
again; those who win will.
     It is difficult to summarize the data on
repeating candidates. The 49 repeaters are divided
into: three who contested five times; nine who
contested four times; 12 who contested three times;
and 25 who contested twice. Using "W" to indicate
contests won and "L" to indicate contests lost, the
pattern of those contesting four and five times is
presented in Table 37. Two things are particularly
striking here: (1) there is only one Jana Sangh
candidate in the group, and (2) the modal type of
long-time repeating candidate seems to be something

TABLE 37

SIX MUNICIPAL ELECTIONS IN SHAHJAHANABAD: CANDIDATES WHO
CONTESTED FOUR OR FIVE TIMES

Candidate	Number of Contests	Number of Constituencies[a]	Label[b]	Pattern (W=Won; L=Lost)
A	5	1	C	WWWWW
B	5	1	I,C,I,C,C	WWWLL
C	5	2(XXXXY)	I,I,I,C,C	WWLWW
D	4	1	C,I,I,I	WWLL
E	4	2(XYXY)	C	WLWW
F	4	1	C,I,I,C	WWWL
G	4	1	CPI	LWWL
H	4	1	JS	WLWW
I	4	1	C,I,C,I	LLWW
J	4	2(XYXY)	I	LLLL
K	4	1	C	WLWW
L	4	2(XYYY)	C,C,C,C-O	WWWL

[a]X = One constituency; Y = Second constituency.

[b]C = Congress (including Congress[R]); I = Independent; CPI = Communist Party
of India; JS = Jana Sangh; C-O = Congress(O).

of a Congress "maverick"--someone who contests as
an Independent when he is denied a ticket and then
is perhaps re-accepted into the Congress in the
next election. Of the 12 men who contested three
times, four were Congressmen, three were Jana
Sanghis, and the other five had two labels (including one who switched from Jana Sangh to
Congress). And of the 25 who contested twice, ten
were of the Jana Sangh, five of the Congress, three
were Independents, one of the CPI, and six had two
labels. Only three of those contesting twice and
none of those contesting three times shifted constituencies.[9] Five of the 10 Jana Sanghis who
contested twice contested (and won) in 1967 and
1971. The won-lost patterns of Table 37 and this
latter point would suggest that the explanation for
the absence of four and five time Jana Sangh candidates lies in the fact that before 1967, Jana
Sangh candidates lost, and losers tend not to run
again (or, are not asked to run again).
Another way of looking at this data is to
treat each election contest separately, as follows:
there were 37 instances of winners winning in the

next election; 21 instances of winners losing; 14
instances of losers winning; and 16 instances of
losers losing. This tends to confirm the impression that it is incumbents who run again, and that
incumbents more often than not are successful.
Some of these instances of losers losing and losers
winning are contained in the "electoral careers"
of candidates who had been, at one point, winners
(cf. candidates A, D, E, et al. in Table 37);
i.e., the tendency of winners to run again is under-
stated by the above figures. There were only nine
repeating candidates who had never won a municipal
election. One (admittedly inelegant) way of presenting this data is given in Table 38. For
this table I counted all previous elections, not
just the preceding one. (Again, I looked at
instances of winners winning, etc., so that one
person is counted more than once if he contested
four or five times.) This really points to a candidate's eye-view of the matter: for instance, 12
of the winners who had lost had had the experience
of being winners who had won, and one or two may
have also had the experience of being a loser who
had subsequently won. If we think in terms of a
"political bug" "theory" of the motivations for
contesting elections, having won an election is
of great psychological significance.[10]

TABLE 38

SIX MUNICIPAL ELECTIONS IN SHAHJAHANABAD: CANDIDATES CONTESTING
THREE OR MORE ELECTIONS

The Number of instances of:	Who Had Been:			
	Winners who had won	Winners who had lost	Losers who had won	Losers who had lost
Winners winning	13	3	8	1
Winners losing	12	1	3	0
Losers winning	1	4	0	2
Losers losing	3	3	0	3

Most of the 49 repeating candidates did not switch parties (or leave or join a party) and most of them were Congress or Jana Sangh (Table 39). There were 25 candidates who won more than half their contests: nine of them were Congress, eight were Jana Sangh, five contested both as Congress and as Independents, and three were other "double label" contestants. The pattern of those who contested with a Congress label and with an Independent label (e.g., candidates B, C, D, et al., Table 37) is interesting, for it shows both co-optation of successful Independents into Congress and the success of those who for some reason or other were not given the Congress ticket again; it suggests that a significant number of consistently successful candidates have support bases independent of the Congress. And, of course, co-optation of individuals with a support base independent of party ties is done by both Congress and the Jana Sangh (especially in 1967 for the latter). The question that this raises is whether the vote for a candidate is a vote for his party or a vote for him. I will attempt to deal with this question, at least by implication, in my discussion of socio-economic and geographic areas of support, below.

TABLE 39

SIX MUNICIPAL ELECTIONS IN SHAHJAHANABAD: PARTY OF THE
FORTY-NINE REPEATING CANDIDATES

Label	Candidates	Label	Candidates
Congress[a]	15	Congress and Independent	8
Jana Sangh	14	RPI and Independent	1
CPI	2	RPI and Jana Sangh	1
Independent	4	Jana Sangh and Congress	2
		Jana Sangh and Independent	2

Here I include candidates of the post-split Congress(O) as Congress, on the grounds that they saw themselves as Congressmen.

Only five of the 1967 wards are the same as
wards in 1951 and 1954, and the delimitations of
wards in 1958 and 1962 are unclear. It is therefore not possible to view geographically defined
patterns of party competition in Shahjahanabad for
the period of the six elections. The 1967 delimitation was retained in 1971 and, in addition,
there was a Lok Sabha (Parliamentary) election in
1967, so we can compare voting patterns in those
three elections. Furthermore, some of these patterns can be summarized and plotted on maps which
can then be compared to the 1961 socio-economic
patterns.

Let us first look at the electoral patterns
of these three elections. The 1971 Corporation
election came two months after the nation-wide
landslide victory of the Congress(R) in the mid-
term Lok Sabha poll in Delhi: the Congress won
the six seats it had lost to the Jana Sangh in
1967 and retained the seat it had won then.*
In the mid-term poll, the Congress(R) had been
allied with the CPI, and the Jana Sangh with the
Congress(O), the SSP (Samyukta Socialist Party)
and the BKD (Bharatiya Kranti Dal). That a CPI
candidate contested against the Congress(R) candidate in ward 64 in the 1971 Corporation election
suggests that the former alliance, despite its
success, did not persist; and the fact that the
Jana Sangh did not contest in ward 68 (where the
Congress[O] candidate got 34 percent of the vote)
suggests that the latter alliance continued. But

---

*The results of this election cannot be in-
cluded in this analysis because results were not
tabulated by polling station or single municipal
wards. This was done in order to insure the
absolute secrecy of the ballot, by preventing
politicians from making the sorts of analyses I
have made (particularly of the ward data) and using
them to punish or reward supporters or opponents so
identified.

the fact that Congress(O) candidates contested
against the Jana Sangh in four other wards suggests
the reverse (the newspaper reports, unfortunately,
do not address themselves to this matter). Overall
in these elections, the Jana Sangh retained its
hold on the Corporation, confounding all pre-
dictions. Some critiques of the Congress performance suggested that the battle for Congress tickets
weakened the party; others pointed out that voters
seemed to be able to distinguish between national
issues and local ones.

Looking first at the change in the Corporation
elections; consider Table 40 and Fig. 17. If we
discount the change of label of the two incumbent
councilors who won as Independents, we can note that
only three wards changed hands: two went from
Congress to the Jana Sangh and one went the other
way. In the former instance, the incumbent councilors had chosen the Congress(O)--they are, incidentally, two of the more eminent Congressmen of
Delhi. But the most remarkable feature of the 1971
election is the success of the incumbents. Indeed,
all but two incumbents who contested won, and 11 of
the 16 seats were won by incumbents. Fig. 17 suggests that while the general picture of Congress and
Jana Sangh victories remained the same, there was
some change in voting strength. In 1967 the Congress won three of its six seats by margins of 20
percent or more, but by 1971 won only one seat by
that margin. Although the number of seats the Jana
Sangh won by margins over 10 percent remained the
same (five) between 1967 and 1971, its competitive
position improved: the shift of the mode from the
0.0-4.9 percent category to the 5.0-9.9 percent
category is impressive.

The data on vote percentages for these two
elections are presented in Table 5 of the Appendix,
and in Table 41. The mean percentage of the Congress vote dropped from 40.7 percent in 1967 to
37.7 percent in 1971, and the Jana Sangh vote rose
from 38.6 percent to 43.4 percent. The Congress
lost an average of 3.1 percent of the vote in the

TABLE 40

1967 AND 1971 CORPORATION ELECTIONS IN SHAHJAHANABAD: PARTY
OF WINNERS AND RUNNERS-UP

Ward Number	1967 Winner	1971 Winner	1967 Runner-up	1971 Runner-up
53	JS	JS	C	C
54	JS	C	C	JS
55	C	JS	JS	C(O)[a]
56	JS	JS[a]	C	C
57	JS	JS[a]	C	C
58	JS	JS[a]	C	C
59	C	C	RPI	Ind
60	C	JS	JS	C(O)[a]
61	C	C[a]	JS	JS
62	JS	JS[a]	C	C
63	C	C[a]	CPI	JS
64	JS	JS[a]	C	C
65	C	Ind[a,b]	Ind	JS
66	JS	JS[a]	C	C
67	JS	JS[a]	C	C
68	RPI	Ind[a,c]	JS	C(O)

[a]Indicates incumbent councilor.

[b]This man left the Congress and joined the Muslim League shortly
before the election; after the election he rejoined the Congress(R).

[c]This councilor is still identified with the RPI.

16 wards it contested in both elections, and the
Jana Sangh gained an average of 4.3 percent in the
15 wards it contested (Table 41). In addition,
these figures serve to underline the fact that in
most cases, it is the Congress and the Jana Sangh
alone which are the real contestants. This can be
easily seen in Fig. 18a (p. 264, below): note that
two of the wards shown as having Congress/Jana Sangh
winners/runners-up in 1967 are those in which the
runner-up to the Jana Sangh in 1971 was the incumbent Congress(O) councilor, so that these two wards
also, in a sense, fit the pattern. A glance at Fig.
11 (p. 150, above), suggests the most likely explanation of this pattern: there is weak Congress-
Jana Sangh competition in the Muslim areas of the
city, and Muslim Independents provide the main challenge to the Congress, as in Kucha Khirkiwala.

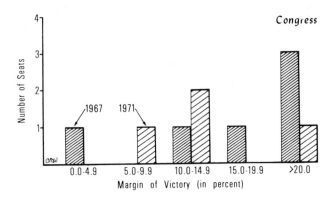

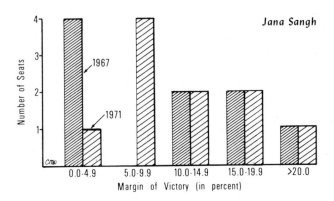

Fig. 17 1967 and 1971 Corporation elections
in Shahjahanabad: margins of victory.

TABLE 41

1967 AND 1971 CORPORATION ELECTIONS IN SHAHJAHANABAD: CHANGE
IN VOTE PERCENTAGE[a]

Ward	Congress	Jana Sangh	Other Parties and Independents
53	+ 8.0	- 3.1	- 4.9
54	+12.9	- 2.9	- 9.9
55	-35.1	+10.5	+24.4
56	+ 9.6	+12.9	-22.4
57	+ 7.7	- 5.8	- 1.8
58	+ 6.4	+19.2	-25.6
59	- 1.2	+ 2.8	- 1.6
60	-27.3	+ 9.6	+17.6
61	+25.0	+14.2	-39.3
62	- 2.9	+ 8.1	- 5.2
63	+18.7	+ 4.9	-23.4
64	- 2.3	+ 3.6	- 1.4
65	-46.5	- 5.7	+52.3
66	- 9.5	- 9.0	+18.5
67	+ 3.8	+ 5.3	- 9.0
68	-16.2	....[b]	+47.3
Mean	- 3.1	+ 4.3[c]	+ 1.0

[a]The three column figures for each ward do not always total 0.0 due to rounding error.

[b]Jana Sangh did not run a candidate in 1971.

[c]Based on 15 wards; if the ward 68 figure is included (-31.2), then the mean becomes +2.1 and the means of the three columns total 0.0, as they should.

If it is true that the Jana Sangh retained the majority in the 1971 Corporation election despite the Congress tide of two months before because the voters made a distinction between national candidates and local candidates, then the pattern that emerges from a comparison of the 1967 election for the Corporation and for the Lok Sabha is not surprising (Table 6 of the Appendix, and a summary version, Table 42). Overall, of course, the Jana

Sangh Lok Sabha candidate won, and nine of the 16
Corporation seats went to the Jana Sangh, but Table
42 indicates that the Jana Sangh Lok Sabha candidate consistently ran ahead of his ticket mate
(in 11 of 16 wards). The Congress Lok Sabha candidate ran ahead of his Corporation ticket mate in
only one ward, and indeed did far worse, on the
whole, in those wards that were won by Congress in
the Corporation election. Part of the explanation

TABLE 42

1967 LOK SABHA AND CORPORATION ELECTIONS IN SHAHJAHANABAD: DIFFERENCE
IN VOTE PERCENTAGE (PERCENTAGE IN LOK SABHA ELECTION
MINUS PERCENTAGE IN CORPORATION ELECTION)

Ward	Congress	Jana Sangh	RPI
53	- 5.1	+ 6.1[a]	
54	- 2.4	+ 8.4[a]	
55	-10.4[a]	+12.1	
56	- 3.5	+ 4.3[a]	- 1.3
57	- 6.8	+ 3.0[a]	
58	+ 3.1	+16.8[a]	
59	-21.7[a]	- 0.5	- 5.5
60	-15.9[a]	- 1.3	- 2.8
61	- 2.2[a]	+11.5	
62	-10.5	+ 4.8[a]	
63	-20.3[a]	+ 3.9	
64	- 6.1	+13.1[a]	
65	-29.9[a]	- 0.7	
66	- 6.7	- 3.1[a]	
67	- 6.4	+ 7.1[a]	- 1.1
68	- 1.4	- 0.8	-18.1
Mean	- 9.1	+ 5.3	- 5.8

[a]Party of the winner of the Corporation seat.

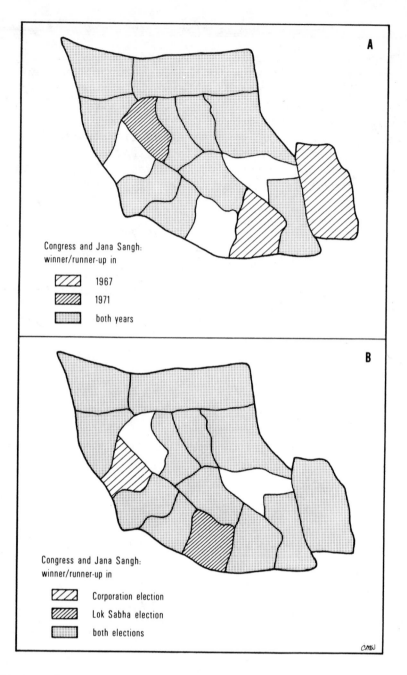

Fig. 18   Areas of Congress and Jana Sangh
competition in Shahjahanabad:
     a: 1967 and 1971 Corporation elections
     b: 1967 Lok Sabha election and 1967
           Corporation election

of this result lies in the fact that there was an
Independent Muslim candidate contesting for the
Lok Sabha in 1967 who received a large number of
votes which had probably gone to Congress candidates in the Corporation contests. The wards
which remain blank in Fig. 18b are those which
the Independent Muslim candidate "won." Note
how closely the pattern fits that of Fig. 18a.

This pattern can be broken down further
if we rank the wards by percentage of vote
received for each party and plot on a map the
"top ranked" wards (wards in which the vote percentage was above the median for all wards of
Shahjahanabad) of each party (Fig. 19). Fig. 19a
can be read as follows: in the 1967 Lok Sabha
election, the Congress did well in the wards
where the Jana Sangh did well. Again, the blank
wards suggest a vote-splitting candidate--the
Muslim Independent. Fig. 19b presents an
entirely different picture: the Congress and
Jana Sangh seem to have strength in largely
separate areas of Shahjahanabad, and here it is
in the Muslim areas that the Congress received
its highest vote percentages. The Jana Sangh
(comparing Figs. 19a and 19b) clearly has a well-
defined set of wards in which it is strong.

The ranking of the wards by percentage of the
vote obtained permits us to test, at least partially, the "territorial stability" of the party
vote. (The view of many in Delhi is that Jana
Sangh voters are more likely to vote a straight
party ticket than Congress voters; the statistics
I am about to present are only an indirect indication that this may be true.) The Spearman's R
rank correlation of the ranks of wards by Congress
vote in Lok Sabha and Corporation election is only
.36 while for the Jana Sangh it is .83. A similar
computation of the rank-order correlation between
the Congress and Jana Sangh vote in the Corporation
elections of 1967 and 1971 reveals a Spearman's R
for the Jana Sangh of .66. This suggests that the
bases of Jana Sangh support (at least between 1967

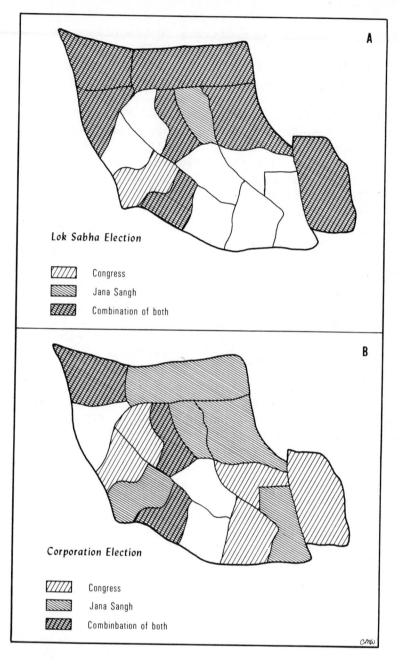

Fig. 19   Areas of Congress and Jana Sangh
electoral strength in Shahjahanabad:
     a: "Top-ranked" wards in the 1967 Lok
         Sabha election
     b: "Top-ranked" wards in the 1967 Corp-
         oration

and 1971), defined territorially, remains remarkably stable, while Congress support areas have
changed.[11]

Most of the patterns of voting, both for the
Corporation and the Lok Sabha, seem to be explained
by the presence of Muslim candidates in Muslim
areas. Are there any further socio-economic vari-
ables which fit with those patterns? Fig. 14, for
instance, shows the "top-ranked" wards in terms of
literacy. As would be expected if the Kucha
Kirkiwala data reflect general patterns (see above,
p. 139), these tend to be the areas of Jana Sangh
strength (caveat: Muslims tend to have a lower
literacy rate than Hindus; literacy may be at best
an intervening variable). There is no way of
inferring that the "typical" Hindu Congress voter
is more, or less, likely to be literate than the
"typical" Jana Sangh voter. Similarly, scheduled
caste residence patterns plotted against voting
patterns will not show much--the scheduled castes
are too small a percentage of each ward. The
occupation data I have presented (Fig. 12) reveals
no pattern which could be interpreted easily, since
the boundaries differ.

SUMMARY

We are left with some fairly reliable conclusions about voting patterns in Shahjahanabad:
the competition of the Jana Sangh is the Congress,
but the competition of the Congress is either the
Jana Sangh, or the Independent or third party candidate, especially if the latter two are Muslim.
Jana Sangh voters probably vote more consistently
Jana Sangh than Congress voters vote Congress,
which suggests that party commitment is important
in all elections, though possibly more for Lok
Sabha elections (the Jana Sangh Lok Sabha candidate
in 1967--by no one's reckoning a charismatic or
even particularly noteworthy candidate--ran ahead
of his Corporation ticket mates).

Being an incumbent seems to be a very real
advantage in getting reelected, particularly in
the 1971 election. This fits with the emphasis
that the councilor puts on direct personal contact
with his constituents, without intermediaries and
with minimal reference to party. It is the person
who gets elected as much as the party, although
again this is probably less true of Jana Sangh
candidates than of Congress candidates. There is
a fit here with the differing campaign style of
the two parties--the Jana Sangh candidate under
the "command" of the party, the Congress candidate
being his own in-charge. The politics of getting
elected is thus "congruent" with the councilor's
style in the day-to-day work of his ward and of the
zone, and it remains an open question as to how
much of the politics of the city is "congruent"
with the (national) politics within the city.

8. The Delhi Municipal Corporation: History and Operation

With this chapter, I return to the all-Delhi level which I discussed briefly in the introductory chapter. Here I shall be outlining the history of the Delhi Municipal Committee and then describing in some detail the working of its successor body, the Municipal Corporation of Delhi, including an analysis of the Corporation's budget. The chapter concludes with a brief sketch of the interactions of the Corporation with other government bodies in Delhi: both "inward," in the interactions with its committees, including zonal committees, and "outward," in the interactions with officials and bodies of the Delhi Administration and the central government.[1]

The history of the Delhi Municipal Corporation* is important to trace for my purposes because so much of what exists today in the practice of the Corporation has its roots in the older local body. When one thinks of the changes that have occurred in Indian government in the last century--the rise of the nationalist movement, the expansion of the franchise, the years of Independence--this continuity is

---

*The official name in English is "Municipal Corporation of Delhi," but both names are in use: abbreviations are MCD or DMC (the latter is also, of course, the abbreviation for the Delhi Municipal Committee).

even more striking. In a sense, the whole sphere
of municipal government in Delhi resembles the
budgetary processes of the Corporation (see below,
pp. 296-309): there are no major shifts from year
to year, but only gradual increments or decreases
in individual items. The most important factor in
shaping the range and intensity of municipal
politics and government seems to be the model of
the previous year's municipal body.

This chapter also highlights a theme of
earlier chapters, when the scheme of "deliberative
wing" and "executive wing" is outlined. At the
Corporation level of government (that is, the level
which encompasses wards and zones; the "top" level
of the Corporation), this division into "wings"
seems to have its greatest validity, since the
councilors sitting in Corporation meetings do constitute a body which can decide matters of policy,
and the decisions can be implemented by a clearly
demarcated administrative apparatus, headed by the
Municipal Commissioner. But the review of the
history of the Delhi municipality will suggest
that policy changes can at best be only incremental: the councilors can change the level of
taxation, can decide which language is to be the
language of administration (Hindi, Urdu, Punjabi,
English?), etc., but the fields of action (things
like sanitation, education, water supply) have in
a sense been determined by the historical evolution
of the body, and are indeed legally determined by
the provisions of the chartering Act, a bill passed
by Parliament in 1957. Councilors of the Corporation level thus spend far less of their time in
"deliberation" than they do in an involvement in
the executive wing actions. Here, as in the ward
and the zone, the councilor and administrator are
not members of the different "wings," acting seri-
ally (the councilor decides, the administrator
executes); but are participants in a governmental
process which is both "deliberative" and "executive,"
and in which both actors share both functions.

This is not to say that the interface between
councilor and administrator is the same at all
three levels. I have shown that in the ward the
councilor in a sense appoints himself an administrative superior of certain low-level officers.
He not only supervises and criticizes their work,
but also, through the use of the constituency fund,
directs the work to be done in specific directions.
In the ward, the councilor quite clearly has the
upper hand over the administrative officers of the
ward. At the level of the zone, the councilor and
administrator stand on equal footing. The councilor at this level no longer acts as an individual,
but as a member of a structured body, the zonal
committee. The administrators with whom he works
are no longer junior officials but senior men who
can, as we have seen (above, pp. 203-06) pursue
various ways of "escalating" conflict and decision-
making into the higher reaches of both the administrative network and the parallel political structures. What was a face-to-face interaction in the
ward, becomes a structured interaction, with
minutes of meetings, formal resolutions, etc. in
the zone. When we consider the interface at the
level of the Corporation, we discover that the
shift of balance in favor of the administration is
completed. We shall see how broad the power of the
commissioner is, and how restricted the power of
the elected council is, except, perhaps, for the
few councilors in leadership positions.

I would suggest that one reason for this shift
in balance has to do with the varying explicitness
of the definition of the councilor's role. At the
Corporation level, his rights and duties are spelled
out in law, and questions of behavior and power in
the context of a Corporation meeting are determined
by well-known parliamentary traditions. The councilor in the ward, on the other hand, is involved,
at least in part, in developing traditions of
rights and duties, since these are neither spelled
out in legal terms (except by implication from
those defined for the Corporation level) nor

determined by previous traditions or party policy.
Ironically, the councilor is not really supposed
to have any real role in the government of his
ward (which "ought" to be a purely administrative
matter), and so he is free to create one for himself, while he is restricted at the higher levels,
where he is to have a role, because someone else
has determined it for him. The fact that the
officers he deals with at the ward level are
probably younger, less experienced, and of lower
status than he, while those in the Corporation are
his age or older, of as great or greater experience in government, of equal or higher status (as
a member of the Indian Administrative Service
would be, for example), with ties to governments
"beyond" the Corporation, goes a long way toward
explaining why the balance in the interface shifts
as it does.

That balance might be altered somewhat, I
would argue, if the citizen played the role at the
Corporation level that he does at the ward and zone
levels. The administrator in the ward is exposed
to the public and at the Corporation level he is
insulated from the public. The officer doing work
in the ward is out there, in the galis, where citizens can and do approach him with complaints and
information. This exposure is reinforced when the
"interpreter" between citizen and administrator,
the councilor, is there, the more so when the
context is the councilor's rounds. Administrators
must keep office hours at the zonal offices, and
they too can be called for a councilor's round.
The zonal offices are relatively near the citizen's
home, and the citizen can easily be accompanied to
the administrator's office by the councilor or some
other political worker.

The administrator can insulate himself from
this contact, in part, by interposing subordinates
(those same ward-level officers, typically, but also
the apparatus of private secretary, clerk, peon
[here "office servant"], et al.) between himself and
the public. Or he can remove himself, going to Town

Hall by preference. Those administrators who are
already at Town Hall, the senior Corporation officials, are well and truly insulated. Physically,
Town Hall itself is almost by definition far away
from the citizen's home, and it is also a labyrinth
of offices and outer offices and corridors (not to
speak of the forbidding people in them), and it
takes a bold soul to penetrate it. These officers
are, indeed, not supposed to be in contact with the
public--they deal, after all, with the decisions of
the public's representatives--and so, except for
the occasional darbar ("public audience"), in which
the commissioner, for example, will admit citizens
and their complaints for an hour a week, the contact of administrator and citizen is minimal.

It is of course true that the citizen's
concern with "Town Hall" matters is not on the
order of the immediate problem of a clogged sewer
line in his mohalla; the citizen, seen as the
average city-dweller, would have little to say to
those whose job it is to draft budgets for a large
school system. (I might add that one does see the
"ordinary citizen" at Town Hall, attending the
meetings of the Corporation, getting some administrative work done, etc., although they are few and
far between.) But in Delhi what might be called
the "extended" citizen--associations of citizens
such as trade unions, cooperative societies, merchants groups, or pressure groups concerned with
a specific issue--is conspicuous by his absence.
Elsewhere in India, councilors have used such
groups as bases of power and influence in Corporation affairs.[2] These groups do exist in Delhi,
though they are not prominent, but with few exceptions they are not involved with municipal government.

I am relying, in this chapter, largely on
secondary sources: histories of the Delhi Municipal Committee, annual reports of the Committee,
etc. for the first part, and newspaper accounts,
minutes of the Corporation meetings, the published
budgets, etc. for the second part. I did attend

some Corporation meetings, and talked with several
informants about Corporation level affairs, but I
had no structured interviews and no plan of detailed observation. I cannot even confirm some of
the newspaper accounts independently, and such confirmation is often needed. I hope to fill in some
of the gaps in this data by inferences drawn from
my more reliable ward and zone level data.

MUNICIPAL GOVERNMENT IN DELHI: A HISTORY

Let me begin this section by recapitulating
briefly the history of Delhi as a political unit,
which I presented above (pp. 22-28). In the period
from 1858-1912 Delhi was not the capital of India,
it was a district of the Punjab. It became a Chief
Commissioner's Province after the shift of the
capital, and, after Independence, a Part C State.
In 1956, with the reorganization of the states, it
became a Union Territory. As the capital city
area, Delhi has always had strong central government control over its affairs (especially law and
order), and until Independence there was no elected
body for the whole state. The assembly of the
Delhi State (1952-1956) and the current Metropolitan
Council (1966-   ) share a certain powerlessness and
thus subordination to the administrative structure,
in the person of the Chief Commissioner (to 1956)
and Lt. Governor (1956-   ). Thus for most of
Delhi's modern history, the various municipal
bodies, and the Delhi Municipal Committee in particular, stood out in importance. They have been
the arena of electoral politics for local affairs
(there have been representatives to national councils and legislatures elected from Delhi), and in
1969-70 the Corporation overshadowed the Metropolitan Council.

Origins and Early Development

The roots of municipal government in Delhi
go back to before the Revolt of 1857: the Moghuls
had a system of municipal administration based on
the mohalla.[3] But the beginning of significant
municipal government was the institution of the
Delhi Municipal Committee in February 1863,[4]
although there is some doubt about how the city
was administered between 1858 and 1862:

> Delhi appears already at that time [late
> 1862] to have been a sort of Municipality.
> At any rate in a letter, dated 26th August
> 1862, the Commissioner of Delhi was asked
> whether any publicity was given to the
> proceedings of the Municipal Committee of
> Delhi and if so what practice was followed.
> The reply of the Deputy Commissioner, dated
> 15th September 1862, mentions 50 copies of
> a vernacular complication [sic] summarizing
> the proceedings as being struck off at the
> expense of the Municipal fund.[5]

The municipality was constituted under Act XXVI of
1850, with the notification made by the Punjab
Government.[6] The Committee constituted by this Act
had powers of taxation over "persons and property,"
the power to frame ordinances (and levy fines up to
Rs 50 for their infringement), and the responsibility for conducting the municipal administration.
The members of the Committee were appointed by the
"Governor or Governor in Council or Lieutenant-
Governor of any Presidency or place within the
territories under the Court of the East India
Company."[7] The main difference between this Act
and the first formal Act for constituting municipalities in India (Act X of 1842) is that indirect
taxes are permitted, and instead of the initiative
for founding the municipality coming from the
inhabitants of the town it would come from the
government. Still, relatively few municipalities
were constituted under this Act.[8]

From the inception of the Delhi Municipal
Committee until 1884, all its members were either
ex-officio (the Deputy Commissioner was ex-officio
President; the Civil Surgeon, the District Superintendent of Police, et al.), or nominated non-
officials, some of whom were "Europeans" and some
Indian. The precise number of members varied from
year to year, but 1881-82 is sufficiently representative:

> The Committee consisted of 21 members, of
> whom 6 were officials and 15 non-official.
> Of the latter, three were Europeans, six
> were Hindu and six Mohammedans. The non-
> official members were nominated and usually
> held office for two years. Owing, however,
> to the difficulty of obtaining men of
> influence, the same members were frequently
> appointed.[9]

A municipal Act of 1884 changed the Municipal Committee into a body half of whose 24 members were
elected.[10] This composition continued (roughly)
until 1922, when the Committee was expanded to 36
members, "24 elected, six appointed and six official. The 24 elected members were divided equally
between 12 Hindu and 12 Muslim members."[11] The
rules of election had been changed in 1913, and 11
members of a Committee of 22 were elected; three
members were ex-officio, eight were nominated (all
non-officials).[12] The balance of European, Hindu
and Muslim members changed over time as well. Until
1912 the number of Europeans (one of whom was
usually elected from the Civil Lines) was seven;
until 1906 there were slightly more Muslims than
Hindus (e.g., ten Muslims and eight Hindus, nine
Muslims and seven Hindus, etc.), and from 1906 to
1912 varying numbers, but more Hindus than Muslims
(13 Hindus and five Muslims in 1910-11, but nine
Hindus and eight Muslims in 1912-13). Between 1913
and 1921 there were five or six Europeans and approximately equal numbers of Hindus and Muslims.

In the period after 1912 there were two
general elections, but the pattern in the earlier
period was three or four elected members chosen
by lot, to retire and stand again. Typically,
these men were re-elected unopposed; similarly,
nominated members whose terms expired were usually
renominated. With few exceptions, the non-contested
election was the norm; Madho Pershad, however, notes
the beginnings of electoral interest in 1893-94 and
writes about the "keen contest" in one ward in
1896:

> It was alleged that many voters had been
> cajoled out of their certificates by the
> agents of either party, so that they
> might not be able to vote on the date of
> polling. The local vernacular papers
> took up sides too, and notices setting
> forth the virtues of one candidate or
> the other were posted up in the bazars.
> Party feeling ran so high that special
> precautions had to be taken to keep the
> peace and to prevent interference during
> polling. . . .[13]

The electorate of one ward in 1915 numbered 1,772
(of whom 700 voted).[14] Ferrell remarks of the
period 1911-1921, "The status of [the Municipal
Committee's] members was fairly low . . . but they
did control a certain amount of power. Very few
men of the Committee held a title, but continuous
membership in the Committee usually ensured some
type of honorary recognition."[15] In discussing the
intense national political activity in Delhi in
this period, which centered on the Khilafat Movement, the Rowlatt Bill Satyagraha and other national
issues, Ferrell mentions numerous men and organizations; almost none of them are to be found in the
Municipal Committee and the Committee itself is
never mentioned. In sum, the Municipal Committee
did not attract those active in national politics.

The meetings of the Committee dealt with
matters of municipal administration, and in this
it was very active. For example, in 1895-96:

> During the year the Committee held 51
> meetings. . . . The average attendance of
> members was 10.62 out of a possible 24.
>   The number of resolutions passed by
> the Committee was 908, and the members
> worked together very harmoniously, cheer-
> fully forming themselves into sub-committees
> to investigate doubtful or intricate cases
> by careful perusal of files, or by visiting
> localities. No less than 74 temporary sub-
> committees of this sort were appointed.[16]

There were also ceremonial functions, and the
municipality presented an "address" to the King
Emperor and Queen Empress at the 1911 Delhi Durbar.
By 1912-13, the Committee was framing by-laws
covering everything from water supply to "rules
regarding the use of steam whistles by the owners
of mills and factories."[17] The president of the
Committee in his report for the year 1912-13 notes
that the situation of Delhi's administration until
December 1911 "when Delhi came so prominently before
the Indian World" was that "the Municipality had been
developing on kachha [the opposite of pukka, which
means, among other things "well-built," "solid"]
irrational lines, like any minor municipality in a
rural district."[18] Needless to say, things
changed under his regime.
   The size of the municipal budget (which was
kept well in the black) grew steadily: in 1870-71
expenditure was Rs. 202,232; in 1884-85 it was Rs.
300,000; and by 1911 it was Rs. 812,318. Following
the increased burdens brought on by the acquisition
of the status of being the capital, expenditure went
up by 75 percent to Rs. 1,417,722 in 1912 and by
1921 it was Rs. 2,253,102. There was a closing
balance in that year of Rs. 600,861.)[19] For the
period up to roughly 1880, the largest expenditure

(about 25 percent of the total) was on the police.
In the 1880's public works, administration, and
sanitation take shares of the budget equal to that
of the police.[20] Throughout the period the largest
part of municipal income came from the octroi (a
tax levied on goods entering a town): (Rs. 273,057
out of Rs. 344,513 in 1886-87; Rs. 804,044 out of
Rs. 984,402 in 1917-18),but by 1920 less than half
the income came from taxation: the rest came
(presumably; Madho Pershad doesn't say) from
central government grants.[21]

The Period After 1920

As part of the Montagu-Chelmsford Reforms,
which brought the system of dyarchy to the Indian
provinces (in which local self-government was one
of the "transferred" subjects, i.e., under Indian
control), the Government of India set out to democ-
ratize local self-government by the extension of
the franchise, the replacement of official chairmen
(presidents) by non-officials, and expansion in the
proportion of elected members.[22] The proposals also
included an expansion in the powers of taxation and
the control of services for which the local authority was paying. All of this was seen as a further
step on the road to responsible self-government for
India, with the local bodies to remain a training
ground for political leaders. After an initial
period of boycotting the reforms, the Congress, in
the mid-1920s, cooperated with them in some instances with the idea of wrecking them by obstruc-
tionist tactics once they were elected.[23] It was
in this period that incipient or active national
leaders such as Jawaharlal Nehru and Vallabhbhai
Patel served on municipal councils.
The Delhi Municipal Committee had not proven
to be an arena for the politically active in the
1919 non-cooperation movement.[24] The citizens of
Delhi were not citizens of a province with "transferred" subjects, and so one might expect that the

politically active would join a Municipal Committee
which was given greater powers and a larger representation of elected members.[25] The first election
to the "new" Municipal Committee was held in March
1922, and Ferrell sees it as a referendum on the
non-cooperation movement, arguing that the electorate both rejected the movement (only six Hindu
Congress candidates won) and accepted it (all the
Muslim candidates picked by the nationalist leaders
Dr. Ansari and Hakim Ajmal Khan won).[26] The new
Committee apparently[27] continued to have the
deputy commissioner as its president.

    I can say very little about the Municipal Com-
mittee in the period between 1922 and 1946 due to a
lack of sources.[28] The communal problem was very
much in evidence: there were communal riots in
1924, 1925 (on election day), 1927, and 1928.[29]
This affected the Municipal Committee--by the end
of 1922 the municipal Congress party had almost
broken apart.[30] Lala Shri Ram hints at this:

> In the absence of any constructive policy
> before it, the Municipality has for some-
> time past been engaged in futile discussions
> and, what is perhaps more reprehensible,
> discussions characterized by a spirit of
> communalism. . . . A sense of civic respon-
> sibility should transcend communal bias, and,
> fortunately for Delhi, instances of the
> exhibition of such bias have been few and
> far between . . . councilors should vie with
> one another in the interest they take in
> municipal affairs rather than try to rival
> others in breaking building bye-laws and
> taking up the cause without justification
> of their undeserving co-religionists
> amongst the staff.[31]

But the main arena of political action from 1928
onward continued to be the national one, and the
Delhi Municipal Committee in all probability remained a backwater. The focus of political activity

after 1928 shifted to the national scene--men like
Jawaharlal Nehru took up national issues once
again--and while municipal politics were linked
to national movements, especially the Congress,[32]
the implementation of the 1935 Government of India
Act, which permitted provincial ministries, opened
up possibilities of holding province-wide office
to aspiring political leaders. The municipal arena
became one of many formal arenas.

    The electoral rules were changed at least
three times (I have imperfect evidence) in the
1930s: in 1934, "according to the present rules a
Hindu can vote for a Hindu candidate and a Mohammedan for a Mohammedan candidate; other electors
may vote for either candidate";[33] in 1935-36, "A
Hindu can vote for a Hindu candidate; others may
vote for either candidate";[34] and in 1937, "A
Muslim can vote only for a Muslim candidate while
a non-Muslim must vote only for a non-Muslim candidate."[35] These changes (and recall that in the
1920s there was a system of double-member constituencies with seats reserved for both communities), particularly the last one, suggest
strongly that the Muslim separatist movement was
emphasizing the unity of the community over the
preservation of minority interests, but unfortunately I have no corroborative evidence, nor do
I know how these rule changes were brought about.
The balance of the Municipal Committee during this
period would probably be like the one of 1937-38:
20 Hindus, 18 Muslims, one Sikh, one Indian
Christian, and four Europeans.[36] The membership
was expanded to 44 that year with 14 double-member
wards, three councilors ex-officio, six councilors
from special interests (two from the Punjab
Chamber of Commerce, one from the Delhi Piece
Goods Association, one from the Delhi Hindustani
Mercantile Association, one from the Delhi Factory
Owners, and one from the Anjuman Vakil-i-Qaum
Punjabian [a Muslim group], and the remaining
seven nominated from the general community.[37]

The size of municipal budgets continued to
grow: in 1931 revenue was Rs. 2,583,400 and
expenditure Rs. 2,605,809. Of the former, 44
percent came from the terminal tax (the successor
to the octroi), and about 15 percent of the latter
went to engineering, 15 percent to sanitation, and
15 percent to education.[38] By 1946-47 (the last
year before Independence) income was Rs. 6,872,000
and expenditure Rs. 6,890,000.[39] An Improvement
Trust carried on schemes of urban development in
the late 1930s and 1940s, expending 3,746,513
rupees in 1939-40 and 1,747,735 rupees in 1940-41.[40]

The relocation of the capital to Delhi brought
with it a proliferation of local bodies around the
old city: the New Delhi Municipal Committee was
formed in 1916; the Notified Area Committee, Civil
Station, in 1913; the West Delhi Notified Area Committee, in 1943; the Notified Area Committee, Fort,
in 1924; the Shahdara Municipal Committee, in 1943
(it had been a Notified Area Committee since 1916);
and the Mehrauli Notified Area Committee, in 1901.[41]
According to the Delhi Municipal Organization
Enquiry Committee, dissatisfaction with the working
of the DMC began in 1935 and by 1938 the DMC itself
had moved a resolution asking for either a responsible provincial legislature or a Corporation form
of government. The first proposal apparently was
not pressed and the latter ran into difficulties.
The purpose of establishing a Corporation would
have been not only to expand the powers of the
municipality but also to amalgamate the various
local authorities into one municipality.[42] World
War II intervened and the question of what would be
the appropriate municipal organization for Delhi
was not studied until 1946, with the appointment of
the Delhi Municipal Organization Enquiry Committee.
The coming of Independence overtook this committee
and its recommendations, so that municipal reorganization did not occur until 1958 (Delhi had of course
received a responsible legislature for a while in
the interval).

The normal three-year term of the Municipal Committee had been extended during the war and the next election was held in 1945. In 1946 the first non-official (and the first Indian) president was elected. This Committee's life was extended for one year and then, after a period of two years when the whole Committee was nominated, elections were held in 1951.[43] These were based on adult franchise, and Delhi was divided into 47 wards, in three of which there was an extra scheduled caste seat, making a total of 50 elected members. In addition there were four ex-officio members, three nominees of the chief commissioner, four seats allotted to industrial and commercial associations, and two to Labor, making a total of 63 members.[44] The elections were held six months before the general election of that year. Toward the end of the term of this Committee, three more constituencies (in the west of the city) and three more scheduled caste seats were added, bringing the total membership to 69, of which 56 were elected.[45] This was also the composition of the last Municipal Committee, for which elections were held in 1954.

In the last year of the Municipal Committee, 1957-58, the estimates of income and expenditure were as reported in Table 43. A very rough estimate--Delhi was growing very rapidly at this point--of the population covered by the municipality would be 1.5 million, making the per capita expenditure approximately Rs. 25.0 (i.e., about 151 percent more than 1946-47 levels). Prices in India had risen by 45 percent in the 1947-57 decade,[46] so there probably was a significant rise in real per capita expenditure.[47]

The president of the Committee, R. N. Agarwala, having given the details of the work of the Committee in its last three years, added: "In judging our record of work it must be borne in mind that we have been functioning under certain limitations imposed by the outmoded Punjab Municipal Act of 1911."[48] He began by noting the Committee's role as "dispenser of hospitality" to visiting dignitaries, and moved

TABLE 43

ESTIMATED INCOME AND EXPENDITURE, 1957-58,
DELHI MUNICIPAL COMMITTEE

Heading	Amount (in Rupees)
Income	
House Tax	5,800,000
Terminal Tax and Toll Tax	9,800,000
Motor Tax	890,000
Other Sources	8,457,000
Government Grant.	1,871,000
Government Loan	3,906,000
Total	30,724,000
Expenditure	
General	7,773,000
Education	5,384,000
Medical	1,095,000
Public Health	8,740,000
Water Supply.	6,053,000
Veterinary Department	20,000
Municipal Works	8,355,000
Total	37,420,000

Source: Moti Ram, ed. *Survey of Activities [of the*
DMC], 1954-1958 (Delhi: Delhi Municipal
Committee, 1958?), p. 13.

on to achievements in improving and expanding street
lighting, water supply, sewers, roads, staff
quarters, etc., and programs for katras, labor
welfare, gardens, taxation, education, social education, public health and sanitation, child welfare,
family planning, and flood relief.[49] He left out
some of the less interesting activities: recording
births and deaths, maintaining the cremation
grounds, sanctioning building plans, etc. In 1870-
71 the concerns of the Committee as reflected in the
major items of expenditure that year were: road
building and road repair, municipal building construction, police, menagerie, lighting, planting and

preservation of trees in public roads, grants to
scientific and charitable institutions, dispensaries, conservancy, watering of roads (to keep down
the dust), education, establishment (administration), and debt repayment.[50] Much the same ground
is covered in both these lists, and my suspicion is
that the actual administration of the expenditure
was as much in the hands of the expert officers in
1957 as it was in 1870, changes in the electoral
system notwithstanding.

THE DELHI MUNICIPAL CORPORATION

     In 1958 all but two of the local authorities
in Delhi were consolidated into the Delhi Municipal
Corporation. The two exceptions were the Delhi Cantonment and a New Delhi Municipal Committee of reduced size. The report of the Rural Urban Relationship Committee takes note of the demand of larger
urban areas for a Corporation form of government:
"The idea of a Corporation carries with it a certain
amount of prestige and civic pride but it also
creates responsibilities for raising higher financial resources."[51] In the course of a description
of the Municipal Committee, the following is said:
"the Council has a Chairman who is also the executive head. The State Government exercises greater
control over the Municipal Councils through the
District Officer and the Divisional Commissioner
than over the Corporation."[52] The Corporation is
thus seen as a more autonomous body, with greater
powers--actually, with an increased number of func-
tions--than the Municipal Committee. The "model"
Corporation was that of Bombay, where men of national stature like Pheroze Shah Mehta had served, and
the Corporation form was thus seen as an "advance"
toward a more popular municipal government.
     The formation of the Municipal Corporation in
Delhi drew on two strands of thought about local
self-government: that local government was to
provide a forum of democratic expression and a

"training ground" for political leadership, and
that it was an administrative necessity to decentralize government to make local affairs manage-
able.[53] With greater autonomy and powers, the
establishment of the Corporation would in some
degree compensate for the loss in democratic
representation after States Reorganization; but,
primarily, it filled an administrative need. In
this instance, it was not the need to decentralize
administrative authority (which was the impetus
behind nineteenth-century grants of powers to local
authorities), but the need to coordinate the pleth-
ora of local bodies in the Delhi Territory, all of
which were interrelated in economic terms already
and some of which had grown together to a point
where the built-up area was continuous, and
boundaries were visible only on maps.

The Corporation absorbed all but two of the
existing local bodies and covered the entire Union
Territory. Certain statutory boards were also
placed under the Corporation (although they remained independent undertakings, with some of their
membership appointed from outside the city government): the Delhi Transport Undertaking (DTU),[54]
the Delhi Electric Supply Undertaking (DESU), and
the Water Supply and Sewage Disposal Undertaking
(WSSDU). The Corporation is divided into the
usual executive wing, consisting of the municipal
commissioner, deputy commissioners, and the various
departments; and a deliberative wing of a hundred
councilors and six aldermen and their various committees: the Standing Committee (elsewhere in
India called the Executive Committee--it is the
committee in which the budget is first presented),
committees for each of the autonomous undertakings,
an Education Committee, a Works Committee, etc.

The Corporation meetings are presided over by
the mayor, who is elected each year. As presiding
officer, he of course has considerable power--he
can ask an offending member (e.g., someone who
refuses to yield the floor) to leave, and he can
adjourn the meeting at any time. He also has the

power to call for any file, and though he cannot
pass orders, he can make notations on it; this
constitutes a lever of no mean importance. It is
not surprising, therefore, that in the early days
of the Corporation, when the political balance
was more tenuous than it has been recently, the
mayoralty was a hotly contested position.[55] There
is also a deputy mayor, a leader of the House, and
a leader of the Opposition.

Meetings of the Corporation

The meetings of the Corporation* are the
locale quite frequently of a confrontation of councilors and administrators. While I have no wish
to overemphasize the point, it seems to me that
the physical set-up (Fig. 20) is symbolic of this.
The mayor's podium and the long table at which the
commissioner and/or his deputies sit are raised a
few feet. The seating positions of the parties
are assigned at the start of each new Corporation
year, but within their area, councilors seem to
sit pretty much where they please, except for the

_____

*
  There were 75 days on which meetings were
held in 1969-70. I was able to obtain a set of
the minutes of that year, which report the attendance of the councilors, roll call votes, and a summary of the proceedings along with relevant documents which the Corporation was considering. Each
month (roughly) sees the start of a new "meeting,"
which are adjourned and adjourned again until the
agenda is disposed of; sometimes this process can
be very long indeed: on October 27, 1969, for
example, the adjourned July (1967) [sic] meeting
took place, beginning at 2:30 PM. It was followed
by the adjourned August (1969) meeting at 3:00 PM,
which was adjourned until the next day, at 6:54 PM.
Having three different meetings scheduled on one
day--one might be a "special meeting"--is not
unusual.

various party leaders (and, to be sure, they move
around to consult with a colleague, etc.). There
is some spatial opposition of the ruling party and
the opposition, although by parliamentary convention (and indeed usually this is practiced) they
are to address the mayor when they are making a
speech.[56] But more significantly, the mass of
councilors sit "opposed to" the commissioner and
his supporting administrative staff. The "Treasury
Benches" are, in effect, occupied by the senior
officers of the executive wing.

The rules of procedure for the conduct of
meetings, the calling of special meetings, etc.,
are set down in the Delhi Municipal Corporation
Act (sections 72-88). These detail the method
of electing the mayor and deputy mayor, the number
of members needed for a quorum, the rights of the

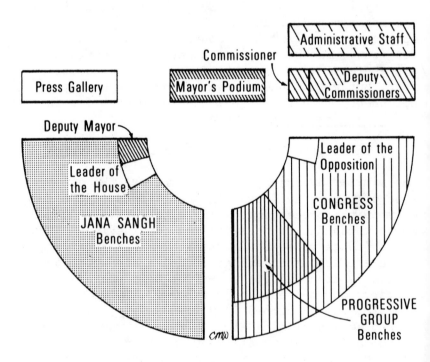

Fig. 20   The Corporation Meeting Hall, 1969-7(

commissioner and his assistants to participate in
debate, the availability of the minutes, and other
similar questions. One of the most important rules
is found in subsection (2) of section 81, which
reads: "A councilor or alderman may, subject to
the provisions of sub-section (3), ask the Commissioner questions on any matter relating to the
municipal government of Delhi or the administration
of this Act or the function of any of the municipal
authorities." Sub-section (3), has a provision
that questions must be submitted in writing seven
days in advance (with supplementary questions permitted), and contains a list of 13 additional
conditions, which reads, in part:

> [no question shall]
>   (i) bring in any name or statement not
> strictly necessary to make the question
> intelligible,
>   (ii) contain arguments, ironical expres-
> sions, imputations, epithets or defamatory
> statements,
>   (iii) ask for an expression of opinion or
> the solution of a hypothetical proposition,. . .
>   (v) relate to a matter which is not pri-
> marily the concern of the Corporation or any
> of the municipal authorities, . . .
>   (ix) ask for information on trivial
> matters, . . .
> (xiii) ask for any information on matter
> which is under adjudication by a court of
> law.

The question of whether or not a member's question
falls within these guidelines is decided by the
mayor. There is a further proviso in sub-section
(5): "The Commissioner shall not be bound to answer
a question if it asks for information which has been
communicated to him in confidence or if in the
opinion of the Mayor it cannot be answered without
prejudice to public interest or the interest of the
Corporation." A similarly worded proviso (section

70, sub-section [2]) modifies the right of the
Corporation to demand that the commissioner
produce "records, correspondence, plan or other
documents" (i.e., the files).

The role of mayor, while modeled on the
impartial, non-party Speaker, clearly has the
potential of being infused with far greater
significance when his ties to the "ruling
party," which elects him, are taken into account.
Mayors in Delhi have typically been politically
powerful figures who have not divorced themselves
from party affairs after their election.   The
mayor in 1973, for example, was the former leader
of the House and probably one of the two or three
most powerful Jana Sangh leaders in Delhi.   It
is no accident that many of the "disorders"
(which are usually shouting matches, but not
infrequently near-brawls) revolve around rulings
by the mayor on procedure.   There are items of
procedure which are not in the Act: "short
notice enquiries" are permitted and typically
constitute the first order of business.   These
deal with important problems of immediate
interest--a large fire, for example--and can
be debated after the commissioner makes his
statement.

A meeting (caveat: not a sitting) will
typically consist of (1) the confirmation of the
minutes of previous meetings (which is usually a
formality); (2) a short notice enquiry, the
commissioner's reply and a debate; (3) regular
enquiries, the commissioner's statement, and
supplementary questions and answers; (4) items of
business (usually these are labeled "urgent
business"), which result in resolutions, and the
debate and voting on resolutions and amendments.
(This is not necessarily the order of action, and
many meetings will not have one or more of these
features.)

The councilor receives Rs. 25 for every day
on which he attends a meeting of the Corporation
or one of its committees, up to a maximum of Rs.

300 per month. The office of the secretary of the
Corporation maintains a register of attendance, and
I was told that councilors found it easy to sign in
for several days at a time, or they may simply come
to Town Hall on a meeting day in order to sign the
register, and will sit in the meeting chamber for
only a short time, if at all. Indirect confirmation
of this can be found in the minutes. The names of
members present are listed at the beginning of the
minutes of each meeting session, and the attendance
is typically less than one hundred. In 1969-70
there were 32 roll-call votes, all of them won by
the Jana Sangh.[57] The number of councilors "ab-
staining" in the 32 roll-calls averaged 25. If we
disregard the nine votes taken on two days of budget
debate (which is well attended, by all accounts)
the number of abstentions averages 30 per vote.
The range is from eight abstentions to 56; during
the budget debate it was from nine to 18. In a
system of party discipline--which functions with
rare exceptions in Delhi--these "abstentions"
clearly represent councilors who were not present
when the vote was taken. Councilors actually in
Town Hall would be called in to vote. The number
of councilors sitting in the chamber, then, is
little more than half the membership. (I might add
that this was also my impression on the occsions
when I observed meetings.)
　　Seventy-five sittings of the Corporation
occurred in 1969-70.* The sitting usually begins

---

*While I was in Delhi I read three of the major
English language dailies (the Statesman, the Hindustan Times, and the Times of India). Of the 52 sittings of 1969-70 held during the period that I collected clippings, only 25 were reported in any paper
(with three reported in all three and six more
reported in at least two). Many of these meetings
were those (apart from the budget session) in which
"disturbances" took place. It is hardly surprising
that the public image of a Corporation meeting is
one of "shameful scenes."

with questions asked of the commissioner. These
can be quite detailed. I give the following
example, selected at random:

Question No. 3
Shri Nakul Bhargava:
    Will the commissioner please state:
(a) . . . how many [law] cases the
    Municipal Corporation won or lost in
    the year 1966-67? [58]
(b) What was the financial implications in
    the cases involved?
(c) Will the Commissioner state the position
    of the case against Ad New Vistas?
(d) Is it a fact that the lawyers do not
    attend the Court till 12:00 noon?
Commissioner:
(a) The number of cases lost from January,
    1966 to March, 1967, is 162 whereas
    the number won during the aforesaid
    period is 3,260. The cases were lost
    mostly on merits and also a very few
    for want of proper evidence, i.e., non-
    availability of witnesses or documents.
(b) No financial implication is involved
    in the cases lost.
(c) The case of Ad New Vista is fixed for
    18-12-67 for filing the written state-
    ment in the Court of Shri Hira Lal Garg,
    Sub-Judge 1st class, Delhi.
(d) It is not correct.[59]

In the normal course of a Corporation meeting,
speeches are made which likewise go into considerable detail on very particular problems. It is not
surprising that service in the municipality has
had, and continues to carry, the implication of
exhausting, dull work over petty detail. The typical Corporation meeting is at best uneventful and
at worst deadly dull.
    But every now and then the Corporation erupts
into a "disorder," which is anything but dull. One

of the most severe during 1969-70--it occasioned
some serious discussion in the following days--
occurred on July 27, 1970. The newspaper account
is worth quoting in its entirety:

> The Delhi Municipal Corporation meeting
> was adjourned five times in four hours on
> Monday, the adjournment durations ranging
> from 10 minutes to one hour.
> It was one of the most chaotic and
> noisiest meetings of the civic body. The
> Opposition, barring members of the Con-
> gress(O), was in a defiant mood and made
> continuous attempts to have their say.
> Every time the House reassembled the Oppo-
> sition renewed its tirade with redoubled
> vigour and determination and made it
> impossible for the Commissioner, Mr. B. S.
> Manchanda, to read a statement on a short-
> notice inquiry raised by the leader of the
> Congress(R), Mr. Kishore Lal.
> But the acting Mayor, Mr. Balraj Khanna,
> and the ruling Jana Sangh proved more than
> a match for the vociferous Opposition. At
> about 6-15 p.m. he ruled that the time for
> the short-notice inquiry had lapsed and took
> up the agenda. And in less than 20 minutes,
> as many as 121 items, 82 urgent and 33 ordi-
> nary, were cleared, the Opposition protests,
> catcalls, shouting, and slogans notwith-
> standing.
> Opposition members stood up and shouted,
> raised points of order and slogans like
> "Tanashahi nahi chalegi." Three of them
> stood up on their bench and picked up the
> microphone and shouted hoarse [sic]. One
> of them, Mr. B. D. Verma (C-R) walked on
> tables to get near the Mayor in a vain bid
> to make him listen to his protestations.
> Mr. R. P. Gupta (Ind) walked to the Mayor's
> dais and left a note in front of Mr. Khanna,
> and Mrs. Sheila Khanna (C-R) approached the

acting Mayor and tried to whisper something into his ears [sic]. But Mr. Khanna turned a deaf ear.

Undaunted, Mr. Khanna kept up his tempo of calling the item number, one after the other, and the ruling party chief, Mr. Kidar Nath Sahni, promptly proposed it; his deputy, Mr. O. P. Jain, seconded it and all Sangh members raised hands to indicate the "aye." It became an almost mechanical process.

The climax of the Opposition's defiant mood was the reported hurling of a paperweight and a glass tumbler at the acting Mayor from the Opposition benches. Mr. Khanna said the paperweight was intercepted by the Commissioner while the tumbler hit the dais and broke into pieces. Mr. Kishore Lal, leader of the Opposition, denied the allegation.

The Opposition's main point was what it described as "political" pressure being exerted by the ruling party in view of the coming elections. It demanded an assurance from the acting Mayor to issue a directive to the Commissioner "not to be pressurized" [sic]. Mr. Khanna said he could not issue a directive to the Commissioner "relating to executive matters."

In the verbal battle between the acting Mayor and the Opposition, allegations were levelled against him. "I can't reply in your language," he retorted. He named Mr. J. P. Goel (Progressive Group) who refused to leave and kept sitting and jibed at him. There were broad smiles in the visitors' gallery as the ruling party clashed with the Opposition several times during which names were called and allegations exchanged.

Earlier, the House mourned the death of Pattam Thanu Pillai, Mr. Madan Lal, a former councilor, and victims of the Alaknanda tragedy.

Mr. Khanna announced that a preamble
seeking to sanction an ex-gratis payment
of Rs. 10,000 to the family of the late
Mr. T. S. Titus, Additional General Manager,
DTU, who died recently, would be put up for
the approval of the House. Members demanded
a higher allocation and he said that it was
for the House to take a final decision on
it.

Mr. Kidar Nath Sahni felicitated the
winners of gold medals in wrestling in the
Commonwealth Games and said that the Corporation would accord them a civic reception
on their return.[60]

The "railroading" of agenda items apparently
became an annual feature--the Hindustan Times of
June 22, 1971, reported that 202 resolutions were
passed in 27 minutes at the previous day's Corporation meeting. The throwing of objects, though
not unprecedented, is not common. The trading of
insults, however, is far more common, and a major
cause of walkouts and adjourned meetings is the
insistence of one councilor that an opponent
apologize for and/or withdraw an "unparliamentary"
remark. The mayor may ask the offender to do this,
and the latter as often as not refuses to leave
when "named" (i.e., asked to leave), and sometimes
refuses to stop speaking. At this point, typically,
the mayor adjourns the meeting. Occasionally, the
leader of the party of the offending member may
apologize for him.

During 1969-70 there were at least six occasions of "grave disorder" occurring, according to
the minutes.[61] On two occasions, the political
leadership requested the mayor to adjourn a subsequent meeting so that the "disgraceful incidents"
could be discussed informally, and the mayor com-
plied. If we consider the less than "grave" disorders and the walkouts that occur (usually staged
by one councilor or a small group who then typically come back to the chamber shortly afterwards;

but the entire opposition walks out not infrequently), it would be fair to say that "unparliamentary" behavior is a prominent feature of many
Corporation meetings. One informant (a newspaper
reporter) claimed that this could be explained by
the decline in quality of the average councilor
after the "best" men decided to contest for the
Metropolitan Council in 1967 (with the expectation
that the Corporation would be superseded), so that
only the illiterate and the uneducated were left.
But the "disorder phenomenon" is too widespread in
India (and is of course not unknown elsewhere,
from the U.N.--vide Kruschev and his shoe--on down)
to make this explanation plausible. There are
other reasons why disorders occur. Inter alia,
there may be considerations of political tactics
involved (it's one way of making it into the papers,
for example), and possibly the venting of the
frustration of having very little chance of influencing anything in the forum of the Corporation
meeting.

The "form" of the "deliberative wing" which
I have been describing is comparable to other
legislative bodies in India.[62] It is a body in
which all councilors can and do participate,
individually, whether in making speeches or
creating "disorders." I now move to a discussion
of the budget, where the Corporation members act
as a structured body, as "government" and "opposition," and as "the Corporation" vis-à-vis the
administrative wing and the municipal commissioner.

The Corporation Budget

Undoubtedly the single most important set of
meetings--they last several weeks of almost daily
sitting--is that which deals with the budget, or
actually budgets: that of the Corporation, and
those of the three statutory bodies, the DTU, DESU,
and WSSDU.[63] The debate is serious and prolonged;
careful and detailed amendments are offered, some

of which are accepted, but most of which are
voted down; and proceedings are on the whole
"uneventful."[64]   In what follows, I consider
the Corporation budget; the procedure with
respect to the budgets of the statutory bodies
is similar, except that they are presented to
the Corporation by the chairman of the appropriate, corresponding statutory committees (see
below, pp. 317-18), and the initial estimates
are prepared by the manager of the Undertaking.

The Budgetary Process
     The budget is prepared by the executive
wing and presented by the commissioner to the
Standing Committee. It is then presented to the
House by the chairman of the Standing Committee
in a lengthy address (he also replies to the
debate just before voting).[65] The minutes are
not helpful in reporting the debate, since they
merely list the names of those councilors who
spoke. In the 1970 debate, some 46 members were
heard (the minutes read "participated in the
discussion") in the debate on the General Wing
budget. At the end of the debate, the budget
(revised estimates for the current [in this
instance, 1969-70] year, and estimates for the
coming year) is moved as a resolution. Amendments are offered to each section as it is presented. A typical sequence (except that there
is usually more than one amendment) is as follows:

     Amendment No. 1:
     Shri Ram Lal [Congress] moved and Shri
     Narain Singh [Congress] seconded the
     following amendment:--
          That the following be added at the end
     of the motion:--
          "with the modification that the rate
     of tax on cycle-rickshaws be reduced to
     Rs 3/- per year per vehicle [from Rs 6/-]
     and licenses be issued to all the rickshaw
     pullers." [It has been Corporation policy

to phase out the use of these vehicles
by not granting new licenses].
   Amendment No. 1 was put to vote and
rejected by 52 to 37 votes.
   (All the members of Opposition present
in the meeting dissented.)
   Thereafter the motion of Shri Sahni [the
Standing Committee Chairman] relating to
Tax on Cycle-rickshaws was carried.[66]

An occasional amendment proposed by the member of
the ruling party is carried (and, of course, the
commissioner's original proposals have been amended
already in the Standing Committee). In addition to
substantive amendments (like the one quoted above),
the following occurs often: "Shri Ram Lal moved
and Shri Narain Singh seconded the following amendment:--Resolved that the Budget Estimates (General)
for the year 1970-71 as prepared by the Standing
Committee be referred to the Standing Committee for
further consideration."[67] These amendments were
rejected. A few amendments were referred to the
commissioner "for final disposal" usually on the
initiative of the Jana Sangh, but in one case at
least on the initiative of the Opposition.
   The budget thus goes through three stages: as
proposed by the commissioner; as amended and presented by the Standing Committee; as approved by the
Corporation. The changes that occurred at each step
are shown in Tables 44-47. The Revised Estimates
for 1969-70 were prepared on the basis of the
receipts and expenditures of the first six months
of the fiscal year. The Corporation clearly follows
the lead of the Standing Committee in virtually
every item, both on the income and expenditure
sides. On the revenue side (Table 44, column 4
minus column 2), the increase of 300,000 rupees (to
be realized from the Terminal Tax) was proposed by
the Jana Sangh, and the increase of 50,000 rupees
on the expenditure side (Table 45, column 4 minus
column 2) on "General Supervision," etc., and the
increase of 250,000 rupees for "Improvement Schemes,

slum clearance" were both proposed by the Jana
Sangh; the former to "provide for decorations on
Republic Day, Diwali and other festivals"[68] and
the latter for the improvement of private katras.
(Recall the description of the katra improvements
given in Chapter 3, pp. 74-82.)

More interesting are the changes made by the
Standing Committee in the proposals of the commissioner. On the income side, in 1969-70, five
of the 13 items were increased, but four of those
were in the seven major sources of increase and
the largest amount (Rs. 25,476,000) in the major
source. This increase was due largely to the
provision of an addition of Rs. 14,000,000 to be
realized from the sale of electricity to the New
Delhi Municipal Committee and the Electricity
Board of the state of U.P. These payments were
in fact a matter of continuing dispute between
the Corporation and the governments concerned,
and it may well be that the inclusion of the
income from these sources was seen as a necessary
part of the Corporation's case (or a lever in the
negotiations). The Congress Party in the Corporation debate attempted to get that amount (the
14,000,000 rupees) deleted.

On the expenditure side, the amount of nine
of the 18 items proposed by the commissioner was
let stand; aside from that for "Roads and Public
Lighting" these were again the smaller items
(totaling only 12-13 percent of the budget). Six
of the nine changes were increases, but with one
exception ("Water supply"), these were relatively
small amounts: 500,000 rupees or less. The
exception shows a decrease of 10,000,000 rupees,
which involves payment to the Water Supply and
Sewage Disposal Undertaking, which was also a
matter of dispute (i.e., the Corporation did not
believe it owed the WSSDU the 10,000,000 rupees
it had been billed). Both income and expenditure
items were changed in the Standing Committee with
votes of seven to seven with the chairman exer-
cising his casting vote. The Standing Committee

TABLE 44

REVISED ESTIMATES OF INCOME, DELHI MUNICIPAL CORPORATION, 1969-70 (IN RUPEES)

Head of Account	(1) Proposed by the Commissioner	(2) Approved by Standing Committee	(3). Column 2 Minus Column 1	(4) Approved by Corporation[a]	(5) Percentage of Total (Column 4)
1. General tax, indirect taxation and miscellaneous revenue	182,767,500	208,243,500	25,476,000	208,543,500	78
2. Water supply[b]					
3. Education	39,136,000	39,136,000	0		15
4. Libraries[b]					
5. Public health	794,100	794,100	0		0
6. Medical relief	153,000	153,000	0		0
7. Conservancy and street cleaning	310,000	510,000	200,000		0
8. Scavenging, drains and sewers[b]					
9. Roads and public lighting	3,117,500	3,117,500	0		1
10. Building acquisition and management	4,251,000	4,251,000	0		2
11. Fire brigade	8,000	8,000	0		0
12. Licensing, removal of encroachments, etc.	3,169,000	3,269,000	100,000		1
13. Gardens and open spaces	200,000	200,000	0		0
14. Markets and slaughter houses	4,425,000	4,525,000	100,000		2
15. Improvement schemes, slum clearance, etc.	2,025,000	2,125,000	100,000		1
16. Transfer from other accounts[b]					
22. Development charges	500,000	500,000	0		0
Totals	240,856,100	266,832,100	25,976,000	267,132,100	100
Opening balance (April 1, 1969)	- 1,747,009	- 1,747,009		- 1,747,009	
Grand total, income	239,109,091	265,085,091		265,385,091	

[a] Equal to column 2 if left blank.

[b] Listed in the budget but with no revenue anticipated.

REVISED ESTIMATES OF EXPENDITURE, DELHI MUNICIPAL CORPORATION, 1969-70 (IN RUPEES)

Head of Account	(1) Proposed by the Commissioner	(2) Approved by Standing Committee	(3) Column 2 minus Column 1	(4) Approved by Corporation^a	(5) Percentage of Total (Column 4)
I. General supervision, collection of revenue	10,414,200	10,437,700	23,500	10,487,700	4
II. Water supply	28,000,000	18,000,000	-10,000,000		7
III. Education	72,982,000	73,082,000	100,000		28
IV. Libraries	256,000	256,000	0		0
V. Public health	8,679,000	8,653,000	-26,000		3
VI. Medical relief	24,830,000	24,695,000	-135,000		9
VII. Conservancy and street cleaning	26,840,000	27,290,000	450,000		10
VIII. Scavenging, drains, and sewers	2,342,750	3,042,750	700,000		1
IX. Roads and public lighting	16,461,000	16,461,000	0		6
X. Building, land acquisition and management	7,126,100	7,126,100	0		3
XI. Fire brigade	3,139,000	3,139,000	0		1
XII. Licensing, removal of encroachments	765,500	765,500	0		0
XIII. Gardens and open spaces	6,030,000	6,030,000	0		2
XIV. Markets and slaughter houses	365,000	365,000	0		0
XV. Improvement schemes, slum clearance	17,525,300	17,545,300	20,000	17,795,300	7
XVI. Miscellaneous	47,013,600	47,550,600	537,000		18
XVII. Reserve for unforeseen charges	293,000	293,000	0		0
XXXVII. Development charges	500,000	500,000	0		0
Less credit to be taken from anticipated savings under the establishment heads	-500,000	-500,000		-500,000	
Net expenditure	273,562,450	264,731,950		265,031,950	99
Closing balance, March 30, 1970	-34,453,359	+353,141		+353,141	
Grand total	239,109,091	265,085,091		265,385,091	

^a Equals the figure in column 2 when blank.

TABLE 46

BUDGET ESTIMATES OF INCOME, 1970-71 (IN RUPEES)

Head of Account	(1) Proposed by the Commissioner	(2) Approved by Standing Committee	(3) Column 2 Minus Column 1	(4) Approved by the Corporation[a]	(5) Percentage of Total (column 4)
1. General tax, indirect taxation and miscellaneous revenue	190,501,500	214,077,500	23,576,000	215,077,500	79
2. Water supply[b]	40,710,000	40,710,000	0		15
3. Education					
4. Libraries[b]					
5. Public health	794,100	794,100	0		0
6. Medical relief	153,000	153,000	0		0
7. Conservancy, street cleaning	320,000	320,000	0		0
8. Scavenging, drains and sewers[b]					
9. Roads and public lighting	3,117,500	3,617,500	500,000		1
10. Buildings, land acquisitions and management	4,306,000	4,631,000	500,000		2
11. Fire brigade	8,000	8,000	0		0
12. Licensing, removal of encroachments, etc.	3,169,000	3,269,000	100,000		1
13. Gardens and open spaces	200,000	200,000	0		0
14. Markets and slaughter houses	1,925,000	2,025,000	100,000		1
15. Improvement schemes, slum clearance	2,025,000	2,625,000	600,000		1
16. Transfer from other accounts[b]					
22. Development charges	500,000	500,000	0		0
Totals	247,729,100	272,930,100	25,201,000	273,930,100	100
Opening balance (April 1, 1970)	- 34,453,359	+353,141		+353,141	
Grand total, income	213,275,741	273,283,241		274,283,241	

[a]Equal to column 2 when blank.

[b]

BUDGET ESTIMATES OF EXPENDITURE, 1970-71 (IN RUPEES)

Head of Account	(1) Proposed by the Commissioner	(2) Approved by Standing Committee	(3) Column 2 Minus Column 1	(4) Approved by Corporation	(5) Percentage of Total (Column 4)
I. General supervision, collection of revenue, etc.	10,702,600	11,180,600	478,000	11,265,600	4
II. Water supply	28,000,000	28,000,000	0		10
III. Education	76,364,300	78,034,300	1,670,000	78,084,300	29
IV. Libraries	258,000	258,000	0		0
V. Public health	8,955,500	9,324,500	369,000	9,349,500	3
VI. Medical relief	26,669,500	27,659,500	990,000		10
VII. Conservancy, street cleaning	27,403,000	27,803,000	400,000		10
VIII. Scavenging, drains and sewers	2,377,600	4,827,600	2,450,000		2
IX. Roads and public lighting	17,411,000	18,111,000	700,000		7
X. Buildings, land acquisition and management	6,670,300	6,670,300	0		2
XI. Fire brigade	3,705,000	3,705,000	0		1
XII. Licensing, removal of encroach-ments, etc.	792,400	792,400	0		0
XIII. Gardens and open spaces	6,530,000	6,930,000	400,000		3
XIV. Markets and slaughter houses	368,000	368,000	0		0
XV. Improvement schemes, slum clearance	8,732,800	8,932,800	200,000	9,682,800	4
XVI. Miscellaneous	35,405,000	39,108,000	3,703,000	39,258,000	14
XVII. Reserve for unforeseen charges	413,000	378,000	-35,000		0
XXXVII. Development charges	500,000	500,000	0		0
Totals	261,258,000	272,583,000	11,325,000	273,643,000	99
Closing balance	-47,982,241	+700,241		+640,241	
Grand Total	213,275,741	273,283,241		274,283,241	

a Equals column 2 when left blank.

in addition rearranged the commissioner's budget,
typically distributing provisions for "ad hoc"
expenditure into expenditures on specific items.

The tendency obviously is for the Standing
Committee and the Corporation to be optimistic
about the amount of revenue to be realized, in
order to permit themselves to be more generous
on expenditure. One would expect that in the
estimates for the coming fiscal year, this
tendency would be more pronounced than for the
fiscal year which was half over. Tables 46 and 47
show that the Standing Committee increased the
commissioner's estimate of income by Rs. 25,201,000
(i.e., about 10 percent of the total budget), and
expenditure by Rs. 11,325,000. (And their estimates of the closing balance are in consequence far
rosier than the commissioner's, and the estimate of
the opening balance--which comes from the 1969-70
revised estimates--is also optimistic.) Again,
the lion's share of the estimated increase in
income was under the largest head ("General tax")--
Rs. 23,576,000. The major increase in that item
was a provision for a "Rural Area Grant" for
10,000,000 rupees, which the Corporation would
presumably get from the Government of India; a
Congress amendment in the Corporation sought to
delete this since there was "no commitment" for
it.[69] The other major expectations of increase
were: 2.3 million for taxes on private property;
3.1 million from terminal tax; 2.6 million from the
tax on motor vehicles; and 3.2 million from another
Government of India grant.

The Standing Committee reduced the estimated
expenditure under one head only, and there by a
miniscule amount. Eight of the ten increases were
between 2 and 6 percent (four of them of 4 percent,
three of 2 percent, and one of 6 percent) over the
commissioner's proposals. The expenditures under
"miscellaneous" were put up by 10 percent, mainly
for the 19 categories of "new works," ranging from
Rs. 50,000 for the construction of ladies' urinals
to Rs. 1,000,000 for "works in constituencies" and

including items such as Rs. 200,000 more for
improvement of street lighting, Rs. 140,000 more
for "provision of statues" and Rs. 500,000 "ad
hoc provision for harijan bastis." But the major
increase (although it amounted to only a 1 percent
increase in the budget as a whole) was the 100
percent increase in the provision for "scavenging,
drains, and sewers." Rs. 2,000,000 of this was
for payment to the WSSDU, and so it may well be
related to the cut of 10,000,000 rupees mentioned
above: 2,000,000 rupees may be what the Corporation thought it should be paying on a 10,000,000-
rupee bill.

In the final stage of approval of the budget,
five of the 18 allocations were increased further
in the Corporation meetings, and six amendments
were involved. Two proposals by Congress members
simply shifted the expenditure from one heading to
another. The four proposed by Jana Sangh members
were more substantial: the largest item was for
an increase of Rs. 750,000 "to provide for the
improvement of private katras," and the smallest,
a provision of Rs. 10,000 more "for the progress
and propagation of the Punjabi language."[70] The
Corporation also included an increase in estimated
revenue from terminal tax of 10,000,000 rupees, in
an amendment moved by Jana Sangh councilors.

There were 258 amendments to the 1970-71
expenditure estimates proposed, with the largest
number (77) under the "miscellaneous" heading.
Councilors tended to propose amendments dealing
with specific improvements, frequently, of course,
in their own constituencies: new schools, road
improvements, etc. These amendments were typically
"referred to the Commissioner for final disposal,"
on the initiative of the Jana Sangh leadership.
Other amendments (all but six) were voted down, a
few with roll-call votes. Virtually every amendment proposed--unsurprisingly--was proposed by an
opposition member.

An indication of just how sanguine the Corporation's estimates are can be had by examining the

past record (see Tables 48 and 49 and compare with
Tables 44 and 45 for the Commissioner's proposals).
On the income side, it can be seen that while the
commissioner's proposals for the revised estimates
under the "General tax" head was some 10,000,000
rupees less than the original budget estimates
(and the commissioner may be "professionally pessi-
mistic" about the size of receipts, as a device to
limit the expansionary zeal of the Corporation),
the revised estimates add another 17,000,000 rupees,
or 27,000,000 rupees more than the commissioner's
proposed estimate. The upward revision under the
"Markets" head is due to a far higher than expected
level of receipts in the first six months of 1969-70.
As far as expenditures go, there seems to be no
inclination to cut back on the budget estimates in
the revised estimates, and the latter are indeed
often increased, though by modest amounts. The
actual figures for 1968-69 give some indication
of how rapidly resources would have to expand to
take care of the significant rise in expenditure:
the revised estimates project an increase of 25
percent in "General tax" revenue, which would seem
somewhat optimistic (to understate the point). The
commissioner in his note on the proposals for the
revised estimates writes:

> Section 111 of the D.M.C. Act requires that
> if at any time during the year it appears
> to the Corporation that the income of the
> Municipal Fund during the same year will
> not suffice to meet the expenditure sanc-
> tioned in the budget estimates of that
> year . . . then it shall be incumbent on
> the Corporation to sanction forthwith any
> measures which it may consider necessary
> for adjusting the year's income to the
> expenditure [by increasing taxes or reducing
> expenditure] . . . . It will be necessary
> to take steps in this direction considering
> the huge gap between likely income and
> expenditure during the year. The matter

TABLE 48

INCOME ESTIMATES AS APPROVED BY THE CORPORATION,
1968-69 AND 1969-70 (IN RUPEES)

Head of Account[a]	Actuals 1968-69	Budget Estimates 1969-70	Revised Estimates 1969-70
1. General tax	160,829,023	191,323,800	208,543,500
2. Education	20,082,571	40,232,000	39,136,000
3. Public health	637,783	714,500	794,100
4. Medical	206,664	303,000	153,000
5. Conservancy	635,283	200,000	510,000
6. Scavenging	876	. . . .	. . . .
7. Roads, public lighting. .	2,587,890	3,140,000	3,117,500
8. Buildings	3,808,146	4,930,000	4,251,000
9. Fire brigade.	8,288	8,000	8,000
10. Licensing	2,911,893	5,348,000	3,269,000
11. Gardens	188,453	200,000	200,000
12. Markets	1,526,545	1,700,000	4,525,000
13. Improvement schemes . . .	1,921,260	2,975,000	2,125,000

The full heading is the same as in Table 44 and 46.

has already been referred to the Standing
Committee and is pending decision.[71]

It is not clear what happens if the Corporation
does not make the adjustment; 1968-69 began with
an "opening balance" of minus Rs. 1,747,000. That
is, modest deficits seem to be tolerated. In any
event, the Corporation seems willing to cut its
budget to accommodate the real situation only after
the actual income is in hand; there is no evidence
that increases of the revised estimates over the
budget estimates were in any way justified by
"genuine" (as opposed to "politically optimistic")
expectations of actual increases.

I might briefly note here a comparison with
the budgetary process in America. Herbert Simon

TABLE 49

EXPENDITURE ESTIMATES AS APPROVED BY THE CORPORATION,
1968-69 AND 1969-70 (IN RUPEES)

Head of Account[a]	Actuals 1968-69	Budget Estimates 1969-70	Revised Estimates 1969-70
I. General supervision . . .	9,049,844	9,818,000	10,487,700
II. Water supply.	7,053,628	30,000,000	18,000,000
III. Education	56,407,499	71,763,000	73,082,000
IV. Libraries	112,522	258,000	256,000
V. Public health	6,106,075	7,108,000	8,653,000
VI. Medical relief.	18,265,511	23,692,400	24,695,000
VII. Conservancy	20,133,238	24,398,600	27,290,000
VIII. Scavenging.	932,517	1,121,400	3,042,750
IX. Roads, public lighting. .	15,753,895	14,813,500	16,461,000
X. Buildings	4,950,580	6,042,600	7,126,100
XI. Fire brigade.	2,571,470	3,061,000	3,139,000
XII. Licensing	618,918	727,500	765,500
XIII. Gardens	4,497,230	5,585,200	6,030,000
XIV. Markets	282,799	296,000	365,000
XV. Improvement schemes . . .	2,284,831	10,016,000	17,795,300
XVI. Miscellaneous	33,076,167	47,469,000	47,550,600
XVII. Reserve	161,049	558,000	293,000
XXXVII. Development	. . . .	700,000	500,000

[a]The full heading is the same as in Tables 45 and 47.

has pointed out that "in considerable part, public
budgets are the product of precedent. In first
approximation, this year's budget is equal to last
year's."[72]   Crecine's survey of municipal budgets
confirms this assertion.[73] The details of his conclusions suggest that Delhi would fit in nicely as
an "American" city. That is, the Delhi budget too
is clearly written as a modification of the previous
year's budget, and Crecine's remarks on the constraints of a statutory requirement of a balanced
budget, the "organizational inertia" of municipal
operating budgets, etc., which work against making
the process one with "a great deal of political
content"[74] seem equally applicable in Delhi.

The Budget in Final Form.
Crecine notes that "wages account for 65-80 percent of a city's total operating expenses" in America.[75]   In Delhi, 60 percent of the Corporation's expenditure (apart from the water supply category, which is in a separate budget) goes in payment of salaries (called "establishment" expenditure--the salary of every job of every department of the Corporation is listed in a "Schedule of Establishment," a public document), and a sizeable part, about 25 percent, into teacher's salaries. This data is presented in Table 50.

TABLE 50

EXPENDITURE AND ESTABLISHMENT COSTS, 1968-69

	Head of Account[a]	Expenditure	Establishment	Percentage
I.	General supervision . . .	9,049,844	6,479,952	72
III.	Education	56,407,499	48,827,012	87
IV.	Libraries	112,522[b]	. . . .	..
V.	Public health	6,106,075	4,063,869	67
VI.	Medical relief.	18,265,511	11,147,301	61
VII.	Conservancy	20,133,238	17,032,661	85
VIII.	Scavenging	932,517	621,325	67
IX.	Roads	15,753,895	2,167,985	14
X.	Buildings	4,950,580	2,929,193	59
XI.	Fire brigade.	2,571,470	2,057,478	80
XII.	Licensing	618,918	585,960	95
XIII.	Gardens	4,497,230	2,119,401	47
XIV.	Markets	282,799	220,587	78
XV.	Improvement schemes . . .	2,284,831	1,549,387	68
XVI.	Miscellaneous	33,076,167	4,057,837	12
XVII.	Reserve	161,049	42,999	27
	Total	175,204,145	103,902,949	59

[a]Full headings as in Tables 46 and 47.

[b]Grants-in-aid to autonomous institutions.

I use the 1968-69 figures (which represent the
actual amounts rather than estimates), but I
suspect that the proportions do not change very
much. In addition, the difficulties of estimating the purchasing power of the rupee in Delhi
for even the recent period (and there has been
considerable inflation) are great if not impossible with the data at hand, and so I have been
unable to compute the real per capita municipal
expenditure for this period. The size of the
budget has however expanded tremendously with the
coming of the Corporation: it was some 30,000,000
rupees in the last year of the Municipal Committee
(1957-58)--which of course did not cover the entire
area of the Corporation, and had perhaps two-thirds
the Corporation's population--and well over
200,000,000 rupees by 1970-71.

Let us turn now to the "shape" of the budget
in its final form. Consider column 5 of Tables
44-47. The income picture is clear: nearly 80
percent of revenue comes from taxes (as opposed to
fees) and grants from the central government.
Indeed, the increase under "Education" is derived
almost entirely from a central government grant
for primary education (only Rs. 150,000 were
expected to be realized from fees and fines in
1970-71). A rough breakdown of the "General tax"
heading is given in Table 51 (though within the
table minor sources of income are omitted). The
major difference between the 1969-70 revised estimates and the 1970-71 budget estimates is found
under the head "Electricity tax"--the near halving
of the expected income from this source comes from
the (apparent) acceptance that "arrears" due (in
the Corporation's view) from the New Delhi Municipal
Committee and the U.P. State Electricity Board were
not likely to be paid. This was to be compensated
by the (fictitious?) rural areas grant from the
central government. Central government grants
provide rather a small (5 percent) part of the
budget: the "Assigned taxes" are those paid into

INCOME FROM "GENERAL TAXES, INDIRECT TAXATION, AND MISCELLANEOUS REVENUE," 1969-70 and 1970-71

Tax[a]	Revised Estimates 1969-70	Percentage of Total	Budget Estimates 1970-71	Percentage of Total
I. Domestic taxes				
A) Property tax	29,600,000	14	36,500,000	17
B) Tax on vehicles and animals	782,000	0	884,000	0
C) Duty on transfer of property	6,700,000	3	7,000,000	3
D) Electricity tax	27,500,000	13	15,300,000	7
Subtotal of I.[a]	91,442,000	44	88,984,000	41
II. Contributions from the central government				
A) Assigned taxes				
1) Terminal tax	67,000,000	32	72,700,000	34
2) Entertainment tax	22,100,000	11	19,200,000	9
3) Motor vehicle tax	14,900,000	7	15,100,000	7
Subtotal of A[a]	104,000,000	50	107,000,000	50
B) Grants in aid				
1) Transferred institutions	9,678,000	5	6,452,000	3
2) Rural area grant	....	..	10,000,000	5
Subtotal of B[a]	10,258,000	5	16,932,000	8
Subtotal of II.[a]	114,258,000	55	123,932,000	58
III. Other receipts (fines, etc.)	2,843,500	1	2,161,500	1
TOTAL INCOME[b]	208,543,500		215,077,500	

[a]Not all taxes are listed here. The subtotal figures include all taxes under that head; i.e., they are not the subtotals of the listed numbers. The percentages in these lines are the percentages of the total (the bottom line) derived from this tax.

[b]Includes taxes not listed; 14 percent of the income derived from this tax is provided by taxes not listed in this table.

the central account (although the terminal tax is
collected by the Corporation and the administrative costs for collecting it are paid to the
Corporation by the central government), all or
part of which are "assigned" to the Corporation.
The terminal tax is clearly the single most important source of revenue, providing some 27 percent
(1970-71) of the total budget income. The next
largest source (the property tax) provides 13
percent of the total income. The tax base of the
Corporation is thus relatively diffuse.

Turning to the "shape" of expenditures, it is
worthy of note that those items which seem important in the context of the ward and the zone--
sanitation, water supply, roads, etc.--not unnat-
urally account for the major expenditures. The
exception here is education, on which the largest
amount is spent (but recall that the "education
budget" contains a large contribution by the central government), but which is not a political
issue in the ward or the zone.

About half of the expenditure under the head
"Miscellaneous" (i.e., about 10 percent of the
total expenditure) is on "new works"--in the 1970-71
budget estimates, Rs. 20,890,000 of the Rs.
39,258,000 of the item as a whole (the other
"miscellaneous" items are the motor workshop, the
municipal press, etc.). This includes the constituency funds (i.e., Rs. 50,000 per councilor,
or Rs. 5,000,000) as well as items such as "improvement of street lighting," "beautification of the
city," "providing of basic amenities in unauthorized
colonies," [housing built in violation of zoning
rules] etc.; some 39 items in all. It is under this
head of "miscellaneous" that the councilors offered
so many amendments.

This description of the budget and the budgetary process is hardly comprehensive; (I sorely
miss more direct data which I might have obtained
through interviews if I had had the time). The
budgetary process can be linked with the patterns
of councilor participation in Corporation meetings

and the history of municipal government in
Delhi which preceded it by noting the "incremental" nature of all three: budgets are the
product, largely, of previous budgets; councilors act in "parliamentary" fashion, in a way
that differs only slightly from the predecessor
members of the Municipal Committee; the range
of areas of municipal concern reflected in the
early history of the Delhi Municipal Committee
is strikingly similar to the lists of functions
of today's Corporation. But this is not to say
that the changes which have occurred are
unimportant.

Not only has the Corporation, armed with
greater resources and political autonomy than
its predecessors, penetrated further downward,
it has also probably had a far greater quantitative impact. The recurrent suggestion by councilors that the Corporation's structure should be
altered to a Mayor-in-Council form (a "cabinet
system") to give the elected representatives
legitimate executive authority in administrative
matters, and the equally recurrent central government proposals for superseding the Corporation
indicate, however, that the valuation of that
penetration and impact is not uniform. What
marks the Corporation off from its predecessors
lies in the area of system-level interactions,
among the Corporation and the other authorities
(of central government provenance) in Delhi,
the autonomous operating authorities (DTU etc.),
and its own sub-units--i.e., committees, zonal
and other. It is to an examination of these
interactions that we now turn.

INTER-GOVERNMENTAL INTERACTIONS IN DELHI

As discussed above (pp. 271-73), at the
Delhi city level the nature of the three "interfaces," discussed in relation to the ward and the
zone, changes. The interaction of the "average"

citizen is minimal at this level.* Similarly, the
nature of the councilor-administrator interface is
different at the all-city level: briefly put, on
the councilor's side there is the interposed structure of the party apparatus which tends to mediate
contact, even in the Corporation meetings (where
the leaders of the party can apologize on behalf
of party members); on the administrator's side, it
is easier to resist "out of channel" political contact, and the administrative structure and chain of
command, headed by the commissioner, mediates
between the city-level administrator and the councilor. There continue to be lateral contacts, of
course, especially as administrators are promoted
up from the zones where ties with councilors had
already been established, and, as noted above
(p. 204), administrators may themselves seek ties

---

*I am forced to neglect the issue of corrup-
tion, which is a common instance of contact between
citizen and administrator (with the councilor not
infrequently also involved). The Corporation is
the hearing authority (of cases passed through the
Standing Committee) for charges of corruption
against high-level officials (Z.A.C., Executive
Engineer, Zonal Engineers, etc.). In 1969-70
some 20 cases were presented to the Corporation,
with charges ranging from being drunk on duty, to
running a private school, to stealing auto parts
from the municipal workshop. The Corporation may
be asked to approve a departmental enquiry, or give
permission to prosecute the officer, or dismiss him
from the service. (There may be other possible
sanctions, this list is drawn from those 20 cases
which appeared in the minutes.) Although the
minutes present the carefully detailed charge-
sheets and occasionally the defense of the officer,
the whole question of corruption was one which I
avoided when interviewing, and there have been
few studies, understandably, dealing even in passing
with the subject.[76]

with councilors as insurance against political pressure. The transformations of the nature of the
three interfaces tend to reduce their salience at
this level.

What becomes important rather is the interplay
between the levels of government and the various
components of the Corporation--the interactions that
"count" are between committees of the Corporation
and the Corporation; between the Corporation and the
Delhi Administration and the Metropolitan Council;
between the Corporation and the various autonomous
agencies in which the Delhi Administration and the
central government participate, most notably the
Delhi Development Authority (DDA); and between the
Corporation and the central government (directly;
the Delhi Administration is the central government
at one remove).

An exhaustive discussion of these interactions
cannot be attempted here. The news coverage of
Corporation affairs, as has been noted above, is
sketchy, and while the Corporation minutes are
voluminous, they refer to only a part of the work
of the Corporation. Most of what the Corporation
qua elected body does is "internal," in the work of
various committees. I will discuss these first, and
then introduce the interactions of the Corporation
with actors "outside" by a detailed description of
one "case" in which Corporation committees, the
Delhi Administration, and other authorities all take
a hand. This case is particularly helpful in setting out the dimension of these interactions: the
time span involved, the intrusion of "political"
concerns in something apparently a matter for
"technical" determination, and so on.

The kinds of interactions that occur are then
presented, with brief illustrative examples. The
conclusions emerging from these are that interactions are sporadic; that the individuals concerned are almost always leaders (not back-bench
councilors or officials lower than deputy commissioner); and that there is a very careful noting of
jurisdictional boundaries, coupled with a general

willingness on the part of all actors to extend
their own sphere of activity and yet charge "interference" when others do the same to them. I should
emphasize here that Delhi is nowhere more obviously
a "special case" Corporation than in these interactions: no other Corporation in India has both the
autonomy, which is a result of the absence of a
state government, and the direct lines of communication to the national government. The members of
the national cabinet are in some sense equivalent
to state government political leaders, in their
control function, but very different in their
minimal concern with Delhi politics.

Interaction here encompasses "cooperation" and
"conflict." "Conflict" is perhaps not the right
word, except in a few instances. Situations tend
to involve the presentation of demands, requests
and criticisms (sometimes all at once) to, say,
the central government; they may involve the support of one party against the charges of another;
etc. One factor that is important is that the
length of time needed to settle questions--months,
if not years--militates against the "temperature"
of a dispute reaching the boiling point. Disputes
that threaten to erupt into battles will be "cooled
off" by reference to an enquiry commission or the
good offices of a respected leader. What one has,
then, are situations of conflict and support, of
feint, bluff and counter-bluff, of tactical maneuver. Decisions are in a sense not "made" at any
level, but rather "arrived at" at all the levels,
in the modal instance. I did not come across
instances of a "conflict to the finish" in which the
authority at one level "won" while others "lost,"
although there are many instances of decisions
"going against" the Corporation. In this sense,
the "conflicts" are part of the co-operation; they
are an integral part of the normal governmental
process, not deviant behavior.

Committees of the Corporation[77]

The Corporation Act provides for six named committees, which are:

1. The Standing Committee
This is the most important committee; in other Corporations it may be called the "Executive Committee" and this gives an idea of its scope: virtually all resolutions pass through it; the commissioner first presents the budget to it; it has the powers of the Corporation in matters of lesser importance (the power to institute inquiries about the performance of a low-level municipal employee, for example); etc. There are 14 members of the Standing Committee, and it has a chairman (with casting vote) in addition.

2. The Rural Areas Committee
This consists of all the councilors from the rural area. Its job is to consider the Corporation's work in the rural areas, and it is required to be "consulted" in such matters.

3. The Education Committee
This committee consists of seven members, no more than three of whom "shall be nominated by the Corporation from among experts in education who are not members of the Corporation" (Corporation Act section 39[5]).

4. The Delhi Electrical Supply Committee

5. The Delhi Transport Committee

6. The Delhi Water Supply and Sewage
     Disposal Committee

These three committees each have a membership of from seven to nine, with four to six municipal councilors and the remaining three members (who would be experts) nominated by the central

government. These committees are thus directly
involved in levels of government "outside" the Corporation. The chairman, in his budget speech for
example, may well refer to the recalcitrance of the
central government in providing loans for new buses.
And from the other direction, questions on the
workings of the three authorities are raised in
Parliament, and the central government ministries
(for instance the Ministry of Power and Irrigation)
may involve themselves in enquiries into their day-
to-day working.[78]
    The Corporation is also empowered to set up
"special committees" and "ad hoc committees," and
it has made considerable use of this power. The
Special Zonal Committees are one set which I have
discussed in detail. The total number of committees
has fluctuated, but with a marked tendency to increase: there were 11 committees in 1958-69; 20 in
1964-65; 25 in 1969-70; and 33 in 1970-71.[79]
Several committees have subsequently been abolished,
and a number have been re-established. Eight of the
31 committees listed in Appendix B of the Dass study
have had consistently less than ten meetings a year
over the past few years (1968-71)--these are all ad
hoc committees, including those for "Hindi,"
"Erection of Statues," "Revision of Master Plan and
Amendments to Building Bye-laws." Other ad hoc committees ("Appointments, Promotion, Disciplinary and
Allied Matters," "Slum Clearance and Improvements")
have met slightly more frequently, as have four of
the special committees: the Garden Committee, the
Market Committee, the Assurances Committee, and the
Law and General Purposes Committee. These meet
between ten and 20 times a year. The Medical
Relief and Public Health Committee met 35 times in
1970-71, but less frequently in previous years.
The Works Committee is the most active of the
special committees, meeting more than 30 times a
year. The statutory committees (i.e., the six
listed above) met from 31 times (the Education Committee in 1968-69) to 80 times (the Rural Areas
Committee in 1968-69 and 1970-71) but generally

around 60 times a year (in short, weekly).

There is some duplication in effort by some of these committees; new works in gardens are considered by both the Gardens Committee and the Works Committee, and one proposal of the Dass study is that some of these committees be amalgamated, with several being absorbed into the Works Committee.[80] But more interesting from our point of view is the items which are referred to the "functional" committees by the "territorial" committees, especially the zonal committees.

The "case" which I outline below involves a recommendation of an action by a zonal committee which is then referred "upward" to a Corporation committee. A number of governmental actors are involved in what would seem to be a "technical" decision, and things like "the press," as well as political actors, enter in. The case takes longer than most to resolve, and is perhaps more convoluted than others, but it is not unusual, and it demonstrates nicely how many dimensions there can be to a "simple" decision of municipal government. Since it is a "case" (so named in the minutes), let us title it "The Case of the Closing of Racquet Court Road."

The case came up in the adjourned May (1969) meeting of the Corporation held on August 25, 1969.[81] The subject of the resolution was the "Closure of the Racquet Court Road for vehicular traffic," and the first item in the file, dated April, 1965, was a letter from the ZAC (presumably of the Civil Lines Zone) in which he writes: "There have been numerous accidents on the junction of Rajpur Road, Racquet Court and Flagstaff Road. In this behalf, the S.P. [Superintendent of Police] (Traffic) was consulted who advised . . . closure of the Racquet Court Road." The zonal committee then recommended to the Works Committee that the road be closed. The next month the Works Committee approved the suggestion and passed the resolution on to the Corporation. At the end of that month (May, 1965) the Corporation

approved the closure, which was then, presumably,
effected.

Two years later the commissioner wrote to
the Works Committee, "After closure there has been
adverse criticism in the press that it has been
closed wrongly. The matter has been reconsidered
and it is recommended that the road should be
opened to vehicular traffic." It is here that the
intricate "movements" begin. The Works Committee
a fortnight later referred the case back to the
commissioner and instructed him to report after
consulting with the S.P. (Traffic). The commissioner did consult and was advised (he reports in a
letter of August, 1967) to keep the road closed.
At the end of September, 1968, (a full year later),
the Works Committee "resolved that the case be
referred back to the Commissioner for a further
report in the light of discussion held in the
meeting." A letter of the commissioner to the
Works Committee in October, 1968, reveals that the
road had been opened a year previously and had
then been reclosed; the Works Committee in the next
month then recommended that the road be reopened.
The Corporation, however, acting a month later,
referred the case back to the Works Committee. The
Works Committee in March, 1969, reaffirmed its
earlier recommendation, with members of the opposition parties dissenting. (The S.P. [Traffic] had
in the meantime changed his mind and recommended
the opening of the road.) The Corporation in April
again referred the case back to the Works Committee
for reconsideration, and after the Works Committee
had again recommended the opening of the road
(acting in July), the Corporation so resolved in
August.

Reading between the lines ("press reports,"
the dissent of the Opposition, the multiple refer-
rals back to the Works Committee), it is clear that
this question was not simply a technical one (i.e.,
how to lower the high rate of accidents), dependent
on the expert advice of the S.P. (Traffic). What
is important here is how a resolution originally

introduced at the zonal level (at which point
already the police--an agency of the central
government under the lieutenant governor--were
consulted), moves between the Corporation, one
of its committees, and the commissioner, with
the police continuing to be involved. There is
evidence of what might be termed "co-ordinative"
decision making, in which members of the "deliberative wing" took an active part, in what might
seem to be a purely "technical" matter clearly
within the purview of the "executive wing." As
noted above, this case is far more complicated
than others, but the "movement" of the case is
not unusual.

A feature of this case, and of our discussion of the committees of the Corporation,
which is significant for the functioning of the
"deliberative wing" of the Corporation as a whole,
is the implication that members of committees--
in this instance, the Works Committee--spend a
great deal of time in considering decisions, that,
indeed, "deliberation" by elected representatives
occurs in committee rooms rather than in general
body meetings (making note of the small scope of
deliberation overall, I should add). Zonal committees resemble the other committees in this
regard: recall the number of meetings devoted to
general consideration of problems of the zone.
The "deliberation," again, does not stand "opposed
to" the "executive" function; it is indeed part of
it. Certainly if we include the zonal committees,
and even otherwise, it can be said that the committees of the Corporation are, in a sense, the
Corporation in its "political" aspect, while the
meetings of the Corporation are just a public face,
into which individual councilors, to be sure, can
invest a great deal of effort and emotion.

The Interaction of the Corporation with
"Outside" Authorities

The rights and duties of the various governmental bodies in Delhi are spelled out by statute,
and their interaction "should" be, in that sense,
"regular." That is, almost all matters of business
which concern more than one authority would be
handled without dispute and according to rule.
There is some evidence of this in the fact that an
examination of a year's newspaper reports of Delhi
politics reveals few conflicts between authorities,
and these are more sporadic than chronic: when
they occur they are of relatively short duration
and they tend not to recur.

The contact at this level concerns leadership
almost entirely: the Lieutenant Governor, the
Chief Executive Councilor, the Mayor, the leader
of the House, the Municipal Commissioner, the leader
of the Opposition (in both Corporation and Metropolitan Council), and central government ministers.
Back-bench councilors are not involved, except when
they are mobilized, say, for a protest march. The
leaders, on the occasions when there are disputes,
tend to be concerned with jurisdictional boundaries
--typically, they charge that their sphere of authority is being "interfered" with--and manipulate
the fuzziness of some of those boundaries, or over-
lapping functions, to their advantage. It is important to note that in these instances appeals for
judicial determination are rare: I discovered but
one instance of a councilor challenging the ruling
of the mayor in court (this involved the election
of a councilor to the DDA), and while there are
appeals to institute judicial enquiries on incidents, particularly those of "disorder" (during the
sweepers' strike, for example), I know of no enquiries which were granted in 1969-70. This lack
of resort to judicial arena may be more a result of
the possibility of solution in some political arena,
which would, not unimportantly, take less time.

These disputes have what might be called
"direction": Corporation leaders may try to
shift the conflict "outward" to coordinate
authorities or "upward" to superior authorities.
Conversely, the central government, or other
"higher" authority, may try to influence the
Corporation, by selective granting of financial
aid, for example, to change its policy in areas
clearly within the sphere of authority of the
Corporation. While these latter instances are
of obvious interest, I would like to confine
myself here to disputes viewed, so to speak,
from the Corporation's point of view.

On occasion, the Corporation acts without
partisan division in interacting with other
authorities. The Corporation is not unwilling
to address itself to national and international
events, passing resolutions to send a message of
congratulations to a victorious cricket team or
to sanction a cash grant for flood victims in
Gujarat (in addition to condolence resolutions).
Acting as a body, it may ask the mayor to approach
other authorities on matters clearly beyond its
jurisdiction with requests (or "to convey the
sentiments of the Corporation," "raise the matter,"
etc.). In one case, the Corporation wished to
express its concern at the showing of certain
films (deemed to be "improper") at the Delhi
International Film Festival.[82]

Most of the interactions of the Corporation
with other authorities quickly take on partisan
overtones, however. An important factor here is
the fact that different authorities are controlled
by different parties (and in this, the Delhi
Corporation is in a situation similar to that of
Corporations "under" state governments elsewhere
in India), so that the Congress party in the Corporation, frustrated by the "ruling" Jana Sangh,
may appeal to the (Congress) cabinet minister.
Jana Sangh Corporation leaders may seek to involve
the chief executive councilor (in 1969-70, a member
of the Jana Sangh) in such a dispute as a counter-

weight. During the strike of a Congress-affiliated
sweepers union in January-February 1970,[83] for
instance, the Congress leaders of the Corporation
appealed to the Union Health Minister against what
was called the "vindictive attitude" of the Jana
Sangh toward the sweepers and their "just" demands.[84] The Jana Sangh accused the Congress(R)
of "master minding" the strike, and a Jana Sangh
delegation went to the lieutenant governor to
complain about the lack of police protection of
"loyal" sweepers. All of this action took place
in a dispute which, in theory, was being handled
by the municipal commissioner, who was in charge
of negotiations with the sweepers. When senior
Corporation administrators and representatives of
the sweepers met with the Union Health Minister, the
Jana Sangh leader of the House objected strongly to
the "interference."[85] In much the same way that
councilors and administrators at the zonal level
attempt to "escalate" conflict to authorities which
they see as more favorable (see above, pp. 204-06),
here the three sides involved--the municipal commissioner, the Jana Sangh Corporation Party, the
Congress(R) Corporation Party--all tried "escalation" to the Delhi Administration, the Metropolitan Council, and the Union Cabinet.

    I have discussed in some detail the "politics"
of the katras of Kucha Khirkiwala (see above, pp.
65-69 and 74-82). I noted there that katras are
widely believed to be strongholds of Congress
(because their residents are both poor and may also
be scheduled caste). I also described the program
the Corporation had set in motion for katra improvement. As part of that program, apparently, the
Delhi Jana Sangh sponsored a padyatra (literally,
"foot pilgrimage"; here something like "walking
tour") by the chief executive councilor to the
katras of Delhi in order to allocate Rs. 1,500,000
for their improvement. Since this event sets out
clearly the points I have been stressing in this
section--the sporadic nature of conflicts, the
involvement of leaders, the questions of

jurisdictional boundaries, and the "escalation"
of disputes to higher authorities--I would like
to portray the full event.

The padyatra was announced on November 26,
1969, and occurred on four different days, the
first of which was January 7, 1970. On the first
tour, in which he visited some 70 katras, the
chief executive councilor was accompanied by the
(Jana Sangh) M.P. of the area, the chief whip of
the Jana Sangh in the Metropolitan Council, the
two area councilors (both Jana Sangh), the deputy
mayor, and a host of others. The padyatra was
immediately denounced by the Congress leaders of
the Corporation as a "political stunt" and "direct
interference" in the affairs of the Corporation.[86]
The improvements were in fact to be carried out by
the Corporation (which had a Rs. 2,000,000 katra
improvement program of its own), which would be
then reimbursed by the Delhi Administration. The
chief executive councilor countered by calling the
Congress leaders' criticism "anti-people" and
pointed out that he had Corporation backing--i.e.,
its Jana Sangh leadership--for the padyatra.[87]

When the padyatra moved to a Congress ward on
January 10, the demonstration against it threatened
by the Congress did not materialize, but the Congress councilor did not join the group. But on the
next tour, three days later and in a different area,
the Congress councilors (one from the Metropolitan
Council) did join, one saying "no politics should
be injected into the problem of improvement of
slums and katras."[88] Not only were decisions made
on the spot during the padyatra, it was reported
that estimates were prepared in 24 hours and
tendered bids accepted within a week.[89] A few
days later the padyatra had faded from the head-
lines.

But on January 23, the central government
announced that it was drastically cutting the
allocation of funds for katra improvement. The
move was immediately denounced by the Jana Sangh
leadership of the Corporation as politically

motivated. According to one report: "The local
political parties, including the Progressive Group
in the Corporation, see in the move an expression
of frustration of the local warring Congress
factions who might fear losing even the present
number of seats in the Corporation in the coming
civic elections."[90] The central government reversed its decision on February 2, after imposing
some conditions on the use of the grant, which the
Administration accepted.[91] There was a report at
the end of February telling of plans by the chief
executive councilor to resume the padyatra to
check if improvements had been made.[92] But there
were no reports of him having done so.

Although the padyatra as originally projected
was to have covered all the katras of the city,
that goal was clearly not reached. (I would estimate that less than a quarter of the "official"
katras were visited, and only a small fraction of
the katras defined by the "50 persons or ten
families" rule [see above, p. 65]). There was no
report on why the padyatra was curtailed, and
whether Congress opposition, in the Corporation or
by the Home Ministry, had anything to do with it.

It is clear from this case that these interactions between authorities in Delhi are not
matters of "interference" with the "proper" sphere
of action of each, but frequently a way of influencing policy--here katra improvement--by probing
the resiliency of the jurisdictional boundary.
The action here is "political," as opposed to
"bureaucratic" or "administrative," because the
authorities involved rely on their political
position vis-à-vis each other rather than the
legal definition of their relationship. At least
in this respect the question of katra improvement
at the ward level is similar to the question at
the all-city level--the councilor in the ward uses
his political position to involve himself in a
supposedly administrative process.

SUMMARY

This chapter has touched on many "themes"
of earlier ones--the difficulty of separating
"deliberative" and "executive" functions into
their respective "wings" of the Corporation,
for instance--but has also revealed an arena of
municipal government which, as one would expect,
differs significantly from the arenas of ward and
zone. The importance of historical factors such
as the range of functions and the size of the
budgets of the municipal bodies, particularly the
Delhi Municipal Committee, which constitute the
Corporation's ancestry, is far clearer at this
level. The parametal factors shift from being
socio-economic to being more institutional: the
citizenry fades in importance and the interface
between councilor and administrator becomes more
complex, as the councilor "side" is divided along
party lines (and the party groups at this level
have ties "outward" to the Metropolitan Council
parties and the national government), and the
administrator "side" goes beyond a clear hierarchy
(topped by the municipal commissioner) into an
arena of competing jurisdictions with other administrators such as the lieutenant governor in the
field. The style of councilor and administrator,
as revealed in the meetings of the Corporation, is
also different. But this chapter has, at least,
filled out the "portrait" of the Corporation councilor and administrative officer and begun to
indicate the complexity of interaction between
these actors, both "internally" in committees and
"externally" in the Delhi arena.

9. Summary, Conclusions, Implications

There should be no need to emphasize that the major payoff of this study is the "political ethnography" it presents. The complex interrelations between social, economic, and historical factors, and the "vocabulary" and "phrases" of city government in Delhi cannot be summarized but only briefly surveyed once again. In this survey I shall emphasize what might be called the recurring "motifs" of the study, from katras and their politics to the question of how significant formal social structures are, at each level--ward, zone, and city--of the Corporation.

Some of these "motifs" can be clustered to form "themes": e.g., the "ombudsman's" role of the councilor derives from his view of his relationship to his constituents--his link role--and his formal role as supervisor of administrative action at the zonal level (as a member of the zonal committee) among other things. Other "themes" are broader in scope. We have already considered, for instance, the relationship of "politics" and "administration" in India at the district and state levels (Chapter 6). These themes will be put in the context of studies of urban politics in other large cities in India.

It is appropriate at this point to note briefly some dimensions of Delhi municipal government, which have been touched on only lightly due to lack of time and readily available data. The most important is the absence of a systematic

consideration of citizen opinion and experience. A
carefully designed survey of the residents of Kucha
Khirkiwala would have opened up the possibilities
of a detailed analysis of the social, economic, and
ideological basis of party support in the ward, for
instance. And a large sample of citizen opinion of
the councilor, of low-level administrators, and of
municipal government in general would have enriched
the study immensely.

    Another dimension which was similarly neglected
is that of party competition. One aspect of this
is the questions of just what the position of the
Jana Sangh and the Congress have been, in electoral
terms, in issue terms, etc., and what effect party
organization and leadership may have had on municipal government. (For instance, does it really make
any difference which party is the "ruling party"?)
It should be noted that in the Delhi municipal
arena--and Delhi is similar to other Indian cities
in this regard (see the discussion below, p. 338)
--one does not find a one-party-dominant system,
which has been the hallmark of India's party system
(and which, in the Indian countryside, quite often
resembles the old-style American big-city machine).
It is of crucial importance, I suspect, that competition between candidates for municipal office
takes place in an electoral arena rather than as
a factional struggle within a dominant party. The
balance of Congress and Jana Sangh in Delhi helps
to keep individual councilors actively nursing
their constituencies; there are few "safe" seats in
Delhi. This dimension has not been absent from the
study, to be sure, but a full analysis of its impact
has not been attempted.

A RAPID RECAPITULATION:
FACTS AND MOTIFS

    In the second part of the Introduction, I out-
lined the governmental context in which the Municipal Corporation of Delhi operates. The Corporation

is supervised by various national ministries, in
contrast to Corporations in the states of India,
which are "under" the state government (where the
electorate is overwhelmingly rural). Delhi's
peculiar position, because of its status as
national capital, has a history of some 60 years.
The important point here is the autonomy that the
Delhi municipal government can maintain because
of this arrangement.

The various areas of the Delhi Union Territory have differing municipal problems and indeed
differing political characters. The rural areas--
some 300 villages with a population of about
500,000--hardly have "municipal" problems at all,
and are heavily Congress. The colonies of Punjabi
refugees are strongly Jana Sangh, and have problems
which are not quite those of the densely populated
wards of the old city (sanitation, water supply,
lighting, etc.), but also not quite those of the
newly-expanding "suburban" colonies which surround
Delhi, where questions of zoning and the installation of public services, including roads, are
more important. Delhi also has within it industrial zones, areas of "unauthorized" colonies,
villages which have been swallowed up or encysted
by the urban sprawl, and the older, spacious
"garden" areas of the government buildings in
New Delhi and the Civil Lines.

The institutions of government in the Union
Territory include, beside the Corporation, the
Delhi Administration, which is headed up by the
lieutenant governor, and which is "advised" by a
virtually powerless elected body, the Delhi Metropolitan Council. The Delhi Administration has
formal authority for things like law and order
throughout the entire Territory, though the actual
authority in the Delhi Cantonment (army base)--
including supervision of the partly elected
Cantonment board--is exercised by the Ministry
of Defense. The New Delhi Municipal Committee
is quite securely in the control, albeit at one
remove, of the lieutenant governor. The Delhi

Development Authority, which is in charge of the
Master Plan implementation, is an autonomous body
with close links--crucially, an "interlocking
directorate" of administrators serving both in
the Town and Country Planning Organization of the
Ministry of Health and in the DDA--to the central
government, but with important ties to the Delhi
Administration and the Corporation. There are
similar, though less important, autonomous bodies
operating within the Territory.

Chapters 2 through 5 of this study dealt with
municipal government at the ward level, through
the device of a detailed examination of one ward,
"Kucha Khirkiwala." Kucha Khirkiwala, a ward of
the walled city of Shahjahanabad, presents a
picture of compressed humanity (nearly 1,000
people per acre are in residence there), and a mix
of commercial and industrial use of buildings, yet
it is an urban environment which is not oppressive
and which, indeed, works well in permitting
relatively quick communication and transport
(i.e., on foot) in a poor country.

A problem of much prominence in the ward is
sanitation, and an examination of the sweepers'
strike outlines the involvement of the councilor
in the process of day-to-day administration, as
well as providing the first indication that the
hypothesis that a well articulated social structure, based on the residential mohalla (neighborhood), exists, might well have to be discarded.

The 1961 and 1971 censuses for Delhi provide
a wealth of detail, which I have analyzed by
polling station (electoral precinct), on the types
of work done by residents of the ward, and on the
number of literates, scheduled caste people, and
"industrial establishments." The voting list was
used to provide a breakdown on religious lines,
between Muslim and Hindu. The workers turn out to
be largely in manufacturing, trade and commerce,
and services; they can be located geographically,
and correlations with the other factors made, so
that intra-ward areas of a specific character can

be defined. Chapter 2 ended with a discussion of
the katra, and the involvement of the Corporation
government with its problems.

The next chapter, concentrating on the councilor of the ward, began with a re-examination of
the katra (which thus qualifies as a "motif" and
which reappears in Chapter 8 as the focus of an
all-city issue) from the political angle, looking
at the number of voters the katras contain, and
the social structure which some do have that permits
a politics of intermediaries ("brokers"). On the
whole, however, the councilor attempts to establish
as direct a link to his constituents as possible,
and this is nowhere made more explicit than when
he is on his "rounds" of the ward. The councilor
exposes himself to the citizenry in his office or
in a place of "public audience" (darbar) as well
as on rounds. The round is also a context in which
there is a structured relationship between the
councilor and the low-level administrator; the
latter is "supervised" by the former, quite in
disregard of the formal niceties of a distinction
between "politics" and "administration" (and
"deliberative wing" and "executive wing," another
motif). The councilor's role generally is both
that of ombudsman, where he transmits citizen
complaints to the bureaucracy and indeed follows
them up, and of a link from the government to the
citizens, as he uses his constituency fund to
divert the flow of administrative expenditure in
directions he desires.

Elections reveal certain features of the
councilor-citizen interface even more clearly. The
campaign, conducted mainly as door-to-door canvassing, "corner" meetings, large "public" meetings,
and with topical posters and slogans, differs in
style in the two major Delhi parties: the Congress
candidate typically is the chief strategist of his
campaign while the Jana Sangh Party organization
of the ward runs the campaign for its candidate.
The lack of a network of "influentials" who could
"deliver" votes to the candidate, except possibly

in some of the katras, fits the previously noted
finding that mohalla or other local associations
are weak or nonexistent in Kucha Khirkiwala. The
candidates thus treat the ethnically defined
groups--the Muslims, the "Banias," the "katra
people," the "Punjabis," et al.--as categories in
their analysis of the voting strength of the ward,
and not as groups whose corporate structure could
be mobilized in their favor. Electoral appeals
are made in general terms to attract specific
groups--a stand in favor of Urdu as an official
language of the Corporation would be calculated
to win Muslim votes, for example--but the main
effort goes into direct contact with individual
voters, a style that conforms to the councilor's
mode of operation in his day-to-day nursing of his
constituency.

A few of the socio-economic data on the ward
were found relevant to voting patterns: Muslims
did not vote for the Jana Sangh, but divided their
votes between the Congress and Independents (not
necessarily Muslim). The competition of Jana Sangh
and Congress thus took place in the Hindu areas of
the ward, and there is some evidence that the Jana
Sangh derived more of its support from the "Bania"
areas of the ward. This result, and, indeed, the
initial mesh of religious, economic and demographic
data which emerged in the analysis in Chapter 2,
would surprise no one who is familiar with Delhi
politics. Inferences based on it can therefore be
made, with some confidence, for City Zone and all-
city arenas.

Chapter 5 through 7 dealt with the area of
Delhi defined first as "Shahjahanabad"--the old
walled city with its 300-year-long history and
distinct physical character--and then as the "City
Zone," comprising 16 wards of Shahjahanabad plus
two sparsely populated wards to the south, an
administrative unit of the Municipal Corporation
which is a feature of the scheme of decentralization instituted in 1963.

Shahjahanabad is portrayed as a cultural
entity, noting its "Islamic" nature. The Hindu-
Muslim difference, which we first met in Kucha
Khirkiwala, reappears, and it becomes clear that
no ethnic group, or caste, could be in any sense
"dominant" in the city. An examination of the
economic and demographic data of the 1971 census
reveals an even balance of workers in manufacturing, workers in commerce and trade, and workers
in services, plus "industrial" areas of the city,
in a pattern similar to that of Kucha Khirkiwala.
The environment--geographical (including the configuration of houses and streets in that term),
economic, social, and cultural--is thus probably
similar for almost all the councilors of the City
Zone.

In the City Zone, the role of councilor and
administrator differ from that of the ward arena.
In individual interactions, the councilor must
deal with a man of greater age, experience and
status than the junior staff of the ward. In the
zone, the administrator is someone who is able,
through long-standing contacts with political
figures of the Corporation as well as by use of
his position in the administrative chain of command, to "escalate" conflicts brought on by a
councilor's "order" to higher, more insulated
levels of the Corporation. The differing levels
of expertise demanded may well have an influence
on the "direction" of the relationship between
councilor and administrator: in the ward the
councilor is likely to have more familiarity,
through years of experience, with municipal
regulations than the newly-posted subordinate
official, and, indeed, probably knows enough of
the "technicalities" (including both engineering
questions and administrative details) involved
in repairing a street or putting in a new water
line to be able confidently to "order" a junior
engineer to do something. At the zonal level, the
engineers are also involved in large-scale projects which are technically too complex for the

average councilor to make any judgments about, and
the greater length of service of the senior officials means that they and the councilor are on at
least equal footing when the intricacies of rules
and regulations are at issue.

Municipal government at the zonal level thus
centers on a more formally structured relation
between "politics" and "administration" and the
holders of the respective roles of councilor and
senior administrator. (The formal structure,
which defines the rights and duties of the zonal
committee of councilors, may itself inhibit the
councilor from stretching his influence into the
spheres "reserved" for administrators.) The system
of zones has as its core rationale, with which both
councilors and administrators agree, the idea that
a decentralized administration is more efficient
and more convenient for the public. What irri-
tates the administrative officers is what the
councilors wholeheartedly support: having the
zonal committee as a supervisor of administrative
action, instead of its being only the local "deliberative wing," confining itself to questions of
priorities for the zone or general inquiries on
policy.

The minutes of the zonal committee meetings
reveal that the councilors must take this part of
their municipal duties quite seriously, for their
attendance at meetings is high, the "politics"
(i.e., partisan conflict) almost nonexistent, and
the scope of concern large. As one would expect,
the topics of interest are largely street repair,
water supply, electricity, sanitation, and administrative procedures. In 1969-70, the largest number
of resolutions asked the Zonal Assistant Commissioner to report on a matter to a later meeting;
other resolutions, in order of frequency, dealt
with the sanctioning of estimates, the recording
of reports, final decisions on zonal matters,
"cases" submitted to superior authorities of the
Corporation, and "formal" resolutions such as the
expression of condolences.

Interviews with the councilors of the zone,
analyzed in Chapter 7, reveal patterns similar to
those found in Kucha Khirkiwala: an emphasis on
ceaseless contact with the citizenry--unmediated
contact--and the role of "ombudsman" accepted and
even gloried in, plus the use of "rounds." Election
results for Shahjahanabad, extending back into the
era of the Delhi Municipal Committee, indicate considerable vote stability and a definite advantage
to the incumbent councilor. The stability in
electoral identification is supported by the
marked geographical areas of party support in
the walled city.

Municipal government for the whole of Delhi
is carried on with various traditions and within
many arenas. A very significant determinant of
the shape of municipal concerns and indeed the
very structure of government in Delhi is the
previously existing municipal government. The
history of the Delhi Municipal Committee (1862-
1958) is examined in some detail at the beginning
of Chapter 8. The Municipal Committee (with some
members elected by a restricted electorate and
others nominated by "government," and run, on the
whole, by "officials") was not an important
political body, particularly after the rise of
the nationalist movement. Still, it concerned
itself with by now familiar problems--sanitation,
education, street repair, etc.--and the budget,
even expressed in terms of per capita expenditures,
steadily increased.

With the advent of the Corporation, the form
of government changes, though the officials,
headed by the Municipal Commissioner, still occupy
the "treasury benches." (Another tradition on
which the Corporation draws, especially in its
formal proceedings, is the parliamentary one:
meetings are presided over by the mayor, who is
much like a Speaker, and, more significantly,
virtually all votes divide on party lines.) The
"deliberative wing" and "executive wing" structure is fully articulated at this level, and one

senses in the conduct of the councilors at Corporation meetings that the role of policy maker and
policy maker alone is felt to be constricting. At
this level, the "tilt" of the relationship between
councilor and administrator is quite definitely in
the latter's favor. An analysis of the Corporation
budget for 1969-70 reveals that, much like the
practice in the United States, the most important
influence on the shape of the budget is the previous year's budget, in which one finds only
incremental increases and decreases.

Chapter 8 ended with a brief discussion of
intra-Corporation and inter-government interactions.
The actors here are the committees of the Corporation, the Municipal Commissioner, the Metropolitan Council and the Chief Executive Councilor, the
Lieutenant Governor, and several branches of the
national government. The features revealed include
the sporadic nature of conflicts between the authorities (the tip of the iceberg of a smoothly
functioning governmental system), the involvement
of political leaders and heads of authorities
rather than "back-bench" councilors or junior
officials, the importance of conflicts over jurisdictions, and the practice of "escalation," a
feature familiar from our discussion of conflicts
at the zonal level.

THE BIG CITY CORPORATION IN INDIA:
DELHI AND OTHERS

We can divide our consideration of the larger
"themes" which emerge from this study into a discussion of the contexts (political, historical,
social, economic, cultural), the institutions, and
roles of the participants in Corporation govern-
ment--councilor, administrator, and citizen.

Contexts

The use of the word "Corporation" is a tip-off
to one aspect of the political context, which we
will consider below under "institutions," the
council-manager-like form. But the Corporation
form of government is descriptive of the larger
cities of India,[1] and I use the term as a useful
way of referring to the form while implying the
size. The Corporation form is granted by the
state legislature, in most instances. The most
significant political context of municipal government is the state qua bureaucracy and qua state-
level political parties, especially the ruling
party (i.e., the State Ministry).[2] The state government, for most cities in India, is not only the
"founding father" of the Corporation, setting out
in the chartering Act the precise form and functions of the body, but, more important, continues
to exercise directly a great deal of power within
the city--control of the police is the most obvious
instance--and indirectly by the supervision of the
Corporation, by its staffing the administrative
wing with state civil service officers in the
upper levels, and by the ultimate threat of super-
session.[3] Delhi differs from other Corporation
cities in this very important particular, and
though we have seen, in Chapter 8, that conflicts
concerning the Corporation may reach central government ministers, still it seems clear the Delhi
does not have the salience for the national
cabinet that Lucknow, for instance, might have
for the Uttar Pradesh cabinet, both governmentally
and politically.

Another facet of the Corporation's political
context is the party system in Delhi. The competition of Congress (today, the Congress[R]) and
the Jana Sangh extends, by and large, through all
the levels of the Corporation, in all the geographic
areas of Delhi. I have noted that the social bases
of the parties differ as one looks at the levels
(in the city as a whole the Congress draws strength

from the rural areas and the Jana Sangh from the
Punjabi localities; in the City Zone, and in Kucha
Khirkiwala, where neither of these groups live in
large numbers, the cases are different), but it is
significant that the two-party system nonetheless
pervades all levels. This certainly has something
to do with party organization, as the Delhi parties
are able to shift financial and manpower resources
into areas where they are not locally strong, and
there is possibly some tie to the socio-economic
contexts as well: a city with no strong ethnically or otherwise defined "splinter" parties. To
put it another way, the reliance on issue and
personal appeal which we have found in Kucha
Khirkiwala and in Shahjahanabad (which one would
expect to be the most socially structured area of
a rapidly growing city like Delhi) suggests a "for
and against" system: one supports or opposes the
incumbent ruling party, etc.

I cannot hope to deal with this hypothesis in
an all-India context here, particularly the socio-
economic facets; the data simply do not exist.
The party position in some other Corporations in
India, for elections close to 1969-70, is given in
Table 52. That the four metropolitan cities seem
to have essentially two-party systems while the
smaller, more "provincial" cities present a picture
of more diffuse party strength (note particularly
the number of Independents) is quite striking,
though one would have to examine the particular
circumstances of each city before assigning reasons.
Still the hypothesis clearly bears further investigation.

The historical context of Delhi government
clearly cannot be readily separated from the
political and cultural contexts particularly. The
position of the Congress party in Delhi, to take
one instance, is obviously not unconnected with
the importance of the nationalist movement in the
city.[4] The history of the municipalities of Delhi
is also clearly related to Delhi's political
position: recall the leap in municipal budgets

TABLE 52

RECENT MUNICIPAL CORPORATION ELECTION RESULTS, SELECTED CITIES[a]

City	Date of Election	Party (Number of Seats Won)							Total Number of Seats[d]
		Congress	Jana Sangh	Shiv Sena	United Front[b]	DMK Front[c]	Others	Inde-pendents	
Bombay	1968	65	6	40	n.a.	n.a.	23	6	140
Calcutta	1969	22	2	n.a.	71	n.a.	..	5	100
Delhi	1971	41	54	n.a.	n.a.	n.a.	2	3	100
Madras	1968	52	..	n.a.	n.a.	68	..	..	120
Kanpur	1968	35	9	n.a.	n.a.	n.a.	9	17	72
Poona	1968	34	14	n.a.	n.a.	n.a.	17	7	72
Nagpur	1969	21	11	n.a.	n.a.	n.a.	19	20	75
Lucknow	1968	33	8	n.a.	n.a.	n.a.	8	15	64
Agra	1968	21	22	n.a.	n.a.	n.a.	10	7	60

Sources: Bombay--Civic Affairs, April, 1968, p. 84; Calcutta--Civic Affairs, June, 1969, pp. 47-48; Delhi--Organiser, May 15, 1971; Madras--Civic Affairs, November, 1968, p. 50; Kanpur--Civic Affairs, June, 1968, p. 46; Poona--Donald B. Rosenthal, The Limited Elite: Politics and Government in Two Indian Cities (Chicago: University of Chicago Press, 1970), p. 274; Nagpur--Civic Affairs, April, 1969, p. 46; Lucknow--Roderick Church, "The Politics of Administration in Urban India: Citizens, Municipal Councilors and Routine Administration in Lucknow" (unpublished Ph.D. dissertation, Duke University, 1973), p. 78; Agra--Rosenthal, The Limited Elite, p. 260.

[a]As far as I know, there is no source which would give even the dates of recent Corporation elections; I selected these cities by searching my memory and skimming through the journal, Civic Affairs.

[b]The United Front of Calcutta comprised: CPI(M)--31; CPI--10; 8 other left parties; and 6 Independents.

[c]The DMK won 54 of the 68 seats of the front.

[d]The results for Kanpur and Nagpur were not given completely; the totals are the actual seats, not the sum of the row figures.

after the shifting of the capital to Delhi in 1912.
These apart, the continuity of the scope of municipal concern, the sources of money, and the proportions of expenditures made under each head, and
other features of municipal government in Delhi,
from 1862 to the present, is significant. This
continuity bridges the gap between pre- and post-
Independence India, despite the expansion of the
franchise (from "rate-payers" or other measure of
the propertied/educated, to adult franchise), which
one would expect to alter the demands on the municipality, and despite the legitimation of democracy
for its own sake, with the transformation of the
bureaucracy from an instrument of imperial tyranny
to a presumed public service, etc., etc. An impressive continuity indeed.

The notion that Shahjahanabad is an "Islamic
city," combined with the political relevance of the
Hindu-Muslim cleavage, is one part of the "cultural"
context of municipal government, if Muslim solidarity derives at least in part, as I believe it
does, from a feeling of a shared cultural history
and a pride in the Mughal Delhi and the Delhi that
is one of the major centers of Urdu. Other aspects
of the cultural context are not so clear: Delhi's
position as capital is not only important because
councilors have quick access to national leaders,
but also there is a pride in the city as a cosmopolitan center and as a city which should be ahead
of others in India in, say, cleanliness and beauty.

I have not discussed the social and economic
contexts of the entire city, but some of the
generalizations about Shahjahanabad--and Kucha
Khirkiwala--hold true in the larger arena. In
social-structural terms, there is no dominant caste
group nor even a coalition of caste or other ethnic
groups organized in some fashion, no indication
that the entire city can be thought of as a conglo-
merate (or pyramid?) of mohallas and other neighborhood units.[5] Areas in the new colonies which are
"Bengali" or "Madrasi" (= South Indian) areas may
have cultural associations and other groups which

look like the interest groups of the American urban scene,[6] but their activities are marginal.

Secondary associations are also not a major part of the Municipal Corporation landscape, with the exception of a few trade unions. Cooperative societies, if they exist in any great number, are certainly not very visible,[7] and the same is true of merchants' associations. We cannot infer from the lack of a "power elite" in any mohalla of Kucha Khirkiwala or in the ward as a whole, the lack of some sort of organized, small group of men with great economic power or social status with whom the Corporation has to deal. But I am tempted to say that if such a "power elite" exists, it is probably the national government, which does indeed wield tremendous economic and social power vis-à-vis the Corporation. Delhi has "leading citizens," to be sure, but none who "run" the city.

This quick survey of the contexts of Corporation government in Delhi featured, it should be noted, a constant return to the institutional bases of Corporation government. It is not some dominant social group, or powerful economic interest, or even the dead hand of historical tradition which governs Delhi city: the formal institutions of ward, zone, and Corporation have an independence of action and power, even vis-à-vis the national government.

Institutions

Two major themes concerning the formal institutions of Delhi government have emerged in this study: the importance of the scheme of decentralization--the zonal system, and, equally important, the ward "system" grounded in large part on the constituency fund--and the blurring of the boundary between "politics" and "administration" at all levels and in most arenas of Delhi city government. A theme which lies behind these two, and which I have not dealt with explicitly, is that the "stage"

for government is not the articulation of demands
or other facets of the "input side" of the decision-
making process, but rather the influencing of the
distribution of services.

Roderick Church, in his study of Lucknow,
refers to the process of routine administration
and the councilors' involvement in it, as an intermediary between citizens and administration.[8]
Church relies largely on survey research (using
extensive interviews with all the councilors of
Lucknow's two councils and a large sample of citizens drawn from all the wards of the city), and
his data complement mine nicely--on things such as
the councilor's perception of his role--and there
is almost nothing in his conclusions that could
not be applied, almost verbatim, to Delhi.

I will refer to Church's work when I discuss
the roles of actors in Delhi Corporation government, but let me note that Church answers his
question of why the Lucknow councilor involves himself in routine administration by pointing out the
institutional constraints, the imperatives of
economic development, and the character of administration and administrators. With regard to the
institutional constraints, he notes "two aspects
of the legal structure of municipal government"--
. . . [one is] the very restricted policy role of
the Corporation . . . [the second is the vesting
of] formal executive and administrative authority
almost entirely in the hands of the administrators."[9] Under the "imperatives of economic
underdevelopment," he lists, as "important factors
shaping the administrative process," general
scarcity, poor communication facilities, and low
levels of education.[10] The character of administration refers to its "slackness"--inefficiency and
corruption--so that "there need be little correspondence between policy statements or by-laws on
the one hand and the way policy is administered on
the other," which means that "Councillors who want
to be effective must necessarily get involved in
administrative matters."[11] Finally, by the climate

of administration, Church indicates that councilors "have a more favorable public image than
administrators" (and the administrators have a
very poor image, with, Church notes, considerable basis in the facts of citizen experience).[12]
Church also discounts cultural factors: "Faced
with a situation similar to that in Lucknow, one
suspects that anyone, whatever his cultural background, would behave in much the same way as
Lucknow's citizens and councilors do."[13] It can
be seen that Church's conclusions neatly complement mine, especially on the question of institutional constraints.

The "decentralization system" theme and the
"distinction between 'politics' and 'administration'" theme blend together: it is the system
of decentralization which permits a legitimate
involvement by the elected representative in
routine administration. At the Corporation level
in Delhi, the usual problems with the distinction
between "deliberative wing" and "executive wing"
apply. On the one hand, the questioning of the
executives by the councilors on how policies are
being implemented and the sanctions built into the
structure of the public meetings and the committee
meetings--primarily public exposure--mean that
councilors are involved in the administrative
process, particularly once the executive officer
"learns" and consults with influential councilors.
On the other hand, the power of the executive wing
to frame the budget, to interpret the rules, etc.,
clearly involves them in the policy-making process.[14] And although periodic press reports suggest
that neither wing is entirely happy with the
arrangement of a theoretical separation and an
actual partial intermingling of the two wings,
clearly something of a modus vivendi has been
worked out.

The zonal system, built partly on the "natural"
divisions of the previously existing local bodies
in the Corporation area (Chapter 6, pp. 206-18),
has a two-pronged rationale: to achieve a more

efficient administration, more accessible to the
citizenry to be sure, but a more "logical" arrangement from the administrative point of view; and a
way of moving government "closer" to the people,
as is shown by the inclusion of zonal committees
in the scheme. Both these rationales are deeply
rooted in the history of local government in
India.[15] The provisions which govern the zonal
committee's functions try to preserve the distinction between (mini-)deliberative wing and
(mini-) executive wing, but the range of problems
relevant to the zone, it seems to me, virtually
guarantees that the chasm would be bridged, quite
apart from the "balance of influence" between
councilors and administrators. By the time one
"descends" to the ward level, the constituency
fund provides for the councilors' legitimate entry
into the process of routine administration (which
is why, I am sure, Commissions from the "higher"
levels of government, like the Morarka Committee,
are so horrified by its existence).* The "government culture" at the ward level inserts the councilor, not unwillingly, into the chain of administrative command. Which brings us to the question
of roles and a recapitulation of the schema of the
three "interfaces."

Roles and Interfaces

It is possible to identify all three actors--
councilor, administrator, and citizen--at the three

---

*
Here Delhi differs from Lucknow. Church
writes: "Although the councillor's administrative
role is easy enough to explain, what makes it so
intriguing is that it must be played within an institutional framework which expressly denies councillors any authority in administrative matters."
(Church, "Authority and Influence in Indian Municipal Politics," p. 421).

levels of Delhi Municipal government, but it is
clear that the salience of the three interfaces
varies with the arena. In the Corporation as a
whole the citizen - councilor and citizen-administrator interfaces recede into the background, and
the councilor-administrator interface is more
structured than it is at other levels. Furthermore, the councilors themselves, qua influential
leaders and qua committee members, are dealing
with other governmental authorities in the Union
Territory, using complex political and institutional ties. At the zonal level, the citizen
has a more prominent role than he has at the city
level, but the councilor-administrator interface,
both formal and on the basis of individual interactions, is pivotal. In the ward, citizens are
quite actively involved in the governmental process,
and while the councilor-administrator interface
continues to be the more important of the three,
it does not overwhelm the other two.

The factor which determines the roles that
the councilors play in the ward, as they themselves
point out, is their need to get votes, which in
turn means the necessity to please and appeal to
as broad a base of the citizenry as possible.
Church has found that "The main impact which councillors have . . . is not one that biases administrative decisions in favor of any particular group
or area, but one which ensures relatively equal
access to civic services."[16] The data from Kucha
Khirkiwala supports this, and there is nothing in
the zonal or city level data which would make one
suppose that it does not hold true for Delhi as a
whole.

The Delhi councilor, like his Lucknow counterpart, is primarily an intermediary between citizen
and the administration. This role at the ward
level consists of an "ombudsman" function, in which
the councilor transmits citizen complaints about
services and/or insures that services are performed,
and a "deliverer of services" function, in which
the councilor diverts the stream of municipal

benefits, which are things like street repair, into
"proper" channels. In this role, the councilor not
only supervises the administrator but also is
involved in the decision-making process; he not
only inspects works in progress and works completed,
he also surveys the ward (and "survey" can mean
to look at physical conditions and to sample the
opinion of constituents) to discover where new
works are needed. Roles he does <u>not</u> perform at
this level are those of distributor of patronage
or vote-broker.

At the zonal level, the councilor acts less as
an "ombudsman"--though he in a sense conveys and
investigates complaints that he himself, on behalf
of his ward, may have--but continues as an intermediary, though here the supervisory side comes to
the fore. At the Corporation level, it may be that
leading councilors have certain quasi-patronage
powers (influencing perhaps the letting of contracts
and the transfer and promotion of administrators),
but there is no evidence of a "machine" politics.
The situation Church found in Lucknow is probably
true of Delhi:

. . . just as any person with a reputation
and a record of local service can win election to the council, so any councillor who
has intelligence and speaking ability and
who takes an active interest in Corporation
affairs can carve out a position of influence
within the council.[17]

The point here is that influence derives from
factors intrinsic to the governmental system, and
not things like social status and economic power
(or, conversely, those <u>without</u> status and wealth
are not excluded from positions of influence).
Municipal government is an autonomous arena, and the
councilor's role reflects this.

The administrator's role changes with the
level of government as well, largely because the
incumbents of the role, unlike the councilor, are

348 Summary, Conclusions, Implications

quite different people at the different levels. At
the ward level, the administrator is younger, less
educated, less experienced, and less involved in
shaping the policies he is administering than his
senior colleagues at the all-city level or even at
the zonal level. The administrator's role at the
ward level is that of a subordinate, of both his
administrative superiors and of the councilor (and
even, at times, of the local citizens); at the zonal
level, he is both superior and subordinate administratively, answerable to the councilors as a body,
perhaps, but with considerable room for maneuver
vis-à-vis the individual councilor. At the Corporation level, his role is that of a superior in
the administrative chain of command, but coordinate
authority, so to speak, with his fellow senior
officials within the Corporation and in the other
authorities of Delhi. (Senior men in the Corporation, particularly the Municipal Commissioner,
as members of the Indian Administrative Service
"seconded" to the Corporation, are themselves
[senior] subordinates in the national administrative system.) These variations in role are
matched by variations in the physical isolation
and exposure of the officer, both to councilors
and to citizens. And they are matched by deference
patterns also, between councilors and administrators in particular.

Municipal government in Delhi means different
things to those playing different roles in it. To
the administrator it means his full-time job (and
such jobs in India, I believe, tend not to be a
"vocation" but rather just an "occupation," with
specified duties, specified pay, and a specified
ladder of advancement); to the councilor, in theory
only a part-time participant but in practice
frequently full-time, it is indeed a vocation
(with the overtone of a psychic commitment to the
job and to "service"); to the citizen, it means a
sporadic involvement, usually in connection with
unpleasantness (a blocked sewer, a tax payment).
The involvement of the councilors, and possibly the

dissatisfaction of the administrators, is tied
directly to the institutional arrangements in
which they operate, and in Delhi, in my judgment, the system works well, so that I am quite
willing to disagree with my posited "some people"
and say that indeed "there is a need for democracy
at the municipal level, that municipal administration functions well because of 'political
interference.'"

IMPLICATIONS

It would be important, in the best of all
possible worlds, to move beyond the conclusions
of this study to consider its implications for
more general questions. I would like to be able
to discuss whether there is something called
"urban" politics, as opposed to "rural" politics
in India, once one "factors out" the differences
between the problems of the two--for instance, the
city constituent needing the benefit of a good
sanitation system, and the village constituent
needing the benefit of access to cheap agricultural
credit. Can we take the various definitions of
"urban," having to do with size, density, and non-
agricultural occupation, and turn them into
hypotheses concerning the political system? (What
are the differences between a constituency covering
50 acres in which 30,000 people live, and one of
the same size where 3,000 live?--to take one
possible example.) And equally, can we differ-
entiate between the many kinds and sizes of urban
areas, distinguishing metropolitan cities from
large towns, "service" cities from "industrial"
cities, by some political measures? Could we
look at the councilor-administrator interface
elsewhere in India and then compare it to similar
relationships in municipal systems outside India?
And so on.
One major constraint on this kind of discussion is the lack of data, especially for Indian

cities and the cities of other countries of the
"Third World." There are only a few studies of
Indian city politics per se--for Calcutta, but
not for Madras or Bombay; for Poona and Agra,
but not for Ahmedabad and Allahabad; for Indore
and Nagpur, but not for Patna or Bangalore or
Hyderabad or Jaipur--and most of those focus
heavily on one aspect of urban government, which
makes comparison with Delhi problematic. But
more important is the near impossibility of
keeping at least some of the factors which
impinge on the urban political system constant--
function vs. territorial organization; democratic vs. authoritarian national systems;
small country/region vs. large country/region;
agricultural country vs. industrial country; and
so on ad infinitum. There is an extensive
literature on "Comparative Urban Politics," but
it is mainly (partial) studies of individual
cities, like this one. There is little in the
way of general hypothesis testing, and, in the
absence of more extensive and comparable data,
that is how it should be. I cannot presume, on
the basis of this study, to venture where others
have not.

There are, however, some implications of my
findings which can be put forward as unsystematic
propositions; most of these have already been
touched on in the body of the study. I will therefore simply list some of the more important, as
follows:

--My use of "big city" in the title points to
the implications of city size for urban politics:
the size of the average constituency (since the
size of the municipal council tends not to expand
much with the rise in city population) coupled
with population density and ease of communication
(measured by the number of telephones per thousand
population, for example) has implications for the
ease of face-to-face contact between councilor and
citizen, which in turn would have implications for
the mode of contact and the importance of

intermediaries. In Delhi, the large constituency
is coupled with a lack of intermediaries, while
the small constituencies of Dewas (as reported by
A. C. Mayer) feature intermediaries.

    --The phrase "big city" also has a flavor of
"urbanity" attached, a suggestion of ethnic hetero-
geneity--one wants to say it is something beyond a
conglomeration of villages. That the mohallas of
Kucha Khirkiwala have little in the way of politically relevant social structure is suggestive, as
is the apparent unimportance of secondary associations in the all-city arena. (Here Delhi could
be contrasted with cities like Agra and Nagpur,
large cities, where such structures do exist.)
The people who "run" the government are by and
large people in elective or administrative office,
not influentials of the economic or social
spheres.

    --The significance of Delhi's autonomy,
which goes with its being the capital of India,
a municipality isolated from the pressures of a
rural-area-dominated state legislature and a
place where access to the actors in the national
political system is direct and convenient, is
considerable. The latter point is true, by
extension, for the capitals of the Indian states
as well, but this line of analysis becomes more
difficult when one notes that those same state
capitals are, on the whole, also India's biggest
cities--which variable do we wish to hold constant?
Still, one can venture that the power of the big
city which is also a capital would be enhanced.

    --The discussion of the significance of the
constituency fund and the system of zonal decentralization in Delhi points to a complementary
suggestion to the previous two: institutional
as opposed to economic or social-structure of
even political (narrowly defined to mean the
party and/or ideological system) constraints are
crucial to understanding Delhi municipal government. I suspect, therefore, that the first
place one must look to explain why an Indian

municipal councilor acts as he does is to the
institutional framework in which he operates, and
only afterwards at his wealth, caste, or whatever.
If the focus is on the administrative officer,
his insulation or exposure vis-à-vis the councilor would be a necessary starting point.

--A point which hardly needs underlining is
the extent to which "informal" relationships
emerge in the "formal" structure of municipal
government; indeed, we have noted that the role
of the councilor at the ward level, for instance,
is largely acted outside the formal definitions--
since by definition of his function, the councilor should have virtually no role at all at
that level--and becomes more flexible (the
administrator might say, more tyrannical) for
that reason. This implication of the study off-
sets the previous point to a degree: one is ill-
advised to consider the institutional arrangements one finds on paper.

--We have not dealt with change over time in
any detail; indeed, the import of much of the
discussion of the history of the Municipal Committee was that there has been surprisingly little
change. But it is worthwhile to consider what
will happen as Delhi continues to progress, when
more people are educated and have access to a
telephone, when the obvious problems of city living
are solved (there is an adequate water supply, all
the sewer lines have been laid, etc.), to give some
possible changes; the implication is that the councilor's role and activity would diminish, because
we have seen that the councilor is not so much a
democratic representative concerned with "policy"
as an adjunct to the administrative apparatus,
whom citizens use as a convenience (as they would,
one suspects, use an ombudsman appointed by the
municipal commissioner). The "decline" in "civic
consciousness," which so many of my friends and
informants allege has occurred in Delhi, may thus
turn out to be, paradoxically, merely a sign of a
future which is to be desired.

This is far from an exhaustive list of the implications of this study, but I fear that were I to continue, others would be even more difficult to present concisely. And it would be best for someone other than a person immersed in Delhi to add to them.

APPENDICES

APPENDIX, TABLE 1

1971 CENSUS DATA, BY POLLING STATION, KUCHA KHIRKIWALA

Polling Station	Houses	House-holds	Popu-lation	Scheduled Caste	Literates	Workers	Workers in Categories: I-IV	V(a)	V(b)	VI	VII	VIII	IX
1	201	302	1,703	123	1,292	523	..	3	116	15	145	28	216
2	143	271	1,540	2	774	466	..	1	155	10	166	40	94
3	133	294	1,701	7	854	487	..	5	194	11	160	49	68
4	148	264	1,813	10	771	519	2	15	263	14	109	18	101
5	122	245	1,903	..	975	546	..	38	255	11	101	36	102
6	181	316	2,145	..	932	568	..	64	238	11	132	23	100
7	237	301	2,163	..	921	590	..	75	283	44	114	9	65
8	113	278	1,897	..	760	535	9	34	246	21	116	25	84
9	207	221	1,345	13	821	375	9	5	66	8	156	32	99
10	146	208	1,403	6	863	383	1	26	98	6	153	7	92
11	124	315	2,103	..	1,197	581	1	42	199	4	218	14	103
12	89	250	1,474	90	1,024	402	..	3	85	7	162	30	115
13	84	244	1,502	95	1,036	423	1	4	88	5	149	29	147
14	125	319	1,874	23	1,297	455	..	4	100	62	192	19	78
15	80	277	1,610	235	936	449	..	3	103	21	213	27	81
16	156	243	1,408	..	1,063	404	1	12	58	11	196	22	104
17	154	264	1,434	4	974	432	1	11	99	14	153	38	116
18	190	228	1,718	338	781	522	3	3	242	7	166	28	73
Totals	2,633	4,840	30,736	946	17,271	8,660	29	348	2,888	282	2,801	474	1,838

Source: India, Census 1971, Series 27, Delhi, Part X, A & B, District Census Handbook, Delhi (Delhi: Delhi Administration, 1972).

I = Cultivators; II = Agricultural Laborers; III = Livestock, Forestry, Fishing, Hunting and Plantations, Orchards and Allied Activities; IV = Mining and Quarrying; V = Manufacturing, Processing, Servicing and Repairs; (a) Household Industry; (b) Other than Household Industry; VI = Construction; VII = Trade and Commerce; VIII = Transport, Storage and Communications; IX = Other Services

Note: Each polling station contains approximately 2-3 census blocks. Most of the polling stations share a census block with another polling station: these were divided arbitrarily -- either half and half or one-quarter, three-quarters -- to correspond to the number of voters from the census block which would be placed in the two polling stations. While this assumption is likely to produce a reasonable approximation of the population figure, the subdivisions are more questionable: workers of one category are probably not spread evenly throughout the census block area. This must introduce some distortions, particularly in those categories with few members, but would have less effect, I would hope, in the categories with many members, such as "literates."

APPENDIX, TABLE 2

THREE ELECTIONS IN KUCHA KHIRKIWALA, PERCENTAGE OF VOTE BY PARTY

| Polling Station | Party |||||||||||||||
| | Congress ||| Jana Sangh ||| Muslim Ind. ||| Hindu Ind. ||| Others |||
	A	B	C	A	B	C	A	B	C	A	B	C[a]	A	B	C
1	37	43	52	54	36	40	..	5	..	4	15		5	1	8
2	36	35	59	40	30	29	7	18	4	6	14		11	3	8
3	22	29	44	35	29	35	28	31	18	2	7		12	3	3
4	22	20	36	13	9	15	45	62	44	2	5		17	4	5
5	21	26	43	18	10	19	43	47	32	2	14		16	3	6
6	15	23	55	6	5	8	69	57	36	2	12		9	3	1
7	17	22	47	4	3	6	67	28	45	3	44		8	2	2
8	14	20	53	21	14	19	48	25	27	7	39		9	3	1
9	35	31	59	55	49	38	..	2	1	7	16		3	2	3
10	25	24	33	32	20	31	28	35	27	4	18		10	2	10
11	21	19	54	40	27	36	30	11	10	6	41		4	2	1
12	32	33	52	62	42	47	..	2	..	3	22		3	1	2
13	33	31	59	49	35	38	1	2	1	13	30		5	2	2
14	36	39	42	54	27	56	..	1	1	7	32		3	1	1
15	32	35	45	57	41	52	..	1	1	8	21		2	1	2
16	36	36	57	54	39	42	..	1	..	7	22		3	2	2
17	35	40	54	52	38	38	8	9	6	2	10		3	2	3
18	36	36	54	31	25	29	19	26	16	6	12		8	2	1

Legend:

A = 1967 Lok Sabha election.
B = 1967 Corporation election.
C = 1969 Corporation election.

[a] No Hindu Independent got a significant vote in 1969.

APPENDIX, TABLE 3

POPULATION, LITERATES, SCHEDULED CASTE, AND OCCUPATION, SHAHJAHANABAD 1971

| Charge No. | Population | Scheduled Caste | Literates | Workers in Categories: | | | | | | |
				I-IV	Va	Vb	VI	VII	VIII	IX
7	17,609	2,093 (11.9)	11,556 (65.6)	15 (0.3)	110 (1.9)	918 (16.2)	90 (1.6)	1,611 (28.5)	1,139 (20.1)	1,779 (31.4)
8	25,975	1,040 (4.0)	16,311 (62.8)	19 (0.2)	201 (2.0)	1,373 (13.8)	233 (2.3)	3,505 (35.3)	1,693 (17.1)	2,904 (29.3)
9	34,721	2,647 (7.6)	23,503 (67.7)	18 (0.2)	278 (2.6)	1,773 (16.5)	128 (1.2)	4,595 (42.7)	1,518 (14.1)	2,460 (22.8)
10	22,938	833 (3.6)	17,070 (74.4)	4 (0.1)	87 (1.3)	1,073 (16.0)	85 (1.3)	2,809 (41.9)	517 (7.7)	2,127 (31.7)
11	21,605	154 (0.7)	15,696 (72.6)	4 (0.1)	98 (1.6)	1,092 (18.1)	62 (1.0)	3,049 (50.5)	241 (4.0)	1,487 (24.6)
12	52,552	1,558 (3.0)	29,701 (56.5)	57 (0.4)	734 (4.8)	4,004 (26.2)	229 (1.5)	5,720 (37.4)	1,021 (6.7)	3,523 (23.0)
13	54,185	3,365 (6.2)	25,501 (47.1)	38 (0.2)	1,285 (7.9)	5,486 (33.9)	577 (3.6)	3,944 (24.3)	954 (5.9)	3,915 (24.2)
14	46,561	9,975 (21.4)	25,028 (53.8)	51 (0.4)	851 (6.7)	2,899 (22.7)	737 (5.8)	4,316 (33.8)	1,020 (8.0)	2,885 (22.6)
15	42,497	1,218 (2.9)	21,801 (51.3)	37 (0.3)	636 (5.3)	4,237 (35.5)	359 (3.0)	3,612 (30.2)	692 (5.8)	2,371 (19.9)
16	34,212	4,489 (13.1)	13,658 (39.9)	71 (0.8)	245 (2.6)	3,407 (36.5)	377 (4.0)	2,761 (29.6)	563 (6.0)	1,905 (20.4)
17	60,218	4,736 (7.9)	32,771 (54.4)	160 (0.9)	991 (5.6)	4,288 (24.3)	286 (1.6)	5,001 (28.3)	936 (5.3)	6,009 (34.0)
Totals	413,073	32,108 (7.8)	232,596 (56.3)	474 (0.4)	5,516 (4.5)	30,550 (25.0)	3,163 (2.6)	40,923 (33.5)	10,294 (8.4)	31,365 (25.6)

Source: Delhi District Census Handbook 1971, Part X--B, pp. 74-104, passim.

APPENDIX, TABLE 4

SHAHJAHANABAD[a]:   1951 DENSITIES

	Ward[b]	Population	Area (Acres)	Gross Density[c]	Net Density[d]
3	Chandni Chowk	15,103	98.8	152	268
4	Katra Neel	18,735	62.0	202	403
5	Shardhanand Bazar	18,426	87.2	211	480
6	Dariba	23,687	60.0	394	1,128
7	Maliwara	21,722	36.0	603	635
8	Charkhewalan	20,107	48.4	415	437
9	Ballimaran	23,513	47.6	493	520
10	Naya Bans	28,664	60.0	311	445
11	Farashkhana	19,124	49.2	388	457
12	Kucha Pati Ram	24,205	63.6	380	639
13	Kucha Pandit	12,928	92.8	139	291
14	Kalan Masjid	15,502	47.6	326	545
15	Lal Darwaza	16,105	36.6	440	470
16	Churiwalan	15,658	38.0	412	433
17	Matia Mahal	21,154	94.4	224	333
18	Daryaganj	14,946	146.6	101	159
19	Chatta Lal Mian	17,164	47.6	260	613
20	Suiwalan	10,014	68.0	294	412
	Totals	336,757	1,184.4	319 (mean)	482 (mean)

Source: India, Ministry of Health, Town Planning Organization, Interim
General Plan for Greater Delhi (Delhi: Ministry of Health,
1956), p. 100.

[a]Shahjahanabad minus the area north of the railway. When Kashmiri Gate
and Mori Gate wards are added, the population becomes 380,328, the area
1,506.8 acres, for a gross density of 252 persons per acre.

[b]While many of the ward names here are the same as those of the present
wards, the area covered in many cases is marginally different, and in
a few cases, very different.

[c]Persons per acre. The table in the source is headed by two "assumptions
in calculating densities": "1. Each family on an average consists of
five members. 2. Each single storey house contains 1-1/2 families on
an average and a double storey house has three families . . . leaving
few exceptions."

[d]Persons per built-up acre.

APPENDIX, TABLE 5

1967 AND 1971 CORPORATION ELECTIONS IN SHAHJAHANABAD:
VOTE PERCENTAGE, BY WARD

Ward	Congress[a]		Jana Sangh		Independents and Other Parties[b]		Others	
	1967	1971	1967	1971	1967	1971	1967	1971
53	36.2	44.2	55.1	52.0	6.0[c]	....	2.7	3.8
54	42.8	55.7	44.6	41.7	7.2[g]	....	5.3	2.6
55	55.2	20.1	38.7	49.2	6.2[g]	30.5[h]	....	0.1
56	32.0	41.6	44.1	57.0	6.4[d]	....	17.5	1.5
57	38.8	46.5	59.3	53.5	1.8[e]	....	....	....
58	26.3	32.7	42.7	61.9	23.8[g]	1.7[h]	7.2	3.7
59	45.4	44.2	14.5	17.3	18.7[d]	35.8[g]	21.4	2.7
60	42.3	15.0	31.9	41.5	18.5[d]	36.7[h]	7.3	6.9
61	30.1	55.1	26.2	40.4	21.4[g]	....	22.3	4.4
62	45.5	42.6	47.8	55.9	5.8[f]	....	1.0	1.6
63	50.6	69.3	23.6	28.5	23.9[c]	....	1.8	2.3
64	37.7	35.4	40.3	43.9	17.8[c]	20.0[c]	4.2	0.6
65	60.0	13.5	22.5	16.8	17.5[g]	51.9[g]	....	17.9
66	37.1	27.6	48.6	39.6	14.3[e]	19.1[h]	....	13.7
67	42.0	45.8	46.6	51.9	8.1[d]	....	3.3	2.4
68	29.3	13.1	31.2	....	36.3[d]	52.0	3.3	34.9[i]
Mean	40.7	37.7	38.6	43.4				

[a]Refers to Congress(R) in 1971.

[b]The single largest vote getter of this description, if significant.

[c]CPI.   [d]RPI.   [e]SSP.   [f]PSP.   [g]Ind.   [h]Congress(O).

[i]All but 1 percent Congress(O).

APPENDIX, TABLE 6

1967 CORPORATION AND LOK SABHA ELECTIONS IN SHAHJAHANABAD: VOTE PERCENTAGE, BY WARD

Ward Number	Congress		Jana Sangh		RPI		Independent or Other Party[a]		Others	
	Lok Sabha	DMC	Lok Sabha	DMC	Lok Sabha	DMC	Lok Sabha	DMC	Lok Sabha	DMC
53	31.1	36.2	61.2	55.1	0.4	....	4.8	6.0	2.4	2.7
54	40.4	42.8	53.0	44.6	0.5	....	3.4	7.2	2.7	5.3
55	44.8	55.2	50.8	38.7	0.5	....	0.9	6.2	2.9	....
56	28.5	32.0	48.4	44.1	5.1	6.4	14.0	9.5	4.0	8.0
57	32.0	38.8	62.3	59.3	0.3	....	0.7	1.8	4.7	....
58	29.4	26.3	59.5	42.7	0.2	....	1.4	23.8	9.5	7.2
59	23.7	45.4	14.0	14.5	13.2	18.7	46.2	10.3	2.9	11.1
60	26.4	42.3	30.6	31.9	15.7	18.5	25.9	7.3	1.5	....
61	27.9	30.1	37.7	26.2	1.0	....	22.0	21.4	11.4	22.3
62	35.0	45.5	52.6	47.8	0.3	....	10.1	5.8	2.0	1.0
63	30.3	50.6	27.5	23.6	1.6	....	38.7	23.9	2.0	1.8
64	31.6	37.7	53.4	40.3	0.8	....	11.6	17.8	2.6	4.2
65	30.1	60.0	21.8	22.5	3.5	....	40.7	17.5	3.9	....
66	30.4	37.1	45.5	48.6	4.3	....	15.5	14.3	4.3	....
67	35.6	42.0	53.7	46.6	7.0	8.1	0.2	2.8	3.5	0.5
68	27.9	29.3	30.4	31.2	18.2	36.3	21.1	1.9	2.4	1.4

[a]The Independent or party candidate (seven instances) with the largest vote.

NOTES, BIBLIOGRAPHY, INDEX

Notes to the Chapters

Chapter 1

1. A wholly nominated body with restricted powers which administers the area immediately surrounding the major national government buildings in New Delhi.
2. See my "Indian Urban Politics, with Particular Reference to the Nagpur Corporation" (unpublished Master's thesis, University of Chicago, 1968); Donald B. Rosenthal, The Limited Elite: Politics and Government in Two Indian Cities (Chicago: University of Chicago Press, 1969); Hugh Tinker, The Foundations of Local Self-Government in India, Pakistan, and Burma (London: The Athlone Press, 1954).
3. Rory Fonseca, "The Walled City of Old Delhi," Shelter and Society, ed. Paul Oliver (New York: Frederick A. Praeger, 1969) describes the physical plan from an architect's point of view. Marshall Clinard, in his Slums and Community Development; Experiments in Self-Help (New York: Free Press, 1970) suggests that social institutions might be strengthened. See also Ahmed Ali, Twilight in Delhi (Bombay: Oxford University Press, 1966 [original edition: 1940]) for a fictional account of Old Delhi as it was in 1910 or so.
4. Adrian C. Mayer, "Municipal Elections: A Central Indian Case Study," Politics and Society, ed. C. H. Philips (New York: Frederick A. Praeger, 1962); "The Significance of Quasi-Groups in the Study of Complex Society," The Social Anthropology of Complex Societies, Association of Social Anthropology of the Commonwealth Monograph No. 4, ed. Michael Banton (New York: Frederick A. Praeger, 1966); "Systems and Network: An Approach to the Study of Political Process in Dewas," Indian Anthropology: Essays in Memory of D. N. Majumdar, ed. T. N. Madan and G. Saran (Bombay: Asia Publishing House, 1962). A further application of this framework is made by Mark Holmström, "Action-sets and Ideology: A Municipal Election in South India," Contributions to Indian Sociology, No. 3 (New Series) December, 1969, pp. 76-93.
5. F. G. Bailey, Politics and Social Change: Orissa in 1959 (Berkeley: University of California Press, 1963).
6. Robert G. Wirsing, "Associational 'Micro-arenas' in Indian Urban Politics," Asian Survey, XIII, No. 4 (1973), pp. 408-20.

7. For the administrative dimension, a most influential source is the report of the Rural-Urban Relationship Committee, which was appointed by the central government. See also the report of a seminar held at the Indian Institute of Public Administration entitled Improving City Government (New Delhi: Indian Institute of Public Administration, 1969). The relationship between administrator and elected official has been examined, for non-city arenas, by Shanti Kothari and Ramashray Roy, Relations between Politicians and Administrators at the District Level (New Delhi: Indian Institute of Public Administration, 1969) and Richard Taub, Bureaucrats Under Stress: Administrators and Administration in an Indian State (Berkeley: University of California Press, 1969). Two works on citizen interaction which use data for Delhi are A. P. Barnabas, The Experience of Citizens in Getting Water Connections (New Delhi: Indian Institute of Public Administration, 1965) and S. Eldersveld et al., The Citizen and the Administrator in a Developing Democracy: An Empirical Study in Delhi State (New Delhi: Indian Institute of Public Administration, 1968).

8. India, Census of India 1961 [by Baldev Raj and Kuldip Chander Sehgal], Delhi District Census Handbook (Delhi: The Delhi Administration, 1964). Hereafter Delhi District Census Handbook 1961.

9. India, Census of India 1971 [compiled by S. R. Gandotra] Delhi, Part X--A & B, Delhi District Census Handbook (Delhi: The Delhi Administration, n.d.). Hereafter Delhi District Census Handbook 1971. I have been unable to obtain the second volume (Part X--C) or other volumes of the Delhi series, if they have indeed been published, and so data on industrial establishments, migration, and religion are drawn from the 1961 census.

10. Delhi is perhaps the city site richest in archaeological remains in India, largely because so many rulers built their capital there, and because, for a variety of reasons, many new rulers built new cities near the old ones. There are numerous guide books and short histories of Delhi (and, unfortunately, no thorough recent history); among these are: Asok Mitra, Delhi, Capital City (New Delhi: Thompson Press [India] Ltd., 1970); Percival Spear, Delhi: A Historical Sketch (Bombay: Oxford University Press [India Branch], 1937); Y. D. Sharma, Delhi and Its Neighborhood (New Delhi: Archaeological Survey of India, Government of India, 1964); Carr Stephen, Archaeological and Monumental Remains of Delhi (Allahabad: Kitab Mahal, 1967--original edition, 1876); A. C. Lothian, ed., A Handbook for Travellers in India, Pakistan, Burma and Ceylon [Murray's Guide] (17th ed.; London: John Murray, 1955), pp. 229-255; Prabha Chopra, ed., Delhi History and Places of Interest (Delhi: Delhi Gazeteer, Delhi Administration, 1970).

11. See Bridget Allchin and Raymond Allchin, The Birth of Indian Civilization (Harmondsworth, Middlesex, England: Penguin Books, Ltd., 1968), pp. 210-11.

12. Lecture by B. B. Lal (Director-General, Archaeological Survey of India), Spring, 1971, at the University of Chicago.

13. One possible reason for this lies in the Islamic character of all but the last Delhi: "Just as it proscribes the house of several stories, Islam has also encouraged the use of fragile and perishable materials. . . . [In Islamic countries] houses are built for man--not for Allah. Despite the modesty commanded by piety, buildings must be built spectacularly--and quickly. Concern for durability is secondary. The use of fragile materials is a token of the insubstantiality of material things and the unimportance of the

individual." (Xavier de Planhol, The World of Islam [Ithaca, N.Y.: Cornell University Press, 1959], pp. 24-25.)

14. See the novel by Ahmed Ali, Twilight in Delhi, or various works in Urdu, e.g., Shamin Ahmad, Dilli kii ek jhulak (no publication data).

15. Indeed the last Moghul emperor, Bahadur Shah 'Zafar' was tried for treason for his role in the 1857 Revolt; the anomaly of the Sovereign being tried for treason against his nominal subjects was not raised until more than half a century later. (See Percival Spear, Twilight of the Mughals [Delhi: Oriental Books Reprint Corporation, 1969; original edition, 1961], p. 223.)

16. See Narayani Gupta, "Military Security and Urban Development: A Case Study of Delhi 1857-1912," Modern Asian Studies, V, No. 1 (1971), p. 64.

17. In 1961, of the 716,000 residents of Census Zone II (City, Sadar-Paharganj), 361,000 were born in the place of enumeration; another 20,000 were born elsewhere in Delhi. The proportion of people in Shahjahanabad alone resident since birth would be in all probability higher. (India, Census of India 1961, Vol. XIX: Delhi, Part II-C, Cultural and Migration Tables (no publication data), p. 222.)

18. Delhi District Census Handbook 1961, p. 13.

19. The Congress Party is of course the dominant party in India, nationally and in most states. Even after the split of 1969, it includes people of widely diverging views. In Delhi, the Congress(R), the party headed by Mrs. Indira Gandhi, emerged with the greater mass support after 1969. See Walter Andersen and M. K. Saini, "The Congress Split in Delhi: the Effect of Factionalism on Organizational Performance and System Level Interactions," Asian Survey, Vol. XI, No. 11 (1971). The Jana Sangh, founded just before the 1951-52 general elections, is a strongly nationalist party, with a Hindu revivalist bias, whose main supporters in Delhi (as in most of North Inda) are the refugees from what is now Pakistan. See Craig Baxter, The Jana Sangh: A Biography of an Indian Political Party (Philadelphia: University of Pennsylvania Press, 1969).

20. For this brief historical sketch I have drawn on the following works: India, Administrative Reforms Commission, Study Team on Administration of Union Territories and NEFA, Report, Vol. I (Delhi: Manager of Publications, 1969), pp. 159-70 and 247-58 (hereafter: ARC Study Team Report); Jag Parvesh Chandra, Delhi: A Political Study (Delhi: Jag Parvesh Chandra, 1969); Prabha Chopra, ed., Delhi: History and Places of Interest (Delhi: Delhi Administration, 1970), pp. 1-108; and M. K. Yadav, ed., Municipal Corporation of Delhi Yearbook, 1969-70 (Delhi: Municipal Corporation of Delhi, 1970). See also Abhijit Datta and J. N. Khosla, "Delhi," Great Cities of the World; Their Government, Politics, and Planning, ed. William A. Robson and D. E. Regan (3d ed.; London: George Allen and Unwin, 1972), I, pp. 409-436.

21. Chandra, Delhi: A Political Study, p. 27.

22. India, States Reorganization Commission, Report (Delhi: Manager of Publications, 1955), p. 157. The Report's footnote to the above excerpt cites the Government of Part C States Act, 1951, Section 21.

23. Chandra, Delhi: A Political Study, p. 45.

24. India, States Reorganization Commission, Report, p. 157.

25. Ibid., p. 160.

26. Ibid., p. 161.

27. Chandra, Delhi: A Political Study, p. 74.

28. Ibid., p. 85. He gives the source as the Delhi Administration Act, 1966, but gives no section number. According to the ARC Study Team Report, p. 27: "[The] advice [of the Executive Council] is not binding on the Administration."

29. For the situation elsewhere in India, see Rodney W. Jones, "Linkage Analysis of Indian Urban Politics," Economic and Political Weekly VII, No. 25 (June 17, 1972), pp. 1195-1203. See also his Urban Politics in India: Area, Power and Policy in a Pentrated System (Berkeley: University of California Press, 1974).

30. Nur-ud-din Ahmad, et al., Case for Greater Delhi, Memorandum submitted to the States Reorganization Commission on behalf of the Delhi State Government (Delhi: Directorate of Public Relations, Delhi State, 1954), p. 8.

31. Ibid., pp. 9-10. Brahm Prakash, at that time Chief Minister of Delhi, writes in his foreword: "The people of this area . . . have common language, dress, marriage rites, laws of succession, system of land tenure and customs. They are identical in their mode of living and outlook on life. . . . Their culture is a happy and harmonious blend of the diversities for which our country is noted. They have evolved a synthesis of the same. That is why the tract is known as 'Hindustan'--'India in miniature'--and the people and the language as 'Hindustani.' In more than one sense, it constitutes the heart of the country" (Ibid., p. 2).

32. Ibid., pp. 15-16. The proposed new state would have included Agra, Meerut, Rohlikund, and Ambala Divisions (with some districts and tehsils excepted), parts of PEPSU, and Alwar and Bharatpur Districts from Rajasthan in addition to Delhi. The state would have had an area of 53,472 square miles and a (1951) population of about 30 million, which would have made it the sixth largest in India (Ibid., p. 12).

33. See, for example, the Evening News (Delhi) report of January 10, 1970, p. 1. But the feeling for a "Vishal Delhi" is durable: several influential members of the Metropolitan Council, apparently supporters of Brahm Prakash, signed a memorandum to the central government demanding the inclusion of the rural areas and part of the walled city in Haryana (which had just "lost" Chandigarh as its capital); see Times of India (Delhi), January 25, 1970, p. 1.

34. India, Administrative Reforms Commission, Report on Administration of Union Territories and NEFA, pp. 27-39.

Chapter 2

1. Rory Fonseca, "The Walled City of Old Delhi," Landscape XVIII, No. 3 (Spring, 1970), pp. 12-25; Rory Fonseca, "The Walled City of Old Delhi," Shelter and Society, ed. Paul Oliver (New York: Frederick A. Praeger, 1969), pp. 103-15; and the source of both these articles, Rory Fonseca, "Urban Rehabilitation and an Indigenous Settlement: A Case Study of Ward 9 in the Walled City of Old Delhi" (unpublished Master of Architecture thesis, University of California at Berkeley, 1968).

2. Fonseca, "The Walled City of Old Delhi," Landscape, pp. 24-25. His emphasis.

3. Fonseca, "The Walled City of Old Delhi," Shelter and Society, p. 108.

4. R. K. Narayan, The Financial Expert (New York: Noonday Press, 1966), p. 33.
5. According to one councilor, 90 percent of the City Zone is now covered by sewer lines. Most landlords are anxious to install flush latrines to connect with sewer lines when they are put in, even though the cost is high. In Kucha Khirkiwala all except a few very small galis are served by sewer lines and a few are served by old lines of inadequate size which are being replaced. There are still many houses which have only dry latrines.
6. See text, pp. 82–95.
7. Evening News, November 22, 1969, p. 8.
8. Statesman, February 1, 1970, p. 6.
9. Marshall B. Clinard, Slums and Community Development: Experiments in Self-Help (New York: Free Press, 1966).
10. Ibid., pp. 78–79.
11. Ibid., pp. 215–16.
12. Municipal Corporation of Delhi, Department of Community Development, Second Evaluation Study of Vikas Mandals (Delhi: Delhi Municipal Corporation, n.d.), pp. 5.7–5.10 [sic]. The report is summarized in Clinard, Slums and Community Development, pp. 254–55.
13. Municipal Corporation of Delhi, Second Evaluation Study, p. 5.8 [sic].
14. Conducted by an informant who wishes to remain anonymous.
15. Of course I have no way of knowing what the area was like before the project began, but it was certainly in no better shape than other non-project area slums, and while there were local leaders (one of the goals of the Community Development project was to develop local leadership) there was no indication that they arose out of the project--rather they tended to be old-style party workers (like the American precinct captain perhaps) or members of traditional institutions such as a caste association, a temple committee, or a local akhara (gymnasium and wrestling pit). A description of the ward can be found in Walter Andersen and M. K. Saini, "The Basti Julahan Bye-Election," Indian Journal of Political Science, XXX, No. 3 (July–September, 1969), pp. 260–96.
16. Poster of mid-May, 1970. The text was in Hindi and in Urdu and in my translation I have attempted to preserve the "flavor" of the original, which includes the awkward sentences.
17. The dignitary pulls a string that unfurls the flag and lets loose a bunch of flower petals which are inside.
18. Stephen P. Blake, "Dar-ul-Khilafat-i-Shahjahanabad: the Padshahi Shahar in Mughal India: 1556–1739" (unpublished Ph.D. dissertation, University of Chicago, 1974), shows that in the period of Shahjahanabad's glory, social and economic life was organized in amiri mohallas, walled mansions of Mughal nobles, which were small-scale versions of the Emperor's palace.
19. Raymond Owens and Ashis Nandy, "Voluntary Associations in an Industrial Ward of Howrah, West Bengal, India" (paper presented to the 23rd annual meeting of the Association of Asian Studies, Washington, D.C., March, 1971).
20. Cf. Hugh Plunkett, "Pragmatic Politics in a Rajasthan Town: A Case Study of a Municipal Election," Economic and Political Weekly, VI, No. 49 (December 4, 1971), pp. 2442–46. In addition to my interview data I will draw on my three weeks' close observation of the campaign in Basti Julahan.

21. All Jana Sangh councilors I interviewed said these groups met once a month. Walter Andersen, who has studied the Jana Sangh organization in a neighboring Lok Sabha constituency, confirms that these bodies do meet regularly (personal communication).
22. This was given as a rough measure by an officer in the office of the Delhi Chief Election Officer (the authority who compiles voters lists), and I tested it out by looking at the population (1961 figures) and the number of registered voters in 1962 in the Lok Sabha constituencies of Delhi, and also by comparing the number of voters (1969) with the 1971 population in the census blocks of Kucha Khirkiwala; (the mean ratio of population to voters in the latter case was 2.1 to 1.). I am fairly confident that doubling the number of voters in most areas of Delhi will give a good estimate of the population.
23. There are only fifteen or so house numbers in which voters of two different religious communities are listed (counting Sikhs and Jains as part of the "Hindu" community, as people tend to do) in the entire ward.

Chapter 3

1. Roderick Church, "Authority and Influence in Indian Municipal Politics: Administrators and Councillors in Lucknow," Asian Survey, XIII, No. 4 (April, 1973), p. 421. See also Donald Rosenthal, The Limited Elite, pp. 119-22.
2. George J. Washnis, Neighborhood Facilities and Municipal Decentralization (Washington, D.C.: Center for Governmental Studies, 1971), I, p. 15. Noting that a proposal for a city ombudsman was recently turned down, Washnis writes "The fifteen councilmen . . . covet this role for themselves and have no intention of relinquishing it to anyone else." (Ibid.)
3. Most clearly in "machine" systems of politics, of course.
4. William Hampton, Democracy and Community: a Study of Politics in Sheffield (London: Oxford University Press, 1970), p. 183.
5. Some of the other councilors of the City Zone indicated that they would accompany constituents to the police station and would deal with "police matters."
6. Compare the form of our "calling me a liar to my face." I also observed heated arguments in India which did occur face-to-face (and "eyeball-to-eyeball"), but never one in which a councilor was arguing with a citizen.

Chapter 4

1. An M.L.A. (Member of the Legislative Assembly) of Punjab quoted in Satish Saberwal, "The Reserved Constituency: Candidates and Consequences," Economic and Political Weekly, VII, No. 2 (January 8, 1972), p. 76.
2. For other descriptions of municipal elections in India, see Adrian C. Mayer, "Municipal Elections: A Central Indian Case Study," Politics and Society in India, ed. C. H. Philips (New York: Frederick A. Praeger, 1962); Mark Holmström, "Action-sets and Ideology: A Municipal Election in South India," Contributions to Indian Sociology, New Series No. 3 (December, 1969), pp. 76-93; B. A. V. Sharma and R. T. Jangam, The Bombay Municipal Corporation:

An Election Study (Bombay: Popular Book Depot, 1962); Andersen
and Saini, "The Basti Julahan Bye-Election."

3. For procedures in the Congress Party, see Stanley Kochanek, The
Congress Party of India: Dynamics of a One Party Democracy
(Princeton, N.J.: Princeton University Press, 1968),
pp. 207-98; Ramashray Roy, "Election Studies, Selection of Congress
Candidates," Economic and Political Weekly, I, No. 20 (December 31,
1966), pp. 833-40; II, Nos. 1, 2, 6, 7 (January 7, 14 and February
11, 18, 1967), pp. 17-24; pp. 61-76; pp. 371-76; pp. 407-16; W. H.
Morris-Jones, "Candidate Selection: The Ordeal of the Indian
National Congress, 1966-67," Studies in Politics; National and
International, ed. M. S. Rajan (Delhi: Vikas Publications, 1970).
These deal with state and national elections. But since the
central bodies of the parties are far more intimately involved
in Delhi municipal politics than in the politics of other cities
(cf. Walter Andersen and M. K. Saini, "The Congress Split in Delhi:
The Effect of Factionalism on Organizational Performance and System-
Level Interactions," Asian Survey, 11, No. 11 (November, 1971), pp.
1084-1100), the M.L.A. selection process elsewhere is possibly
quite similar to the councilor selection process in Delhi. I made
no direct investigation, however. The more usual pattern for city
politics is described in Donald R. Rosenthal, The Limited Elite:
Politics and Government in Two Indian Cities (Chicago: University
of Chicago Press, 1970), pp. 59-64, and passim.

4. These ballots are sealed separately and are opened if the outcome
is close enough to make them significant. In the Basti Julhan by-
election, the main battle of the campaign was fought in the courts
over the revision of voters' lists. (Cf. Andersen and Saini, "The
Basti Julahan Bye-election.") The Jana Sangh discovered that voters
could be challenged until three days before the polling date, and
to retain one's name on the list one had to make a personal appearance in front of the registration officer, which was difficult for
the generally poor people of this ward. The Jana Sangh therefore
submitted its challenges late enough to make it difficult for the
Congress to hunt up voters and make counter challenges. The great
majority of votes challenged (and removed from the lists) were of
basti dwellers whose basti had been cleared; the Jana Sangh charged
that the Congress was planning to bring these people in from the
new housing into which they had been moved to vote.

5. The Rashtriya Swayamsevak Sangh, which calls itself a "cultural"
organization whose aim is to revitalize Hindu society. It holds
daily meetings of its branches (shakhas) with physical exercises,
patriotic lessons, etc. See J. A. Curran, Jr., Militant Hinduism
in Indian Politics: a Study of the RSS (New York: Institute of
Pacific Relations, 1951) and Walter Andersen, "The Rashtriya
Swayamsevak Sangh," Economic and Political Weekly, VII, Nos. 11-14
(March 11, 18, 25, and April 1, 1972), pp. 589-97, pp. 633-40,
pp. 673-82, and pp. 724-27, respectively. There is a very strong
tie between the RSS and the Jana Sangh which is publicly denied
and privately admitted.

6. Andersen and Saini, "The Basti Julahan Bye-Election," p. 265.

7. See F. G. Bailey, Politics and Social Change, passim, and Mayer,
"Municipal Elections."

8. In Hindi: (1) voT foR / Congress; (2) mohar lagaa do /
   bailon par; (3) diipak bujhaoo / jamhuriyat bachaoo; (4)
   Bharatiya Jana Sangh / kii jai; (5) jiitegaa bhai jiitegaa /
   diipak waalaa jiitegaa; (6) baapujii ne kyaa kahaa thaa?
   / Congress ko toR do.
9. For a discussion of the use of survey data in this kind of
   setting, see Frederick W. Frey, "Cross-Cultural Survey Research
   in Political Science," in Robert T. Holt and John E. Turner,
   eds., The Methodology of Comparative Research (New York: Free
   Press, 1970), pp. 173-294.
10. I recall that during a visit to a village in South India, in
    1965, in an area where the "ex-untouchables" were consistent
    Communist Party supporters, I spoke with an "ex-untouchable"
    who said that at election time, the Communist argument for votes
    was that the benefits the Congress government had given to the
    "ex-untouchables" (and these were admittedly considerable) were
    given only because they had voted Communist, and if they were to
    vote Congress, the flow of benefits would stop. This provides a
    possible clue to why Kucha Khirkiwala voters, especially the
    Muslims, continue to vote for the opposition, and in addition
    suggests that having a vigorous opposition party in Delhi is
    important for the "style" of municipal government.

Chapter 5

1. Y. D. Sharma, Delhi and Its Neighborhood (New Delhi: Archaeological Survey of India, 1964), p. 117.
2. [Jeevan Lal], A Short Account of the Life of Rai Bahadur Jeevan
   Lal, Late Honorary Magistrate, Delhi; and Extracts from His Diary,
   by his son (Delhi: Imperial Medical Hall Press, 1888), Appendix A
   [Extracts from the Diary], p. 26. This is a slightly different
   version of his narrative in T. Metcalf, Two Native Narratives of
   the Mutiny at Delhi (reprint ed.; Delhi: Seema Publications, 1974).
3. Percival Spear, Delhi: A Historical Sketch (Bombay: Oxford
   University Press, 1937), pp. 77-78. Cf. Blake, "Shahjahanabad,"
   pp. 12-13.
4. Carr Stephen, Archaeological and Monumental Remains of Delhi
   (reprint ed.; Allahabad: Kitab Mahal, 1967), p. 246. The original
   edition of this work appeared in 1876. Starting from Fatehpuri,
   Stephen lists the names of the bazars as: Fatehpuri Bazar,
   Chandni Chowk, Jowhri (Jewelers') Bazar, Phul ka Mandi (flower
   market), and the Urdi (military)Bazar. This would make the
   translation of "Chandni Chowk" as "Moonlight Square" quite
   appropriate.
5. Cf. Francois Bernier, Travels in the Moghul Empire 1656-1668
   (reprint ed.; Delhi: S. Chand and Co., 1968), pp. 239 ff. and
   Blake, "Shahjahanabad," passim.
6. Spear, Delhi, pp. 94-95.
7. It is impossible to give even inexact estimates of the numbers
   because the 1961 Census enumeration division for the migration
   category is "Old Delhi" (actually Zone II), which includes Sadar-
   Paharganj, where considerable numbers of refugees have established
   residences and businesses.

8. Xavier de Planhol, The World of Islam (Ithaca, N.Y.: Cornell University Press, 1969). An alternative view is presented by Ira Lapidus, "The Evolution of Muslim Urban Society," Comparative Studies in Society and History, XV, No. 1 (January, 1973), p. 48. See also his Muslim Cities in the Later Middle Ages (Cambridge, Mass.: Harvard University Press, 1967), and A. Hourani and S. M. Stern, eds., The Islamic City (Philadelphia: University of Pennsylvania Press, 1970).
9. de Planhol, The World of Islam, p. 7.
10. Ibid., pp. 7-8.
11. Ibid., p. 9.
12. Ibid.
13. Ibid., pp. 9-10.
14. Ibid., p. 12.
15. Ibid.
16. Ibid., p. 13.
17. Ibid., p. 23.
18. Ibid., p. 24.
19. Ibid., p. 25.
20. Ibid.
21. See Chapter 2, above.
22. The best discussion of the population figures for Shahjahanabad in the period before the censuses began is Blake, "Shahjahanabad," Appendix I, pp. 153-157.
23. There is an immense literature on "1857"; see, for example, Surendra Nath Sen, Eighteen Fifty-Seven (Delhi: Publications Division, Government of India, 1957) and Ramesh Chandra Majundar, The Sepoy Mutiny and Revolt of 1857 (Calcutta: Firma K. L. Mukhopadhyay, 1963).
24. Spear, Twilight of the Mughals, p. 220. Other mosques were kept even longer in British hands.
25. Ibid., pp. 222-228.
26. Cf. Ahmed Ali, Twilight in Delhi.
27. The Muslims of the Indian subcontinent were concerned about the fate of the Caliph, the Sultan of Turkey, after the defeat of the Ottoman Empire in World War I. The Khilafat movement was a mass movement among Muslims, and, at Gandhi's initiative, was supported by Hindus as a way of demonstrating national solidarity. The movement lasted from 1919 to 1924.
28. See Donald Ferrell, "Delhi 1911-1922: Society and Politics in the New Imperial Capital of India" (unpublished Ph.D. dissertation, Australian National University, Canberra, 1969). For a discussion of communal tension in earlier periods, see Sangat Singh, Freedom Movement in Delhi (1858-1919), (New Delhi: Associated Publishing House, 1972), pp. 83-96, pp. 144-154.
29. Census of India 1931, XVI, Part I, p. 127. These were: Chuhra, Dhobi, Gujjar, Jat, Julaha, Nai, Rajput, Tarkhan, and Teli. Lohars were equally divided between Muslim and Hindu members.
30. Imdad Sabri, Delhi Sidiqqi Biraadarii kii Shakhsiiyateen [Personages of the Delhi Sidiqqi Biradari] (no publication data), p. 432.
31. Census of India 1961, XIX, Part II-C, pp. 163-66. See Table 18.
32. There were 155,453 Muslims and 153,247 Urdu speakers in Delhi in 1961, and 127,439 and 128,402, respectively, in Census Zone II. Thirteen percent of the population were matriculates and above, and 16 percent of the people of Delhi knew English; in Zone II the figures were 10 and 12 percent respectively.

33. The most recent summary of the issue of caste in Indian politics is Rajni Kothari's Introduction to the volume he has edited, Caste in Indian Politics (Delhi: Orient Longmans, 1970). The most important earlier statement is found in Lloyd and Susanne Rudolph, The Modernity of Tradition (Chicago: University of Chicago Press, 1967). It should be emphasized that I am here speaking of Shahjahanabad: elsewhere in Delhi the new inhabitants have organized themselves, particularly according to state of origin (Bengalis, Tamils, etc.). Although I have no quantitative data, I believe that large numbers of the Hindus of the old city are members of the Arya Samaj, which has an anti-caste ideology, and this may explain the lack of caste organizations among Hindus.

34. This division is crucial in the neighboring constituency of the old city (Sadar); see Andersen and Saini, "The Congress Split in Delhi," passim.

35. Delhi Administration, Planning Department, Draft Fourth Five-Year Plan (1969 to 1973-74) (Delhi: Delhi Administration, 1968) p. 70.

36. The census categories on occupation are not strictly comparable over time, but they come close. This is a difficult problem not only because of the way the categories have been defined, but also because the definition of "worker" has also changed. In 1941 the primary definition was broken down into four major categories: occupation as a principal means of livelihood; as a principal means of livelihood but with a subsidiary means; as a subsidiary means of livelihood; as a means of livelihood of partly dependents (family members, for example). The 1971 census categories are most simply seen as separating out the "non-workers" first, and dealing with the "partly" employed in various ways. Fortunately (for us), in 1941 the overwhelming number of people enumerated in a given occupation are those who have it as a principal means of livelihood; I have, however, added in the other three categories of workers to make it more comparable to the 1971 census. The three major categories of workers that I am interested in-- manufacturing, trade and commerce, and services--are largely comparable from 1941 to 1971. A table giving a detailed break-down of workers' occupations from 1921 to 1951 can be found in Delhi Development Authority, Master Plan for Delhi (Delhi: Delhi Development Authority, 1962), II, 3-6.

37. Delhi Administration, Bureau of Economics and Statistics, Delhi Statistical Handbook 1970, (Delhi: Delhi Administration, 1970), pp. 120-21.

38. Ibid.

39. Delhi Master Plan, II, p. 128.

40. Ibid., II, p. 84.

41. The data on industrial establishments, found in pp. 445-448 of the Delhi District Census Handbook 1961, are difficult to handle, because the printed figures are frequently hard to read: errors are so easy to make that I will quote only "approximate" figures.

42. I have done this in my Ph.D. dissertation, "Big City Politics in India," pp. 206-213.

43. National Council of Applied Economic Research (NCAER), Commodity Disposition Survey in Delhi, Occasional Papers No. 4 (London: Asia Publishing House, 1959).

44. Ibid., p. 5.

45. Ibid., p. 6.

46. *Ibid*., p. 38.
47. *Ibid*., p. 41.
48. *Delhi District Census Handbook 1971*, Part X-B, pp. 74-104.
49. The source of the basic table, Table 3 of the Appendix, is the *Delhi District Handbook 1971*, Part X-B. The categories in the source are divided by sex, and there is also data on the number of houses and households.
50. India, Ministry of Health, Town Planning Organization, *Interim General Plan for Greater Delhi* (Delhi: Ministry of Health, 1956), p. 100. It is not clear whether these figures were computed from census slips or whether, as is implied by the "assumptions" used (see note to Appendix Table 4), they were estimated from a survey of buildings.
51. The *Delhi Master Plan* (I, p. 23) estimates gross densities for Shahjahanabad (here including the lower density areas north or the railway line and, probably, the old Red Fort Notified Committee area which had a 1951 population of about 10,000 and an area of nearly 600 acres) at 350 persons per acre.
52. Again, this is "literacy" only in the sense that the percentage of literates, including in the population those below the age of five, is a good measure of literacy for comparative purposes.
53. India, Census of India, Delhi, *Tables on Scheduled Castes* (No publication data, but probably Delhi: Manager of Publications, 1965), XIX, Part V-A, pp. 89 and 93.
54. India, Census of India 1961, Delhi, *Cultural and Migration Tables*, pp. 101-02.
55. India, Census of India, 1961, *Delhi*, Vol. XIX, Part I-A: *General Report on the Census* (New Delhi: Manager of Publications, 1966), p. 48 (hereafter cited as *Delhi Census 1961, General Report*). The other cities reported, and their growth: Hyderabad (11.2 percent); Bangalore (53.5 percent); Ahmedabad (37.5 percent); Kanpur (37.7 percent). This spectacular growth in Delhi has continued in the 1961-71 decade (52.93 percent according to the 1971 Census *Delhi District Census Handbook 1971*, p. 7). I use the 1961 census, which is closer to the dates of survey in the comparative data.
56. *Delhi Census, 1961, General Report*, p. 279.
57. *Ibid*., p. 280.
58. *Ibid*., pp. 208-09.
59. *Ibid*., p. 130.
60. Calculated from figures in Tokyo Metropolitan Government, *Comparative Statistical Table of World Large City 1961* (Tokyo: Tokyo Metropolitan Government, 1961), pp. 4-5. See also Horner Hoyt, "Growth and Structure of Twenty-one Great World Cities," in Gerald Breese, ed., *The City in Newly Developing Countries: Readings in Urbanism and Urbanization* (Englewood Cliffs, N.J.: Prentice-Hall, Inc., 1969), p. 207. It should be noted that Los Angeles grew by 54.3 percent and Toronto by 63.3 percent in the decade of the 1950s.
61. For instance, in 1966 the Tokyo percentages had become: I-III: 0.3; V: 34.6; VI: 7.2; VII: 36.6; VIII: 6.4; IX: 14.9. See Tokyo Metropolitan Government, *Statistics of World Large Cities 1968* (Tokyo: Tokyo Metropolitan Government, 1968).
62. Fred Riggs, "Bureaucrats and Political Development: a Paradoxical View," in Joseph LaPalombara, ed., *Bureaucracy and Political Development* (Princeton, N.J.: Princeton University Press, 1962), p. 120.

63. For example, Daniel Lerner, <u>The Passing of Traditional Society</u> (New York: Free Press, 1958).
64. For example, see Sidney Verba, Bashiruddin Ahmed, and Anil Bhatt, <u>Caste, Race, and Politics: A Comparative Study of India and the United States</u> (Beverly Hills, Calif.: Sage Publications, 1971).
65. Lapidus, <u>Muslim Cities</u>, pp. 1-2.
66. <u>Ibid.</u>, pp. 185, 187.
67. <u>Ibid.</u>, p. 186.

Chapter 6

1. There are several <u>tehsils</u> in each district; there are around 275 districts in India.
2. Richard P. Taub, <u>Bureaucrats Under Stress: Administrators and Administration in an Indian State</u> (Berkeley and Los Angeles: University of California Press, 1969), pp. 113-14.
3. P. V. R. Rao, <u>Red Tape and White Cap</u> (New Delhi: W. H. Patwardhan, Orient Longmans, Ltd., 1970), p. 102.
4. <u>Ibid.</u>
5. Shanti Kothari and Ramashray Roy, <u>Relations Between Politicians and Administrators at the District Level</u> (New Delhi: Indian Institute of Public Administration, 1969), p. 167.
6. <u>Ibid.</u>, p. 160.
7. This difficulty is, of course, not confined to India: "Wilson laid down the postulates, later reinforced by Goodnow and hardly questioned for fifty years, that politics and administration are separate studies. . . . We know now that, taken as a description of American administrative institutions, Wilson's postulate simply is (and was) wrong." Herbert A. Simon, "The Changing Theory and Practice of Public Administration," in Ithiel de Sola Pool, ed., <u>Contemporary Political Science: Toward Empirical Theory</u> (New York: McGraw-Hill Book Co., Inc., 1967), p. 87.
8. Kothari and Roy, <u>Relations</u>, p. 148.
9. <u>Ibid.</u>, p. 164.
10. See Rosenthal, <u>The Limited Elite</u>, pp. 129-32, for a discussion of how councilors' mutual esteem cut across caste and party lines, focusing instead on leadership skills and personal qualities.
11. India, Delhi Municipal Committee Enquiry Committee, <u>Report</u> (New Delhi, 1948), pp. 74-75 and schedules 2 and 3 (map).
12. Much of the following material on the zonal system in Delhi is drawn from the working paper prepared by Mr. H. B. Dass for the "Seminar on Decentralization of Municipal Administration in Delhi," organized by the Corporation and held at the Indian Institute of Public Administration in Delhi in March, 1969. (Mimeographed.)
13. Dass, Working Paper, p. 3.
14. Delhi Municipal Organization Enquiry Committee, <u>Report</u>, p. 74.
15. These ideas are not confined to India: "the objectives of this program [Branch City Halls in Los Angeles] are to effect greater efficiency, hold down citizen alienation, and alleviate transportation problems for both citizens and employees." George J. Washnis, <u>Neighborhood Facilities and Municipal Decentralization</u> (Washington, D.C.: Center for Governmental Studies, 1971), I, p. 14.

16. For simplicity's sake, I shall confine myself to a discussion of these ideas in India, since that is what has helped mold the attitudes of councilors, administrators, and citizens in Delhi. There is, of course, a large literature on the subject, particularly concerning North America; e.g., Harold Kaplan, Urban Political Systems: A Functional Analysis of Metro Toronto (New York: Columbia University Press, 1967).

17. India, Ministry of Health and Family Planning, Rural-Urban Relationship Committee, Report (3 vols.; Delhi: Manager of Publications, 1966), I, section 7.27, p. 62.

18. There is much talk of the "multiplicity of authorities" in Delhi, by which is meant autonomous boards dealing with planning, water supply, etc. In other cities, similar boards may deal with electric supply and other services. It is not clear in most discussions just where these bodies would fit into a two-tier system.

19. H. D. Sanwal, "Problems of Citizen Participation in Municipal Government," in Improving City Government: Proceedings of a Seminar (New Delhi: Indian Institute of Public Administration, 1959), p. 168.

20. Rural-Urban Relationship Committee, Report, I, p. 65.

21. Mohit Bhattacharya, "Decentralization of Big City Government," paper presented at the seminar on Municipal Decentralization in Delhi, New Delhi, March 1969. (Mimeographed.)

22. Hira Lal, "An Experiment in Decentralization of Municipal Administration" (Delhi: Municipal Corporation, 1967), p. ii.

23. Delhi Municipal Corporation, Resolution No. 508, dated 29-11-62. This resolution approves the report of the Corporation's ad hoc committee; the quotation is from Chapter III, section 6 of that report.

24. Delhi Municipal Organization Enquiry Committee, Report, p. 10.

25. Class II officers refers to their pay scale (the second highest), but it is also a measure of expertise and/or experience. Different zones have slightly different numbers of officers of this rank.

26. Municipal Corporation of Delhi, Members' Guide 1969-70, p. 248.

27. Ibid., p. 250.

28. See the Delhi Municipal Corporation Act, 1958, section 42. These obligatory functions are virtually identical to those of other Corporations in India; see Abhijit Datta and J. N. Khosla, "Delhi," in Great Cities of the World, ed. William Robson and D. E. Regan (3d ed.; London: George Allan and Unwin, Ltd., 1972), pp. 409-36 and my "Indian Urban Politics," p. 46.

29. There is, of course, the possibility that councilors attend meetings only in order to collect their maximum salary: they are paid Rs 25 for every meeting they attend, up to a monthly maximum of Rs 300. Since they usually attend about eight Corporation meetings per month (= Rs 200), and sit on at least one other committee of the Corporation, which would meet several times a month, many councilors could probably earn the maximum salary without attending any or only a few zonal committee meetings. (If they attend zonal committee meetings in preference to Corporation meetings, the implication is much the same.) Indeed, about 80 percent of the amount set aside for councilor salaries (106 councilors X Rs 300 = Rs 31,800 per month) is actually collected. See Municipal Corporation of Delhi (O & M office),

"A Study of the Committee System in the Municipal Corporation of Delhi" (n.d., but c. 1972), p. 8. (Mimeographed.)

30. Because they are politically or administratively embarrassing: the committee may continue to insist that the ZAC do something which is contrary to what he believes Corporation policy to be, for example. It might be noted that the Corporation in its general meetings frequently deals with resolutions introduced two and three years previously (cf. pp. 287-88).

31. See p. 72, for a description of the constituency fund. The division of the category proved difficult because although I knew one reference number (i.e., a budgetary account number to which the expenditure would be charged) of the constituency fund, the reference number itself was not always given in the minutes. All these estimates were formally "proposed by the ZAC" and all dealt with the paving of various streets. Undoubtedly there were other items "proposed by the ZAC," which were in fact proposed by the councilor as a use of his fund.

32. A clocktower, a Delhi landmark, had stood at that point from 1869 to 1951, when it collapsed, killing several people.

33. Another informant recounts the case of a chief accountant who wished to add a few more assistants to his department, not because it was understaffed, but because he wanted to punish one subordinate by diminishing the size of his "cut" from commissions. I was told that the practice of taking a commission dates from before India became independent in 1947.

34. The same is not true of Standing Committee decisions referred to the Corporation meetings; there are frequently divisions along party lines.

35. I argue this point at some length in my "Indian Urban Politics," especially pp. 22 ff.

36. See Mohit Bhattacharya, ed., Cabinet System in Municipal Government; Proceedings of the Seminar (September 15-16, 1969) (New Delhi: Indian Institute of Public Administration, 1969).

Chapter 7

1. Again, the Congress split while this study was in progress. I retain the singular "the Congress" because the organization and style of the two post-split Congress parties seemed to be indistinguishable in Shahjahanabad, and the differences, even in terms of personal interaction between the members of the opposing Congress parties, had not solidified by the time I left Delhi.

2. This interview was conducted in Urdu, and I found it difficult to take adequate notes: the councilor is ill served by the choppy style my note taking has forced on him. The numbering is mine, as I wrote down the points he made.

3. This is a prominent part of Indian political culture, as it is, of course, of U.S. political culture (e.g., the presidential candidate not being able to deny the will of the people despite his keen awareness of other, more worthy candidates). See Rudolph and Rudolph, The Modernity of Tradition, p. 236, for a discussion of the Gandhian view of political power; one summary sentence reads, "By aspiring to power, a man demonstrates his unfitness to exercise it."

4. In addition there have been a number of by-elections; for example, three between 1967 and 1971. I was unable to find the time to search for the results of these--most would have been found in newspaper reports which are hard to come by--and so they are omitted from the following analysis.

5. The delimitations of the 1967 and 1971 wards are the only ones that I could obtain in "official" form. I'm not sure that records of constituency delimitation are even kept. I used a map from an issue of Rajdhani [the magazine of the Delhi Municipal Committee] (Vol. 6, No. 1 [January, 1955]) to draw the boundaries of the Municipal Committee wards, but the boundaries of the Corporation wards in 1958 and 1962 can only be guessed at.

6. In 1967 there was a mean difference of four votes (in an "average" constituency of approximately 9,000 votes) between votes cast in the parliamentary election and the votes cast in the Corporation election (which were held simultaneously); the turnout was, unsurprisingly, also 73 percent. In 1971, the Corporation election was held, somewhat anticlimactically, two months after the 1971 general elections. The turnout in the 16 wards in the municipal election ranged from 59 to 72 percent, with a mean of 67 percent. All adults 21 years old and above are voters; registration is done by officials going door-to-door.

7. Cf. the case of Nagpur, where there was an average of four candidates per seat in 1952; six per seat in 1957; and nine per seat in 1962. See my "Indian Urban Politics," p. 96.

8. In addition, the Congress had patched up its factional fights that year and won an overwhelming victory in Delhi; see Andersen and Saini, "The Congress Split in Delhi."

9. It is of course possible to file in as many constituencies as you wish (given a certain amount of voter support on your nominating petition), but it is not done in Delhi; in 1967, however, several people filed for both the Corporation and Metropolitan Council contests.

10. Here is one more attempt to put the data on this subject more clearly: in the 18 instances of winners winning, 10 of the candidates had won before and 8 had lost; of the 14 instances of a winner losing, 11 had previously been winners and 3 had lost at one point; of the 5 instances of losers who won, 3 had been winners and 2 losers; and of the 5 cases of losers losing, 3 involved previous winners and 2 previous losers. Here is the frequency distribution of all the patterns:

WW--9	WWW--2	WWWL--2	WWWWW--1
WL--5	WWL--4	WLWW--2	WWLWW--1
LW--3	LWW--3	WWLL--1	WWWLL--1
LL--8	WLL--1	WLWL--1	
	LWL--1	LWWL--1	
	LLW--1	LLWW--1	
		LLLL--1	

11. To test this pattern from a different angle, as it were, I took a 20 percent sample of polling stations of Chandni Chowk constituency and computed the correlation between the vote in the Corporation election and in the Lok Sabha election. As one would expect, the r for the Jana Sangh vote was .912 and for the Congress, .402.

Chapter 8

1. I use "inward" and "outward" rather than "downward" and "upward" in "system-level" interactions, because the latter terms suggest that the "higher" levels encompass the "lower" levels, and this is not quite the case in Delhi: many of the government authorities I discuss have autonomous spheres of action and control.
2. See, for instance, Robert G. Wirsing, "Associational 'Micro-Arenas' in Indian Urban Politics," Asian Survey, XIII, No. 4 (April, 1973), pp. 408-20.
3. For a one-paragraph sketch of the Moghul system--which Delhi shared--see Tinker, Foundations . . . , p. 17. The mohalla official declined in importance when the British ruled Delhi, though the office was retained, according to Donald W. Ferrell, "Delhi, 1911-1922: Society and Politics in the New Imperial Capital of India" (unpublished Ph.D. dissertation, Australian National University, Canberra, 1969), p. 19. See also Dharmendra, "Municipal Government of Delhi--A Historical Perspective," Quarterly Journal of the Local Self-Government Institute, XLI, No. 2 (1970), pp. 177-88, for the period up to 1862.
4. The major source for the history of the municipality in its first 60 years is Madho Pershad, The History of the Delhi Municipality 1863-1921 (Allahabad: Pioneer Press, 1921). See also Dilli kaa raajaneetik itihaas [The Political History of Delhi, in Hindi] (Delhi: District Congress Committee, 1934); Kanwar Kishore Seth, ed., Delhi Municipal Administration Since Independence (Delhi: Delhi Municipal Committee, 1951); and other pamphlets published by the municipality.
5. Pershad, History of the Delhi Municipality, p. 6.
6. The (partial?) text of this Act is contained in M. Venkatarangaiya and M. Pattabhiram, eds., Local Government in India: Select Readings (Bombay: Allied Publishers, 1969), pp. 86-90. See, also, Tinker, Foundations . . . , pp. 29-32.
7. Venkatarangaiya and Pattabhiram, Local Government in India, p. 87. Calcutta, Madras, and Bombay had separate systems of local self-government and were not covered by the Act.
8. Tinker, Foundations . . . , p. 29.
9. Pershad, History of Delhi Municipality, p. 55.
10. According to one source, [Government of] India, the Delhi Municipal Organization Enquiry Committee, Report (New Delhi: Manager, Government of India Press, 1948), p. 4. Madho Pershad reports slightly varying numbers in the following years. This Act was probably part of the Ripon reforms which began with his famous resolution of 1882 which proposed greater local control over government; see Tinker, Foundations . . . , pp. 43-63.
11. Ferrell, "Delhi, 1911-1922," p. 528.
12. Pershad, History of Delhi Municipality, p. 202. The Civil Lines area had been split off from the DMC with the formation of a Civil Station Notified Area Committee in 1913.
13. Ibid., p. 111.
14. Ibid., p. 208.
15. Ferrell, "Delhi, 1911-1922," p. 28.
16. Pershad, History of Delhi Municipality, p. 111.
17. Ibid., p. 181.
18. Quoted in Ibid., pp. 189-90; see also Ibid., pp. 227 ff.

19. In 1875 the population of Delhi city was 160,553 and in 1921 it had risen to 266,692 (see Table 18). The population grew by approximately 75 percent in those fifty years and per capita expenditure thus by about 535 percent (estimating the 1870-71 population, it grew from about Rs. 1.33 per capita to Rs. 8.45). Prices in India rose by about 60 percent from 1870-71 until 1911, and nearly doubled in the next decade (M. Mukherjee, National Income of India: Trends and Structure [Calcutta: Statistical Publishing Society, 1969], p. 94). Over ·the fifty-year period, then, real per capita expenditure approximately doubled (assuming that price rises in Delhi were roughly equal to the national averages).

20. Pershad, History of Delhi Municipality, passim. Unfortunately the detailed breakdown of expenditure is not given for later years.

21. For the all-India situation of local governments in this period, see Tinker, Foundations . . . , pp. 114-25.

22. See Ibid., pp. 129 ff. The text of the Government of India Resolution, 1918 on the subject is reprinted in Venkatarangaiya and Pattabhiram, Local Government in India, pp. 171-92.

23. This period is amply covered in the standard histories; see, e.g., Percival Spear, India: A Modern History (Ann Arbor: University of Michigan Press, 1961), pp. 365-73. For the point of view of some participants, see Michael Brecher, Nehru: A Political Biography (London: Oxford University Press, 1959), pp. 84-103 and Surendranath Banerjea, A Nation in Making (London: Oxford University Press, 1925), pp. 333-91, among others.

24. Cf. Ferrell, "The Rowlatt Satyagraha in Delhi" in Ravinder Kumar, ed., Essays on Gandhian Politics; the Rowlatt Satyagraha of 1919 (London: Oxford University Press, 1971).

25. One feature of the new system of local self-government was the varying devices used to secure representation for the "minority" community (cf. Tinker, Foundations . . . , pp. 132 ff.). In Delhi "The 24 elected members were divided equally between 12 Hindus and 12 Muslim members. The number of electoral wards was expanded from 11 to 12 and each ward was to elect one Hindu and one Muslim with each elector having only one vote (which effectively ensured that Hindu electors would vote for Hindu candidates)." (Ferrell, "Delhi, 1911-1922," pp. 528-29).

26. Ibid., pp. 528-31.

27. Unfortunately, I have no direct sources, and must infer this from a passing remark in a 1951 publication (Seth, Delhi Municipal Administration . . .), p. 1.

28. [Lala] Shri Ram, "Municipal Problems in Delhi" (no publication information) deals with the decade 1921-31, but the author, a municipal councilor, states at the outset "It is not my purpose in this review to deal with the constitution of the Municipality, its progressive democratization, the public interest displayed in its elections or the extent and value of the political education acquired by its citizens" (p. 1).

29. Ferrell, "Delhi, 1911-1922," p. 163n.

30. Dilli kaa raajanaitik itihass, Part I, p. 154.

31. Shri Ram, "Municipal Problems in Delhi," pp. 18-19.

32. See Harold A. Gould, "The Emergence of Modern Indian Politics: Political Development in Faizabad," The Journal of Commonwealth Political Studies, XII, Nos. 1 and 2 (1974), pp. 20-41; pp. 157-188.

33. [Delhi Municipal Committee], Report on the Administration of the Delhi Municipality in the Year 1934-35 (Delhi: Delhi Municipality, 1935), I, p. 1.   Hereafter cited as DMC, Report, with appropriate year, volume, and page(s).

34. DMC, Report . . . 1935-36, I, p. 1.

35. DMC, Report . . . 1937-38, I, p. 1.

36. Ibid.

37. Ibid.

38. DMC, Report . . . 1940-41, I, p. 1.

39. Seth, Delhi Municipal Administration . . . , pp. 12-13.   Per capita expenditure was thus Rs. 7.13 in 1931, and about Rs. 9.84 in 1946-47.   In India as a whole, prices declined by 46 percent from 1921 to 1931, but had increased by 60 percent over 1921 in 1946-47 (Mukherjee, National Income of India, p. 94). "Real" per capita expenditure thus probably declined in this period.

40. Delhi Improvement Trust, Administrative Report for the Years 1939-1941 (New Delhi: Delhi Improvement Trust, 1942), p. 46.

41. [Government of] India, Delhi Municipal Organization Enquiry Committee, Report, pp. 4-5.   Notified Area Committees consist entirely of nominated and ex-officio members.   The New Delhi and Shahdara Municipal Committees were second class Municipalities, which means that the majority of their membership was nominated.

42. Ibid., pp. 6-7.

43. Seth, Delhi Municipal Administration . . . , pp. 1-2.

44. Ibid., p. 4.

45. Ibid., p. 12.

46. Mukherjee, National Income of India, p. 94.   There is only limited data on Delhi, but it is suggestive: the consumer price index for industrial workers in Delhi, using a base of 1949 = 100, was estimated at 127 in 1961.   (Delhi Administration, Delhi Statistical Handbook 1970, pp. 146-47.)

47. The population estimate is mine; the Delhi Municipal Committee area population was 914,700 in 1951 and 2,061,758 in 1961.   I have no way of knowing whether the increase was evenly spread over the decade. The price figures are from Mukherjee (National Income of India).   Again, he uses all-India figures, and Delhi may well have had very different price fluctuations.   The translation into "real" rupees is not a simple one, hence the use of "probably."

48. Moti Ram, ed., Survey of Activities [of the DMC], 1954-1958 (Delhi: Delhi Municipal Committee, 1958?), p. 2.

49. Ibid., pp. 2-6.

50. Pershad, History of Delhi Municipality, p. 17.

51. India, Ministry of Health and Family Planning, Rural-Urban Relationship Committee, Report, Vol. I (New Delhi: Ministry of Health and Family Planning, Government of India, 1966), p. 28.

52. Ibid., p. 57.

53. See my M.A. thesis, "Indian Urban Politics," pp. 10-43, passim, for a discussion of this issue.

54. This was taken away from the Corporation in 1971 and made a central government autonomous corporation.

55. See Civic Affairs, XVII, No. 2(ii) (September, 1969), pp. 7-14, for a brief history of the mayoralty contests.   This is a Delhi Municipal Corporation special issue of Civic Affairs.

56. In the Indian Parliament, the Speaker occupies the position here given to the mayor and the configuration is very similar.   See the diagram in W. H. Morris-Jones, Parliament in India (Philadelphia: University of Pennsylvania Press, 1957), p. 134.

57. There were many more votes recorded with precise numbers (52 for, 38 against), presumably taken by show of hands; voice votes are apparently not used, except for resolutions adopted unanimously. Often a show of hands vote is followed by the demand for a division. For instance, in the meeting of September 6, 1969, a motion won by a vote of 36 to 25, and won in the subsequent roll-call by 44 to 32.
58. These questions were put in the adjourned July (1967) meeting, which was held on September 2, 1969. In the supplementary questions, the commissioner brought the answer up to date.
59. DMC minutes, 1969-70, III, No. 52, pp. 4-5 (the case referred to was still sub judice in 1969).
60. Statesman (Delhi), July 28, 1970, p. 8.
61. I am unable to give the precise figure with certainty, because it is fairly likely that I missed a mention of a "grave disorder" or two in going through the voluminous minutes.
62. See Morris-Jones, Parliament in India, esp. pp. 129-58.
63. See Note 54, above. DTR = Delhi Transport Undertaking; DESU = Delhi Electric Supply Undertaking; WSSDU = Water Supply and Sewage Disposal Undertaking.
64. Which is not to say that things don't occur during the budget debate: members may attempt to bring up unrelated matters (in 1970, it was the sweepers' strike) and disorder may result. The scheduling of debate for only a specified period may result in some members feeling that they have not been given an opportunity to be heard: on February 6, 1970, the Congress(R) staged a temporary walkout for this reason.
65. For a description of the similar proceeding of the Indian Parliament, see Morris-Jones, Parliament in India, pp. 236 ff.
66. DMC Minutes of the Adjourned Special Meeting, held on February 11, 1970, III, No. 116, p. 17. The tax on each category of vehicle (14 in all) was passed separately.
67. Ibid., p. 42.
68. Ibid., p. 37.
69. Ibid., p. 42.
70. Ibid., pp. 47, 49, 55, 69, 95, and 113.
71. Commissioner's Note, Budget Estimates of the Delhi Municipal Corporation, 1969-70 and 1970-71, p. ix [in a separately paginated section].
72. Herbert Simon, "The Changing Theory and Changing Practice of Public Administration," Contemporary Political Science, ed. by Ithiel de Sola Pool (New York: McGraw-Hill Book Co., Inc., 1967), p. 103.
73. John P. Crecine, Governmental Problem Solving: a Computer Simulation of Municipal Budgeting (Chicago: Rand McNally and Co., 1969). See pp. 218-19 for a summary of his conclusions.
74. Ibid.
75. Ibid., p. 218.
76. An exception is Barnabas, The Experience of Citizens Getting Water Connections. See also the excellent discussion by Richard Taub, Bureaucracy Under Stress: Administrators and Administration in an Indian State (Berkeley: University of California Press, 1969), pp. 139-44; he remarks, inter alia, "that corruption is a serious problem in the Indian bureaucracy, or at least in the higher levels of the Orissa bureaucracy, I would dispute" (pp. 142-43).
77. A major source for this section is a "Study of the Working of the Committee System in the Municipal Corporation of Delhi" by H. B. Dass, the O & M Officer of the Corporation (Delhi: Delhi Municipal Corporation, 1971). (Mimeographed.)

78. For one example, see the Times of India, July 31, 1970, p. 10.
79. Dass, "Working Paper," p. 3.
80. Ibid., p. 15.
81. DMC Minutes, III, No. 50, pp. 186–89; this contains the entire record of the "case."
82. Hindustan Times, December 8, 1969, p. 3.
83. We have already looked at this strike "from below," at its impact on Khirkiwala (see above, pp. 39–41). Accounts of the strike were front-page news in the Delhi press from January 22 to February 7, 1970.
84. Times of India, January 29, 1970, p. 3.
85. Hindustan Times, February 1, 1970, p. 5; Statesman, February 1, 1970, p. 6.
86. Hindustan Times, January 8, 1970, p. 3.
87. Times of India, January 9, 1970, p. 9.
88. Ibid., January 14, 1970, p. 3.
89. Ibid., January 15, 1970, p. 3.
90. Evening News, January 23, 1970, p. 1.
91. But on February 17, the Evening News reported that the Administration was violating the conditions.
92. Times of India, January 9, 1970, p. 70.

Chapter 9

1. For a description of the Corporation form (plus a list of Corporations, other data, and recommendations for improvements), see [Government of] India, Ministry of Health and Family Planning, Rural-Urban Relationship Committee, Report, I, pp. 56–72.
2. See Rodney Jones, "Linkage Analysis of Indian Urban Politics." Economic and Political Weekly, VII, No. 25 (1972), pp. 1195–1203, which is drawn from his "Area, Power and Linkage in Indore: A Political Map of an Indian City" (unpublished Ph.D. dissertation, Columbia University, 1970). Cf. also Donald B. Rosenthal, "Symposium on Indian Urban Politics Introduction," Asian Survey, XIII, No. 4 (1973), pp. 383–84.
3. See Roderick Church, "The Politics of Administration in Urban India: Citizens, Municipal Councillors and Routine Administration in Lucknow" (unpublished Ph.D. dissertation, Duke University, 1973), p. 274.
4. Cf. Sangat Singh, Freedom Movement in Delhi, 1858–1919 (New Delhi: Associated Publishing House, 1972) and Donald W. Ferrell, "The Rowlatt Satyagraha in Delhi," Essays on Gandhian Politics; the Rowlatt Satyagraha of 1919, ed. by Ravinder Kumar (London: Oxford University Press, 1971), pp. 189–235.
5. See Owen M. Lynch, "Rural Cities in India: Continuities and Discontinuities," India and Ceylon; Unity and Diversity, ed. by Philip Mason (London: Oxford University Press, 1967), pp. 142–58, and also Lynch, The Politics of Untouchability; Social Mobility and Social Change in a City of India (New York: Columbia University Press, 1969) for a description of a different situation. The Jatavs of Agra, at least, do have a well-developed city-wide social structure, complete with political incarnation. See also Rosenthal, The Limited Elite, passim. I have referred to the various socio-economic studies of Delhi in the course of the study. Aside from the volumes of the 1961 Census of India, publications of the Municipal Corporation, the Delhi Administration, and the Government of India (Enquiry

Committees and the Town and Country Planning Organization),
some of the more important sociological and statistical sources
include: A Bopegamage, Delhi: A Study in Urban Sociology
(Bombay: University of Bombay, 1957); V. K. R. V. Rao and P. B.
Desai, Greater Delhi--a Study in Urbanization, 1910-1957 (Bombay:
Asia Publishing House, 1965); M. S. Gore, Urbanization and Family
Change (Bombay: Popular Prakashan, 1968); Asok Mitra, Delhi:
Capital City (New Delhi: Thomson Press, 1970); and Marshall B.
Clinard, Slums and Community Development: Experiments in Self
Help (New York: Free Press, 1970).

6. See Andrea Menafee, "Voluntary Associations in a Neighborhood
of New Delhi," paper prepared for delivery at the Association
for Asian Studies meeting, March, 1971. (Mimeographed.)

7. For a very different situation, see Robert Wirsing, "Associational
'Micro-Arenas' in Indian Urban Politics," Asian Survey, XIII, No. 4
(1973), pp. 408-420, based on his unpublished Ph.D. dissertation,
"Socialist Society and Free Enterprise Politics: A Study of the
Urban Political Process in Nagpur, India" (University of Denver,
1971).

8. Church, "The Politics of Administration in Urban India . . ."
and Roderick Church, "Authority and Influence in Indian Municipal
Politics: Administrators and Councillors in Lucknow," Asian
Survey, XIII, No. 4 (1973), pp. 421-38.

9. Church, "The Politics of Administration in Urban India . . . ,"
p. 279.

10. Ibid., p. 280. I have not dealt with these or even similar
constraints, like high density housing, with anywhere near the
richness of data that Church has.

11. Ibid., p. 281.

12. Ibid., pp. 281-82.

13. Ibid., p. 279.

14. See R. B. Das and D. P. Singh, eds., Executive and Deliberative
Wings in Local Government (Lucknow: Institute of Public Adminis-
tration, Lucknow University, 1968); Mohit Bhattacharya, ed.,
Cabinet System in Municipal Government; Proceedings of the Seminar
(New Delhi: Indian Institute of Public Administration, 1970); and
R. Srinivasan and B. A. V. Sharma, "Politics in Urban India: A
Study of Four Corporations [Bombay, Calcutta, Delhi, Madras],"
Studies in Indian Democracy, ed. by S. P. Aiyar and R. Srinivasan
(Bombay: Allied Publishers, 1965), pp. 467-514.

15. Hugh Tinker, The Foundations of Local Self-Government in India,
Pakistan and Burma (London: Athalone Press, 1954); C. M. P.
Cross, The Development of Self-Government in India 1858-1919
(Chicago: University of Chicago Press, 1922); R. Argal, Municipal
Government in India (Allahabad: Agarwal Press, 1960); Ramayan
Prasad, Local Self-Government in Vindhya Pradesh (Bombay: All-
India Institute of Local Self-Government, 1963). See also my
unpublished M.A. dissertation, "Indian Urban Politics, with
Particular Reference to the Nagpur Corporation" (Chicago:
University of Chicago, 1968), pp. 10-43.

16. Church, "The Politics of Administration in Urban India. . . ,"
p. 285.

17. Ibid., p. 109.

Bibliography

Books and Articles

Ahmad, Nur-ud-din, et al. Case for Greater Delhi. Delhi: The
  Directorate of Public Relations, Delhi State, 1954.
Ahmad, Shamin. Dilli kii ek jhulak [A Glimpse of Delhi]. No
  publication data.
Ali, Ahmed. Twilight in Delhi. Reprint ed. Bombay: Oxford
  University Press, 1966; original ed., 1940.
Allchin, Bridget, and Allchin, Raymond. The Birth of Indian
  Civilization. Harmondsworth, Eng.: Penguin Books, 1968.
Andersen, Walter. "The Rashtriya Swayamsevak Sangh," Economic
  and Political Weekly, VII, Nos. 11-14 (March 11, 18, 25, and
  April 1, 1972), pp. 589-97; pp. 633-40; pp. 673-82; pp. 724-27,
  respectively.
Andersen, Walter, and Saini, M. K. "The Basti Julahan Bye-
  Election," Indian Journal of Political Science, XXX, No. 3
  (July-September, 1969), pp. 260-76.
Andersen, Walter, and Saini, M. K. "The Congress Split in Delhi:
  the Effect of Factionalism on Organizational Performance and
  System Level Interactions," Asian Survey, XI, No. 11
  (November, 1971), pp. 1089-1100.
Argal, R. Municipal Government in India. Allahabad: Agarwal
  Press, 1960.
Ashraf, Ali. The City Government of Calcutta: a Study in Inertia.
  New York: Institute of Public Administration, 1966.
Bailey, F. G. Politics and Social Change: Orissa in 1969.
  Berkeley: University of California Press, 1963.
Bannerjea, Surendranath. A Nation in Making. London: Oxford
  University Press, 1925.
Barnabas, A. P. The Experience of Citizens in Getting Water
  Connections. New Delhi: Indian Institute of Public Adminis-
  tration, 1965.
Baxter, Craig. The Jana Sangh: A Biography of an Indian Political
  Party. Philadelphia: University of Pennsylvania Press, 1969.
Bernier, Francis. Travels in the Moghul Empire 1656-1668. Reprint
  ed. Delhi: S. Chand and Co., 1968.
Bhattacharya, Mohit, ed. Cabinet System in Municipal Government;
  Proceedings of a Seminar (September 15-16, 1969). New Delhi:
  Indian Institute of Public Administration, 1969.

Bhattacharya, Mohit. "Decentralization of Big City Government."
Paper presented at the Seminar on Municipal Decentralization
in Delhi. New Delhi, March 1969. (Mimeographed.)
_____. "Structure of Urban Local Government in India,"
Journal of Administration Overseas, VII (1968), pp. 351-57.
Blake, Stephen P. "Dar-ul-Khilafat-i-Shahjahanabad: The
Padshahi Shahar in Mughal India: 1556-1739." Unpublished
Ph.D. dissertation, University of Chicago, 1974.
Bopegamage, A. Delhi: A Study in Urban Sociology. Bombay:
University of Bombay, 1957.
Bose, Ashish. Urbanization in India; an Inventory of Source
Materials. Bombay: Academic Books, 1970.
Brass, Paul. Factional Politics in an Indian State. Berkeley:
University of California Press, 1965.
Brecher, Michael. Nehru: A Political Biography. London: Oxford
University Press, 1959.
Breese, Gerald, ed. The City in Newly Developed Countries:
Readings in Urbanism and Urbanization. Englewood Cliffs, N.J.:
Prentice-Hall, Inc., 1969.
Breese, Gerald. Urbanization in Newly Developing Countries.
Englewood Cliffs, N.J.: Prentice-Hall, Inc., 1966.
Census of India, see India. Census of India.
Chandra, Jag Parvesh. Delhi: A Political Study. Delhi: Jag
Parvesh Chandra, 1969.
Chaudhury, M. D., and Hoselitz, Bert. "State Income of Delhi
State, 1951-52 and 1955-56," Economic Development and Cultural
Change, Vol. XI, No. 3, Part II (April, 1963).
Chopra, Prabha, ed. Delhi; History and Places of Interest. Delhi:
Delhi Gazeteer, Delhi Administration, 1970.
Church, Roderick. "Authority and Influence in Indian Municipal
Politics: Administrators and Councillors in Lucknow," Asian
Survey, XIII, No. 4 (April, 1973), pp. 421-38.
Church, Roderick. "The Politics of Administration in Urban India:
Citizens, Municipal Councillors and Routine Administration in
Lucknow." Unpublished Ph.D. dissertation, Duke University, 1973.
Clinard, Marshall B. Slums and Community Development: Experiments
in Self Help. New York: The Free Press, 1970.
Crecine, John P. Governmental Problem-Solving: A Computer Simu-
lation of Municipal Budgeting. Chicago: Rand McNally and
Company, 1969.
Cross, C. M. P. The Development of Self-Government in India
1858-1919. Chicago: University of Chicago Press, 1922.
Curran, J. A., Jr. Militant Hinduism in Indian Politics: A Study
of the RSS. New York: Institute of Pacific Relations, 1951.
Das, R. B., and Singh, D. P., eds. Executive and Deliberative
Wings in Local Government. Lucknow: Institute of Public
Administration, Lucknow University, 1968.
Dass, H. B. "Working Paper for the Seminar on Decentralization of
Municipal Administration in Delhi." Paper presented at the
seminar, 1969. (Mimeographed.)
Datta, Abhijit, and Khosla, J. N. "Delhi." Great Cities of the
World; Their Government, Politics, and Planning. Edited by
W. A. Robson and D. E. Regan. 2 vols. 3d ed. London:
George Allen and Unwin, 1972.

Delhi Administration. Bureau of Economics and Statistics. Delhi
    Statistical Handbook 1970. Delhi: Delhi Administration, 1970.
Delhi Administration, Planning Department. Draft Fourth Five-
    Year Plan (1969-70 to 1973-74). Delhi: Delhi Administration,
    1968.
Delhi Development Authority. Master Plan for Delhi. 3 vols.
    Delhi: Delhi Development Authority, 1962.
Delhi Improvement Trust. Administrative Report for the Years
    1939-41. New Delhi: Delhi Improvement Trust, 1942.
[Delhi Municipal Committee]. Report on the Administration of
    the Delhi Municipality in the Year 1935-36. Delhi: Delhi
    Municipality, 1936.
[_____]. Report on the Administration of the Delhi Munici-
    pality in the Year 1937-38. Delhi: Delhi Municipality, 1938.
[_____]. Report on the Administration of the Delhi Munici-
    pality in the Year 1940-41. Delhi: Delhi Municipality, 1941.
Delhi Municipal Corporation, see Municipal Corporation of Delhi.
Dharmendra. "Municipal Government of Delhi--A Historical
    Perspective," Quarterly Journal of the Local Self Government
    Institute, XLI, No. 2 (1970), pp. 179-88.
Dilli kaa raajaneetik itihaas (The Political History of Delhi.)
    Delhi: District Congress Committee, 1934.
Eldersveld, Samuel J., Jagannadham, V., and Barnabas, A. P. The
    Citizen and the Administrator in a Developing Democracy; an
    Empirical Study in Delhi State. New Delhi: Indian Institute
    of Public Administration, 1968.
Ferrell, Donald W. "Delhi, 1911-1922: Society and Politics in the
    New Imperial Capital of India." Unpublished Ph.D. dissertation,
    Australian National University, Canberra, 1969.
_____. "The Rowlatt Satyagraha in Delhi." Essays on Gandhian
    Politics; the Rowlatt Satyagraha of 1919. Edited by Ravinder
    Kumar. London: Oxford University Press, 1971.
Fonseca, Rory. "Urban Rehabilitation and an Indigenous Settlement:
    A Case Study of Ward 9 in the Walled City of Old Delhi." Unpub-
    lished M. Arch. dissertation, University of California at Berkeley,
    1968.
_____. "The Walled City of Old Delhi," Landscape, VIII,
    No. 8 (Spring, 1970), pp. 15-25.
_____. "The Walled City of Old Delhi," Shelter and Society.
    Edited by Paul Oliver. New York: Frederick A. Praeger, 1969.
Fox, Richard. From Zamindar to Ballot Box: Community Change in a
    North Indian Market Town. Ithaca, N.Y.: Cornell University
    Press, 1969.
Frey, Frederick W. "Cross-Cultural Survey Research in Political
    Science." The Methodology of Comparative Research. Edited by
    Robert T. Holt and John E. Turner. New York: The Free Press,
    1970.
Gazeteer of the Delhi District, 1883-4. Punjab Government: no
    further publication data.
Gore, Madhav Sadashiv. Urbanization and Family Change. Bombay:
    Popular Prakashan, 1968.
Gould, Harold A. "The Emergence of Modern Indian Politics: Political
    Development in Faizabad," Journal of Commonwealth Political
    Studies, XII, Nos. 1 and 2 (1974), pp. 20-41; pp. 157-188.

_____. "Local Government Roots of Contemporary Indian
Politics," Economic and Political Weekly, VI, No. 7 (1971),
pp. 457-64.

Gupta, Narayani. "Military Security and Urban Development:
A Case Study of Delhi 1857-1912." Modern Asian Studies,
V, No.· 1 (1971), pp. 61-77.

Hampton, William. Democracy and Community; a Study of Politics
in Sheffield. London: Oxford University Press, 1970.

Holmström, Mark. "Action-sets and Ideology: A Municipal Election
in South India," Contributions to Indian Sociology, New Series,
No. 3 (December, 1969), pp. 76-93.

Hourani, A. M., and Stern, S. M., eds. The Islamic City.
Philadelphia: University of Pennsylvania Press, 1970.

Improving City Government; Proceedings of a Seminar (September 13-
14, 1958). New Delhi: Indian Institute of Public Administration,
1959.

India. Administrative Reforms Commission. Study Team on Administration of Union Territories and NEFA. Report. Vol. I. Delhi:
Manager of Publications, 1969.

India. Census of India. [International Documentation Company
Microprint Edition.]
1891, Vol. XX, Part II; 1901, Vol. 17-A, Part II; 1911, Vol.
XIV, Part II; 1921, Vol. XV, Part II; 1931, Vol. XVI, Part II;
1941, Vol. XVI; 1951, Vol. VIII, Part II-A.

India. Census of India. Vol. XVI: Delhi, "Tables." Delhi:
Manager of Publications, 1942.

India. Census of India 1961. Vol. XIX: Delhi, Part I-A: "General
Report on the Census." Delhi: Manager of Publications, 1966.

India. Census of India 1961. Vol. XIX: Delhi, Part II-C: "Cultural
and Migration Tables." No publication data.

India. Census of India 1961. Vol. XIX: Delhi, Part V-A: "Tables
on Scheduled Castes and Scheduled Tribes." No publication data.

India. Census of India 1961. Delhi District Census Handbook.
Compiled by Baldev Raj and Kuldip Chander Sehgal. Delhi: The
Delhi Administration, 1964.

India. Census of India 1971. Delhi, Part X-A and B. Delhi District
Census Handbook. Compiled by S. R. Gandotra. Delhi: Delhi
Administration, n.d.

India. Delhi Municipal Organization Enquiry Committee. Report.
New Delhi: No publisher given, 1948.

India. Ministry of Health. Town Planning Organization. Interim
General Plan for Greater Delhi. Delhi: Ministry of Health, 1956.

India. Ministry of Health and Family Planning. Rural-Urban
Relationship Committee. Report. 3 vols. Delhi: Manager of
Publications, 1966.

India. States Reorganization Committee. Report. Delhi: Manager
of Publications, 1955.

Jeevan Lal. A Short Account of the Life of Rai Bahadur Jeevan Lal,
Late Honorary Magistrate, Delhi, and Extracts from His Diary.
[Compiled?] By His Son. Delhi: The Imperial Medical Hall
Press, 1888.

Jones, Rodney. "Area, Power, and Linkage in Indore: A Political
   Map of an Indian City." Unpublished Ph.D. dissertation, Columbia
   University, New York, 1970.
_____. "Linkage Analysis of Indian Urban Politics," Economic
   and Political Weekly, VII, No. 25 (1972), pp. 1195-1203.
_____. Urban Politics in India: Area, Power, and Policy
   in a Penetrated System. Berkeley: University of California
   Press, 1974.
Kaplan, Harold. Urban Political Systems: A Functional Analysis
   of Metro Toronto. Princeton: Princeton University Press, 1968.
Kochanek, Stanley. The Congress Party of India: Dynamics of a
   One-party Democracy. Princeton: Princeton University Press,
   1968.
Kothari, Rajni, ed. Caste in Indian Politics. Delhi: Orient
   Longmans, 1970.
Kothari, Shanti S., and Roy, Ramashray. Relations between Politi-
   cians and Administrators at the District Level. New Delhi:
   Indian Institute of Public Administration, 1969.
Lal, Hira. "An Experiment in Decentralization of Municipal Adminis-
   tration." Delhi: Delhi Municipal Corporation, 1967.
Lapidus, Ira. "The Evolution of Muslim Urban Society," Comparative
   Studies in Society and History. Vol. XV, No. 1 (January, 1973).
_____. Muslim Cities in the Later Middle Ages. Cambridge,
   Mass.: Harvard University Press, 1967.
Lerner, Daniel. The Passing of Traditional Society. New York:
   The Free Press of Glencoe, 1958.
Lothian, A. C., ed. A Handbook for Travelers in India, Pakistan,
   Burma and Ceylon [Murray's Guide]. 17th ed. London: John
   Murray, 1955.
Lynch, Owen M. The Politics of Untouchability; Social Mobility and
   Social Change in a City of India. New York: Columbia University
   Press, 1969.
_____. "Rural Cities in India: Continuities and Discontinuities."
   India and Ceylon: Unity and Diversity. Edited by Philip Mason.
   London: Oxford University Press, 1967.
Majumdar, Ramesh Chandra. The Sepoy Mutiny and the Revolt of 1857.
   Calcutta: Firma K. L. Mukhopadhyay, 1963.
Mayer, Adrian C. "Municipal Elections: A Central Indian Case
   Study." Politics and Society. Edited by C. H. Philips.
   New York: Frederick A. Praeger, 1962.
_____. "The Significance of Quasi-Groups in the Study of
   Complex Societies." The Social Anthropology of Complex Societies.
   Association of Social Anthropology of the Commonwealth Monograph
   No. 4. Edited by Michael Banton. New York: Frederick A. Praeger,
   1966.
_____. "Systems and Network: An Approach to the Study of
   Political Process in Dewas." Indian Anthropology: Essays in
   Memory of D. N. Majumdar. Edited by T. N. Madan and G. Saran.
   Bombay: Asia Publishing House, 1962.
Menafee, Andrea. "Voluntary Associations in a Neighborhood of New
   Delhi." Paper prepared for delivery at the Association for Asian
   Studies meeting, March, 1971. (Mimeographed.)

Metcalfe, C. T., ed. Two Native Narratives of the Mutiny at Delhi.
    Reprint ed. Delhi: Seema Publications, 1974; original edition,
    1898.
Mitra, Ashok. Delhi: Capital City. New Delhi: Thomson Press
    (India), Ltd., 1970.
Morris-Jones, W. M. "Candidate Selection: The Ordeal of the
    Indian National Congress, 1966-67." Studies in Politics;
    National and International. Edited by M. S. Rajan. Delhi:
    Vikas Publications, 1970.
_____. Parliament in India. Philadelphia: The University
    of Pennsylvania Press, 1957.
Mukherjee, M. National Income of India: Trends and Structure.
    Calcutta: Statistical Publishing Society, 1969.
Municipal Corporation of Delhi. Budget Estimates of the Delhi
    Municipal Corporation, 1969-70 and 1970-71. 2 vols. Delhi:
    Municipal Corporation of Delhi, 1971.
_____. Members Guide--1968-69. Delhi: Municipal Corporation
    of Delhi, 1968.
_____. Members Guide--1969-70. Delhi: Municipal Corporation
    of Delhi, 1969.
_____, Department of Community Development. Second Evaluation
    Study of Vikas Mandals. Delhi: Delhi Municipal Corporation, 1965.
_____, O & M Office. "A Study of the Committee System in the
    Municipal Corporation of Delhi" [c. 1972]. (Mimeographed.)
Narayan, R. K. The Financial Expert. New York: The Noonday Press,
    1966.
National Council of Applied Economic Research. Commodity Disposition
    Survey in Delhi. Occasional Papers No. 4. London: Asia Pub-
    lishing House, 1959.
Oldenburg, Philip. "Indian Urban Politics, with Particular Reference
    to the Nagpur Corporation." Unpublished Master's thesis,
    University of Chicago, 1968.
Owens, Raymond, and Nandy, Ashis. "Voluntary Associations in an
    Industrial Ward of Howrah, West Bengal, India." Paper presented
    at the twenty-third annual meeting of the Association of Asian
    Studies, Washington, D.C., 1971. (Mimeographed.)
Pershad, Madho. The History of the Delhi Municipality 1863-1921.
    Allahabad: The Pioneer Press, 1921.
Planhol, Xavier de. The World of Islam. Ithaca, N.Y.: Cornell
    University Press, 1959.
Plunkett, Hugh. "Pragmatic Politics in a Rajasthan Town: A Case
    Study of a Municipal Election," Economic and Political Weekly,
    VI, No. 49 (December, 1971), pp. 2442-46.
Prasad, Ramayan. Local Self-Government in Vindhya Pradesh.
    Bombay: All-India Institute of Local Self-Government, 1963.
Ram, Moti, ed. Survey of Activities 1954-1958. Delhi: Delhi
    Municipal Committee, n.d.
Rao, M. S. A. Urbanization and Social Change, a Study of a Rural
    Community on a Metropolitan Fringe. New Delhi: Orient Longmans,
    1970.
Rao, P. V. R. Red Tape and White Cap. New Delhi: W. H. Patwardhan,
    Orient Longmans, Ltd., 1970.

Rao, V. K. R. V., and Desai, P. B. Greater Delhi: A Study in
    Urbanization 1910-1957. Bombay: Asia Publishing House, 1965.
Riggs, Fred. "Bureaucrats and Political Development: A Para-
    doxical View." Bureaucracy and Political Development. Edited
    by Joseph La Palombara. Princeton, N.J.: Princeton University
    Press, 1963.
Rosenthal, Donald B. "Deurbanization, Elite Displacement, and
    Political Change in India," Comparative Politics, Vol. II
    (1970).
    _____. The Limited Elite: Politics and Government in Two
    Indian Cities. Chicago: University of Chicago Press, 1970.
Rosenthal, Donald B. "Symposium on Indian Urban Politics Intro-
    duction," Asian Survey, XVIII, No. 4 (1973), pp. 380-85.
Roy, Ramashray. "Election Studies, Selection of Congress
    Candidates," Economic and Political Weekly, I, No. 20
    (December, 1966), pp. 835-40 and II, Nos. 1, 2, 6, and 7
    (January, February, 1967), pp. 17-24, pp. 61-76, pp. 371-76,
    and pp. 407-16, respectively.
Rudolph, Lloyd I., and Rudolph, Susanne H. The Modernity of
    Tradition. Chicago: University of Chicago Press, 1967
Saberwal, Satish. "The Reserved Constituency: Candidates and
    Consequences," Economic and Political Weekly, VII, No. 2
    (January, 1972), pp. 71-80.
Sabri, Imdad. Delhi Sidiqqi Biraadarii kii Shakhsiiyateen
    (Personalities of the Delhi Sidiqqi Biraadarii [literally:
    Brotherhood]. No publication data.
Sanwal, H. D. "Problems of Citizen Participation in Municipal
    Government." Improving City Government. New Delhi: Indian
    Institute of Public Administration, 1959.
Sen, Surendra Nath. Eighteen Fifty-Seven. Delhi: The Publi-
    cations Division, Government of India, 1957.
Seth, Kanwar Kishore, ed. Delhi Municipal Administration Since
    Independence. Delhi: Delhi Municipal Committee, 1951.
Sharma, B. A. V., and Jangan, R. T. The Bombay Municipal Corpo-
    ration: An Election Study. Bombay: Popular Book Depot, 1962.
Sharma, Y. D. Delhi and Its Neighborhood. New Delhi: Archaeological
    Survey of India, 1964.
Shri Ram. "Municipal Problems in Delhi." No publication data.
    (Pamphlet.)
Simon, Herbert A. "The Changing Theory and Changing Practice of
    Public Administration." Contemporary Political Science:
    Toward Empirical Theory. Edited by Ithiel de Sola Pool.
    New York: McGraw-Hill Book Co., Inc., 1967.
Singh, Sangat. Freedom Movement in Delhi, 1858-1919. New Delhi:
    Associated Publishing House, 1972.
Spear, Percival. Delhi: A Historical Sketch. Bombay: Oxford
    University Press, 1937.
    _____. India: A Modern History. Ann Arbor: University of
    Michigan Press, 1961.
    _____. Twilight of the Mughals. Reprint ed. Delhi: Oriental
    Books Reprint Corporation, 1969; original edition, 1951.

Srinivasan, R., and Sharma, B. A. V. "Politics in Urban India:
A Study of Five Corporations." Studies in Indian Democracy.
Edited by S. P. Aiyar and R. Srinivasan. Bombay: Allied
Publishers, 1965.

Stephen, Carr. Archaeological and Monumental Remains of Delhi.
Reprint ed. Allahabad: Kitab Mahal, 1967.

Taub, Richard P. Bureaucrats Under Stress: Administrators and
Administration in an Indian State. Berkeley: University of
California Press, 1969.

Tinker, H. R. The Foundations of Local Self-Government in India,
Pakistan, and Burma. London: The Athalone Press, 1954.

_____. "Local Government and Politics, and Political and
Social Theory in India." Local-level Politics. Edited by
Marc Swartz. Chicago: Aldine Publishing Co., 1968.

Tokyo Metropolitan Government. Comparative Statistical Table of
World Large Cities 1961. Tokyo: Tokyo Metropolitan Government,
1961.

_____. Statistics of World Large Cities 1968. Tokyo:
Tokyo Metropolitan Government, 1968.

Turner, Roy, ed. India's Urban Future. Berkeley: University of
California Press, 1962.

Vajpeyi, D. K. "Municipal Corporations in U.P., Elected Representatives and Executive Officers--Their Roles and Relationships,"
Journal of Administration Overseas, V, No. 4 (October, 1966),
pp. 243-50.

Verba, Sidney; Ahmed, Bashiruddin; and Bhatt, Anil. Caste, Race,
and Politics; a Comparative Study of India and the United States.
Beverly Hills, Calif.: Sage Publicatons, 1971.

Venkatarangaiya, M., and Pattashivam, M., eds. Local Government in
India: Select Readings. Bombay: Allied Publishers, 1969.

Washnis, George J. Nieghborhood Facilities and Municipal Decentralization. 2 vols. Washington, D.C.: Center for Governmental
Studies, 1971.

Wirsing, Robert G. "Associational 'Micro-Arenas' in Indian Urban
Politics," Asian Survey, XIII, No. 4 (April, 1973), pp. 408-20.

_____. "Socialist Society and Free Enterprise Politics: A
Study of the Urban Political Process in Nagpur, India."
Unpublished Ph.D. dissertation, University of Denver, Denver,
Colorado, 1971.

Yadav, M. K., ed. Municipal Corporation of Delhi Yearbook, 1969-70.
Delhi: Municipal Corporation of Delhi, 1970.

Periodicals

Civic Affairs (Kanpur).
Evening News (Delhi).
Hindustan Times (Delhi).
Organiser (Delhi).
Rajdhani (Delhi).
Statesman (Delhi).
Times of India (Delhi).

Index

Note: references to words in *Hindi* and *Urdu* are given for the page where they are most fully defined. A list of abbreviations is also incorporated.

Administrative Reforms Commission, 28
administrator, 6, 228, 272–73. *See also*
 administrator-citizen interface; City Zone
 administrators; councilor-administrator
 interface
administrator-citizen interface, 98–101,
 210–11, 272
Agarwala, R. N., 283
Ajmal Khan, Hakim, 280
aldermen, 4
Andersen, Walter, 115
animals in Kucha Khirkiwala, 63–65
Anjuman Vakil-i-Quam Punjabian, 281
Ansari, Dr., 280
Arya Samaj, 164 n.33
ASI. Assistant Sanitary Inspector
Assistant Assessor and Collector, 215
Assistant Chief Accountant, 215
Assistant Education Officer, 215
Assistant Engineer (Planning), 215
Assistant Labour Welfare Officer, 215
Assistant Public Relations Officer, 215
Assistant Sanitary Inspector (ASI), 36,
 38–39, 100; on rounds, 83, 86–87, 93
Assistant Superintendent of Gardens, 215
Assurances Committee, 318

Baker, Herbert, 17 n
Bania, 21, 139, 163
basti, 30
Basti Julahan by-election, 75, 107, 109;
 campaign organization in, 113, 118;
 party strategies in, 121, 368 n.4; result of,
 75–76; vote blocs in, 116; voting
 procedure in, 112–13
Bharatiya Kranti Dal (BKD), 258
Bhargava, Nakul, 292
Bhattacharya, Mohit, 209
BKD. Bharatiya Kranti Dal
biraadari, 43

biraadaris of Delhi, 160–61
Blake, Stephen P., 153 n
Bombay Municipal Corporation, 285
Brahm Prakash, 365 n.31
budget process in America, 307–309
building types, 30
building usage mix, 174

Cantonment, 3–4, 20, 285
census data, 51–52, 167; occupation
 categories in, 371 n.36; as used in the
 study, 11–12, 363 n.9
central government. *See* Government of
 India
chabutra, 63
chalan, 36
Chandni Chowk, 62, 152, 177
charpoi, 65
chaudhari, 46
chhatta, 30
Chief Executive Councilor, 24–25, 76,
 118, 322
chowk, 62–63
chowkidar, 44
Church, Roderick, 71, 343–47
citizen-administrator interface, 98–101,
 210–11, 272
citizen-councilor interface, 95–98, 104–105
citizens: associations of, 273; complaints of,
 36, 96; social and political ties of, 48–50;
 opinion of, 329
City North Zone, 219–20
City South Zone, 220–21
City Zone, 8–10, 21, 148, 219–21;
 geographic definition of, 146, 149, 191
City Zone administrators: attitudes toward
 councilors, 196–97; attitudes toward
 zonal system, 211–12; description of,
 214–16; interviews with, 12, 196 n

[395]